D0998689

The Psychology of Work

Theoretically Based Empirical Research

LEA's Organization and Management Series
Arthur P. Brief and James P. Walsh, Series Editors

The Psychology of Work

Theoretically Based Empirical Research

Edited by

Jeanne M. Brett
Northwestern University

Fritz Drasgow
University of Illinois at Urbana-Champaign

LEA LAWRENCE ERLBAUM ASSOCIATES, PUBLISHERS
2002 Mahwah, New Jersey   London

The picture reproduced on the cover of this book is a formal portrait of a cooper, or barrel maker, taken about 1850. Having a portrait taken then was a formal occasion, and a series of daguerreotypes on the Library of Congress' Web site depicts many occupational photographs in which individuals included the tools of their trade in their portraits. The pictorial historical record suggests that people have long presented themselves to the world identified with their work. The cooper in the photograph represents himself as working on the barrel he is making. Not much has changed in a century and a half. People are still known by what they do. Work is an integral part of self-identity. It is about this vital aspect of individuals' lives—work—that this book is written. We dedicate this volume to the workers of the world whose work still defines them.

Library of Congress, Prints & Photographic Division,
Daguerreotype Pictures and Views 1839–1864, reproduction number 23.

Lawrence Erlbaum Associates, Inc., Publishers
10 Industrial Avenue
Mahwah, NJ 07430

Cover design by Kathryn Houghtaling Lacey

Library of Congress Cataloging-in-Publication Data

The psychology of work : theoretically based empirical research / edited by Jeanne M. Brett, Fritz Drasgow.
    p. cm.
  Includes bibliographical references and indexes.
  ISBN 0-8058-3815-5 (alk. paper)
    1. Work—Psychological aspects—Congresses.   I. Brett, Jeanne M.   II. Drasgow, Fritz.

BF481 .P84   2002
158.7—dc21
                                                                            2001045112
                                                                                  CIP

Books published by Lawrence Erlbaum Associates are printed on acid-free paper,
and their bindings are chosen for strength and durability.

Printed in the United States of America
10 9 8 7 6 5 4 3 2 1

In honor of Charles L. Hulin

Contents

Foreword

Arthur P. Brief
Tulane University

James P. Walsh
University of Michigan

Jeanne Brett and Fritz Drasgow's collection of essays in honor of Chuck Hulin is a testimony to the breadth and depth of what the organizational sciences, in this case Industrial and Organizational Psychology and organizational behavior, have become. Breadth-wise, several essays address a traditional concern of the field—turnover and other forms of organizational withdrawal—but others focus on such topics as cross-cultural perspectives on the motivation to work, patterns of aggressive behavior in organizations, and the effects of ambient sexual harassment of women on men. Depth-wise, one finds, for example, a detailed and provocative analysis of the supposed ubiquity of evaluation. Moreover, the list of contributors is punctuated by some of the field's leading scholars (e.g., Dan Ilgen, Ed Locke, Terry Mitchell, Harry Triandis, and Howard Weiss), so, readers, justifiably, should expect a tantalizing read. We are pleased to feature Brett and Drasgow's collection in our LEA Series.

Introduction

Jeanne M. Brett
Northwestern University

Fritz Drasgow
University of Illinois at Urbana-Champaign

On May 19–20, 2000, colleagues and former students of Charles L. Hulin gathered in Champaign, Illinois, for a conference to honor his contributions to the psychology of work and to celebrate his retirement. This book is the product of that conference, but it is more than simply a series of research papers on the psychology of work or the musings of scholars about the psychology of work. The book can be read to understand the current state of the research on the psychology of work. It can also be read to understand Hulin's unique theoretical-empirical perspective on research about the psychology of work. Doctoral seminars taught by the very best professors provide insight not only into a content area, but also into the professor's way of thinking about and inquiring into that content area. This book was designed to provide insight into the Hulin legacy—a paradigm for thinking about and doing research on the psychology of work.

Part I of the book, The Hulin Legacy, provides direct insight into this paradigm. Hulin's own chapter, Lessons From Industrial and Organizational Psychology, discusses the centrality of work in modern life. Judge's chapter, Back to the Same Place, for the First Time? The Hulin Family Tree, reveals Hulin's intellectual influences passed down from Wilhelm Wundt and Edward Titchener, E. G. Boring, and J. P. Guilford through his mentor, Patricia Cain Smith, and from Thomas Art Ryan, also a professor of psychology at Cornell during Hulin's graduate school days. Hulin's vita is an appendix to the book. Hulin is the son of an autoworker and a union member, who knew the days of organizing the UAW–CIO in the Michigan auto plants. He passed along many of these events and an appreciation of the role of the blue-collar work to Chuck.

Chuck was a scholarship student at Northwestern University where he worked in D. T. Campbell's social psychology laboratory and wrote a BA Thesis with Brendan Maher. He went to graduate school at Cornell, and subsequently spent his entire career at the University of Illinois in psychology. The Society for Industrial and Organizational Psychology recognized Hulin's influence on the field by conferring its Career Contributions award in 1998, noting his direct impact on knowledge about job satisfaction and withdrawal from work and indirect impact through training and collaborating with students and colleagues. What better way to understand that influence than engaging with him as he considers the lessons he has learned about the psychology of work, understanding his intellectual heritage, and becoming familiar with that which has been influenced by his thinking?

Part II, Research on the Psychology of Work, is organized into sections that reflect three recurring themes in Hulin's own research. Each section consists of chapters by authors who have worked with Hulin during their careers. The sections survey the state of knowledge with respect to the conceptualization of psychological constructs, the antecedents and outcomes of satisfaction, and modeling organizational behavior. First and foremost, the chapters in these sections provide content. They review past research, but they also suggest new insights into the psychology of work. Read these chapters for their content and read them to see how the Hulin paradigm is applied in systematic empirical research.

The chapters in Section A emphasize the theme of broad, theoretical constructs. The virtue of viewing constructs broadly is that a wide range of behavioral patterns can be explained by a small number of variables. Research by Hulin and his students has carefully developed and tested theories related to job satisfaction, withdrawal from work, and sexual harassment that demonstrate the conceptual and empirical utility of broad theoretical constructs. The chapters in this section illustrate the use of general constructs with respect to disposition or personality, performance evaluation, and cultural values.

The chapters in Section B illustrate the linkages between job satisfaction and its antecedents and outcomes. Hulin's own research propelled job satisfaction into a central role in theories of organizational behavior, first by demonstrating relationships between job satisfaction and a variety of outcome variables, and then by developing the general constructs of job and work withdrawal and demonstrating relationships between job satisfaction and withdrawal constructs. Two chapters in this section illustrating the precursors and consequences theme focus on "ripple effects" in organizations where sexual harassment of women affects the job satisfaction of men in the same work groups, and where layoffs in a period of growth and economic prosperity transform psychological contracts based on job security to ones based on job insecurity. Two other chapters in this section illustrate one extreme reaction to job dissatisfaction—turnover—and how that decision unfolds. The final chapter describes a different reaction to job dissatisfaction—adaptation.

The chapters in Section C illustrate the theme of modeling behavior in organizational settings. Much of Hulin's recent research has focused on how to use formal models to characterize behavior in organizations. These contributions include applying models derived from item response theory to measures and translations of measures of job satisfaction, using structural equation modeling to test hypotheses about sexual harassment, and, most recently, using computational modeling to account for work withdrawal. Three chapters illustrate this theme using formal modeling procedures to explore patterns of aggressive behavior, faking and self-presentation behavior, and withdrawal behavior.

Colleagues and former students of Chuck Hulin produced this book to share the unique legacy of Chuck's insights into research and theory with a broader audience of scholars in work and psychology. Our enthusiasm for this project stemmed from another unique legacy of Chuck Hulin. Working with him, we learned to respect the people whose work lives we were studying; we learned the importance of our field of research; we learned to do research of the highest quality; we learned to be professionals. We also learned that none of us stands alone at the beginning of a research journey. All of us reached that place following the guidance of those who went before us and whose research has provided roadmaps of where we have been and where we seem to be headed. Without his encouragement, confidence, and behind-the-scenes aid, many of us would not be Industrial and Organizational psychologists. Hulin is not only a fine scholar, but an extraordinary teacher and mentor as well. The contributors to this book and the participants in the conference on the Psychology of Work celebrate Chuck Hulin's career. Thank you, Chuck, for the knowledge, the skills, and the values you gave us.

Part I

THE HULIN LEGACY

Chapter 1

Lessons From Industrial and Organizational Psychology

Charles L. Hulin
University of Illinois at Urbana-Champaign

CENTRALITY OF WORK IN LIVES IN MODERN SOCIETY

Industrial and Organizational (I-O) Psychology, to a greater extent than any other field of behavioral science, is concerned with one of the few fundamental elements of the life of an individual in our world. In the United States and other nations in the industrialized world, our work defines us. You are what you do. To do nothing is to be nothing. Just as doing nothing negates our humanity, we are defined privately and socially by our work.

> Work, whether pleasant or painful, helps define individual identity. Strangers ask, "What do you do?" We reply to casual or ideological queries by naming skills or places of employment. We relate occupation to race, ethnicity, gender, region, and religion in struggling to comprehend the essential reality of self or community. Our daily tasks give lives coherence; by contrast, the lack of work denies our basic humanity. Workers uncomfortable with abstract discourse assert, "I am a workaholic" or "Hard work's my middle name." Philosophers may translate such vernacular lines into "I work, therefore I am." (Green, 1993)

There are changes (but fewer than we think) from the days when we wore our occupation as our name. Our Anglo-Saxon ancestors named Archer, Baker, Bowman, Butcher, Brewer, Carpenter, Cartwright, Clark, Cooper, Cook, Farrier, Fletcher, Hunter, Judge, Miller, Miner, Porter, Sawyer, Sheppard, Scribner, Shoemaker, Smith, Squire, Tailor, Tanner, Teacher, Tinker, Wagner, Weaver, and Wright, among others, were identified by their occupation. Other examples from other languages and cultures are easily found. We did not have to guess about others' jobs nor did they have to announce their job in the first few sentences of a conversation for their place in the world to be known. We truly were what we did. We still are in less obvious but equally defining ways.

What Work Provides

Work is a source of identity. We no longer wear our occupation as our name so "What do you do?" is among the first questions we ask of a new acquaintance (perhaps the most generally exchanged bit of information about ourselves).

Work is a source of relationships outside the family. Our relationships with our work colleagues and supervisors define us and shape our views of the world as surely as do social roles.

Work is a source of obligatory activity. The obligatory activities and time constraints of work provide a structure to our everyday lives. Absent these structuring forces, quotidian activities may resemble all too much time fillers without purpose.

Work is a source of autonomy. In individualist cultures, autonomy is among the most strongly held values. Our autonomy, valued so highly in U.S. culture, rests on the foundation of a job, the money it provides, the goods that can be purchased with that money, and the intangible values of "standing on one's own two feet."

Work provides opportunities to develop skills and creativity. Aside from genetically influenced general cognitive abilities, the important skills and abilities we have are either developed or honed in the performance of a succession of jobs. We establish the base for these skills in the classroom but we develop them on the job.

Work is a source of purpose in life. The importance of family notwithstanding, work provides most of us with a sense of purpose. Among women, changes in the relative priority of marriage and family on one hand and work and a career on the other in industrialized societies suggest the overall importance of work may be increasing, at least among this segment of the population.

Work is a source of feelings of self-worth and self-esteem. Just as work provides a sense of purpose in life, accomplishments related to this purpose provide us with a sense of our self-worth and self-esteem. We gain self-esteem when we accomplish something worthwhile—and work is worthwhile.

Work is a source of income and security. Money is the universal fungible. Work, whatever the nature of the job, provides income that can be spent to acquire goods and services needed or desired. No other value received for work can be exchanged for the range of things that money can. Other values received from work may be more valued but none is as fungible. Money is a nearly universal metric used to measure accomplishments.

Work gives other activities, for example, leisure time, meaning. Absent work and work routines, our other activities would have no defining base. Not everything we do is measured against our work; work is, however, the source of activities that provides the ambient structure against which other activities are compared and defined.

Job Loss

Just as a job still defines today, the loss of a job has fundamental consequences for our lives. For example, when Gary Romans was fired by Caterpillar in Peoria, what troubled him more than the silence of the union was losing the company badge he had carried from the age of 18, as his father did before him for 31 years. Getting fired from the largest employer in a company town like Peoria is ". . . like an industrial death sentence. When you are fired, you have lost your identity, your sanctuary, and security" (Franklin, 1996).

Clifford Mills, executive vice president of Tazwood, a mental health center based in Pekin and serving the Peoria area, said after a prolonged Caterpillar strike that resulted in many employees being fired, "Trying to get these guys to respect themselves again is going to be the hard part for us clinically" (Franklin, 1996).

Clifford McCree returned to his former workplace 14 months after being fired from his maintenance job with the city of Miami. He killed five former coworkers, wounded one, and then killed himself. His suicide note read, "The economic lynching without regard or recourse was—is—something very evil. Since I couldn't continue to support my family, life became nothing. . . . I also wanted to punish some . . . that helped bring this about" ("In Suicide Note," 1996).

"Going postal" is now a part of our everyday language. It almost always refers to somebody killing former co-workers or supervisors because of real or imagined problems at work or the removal of work or a job from one's life. But, just as suicide is the final culmination in a long series of self-destructive behaviors, "going postal" is but the tip of the iceberg of interpersonal aggressiveness and abuse individuals experience and dispense in organizations (Glomb, 1998, in press). The consequences for individuals and organizations of anger and aggression in the workplace are significant and long-term. Patterns of such incidents, both aggressing and being

aggressed against, are predictable by a combination of individual differences and organizational characteristics (Glomb, 1998). These relations
highlight the need for research into an aspect of work in organizations
that may erupt into violence when individuals are denied a job and the
dignity that goes with it.

In the United States, when the size of the population is controlled, the
number of employed persons and the number of suicides are correlated
$-.59$ ($p < .01$) across years (Cook, Dintzer, & Mark, 1980). The direction
of this correlation no surprise; the size of the relationship, describing an
effect size of $\sim.6$ in the relationship between suicide and lack of work
across years, may be somewhat surprising. The results of a lack of a job are
not phenomena restricted to the United States or Western societies. In Japan, they are experiencing the highest unemployment levels in post-war
history and the highest number and largest percentage of people commit-
ting suicide, nearly 33,000 in 1998 (Strom, 1999). These trends in suicide
began in 1990 when the bubble of Japan's economy burst. There was a
44.6% increase in suicide in 1998 over 1997 among men ages 40 to 59.
Forty percent more men in their 20s committed suicide in 1998. These
trends have not changed in the past 2 years. These are noteworthy figures
because this is the period of time when young men traditionally counted on
becoming *shaiin*, members of society by means of entering the work force.
This portal to society is opened only a crack today compared to previous
years. The shame of not having a job is almost unbearable among Japanese
men. Men without a job—even employed men fearful of losing their job—
are killing themselves. The effects of job loss or a lack of a job may be mag-
nified in Japan because the threshold for suicide is reduced; suicide has little of the stigma it has in the United States or other Western societies.

But in other nations, functionally related responses that reflect indirect
self-destruction (Baumeister & Scher, 1988; Faberow, 1980) will be enacted as surely as people are deprived of a job and their pride is eroded.
Few modern societies or cultures have true "coming of age and independence" ceremonies. Jobs and work are the defining elements of adulthood.
Acquiring full-time work is often the only obvious event marking the transition from childhood. The loss of a job, either through layoff, firing, or
retirement is a major life event; it may mark a return to dependency on
one's family, spouse, or the government. In an individualist culture such
as the United States (Triandis, 1994; chap. 5, this volume), dependency is
functionally equivalent to being shunned in a collectivist culture; they are
both threats to one's identity.

When we deny a person's work, we deny many things other than income—things that represent the difference between existence and a life
seen as valuable. We gain self-esteem when we do something worthwhile,
not when we mouth psychobabble slogans about our importance in the

cosmos; our jobs provide the most frequent source of accomplishments. When a job is lost, low self-esteem and its consequences follow. We rarely have to retreat to our own private Walden Pond to learn if we have lived; we do that by examining our accomplishments.

Work, Population Demographics, and Public Policy

Work and jobs and expectations about jobs influence ages, and the changes in these ages, at which we marry (22.5 years for males and 20.6 years for females in 1970, and 26 years for males and 24 years for females in 1990) when we have our first children (21.8 years in 1960 to 24 years in 1990), and even *if* we get married (72% in the 1970s; 61% in 1990). These are *very* large changes in population demographics across approximately 20 years. The birth rate in the United States has dropped to near the replacement rate of ~2.1. Fertility rates are substantially below population replacement rates in many Western, industrialized nations, for example, Sweden, Ireland, and Italy in the European Union. Their birth rates are sufficiently below population replacement rates that they have significant (negative) implications for the nation.

The most frequent reason given for delayed beginnings of families, for limitations on family size, increasing ages of marriage, or even marriage at all, is interference with working careers of potential mothers. When work or a career are seen as limited by marriage and a family, the latter are frequently giving way to the former. Some countries, for example, Sweden, have instituted public policies to increase birth rates and family sizes by making parenthood compatible with working careers. A similar but weaker Family Friendly Leave Act addresses the same issues in the United States.

Changes in women's priorities, balancing or even reversing the relative importance of marriage and family on one hand, and work and career on the other, would have seemed unthinkable a generation ago. Legislation allowing women to pursue marriage and families within the context of jobs and careers speaks eloquently to the importance of work and its role in contemporary lives of both men and women. Changes in thinking about work and careers is needed but these changes must be based on solid empirical data.

Tinkering with work so it is compatible with a family or addressing peripheral issues of work responsibilities is not going to do the job. When work and careers take precedence over marriage and children, changes in social policies to protect the social institutions of marriage and the family within the context of a working family are needed. But we must know what elements of work constitute the core of its meaning in contemporary lives. The study of work is vital to understanding changes in individuals and society. Work may be the impetus for more changes in family life and contemporary society than any other single force.

Work and Development

Work influences us throughout our lives as few activities do. No other choice we make—with the possible exception of our spouse—influences each of us, our families, our children, our values, or our status as much as our choice of a job or an occupation. Throughout our lives, but especially from our late teens and early 20s to our 60s, we spend more time engaged in work activities than any other single pursuit (except sleep, which does not seem to be a pursuit or even an activity). Social roles and social behaviors are developed and grow out of our work roles and work organizations but they are studied devoid of their context within populations of college sophomores who appear as research participants in most experimental research.

Wiggins (1965) argued that personalities are forged by social roles and social interactions. Work roles and work role interactions occur later in our lives than do social roles and social role interactions, but many enter the world of work via part-time and temporary work in their early teens. In 2000, nearly 65% of the teenagers work by the time they are 15 according to a report released by the U.S. Department of Labor. By the time U.S. teenagers are graduated from high school, 80% of them have been employed at least on a part-time basis (Barling & Kelloway, 1999); many occupy full-time work roles by then. The age at which personalities become fixed is unknown and probably varies from individual to individual. If social roles influence our personalities, then the influence of work roles on personalities must be explored because work roles are a large and important part of social roles and because the overwhelming majority of U.S. teenagers have jobs during high school. The influences of social and work roles, early and later in life, are largely unaddressed empirical questions. It will take a major change in how developmental and personality questions are studied; a life-span approach that addresses questions about the continuing importance of work and careers in the lives of individuals and families.

These psychological processes and their impact on nonwork spheres of life are rarely studied *in situ*, in organizational contexts, by social psychologists or personality researchers. Organizations are the settings for most of our nontrivial behaviors. These nontrivial behaviors take place in contexts that directly influence the behaviors. This is not to reopen the personality/situationism debate that was waged by Mischel (1977), Mischel and Peake (1982), and others (Bowers, 1973) but persistent, general, questions remain unaddressed about the role of situations and roles not often represented in traditional studies of personality or social psychology.

There is evidence that events at work create emotions and emotional reactions that spill over onto nonwork behaviors, health conditions, and health satisfactions (Fitzgerald, Drasgow, Hulin, Gelfand, & Magley, 1997; Fitzgerald, Hulin, & Drasgow, 1994; Glomb, Munson, Hulin, Bergman, & Drasgow, 1999; Glomb et al., 1997; Hulin, Fitzgerald, & Drasgow, 1996; Munson, Hulin, & Drasgow, 2000); there is little evidence that the spillover goes in the opposite direction.

Work, Society, and General Perceptions

Federal courts recognize the importance of work and jobs in our society, but they limit freedom of expression when expressions take place within the context of work organizations. Expressions and behaviors constituting gender and sexual harassment, expressions rarely challenged otherwise, are proscribed if they take place within work organizations. Such statements are judged to create hostile and threatening work environments that interfere with an individual's pursuit of a job or career. Harassers and their employing organizations are punished civilly by multimillion dollar fines. The Supreme Court of the United States has effectively ruled that when our fundamental right of freedom of expression conflicts with others' fundamental rights to a job and career, our freedom of speech must give way to these other, fundamental, rights. This recognition by the Supreme Court highlights their contention articulated in the 1954 *Brown v. Board of Education of Topeka, Kansas* that the constitution of the United States must be interpreted within the prevailing values of society. Our society values work and the freedom to pursue a job and a career as much as other freedoms. When they are in conflict, limits may be placed on the conflicting freedoms.

There are numerous other nonscientific testaments about the importance of work other than the decisions of the Supreme Court. Miller's *Death of a Salesman*, the American *Hamlet*, examines the disintegration of Willy Loman's life when he loses his job and his identity. Willy was a salesman. And for a salesman

> . . . there is no rock bottom to the life. He don't put a bolt to a nut, he don't tell you the law or give you medicine. He's a man way out there in the blue, riding on a smile and a shoeshine . . . and when they start not smiling back— that's an earthquake. And then you get yourself a couple of spots on your hat, and you're finished. Nobody dast blame this man. A salesman is got to dream, boy. It comes with the territory. (Miller, 1981)

But without a job, Willy no longer had a dream.

O'Neill's (1937) *The Hairy Ape* traces the collapse of an individual whose job as a coal tender on a ship identified him as a lout, incapable of sensitivity or intellect. His descent followed his realization of how he was seen by society. John Henry, perhaps our most recognized mythic hero, is celebrated in song and story for his fatal victory over a machine designed to take away his job. We have erected a bronze and granite statue of him at the site of the Big Bend Tunnel on the C&O Road. There is no statue honoring the man who designed the steam drill that killed John Henry and took his job. But John Henry, a mythic tunnel stiff, is so honored.

From a different point on the heroic spectrum, we have a song written nearly 200 years ago celebrating being a shoemaker, making shoes.

> *In the days of eighteen and one,*
>   *peg and awl.*
> *In the days of eighteen and one,*
>   *peg and awl.*
> *In the days of eighteen and one,*
>   *pegging shoes was all I done,*
> *Hand me down my pegs, my pegs, my pegs, my awl.*

> .
> .
> .

> *In the days of eighteen and four, peg and awl. (2)*
> *In the days of eighteen and four,*
> *I said I'd peg them shoes no more,*
> *Throw away my pegs, my pegs, my pegs, my awl.*

> *They've invented a new machine, peg and awl. (2)*
> *They've invented a new machine,*
> *The prettiest little thing you ever seen.*
> *I'll throw away my pegs, my pegs, my pegs, my awl.*

> *Makes a hundred pair to my one, peg and awl (2)*
> *Makes a hundred pair to my one,*
> *Peggin' shoes, it ain't no fun.*
> *Throw away my pegs, my pegs, my pegs, my awl.*

Songs addressing basic human needs survive 200 years in oral tradition. Those that do not are unlikely to be found in oral tradition beyond the lifetime of the social writhing that produced them.

Community psychologists performed an important function when they adopted the ideas and approaches advocated and used effectively by Alinsky in his Back of the Yards Movement (1989, 1991) and focused attention on the importance of communities as influences on mental health, psychological development, empowerment, and other aspects of our lives.

However, what may be the most important parts of communities—work organizations, talking circles, and networks of co-workers—and the most important sources of self-esteem—accomplishments on a job or simply having a job—seem excluded from their inquiry. A recognition of the role of jobs and work as important influences on the lives and health of individuals may have developed a healthy cross-fertilization between community and I-O Psychology that would have strengthened both fields.

Contributions, Religion, and Society

Certainly on a normative basis, and perhaps even on an ipsative basis, jobs and careers are rated as more important to professionals than to blue collar workers (Hanisch & Hulin, 1990, 1991). This in no way overshadows the general importance of work, jobs, and the intangible benefits provided by such jobs, as compared to other elements in their lives, to all varieties of blue- and pink-collar workers. The effects of work on individuals is general. Work is work no matter who does it or what they do. It is as important to who we are whether one is a archeologist cataloging old garbage or a garbage collector picking up new garbage. Today, we rarely imbue work with elements of religion; previously, for some, work was painful but gained dignity because of its worthy end, purification for the pride of flesh. For instance, for John Calvin, work was valuable for what it signified in terms of a person's presence among the chosen few.

Contemporary man has replaced God and king with himself at the center of his life. For most people, the self is now defined by work more than any other element of their lives, including God and country. The meanings of work to individuals' lives have been stripped of most religious significance for most of us, but work's importance is not limited by socioeconomic status; its role may vary across groups but it is irrelevant to few. The usefulness of many standard external cues by which others know us—ancestry, religion, land ownership, school, accent, job—have been eroded in the United States by relentless application of democratic political philosophy, dynamic economic conditions, effective academic scholarship programs, and social, labor, and geographic mobility that have homogenized our population. One's job, however, remains as an obvious personal characteristic used by others and by ourselves to identify us.

Nothing links school, work, careers, family life, retirement, and post-retirement activities as do work, work attitudes, work values, and work behaviors. Other influences and processes wax and wane in importance across developmental stages. For some isolated populations, work plays a minor role at best in their lives. But for most, work provides an essential continuity across stages of our lives.

Few researchers now pursue a life-span approach to individuals' lives. Among the important themes such a life-span view of human development would discover are the things work brings to lives—autonomy, self-esteem, self-respect, a sense of purpose in life. These values and attitudes are related to behaviors in all of spheres of life, not just to work behaviors. Work attitudes and work values tie the components of our lives together. Nobody outside of I-O psychologists studies this aspect of the lives of individuals.

CONTRIBUTIONS OF I-O PSYCHOLOGY TO THE LIVES OF EMPLOYEES

Selection and Training

Much empirical and theoretical work by I-O psychologists contributes directly to the welfare of formal work organizations. In the extreme, this has been expressed as I-O psychologists being "handmaidens" of management, serving the goals of greater organizational profits at the expense and exploitation of employees. One need not encounter a Marxist or a member of the counterculture to hear this description of I-O psychologists and their activities. Zickar (in press) reviewed a part of the history of I-O Psychology that details evidence supporting this belief. This is a somewhat myopic view today of the generality and importance of research and application efforts of I-O psychologists. It accurately describes some I-O applied research. It does not describe the field as a whole.

Ideological controversies about the role of general cognitive ability in job and school performance (Andrews, 1990; Brodnick & Ree, 1993; Gould, 1981; Herrnstein & Murray, 1994) may never be resolved but empirically established relations between general intelligence and performance in a variety of complex settings (schools, work organizations) are well established (Hunter, 1980; J. E. Hunter & R. F. Hunter, 1984). Selection research benefits individuals selected into work organizations and, paradoxically, those not selected. Not getting a desirable job is painful at the time for all that having a job provides. The costs of getting a job for which one is not qualified have a deferred payment schedule in the coin of dissatisfaction, work, and job withdrawal (Hulin, 1992). The costs are no less expensive for that delay. The benefits from having a job that one can do well are inestimable. Basic research on selection into work organizations or academic institutions is necessary and valuable; exploiting the database benefits all parties involved.

The value of selection programs, both to society and to an organization, covaries with labor market conditions. During times of very low unemployment, selection blends over into placement programs. The question is not who should be hired but how can those hired be placed to maximize their contributions to an organization. Selection also influences training more when unemployment is very low. How can those hired be trained to enable them to be productive members of an organization? When unemployment is higher, there are more applicants for a job and selection become possible without the necessity of investing in training for those hired.

Selection and training are two sides of a single coin. Depending on the labor market, and within wide limits, selection and training are alternate paths for reaching an organization's goals. They have different costs that are borne by different parties to the selection–hiring–placement–training process. Selection removes skilled and trained individuals from local environments through the hiring process, relying on high schools, community colleges, and training done by other organizations to provide employees with necessary knowledge and skills. Individuals can also be hired randomly from the applicant pool and then trained to perform the jobs in question. In this case, the costs of training are borne by the organization; individuals with newly acquired skills and knowledge are returned, stochastically, to the environment.

Selection and training are elements of an organization's interface with its environment that exploit or enrich environments depending on the relative balance of selection or training. Both processes benefit employees as well as work organizations in different degrees and coins over different time spans. Selection and training are intimately connected to the local labor market; they depend on theory and empirical data developed from basic research by I-O psychologists. If appropriately done, they provide better job/person fits than the ones provided by a random system of selection and unstructured on-the-job training.

On its own merits, organizational training represents an area of direct contributions by I-O psychologists to the worklife of employees. Teaching complex skills and procedures is relatively easily accomplished. The problems with organizational training, and perhaps most training and teaching, seem to be designing the training so it will transfer to work situations and will generalize broadly from the specific skills taught to other, related, skills (Richman, 1998). Individual employees in training courses and work organizations that sponsor the training are direct beneficiaries of research on training that will transfer and generalize. I-O psychologists are pursuing these latter questions, using models of motivated behavior based on goal setting (Ryan, 1970) and models of relapse prevention by Kanfer (1980).

Motivated Behaviors

Research in the area of human motivation by I-O psychologists makes significant contributions to employees as well as to the employing organizations. I-O researchers have borrowed from general psychology for their theories in the past. This nonrecursive borrowing has slowed considerably in the last 10 years or so. Appeals to physiological needs, need hierarchies, psychoanalytic motives, and even self-observations of one's own behaviors (as if these behaviors were the only needed source of information about why we behave as we do), are being discarded in favor of somewhat different starting points. These different starting points are cognitive in nature but the emphasis may be shifting to a recognition of the role of work and work tasks in our lives. The time may have come when there is a reversal of the assumed "appropriate" direction of generalization and influence that has gone from theories of behavior in general to work behaviors. Theories of work behavior should be a foundation for "basic" areas of research; the ecological importance of work behaviors and the lack of clear distinctions between work and nonwork activities are compelling reasons:

- Activity is the normal state of an individual (Naylor, Pritchard, & Ilgen, 1980; Ryan, 1970).
- Work and nonwork constitute fuzzy rather than crisp sets; distinctions among work and nonwork activities are probabilistic. Even if we try to separate the activities from their contexts, the distinctions may be trivial.
- Models and theories of motivation need to account for variance in direction and duration of this ongoing stream of behavior; variance in amplitude will contribute trivially to understanding normal behaviors (Terborg & Miller,1978).
- Behaviors in work settings account for most of the important activity to be explained. When time for eating, sleeping, and routine commuting is subtracted from a day, work activities constitute the bulk of the remaining activities whose variance we want to explain.

These assumptions should lead to a changed direction in motivation research. They suggest that we need not concern ourselves with impetus to action when studying normal adults. Generalizations of a theory of behavior at work to account for variance in less generally distributed tasks and activities have the advantage of being based on data from individuals enacting salient and widely distributed tasks and activities.

The assumption that activity is the normal state and researchers need be concerned only with direction and duration of a stream of activity rather than activity versus nonactivity seems a truism. It could be verified by observations of individuals but hardly seems worth the effort.

We can test empirically the assumption that work and nonwork are fuzzy sets with activities having degrees of belongingness rather than crisp memberships by generating a list of activities and asking observers to classify them, divorced from their contexts, if possible, into work versus nonwork tasks. One person's hobby is very likely to be another person's work and livelihood:

- Some individuals tie trout flies for fun. Other people, some working part-time in small towns in Montana, some from third-world and emerging countries, tie them for money.
- I wrote for a living . . . or, perhaps more accurately, I spent many hours writing and editing manuscripts while "working." Others write for fun and "publish" their products in vanity presses or chapbooks.
- There are more amateur musicians than there are professionals; their musical activities, including performing before an audience who may or may not have paid to hear them, differ but little. Amateurs are unlikely to regard making music as work; professionals regard what they do as work.
- There are more amateur actors in local playhouses than there are professionals on Broadway. They perform before paying audiences. Everything about their task but the pay is the same. The degree to which the task of acting contributes to the self-identity of professional and amateur actors may differ but little. Their "day-jobs" allow them to eat; their "real" jobs allow them to be.

Tasks can be classified into work and nonwork even though the tasks may migrate between work and nonwork depending on the context, who is doing them, and why. We can extract signals about the worklike nature of some tasks and the nonworklike characteristics of others even when tasks have degrees of belongingness of .55/.45 to the two sets. These signals may be informative and important. But, there may be few reliable differences between work and nonwork activities except for contextual factors. Generalizations from theories of work and patterns of organizational behaviors to patterns of behaviors in nonwork settings may help us understand planful and reasoned behaviors in all settings, not just behaviors in work organizations.

Assumptions about the overlap between work and nonwork tasks can be addressed empirically. A relatively small number of unidimensional ratings of task characteristics in a multidimensional scaling study of tasks might contribute significantly to both our understanding of the differences between work and nonwork and the similarities and overlap in the constituent activities of the two sets. These unidimensional ratings might include:

- Paid versus unpaid;
- Supervised versus unsupervised;

- Product or goal determined by someone else versus self-determined product or goal;
- Ownership of the work product versus ownership by someone else;
- Done at hours set by someone else versus done at the pleasure of the person.

Such unidimensional ratings may help us identify the dimensions needed to account for perceived similarities of work and nonwork tasks. The specifications of the dimensions are important evidence about tasks that constitute the nontrivial behaviors individuals enact. Clusters or families of tasks are likely to include both "work" and "nonwork" activities. The distinctness of work and nonwork tasks and the content of the unidimensional ratings accounting for dimensions among tasks will inform us of the likelihood that a general theory of task performance will generalize across the nontrivial tasks individuals do, whatever the setting.

Work may also consist of those things we do well enough so others pay us to do them, and that we can do fast enough to make a living. This elevates pay and others' evaluations of what we do to central roles. *Pro bono* activities, ranging from carpenters building a house for a homeless family to lawyers or professors contributing their time to a legal case or project requiring their talents, cause problems for this definition. If we do the same tasks for a living are they work when we do them *pro bono*? The tasks are identical but the role of pay has changed. The background against which *pro bono* activities are judged, work-for-pay activities, provides the ground that differentiates work from the figure of *pro bono* activities. But we need a definition of work that includes those tasks that are work but excludes those that are not to form the background. The complexity of the construct suggests a multidimensional, "fuzzy" set approach may provide initial understanding that can be supplemented by a more inclusive definition that builds on the insights provided by characteristics of tasks that are related to degrees of belongingness of tasks to work and nonwork sets.

Organizations are excellent laboratories: They control many environmental characteristics that influence means, variances, and the structure of behaviors and constructs of our theories. Research done in these controlled settings provides an excellent empirical basis for generalizations.

This reversal of the assumed "appropriate" direction of generalization from behavior in general to work behaviors will strike many non-I-O psychologists as blasphemy. I-O Psychology, an "applied" area, should be taking its lead from the "basic" areas of psychology. The arguments just outlined suggest a theory of motivation based on individuals enacting behaviors related to work tasks and leading to a different conclusion. We should proceed in an orderly fashion to explore the limits of generality of theories of work behaviors.

Theories of behavior that have emerged from I-O research are intended to account for variance in reasoned activities that humans perform. In addition to accounting for variance in work behaviors in organizations, goal setting theory (Ryan, 1970) and technology (Locke, Shaw, Sari, & Latham, 1981) account for variance in performance across a wide variety of settings. Kluger and DiNisi's (1996) theory of feedback interventions provides a statement about the characteristics of feedback. Naylor et al. (1980) developed a general theory of behavior based on an expansion of subjective utility theory derived from Tolman (1932, 1959) and Peak (1955). Their theory assumed that behaviors are a result of judgments and decisions by individuals influenced by individual differences, situational constraints, and characteristics of tasks that constitute the antecedents of these judgments and decisions. Weiss and Cropanzano's (1996) theory of affect and evaluations—emotions and attitudes—in organizations specifies relations between these different reactions to work and other tasks and salient behaviors that should be observed (Donovan, 1999; Miner, 1999). Differences in relations involving emotions and evaluations about the same object can contribute significantly to our understanding of how individuals react and how they behave in response to their cognitive and emotional reactions to their jobs and other tasks.

These developments have come from I-O psychologists attempting to account for variance in characteristics of human behavior. Organizational behavior was the focus of their efforts; the generality of their formulations may reach well beyond this focus. The general usefulness of these theories rests on the degree of generality of the theories that specifically account for variance in behaviors in organizations to other settings.

Satisfactions and emotions are important parts of theories of motivation and behaviors. The role of satisfactions, viewed as instantiations of attitudes, in theories of job motivation is well known. The role of affect and emotions in theories of job behaviors and general behaviors is less studied. Interest in many aspects of motivation in psychology wax and wane as a function of the currently dominant paradigm dictating what is important—cognitions, emotions, or behaviors. Attitudes have components of each of these; the study of attitudes has remained important whereas the winds of research fashion have brought behaviors, emotions, and cognitions to the fore at different times. However, the demonstrated relevance of job attitudes as consistent correlates of important job behaviors suggests that they would be important to a general theory of motivation. Research on job behaviors has produced evidence (Hanisch & Hulin, 1990, 1991; Hulin, 1992) that predicting patterns of behaviors rather than individual behaviors, as suggested by Thurstone (1931) and Doob (1947), will pay dividends in the study of reasoned behaviors in general. Knowing the antecedents of attitudes and of emotions and the degree of overlap or separation in these sets of antecedents would provide important information regarding why individuals enact their behavioral patterns.

Generalizing theories of work behaviors to behaviors in general, and including attitudes and affect as core constructs in the theories, adds to the mix of empirical findings, generalizations from these findings, and attitude/behavior theories. The consistently significant attitude/behavior relations found between job satisfactions and several job behaviors pose an unacknowledged theoretical problem for attitude researchers. Organizational attitudes predict many organizational behaviors; social attitudes towards objects do not, in general, predict individuals' behaviors toward those objects. This discrepancy may reflect a fundamental difference between social and work attitudes and between social and work behaviors. It should be addressed.

A perspective that stresses the general importance of work tasks and behaviors reverses signal and noise. The normal significant relations between job attitudes and job behaviors become the baseline against which nonsignificant relations between social attitudes and social behaviors are contrasted. Treating the lack of significant relations between attitudes and behaviors as the baserate and ignoring the ecologically more valid findings from I-O Psychology seems counterproductive. Research on attitudes that do predict behaviors may tell us much about social attitudes that do not predict behaviors.

The salience of the tasks that generate attitudes and the attitudes themselves that are used to predict different classes of behaviors, social versus organizational, vary considerably. Salience of attitudes is likely to be related to the ease of access to the attitudes; the omnipresence of job attitudes might be more important than accessibility. It is not just that job attitudes are easily accessible, it is that we cannot escape them for most of our waking days. This is in distinction to attitudes toward general social objects—religion, blood donations, contraceptive usage. How many times a day are these important? The importance of the ubiquity of job attitudes in influencing behaviors that are consistent with cognitive and emotional reactions to jobs may be a potentially important hypothesis to be studied. Working 8 hours a day, 50 weeks a year on a job that one hates is inescapable. A job that provides few of the outcomes an individual desires, or needs, to provide positive motivations to go to work every day or contains many stressors is dissatisfying, stressful, and potentially unhealthy (Fitzgerald et al., 1997; Glomb et al., 1999; Hanisch & Hulin, 1990, 1991; Munson et al., 2000). Opportunity costs involved in holding a dissatisfying job when one might have a satisfying job make the situation even worse. The affect and emotions generated by negative evaluations of a job and the inputs required to maintain the job are unavoidable. Working on a job that provide an individual with most or all of one's desired outcomes may also be obvious. Individuals, while not evaluating their jobs every waking moment, are very much aware of a job's deficits and its advantages. These evaluations form the basis for job satisfactions/attitudes. These also are likely to be among the important antecedents of affect and emotions.

SUMMARY

I-O researchers, alone among psychologists, study work and its roles in the lives of individuals. Without I-O Psychology, the work processes and events that define our personae would remain unexplored or, worse, assumed to be known and turned over to practitioners for implementation. It is critical that the research is done well and that it is grounded in sound theory. Well done I-O research is likely to have immediate implications for public and organizational policies that distribute scarce resources such as jobs, careers, pay, and promotions; so, however, will poorly done research or research done in highly restrictive settings with problematic ecological validity. Bad research, like bad money, will drive out good research; it is almost always full of catchy slogans, simpler, easier to understand, and easier to sell to policy makers. If bad research dominates our field, it will be relied on by those needing guidance in policy decisions.

The research and theory that informs organizational policy, as opposed to public policy, has implications that are nearly as far-reaching. The impact may be on fewer individuals at a time but when this is multiplied across the number of work organizations in the United States, the cumulative impact is nearly as great as research that informs public policy. The quality and rigor are equally demanded.

This is not a plea for sound research on important issues. That may not be a no brainer but it is rather obvious. Few have ever made an argument for sloppy, atheoretical research. But the stakes here seem much different. I-O Psychology is being assaulted on two sides. One group is our colleagues from the practitioner side of the Boulder scientist/practitioner model that held sway in I-O Psychology for many years and did nobody, scientist or practitioner, any favors. See Latham (2001) and Hulin (2001) for two point–counterpoint articles on the role of basic versus applied research in I-O Psychology. On the other side are our colleagues from the so-called basic areas of behavioral science. I-O psychologists are seen as too theoretical by our application oriented colleagues; we are too applied for the rest of our colleagues. The former raise issues that are relatively easy to respond to. The rejection of the fundamental importance of I-O Psychology is less easily handled and these criticism are potentially more lethal, not for their validity but because of the standard, knee-jerk labeling, perception, and treatment of different subdisciplines within behavioral sciences. The importance and scope of work and working careers, the ecological validity of work tasks as a basis for generalizations to other activities, and the interesting contradictions between well-done research in organizational behavior and social and social–cognitive research belie the validity of the argument that I-O Psychology is not a basic area of human behavioral research. A recognition of the basic nature of I-O research could do much to change the nature of the field and its place in the panoply of the behavioral sciences.

REFERENCES

Alinsky, S. (1989). *Rules for radicals: A practical primer for realistic radicals*. New York: Vintage.

Alinsky, S. (1991). *Reveille for radicals*. New York: Vintage.

Andrews, W. J. (1990). Eugenics revisited. *Mankind Quarterly, 30*, 235–302.

Barling, J., & Kelloway, K. (1999). *Young workers: Varieties of experience*. Washington, DC: American Psychological Association.

Baumeister, R. F., & Scher, S. J. (1988). Self-defeating behavior patterns among normal individuals: Review and analysis of common self-destructive tendencies. *Psychological Bulletin, 104*, 3–22.

Bowers, K. S. (1973). Situationism in psychology: An analysis and critique. *Psychological Review, 80*, 307–336.

Brodnick, R. J., & Ree, M. J. (1993). *A structural model of academic performance, socioeconomic status, and Spearman's g*. San Antonio, TX: St. Mary's University of Texas.

Brown v. Board of Education (Topeka, Kansas). 347 U.S. 483, 47 S Ct. 686, 98 L. Ed 873 (1954).

Donovan, M. A. (1999). *Cognitive, affective, and satisfaction variables as predictors of organizational behaviors: A structural equation modeling examination of alternative models*. Unpublished doctoral dissertation, University of Illinois at Urbana-Champaign.

Doob, L. W. (1947). The behavior of attitudes. *Psychological Review, 54*, 135–156.

Faberow, N. L. (Ed.). (1980). *The many faces of suicide: Indirect self-destructive behavior*. New York: McGraw-Hill.

Fitzgerald, L. F., Dragsow, F., Hulin, C. L., Gelfand, M. J., & Magley, V. J. (1997). The antecedents and consequences of sexual harassment in organizations: A test of an integrated model. *Journal of Applied Psychology, 82*, 578–589.

Fitzgerald, L. F., Hulin, C. L., & Dragsow, F. D. (1994). The antecedents and consequences of sexual harassment in organizations: An integrated model. In G. Keita & S. Sauter (Eds.), *Job stress in a changing workforce: Investigating gender, diversity, and family issues*. Washington, DC: American Psychological Association.

Franklin, S. (1996, February 11). For Caterpillar workers, scars lie deep within. *Chicago Tribune*, Section 5, pp. 1–2.

Glomb, T. M. (1998). *Anger and aggression in organizations: Antecedents, behavioral components, and consequences*. Unpublished doctoral dissertation, Department of Psychology, University of Illinois at Urbana-Champaign.

Glomb, T. M. (in press). Anger and aggression in organizations: Antecedents, behavioral components, and consequences. *Academy of Management Journal*.

Glomb, T. M., Munson, L. J., Hulin, C. L., Bergman, M. E., & Dragsow, F. (1999). Structural equation models of sexual harassment: Longitudinal explorations and cross-sectional generalizations. *Journal of Applied Psychology, 84*, 14–28.

Glomb, T. M., Richman, W. L., Hulin, C. L., Drasgow, F., Schneider, K. T., & Fitzgerald, L. F. (1997). Ambient sexual harassment: An integrated model of antecedents and consequences. *Organizational Behavior and Human Decision Processes*, 309–328.

Gould, S. J. (1981). *The mismeasure of man*. New York: W. W. Norton.

Green, A. (1993). *Wobblies, pilebutts, and other heroes*. Urbana: University of Illinois Press.

Hanisch, K. A., & Hulin, C. L. (1990). Retirement as a voluntary organizational withdrawal behavior. *Journal of Vocational Behavior, 37*, 60–78.

Hanisch, K. A., & Hulin, C. L. (1991). General attitudes and organizational withdrawal: An evaluation of a causal model. *Journal of Vocational Behavior, 39*, 110–128.

Herrnstein, R. J., & Murray, C. (1994). *The bell curve: Intelligence and class structure in American life*. New York: The Free Press.

Hulin, C. L. (1992). Adaptation, persistence, and commitment in organizations. In M. D. Dunnette (Ed.), *Handbook of industrial organizational psychology* (2nd ed., Vol. 2, pp. 445–506). Palo Alto, CA: Consulting Psychologists Press.

Hulin, C. L. (2001). Applied psychology and science: Differences between research and practice. *Applied Psychology: An International Review, 50*, 225–234.

Hulin, C. L., Fitzgerald, L. F., & Drasgow, F. D. (1996). Organizational influences on sexual harassment. In M. S. Stockdale (Ed.), *Women and work series, sexual harassment in the workplace: Perspectives, frontiers, and response strategies* (Vol. 5, pp. 125–150). Newbury Park, CA: Sage.

Hunter, J. E. (1980). *Test validation for 12,000 jobs: An application of synthetic validity and validity generalization to the General Aptitude Test Battery (GATB)*. U.S. Employment Service, U.S. Department of Labor. Washington, DC: Government Printing Office.

Hunter, J. E., & Hunter, R. F. (1984). Validity and utility of alternative predictors of job performance. *Psychological Bulletin, 96*, 72–98.

In suicide note, Florida gunman accuses former co-workers of racism. (1996, February 11). *Chicago Tribune*, Section 1, p. 12.

Kanfer, F. H. (1980). Self-management methods. In F. H. Kanfer (Ed.), *Helping people change*. New York: Wiley.

Kluger, A. N., & DeNisi, A. (1996). Effects of feedback intervention on performance: A historical review, a meta-analysis, and a preliminary feedback intervention theory. *Psychological Bulletin, 119*, 254–284.

Latham, G. P. (2001). The reciprocal transfer from journals to practice. *Applied Psychology: An International Review, 50*, 201–211.

Locke, E. A., Shaw, K. N., Saari, L. M., & Latham, G. P. (1981). Goal setting and task performance: 1969–1980. *Psychological Bulletin, 90*, 125–152.

Miller, A. (1981). *Arthur Miller's collected plays: With an introduction* (Vol. 1). New York: Viking.

Miner, A. G. (1999). *Experience and evaluation: An exploration of the structure and function of job attitudes and affect*. Unpublished master's thesis, University of Illinois at Urbana-Champaign.

Mischel, W. (1977). On the future of personality measurement. *American Psychologist, 32*, 246–254.

Mischel, W., & Peake, P. K. (1982). Beyond *deja vu* in the search for cross-situational consistency. *Psychological Review, 89*, 730–755.

Munson, L. J., Hulin, C. L., & Drasgow, F. D. (2000). Temporal dynamics and sexual harassment: Assessing the effects of sexual harassment over time. *Personnel Psychology, 53*, 21–46.

Naylor, J. C., Pritchard, R. D., & Ilgen, D. R. (1980). *A theory of behavior in organizations*. New York: Academic Press.

O'Neill, E. (1937). *The hairy ape*. New York: The Modern Library.

Peak, H. (1955). Attitude and motivation. In M. R. Jones (Ed.), *Nebraska Symposium on Motivation*. Lincoln: University of Nebraska Press.

Richman, W. L. (1998). *Examining the effects of post-training interventions on transfer of training.* Unpublished doctoral dissertation, Department of Psychology, University of Illinois at Urbana-Champaign.

Ryan, T. A. (1970). *Intentional behavior: An approach to human motivation.* New York: Ronald Press.

Strom, S. (1999, July 15). In Japan, mired in recession, suicides soar. *The New York Times*, pp. A1, A8.

Terborg, J. R., & Miller, H. E. (1978). Motivation, behavior, and performance: A closer examination of goal setting and monetary incentives. *Journal of Applied Psychology, 63*, 29–39.

Thurstone, L. L. (1931). The measurement of social attitudes. *Journal of Abnormal and Social Psychology, 26*, 249–269.

Tolman, E. C. (1932). *Purposive behavior in animals and men.* New York: Century.

Tolman, E. C. (1959). Principles of purposive behavior. In S. Koch (Ed.), *Psychology: A study of a science* (Vol. 2). New York: McGraw-Hill.

Triandis, H. C. (1994). Cross-cultural industrial and organizational psychology. In H. C. Triandis, M. D. Dunnette, & L. M. Hough (Eds.), *Handbook of industrial and organizational psychology* (2nd ed., Vol. 4, pp. 103–172). Palo Alto, CA: Consulting Psychologists Press.

Weiss, H. M., & Cropanzano, R. (1996). Affective Events Theory: A theoretical discussion of the structure, causes and consequences of affective experiences at work. In B. M. Staw & L. L. Cummings (Eds.), *Research in organizational behavior: An annual series of analytical essays and critical reviews, 18* (pp. 1–74). Greenwich, CT: JAI Press.

Wiggins, J. S. (1965). Interpersonal diagnosis of personality. In O. K. Buros (Ed.), *Sixth mental measurements yearbook.* Highland Park, NJ: Gryphon Press.

Zickar, M. J. (in press). Using personality inventories to identify thugs and agitators: Applied psychology's contribution to the war against labor. *Journal of Vocational Behavior.*

Chapter 2

Back to the Same Place, for the First Time? The Hulin Family Tree

Timothy A. Judge
University of Florida

In a book written by those who have been influenced by Charles Hulin, it seems fitting to describe those who influenced him. Thus, the purpose of this chapter is to trace the Hulin family tree, working backward from Hulin to the taproot, Wilhelm Wundt. This chapter is organized into three sections. In the first section, the historical figures in the family tree, individuals now deceased, are described. This section describes the research careers of each of these historical figures. The second section of the chapter focuses on Hulin and his most important influence, his advisor, Patricia Cain Smith. In this section, the research careers of Smith and Hulin are briefly summarized and then, in their own words, they describe the influence of their predecessors in the family tree. The final section of the chapter provides a summary of lessons learned for Industrial and Organizational (I-O) Psychology from an analysis of the family tree.

HISTORICAL FIGURES: WUNDT THROUGH RYAN

The Hulin family tree is provided in Fig. 2.1. The tree begins with Wundt. In this section, I provide brief biographies of the individuals in this tree up to Smith, beginning with Wundt. Readers interested in a more general historical account of the leading figures in I-O Psychology should consult Landy (1992, 1997). Those interested in more in-depth accounts of the individuals in this section should consult Boring (1929, 1950) or other sources cited in this chapter.

23

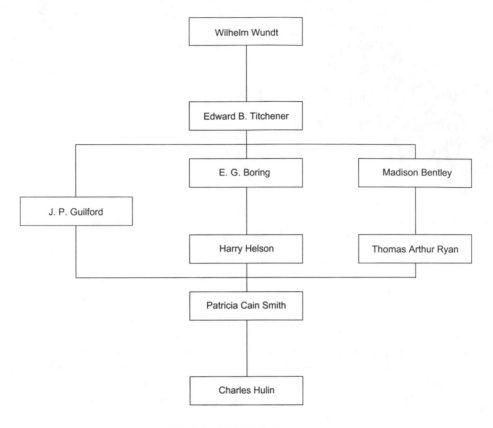

FIG. 2.1. The Hulin family tree.

Wilhelm Wundt

Wundt is commonly credited as being the father of psychology (though paternity may be owed William James). Wundt's laboratory at Leipzig was the first in experimental psychology to be established (James's was purely for demonstration purposes). Before Wundt, psychology had been studied and written about, but the topic was subsumed within a diverse set of other disciplines—most notably, philosophy (e.g., Mill, Kant), physiology (e.g., Müller, Helmholtz), and even physics, or was studied by individuals whose work lay at the intersection of these fields (e.g., Fechner). Much of what Wundt studied and wrote about represented extensions and replications of existing work in these fields, especially physiology, but Wundt explicitly labeled this work as psychology. As this new discipline progressed, much of what Wundt studied, how he studied it, and how he interpreted what he found, diverged from physiology. Physiologists studied the mind to interpret bodily actions; Wundt and his students studied bodily actions to understand the mind. In a transformed manner, this is what many I-O psychologists do today.

Beyond his explicit founding of (physiological) psychology, Wundt's contributions were in the areas of methodology and substantive aspects of experimental psychology. Wundt adapted the scientific method and experimental approach from physics to study human physiological phenomena. Watson (1978) commented, "To Wundt, the use of the experimental method, whenever possible, was mandatory. He replaced the age-old method of meditation with a more exact and exacting method of introspection" (p. 275). For Wundt, the process of introspection was the marriage of observation and experimentation. Wundt's psychology, as experimental physiology, was to be based on an objectively measurable stimulus, applied under explicit conditions, that resulted in likewise objectively measured responses (Murphy, 1949). Unlike "mere" physiology, however, to Wundt's psychology there must be intervening steps—these intervening steps, mental processes revealed through introspection, were what distinguished psychology from physiology.

Substantively, Wundt argued that psychology was concerned with how to: (a) analyze conscious experience into its basic elements; (b) discover if and how these elements are related; (c) determine the lawful nature of these relations. Sensations, aroused whenever a sense organ is stimulated above threshold, were considered by Wundt to be the basic forms of experience. Feelings were the other form of experience, and Wundt held that feelings were subjective interpretations of sensations that had three dimensions (pleasantness–unpleasantness, tension–relief, excitement–depression).[1] Within this framework, Wundt carried out studies in the area of sensation and perception, especially vision, hearing, touch, and taste. Other topics included reaction times in response to various stimuli, attention, feelings in response to various stimuli, and association. Most of the studies completed by Wundt and his students were published in the first psychology journal (created by Wundt), *Philosophische Studien*.

Edward Bradford Titchener

Wundt demanded loyalty from his students and, for the most part, he got it. No Wundt student was more loyal to his mentor than Edward Bradford Titchener. With earlier training at Malvern and then Oxford in his native England, Titchener received his PhD from Leipzig, under Wundt, in 1892. Titchener returned to Oxford but shortly thereafter was called to

---

[1]It is worth noting that most current formulations of affect include two dimensions remarkably similar to Wundt's, most notably pleasantness–unpleasantness and activation–deactivation (see Yik, Russell, & Barrett, 1999). Thus, 100 years ago, Wundt may have essentially had it right, though with one too many dimensions.

the then-new Cornell University. Titchener was to serve 35 years on the faculty of Cornell.

Titchener's studies were in much the same tradition as Wundt's—systematic studies of sensations and of feelings. Titchener coined the term *structuralism* to describe his (and Wundt's) research. The main objective of structuralism was to dissect the mind into its components. And Titchener did dissect the structure of consciousness. In his research, he documented 44,000 sensory qualities, most of them visual. In his career, Titchener supervised more than 50 dissertations and published 216 articles. He also served as associate editor and then editor of *The American Journal of Psychology* from 1895 to 1925. As Wundt is the founder of experimental psychology, Titchener is the founder of experimental psychology in America.

Titchener also sought to establish psychology as a scientific discipline. Titchener's *Experimental Psychology* (1905), published in four volumes, has been characterized as the "most erudite psychological work in the English language" (Boring, 1927, p. 385). The ambitious goal of the work was to establish psychology as a new science. Within the framework of that general goal were comprehensive instructions and guidelines on proper training to perform laboratory research. Titchener, even more pointedly than Wundt, fought against reformations of Wundt's work. He strongly disagreed with "functional" psychology, which had as its goal determination of the adaptive nature of consciousness, to study "is . . . for" questions rather than "is" questions, and psychology in areas that owe much or most of their development to American research (individual differences, applied psychology, behaviorism) that developed out of the University of Chicago and Angell's work. He also rejected the psychological study of animals, children, and clinical patients because they could not introspect. He believed that psychology's status as a science depended on its point of view; there may be other points of view from which to observe behavior, but only one point of view lay within the domain of psychology. In Titchener's view, other sciences were independent of experiences, but the study of experience was the domain of psychology.

Titchener felt isolated from his American colleagues; mostly this was his own doing. He was not taken, as were his colleagues, with the movements sweeping American psychology—behaviorism, Freudian psychology, and so forth. Indeed, he directly opposed them. He avoided publishing in journals, such as *Psychological Review*, that favored perspectives different from his own. Twice he resigned from the American Psychological Association,[2] and rarely attended meetings. He was also isolated in his personal-

---

[2]Titchener felt (apparently, with good reason; see Angell, 1895) that E. W. Scripture had plagiarized his translation of Wundt's work, and unsuccessfully tried to have the American Psychological Association (APA) censure or expel Scripture. When APA refused to act,

ity. He rarely met his students (one student reports meeting with him only twice on his dissertation), use of the telephone was forbidden except in extreme emergencies, and many long-serving faculty members at Cornell had never seen him.

Like Wundt's, Titchener's lectures were extremely popular, though perhaps for somewhat different reasons. In part, Titchener's lectures, like Wundt's, were popular due to his reputation. To a large degree, however, his lectures were popular because of the strength of his personality. Boring (1967) described him as erudite. Watson (1978) characterized his lectures as trenchant and powerful. The conduct of his lectures was patterned after Wundt's—with more histrionics. Titchener assigned topics to his students as had his mentor. In this way, as had Wundt, he used his students to build a unified systematic position.

The hallmarks of Wundtian and Titchenerian psychology, in substance and method, seemed to end with Titchener. Introspection faded as an approach to psychology after 1930 (though sanitized remnants of it in the form of verbal reports, free association, and cognitive psychology remain to this day). Psychologists were showing—from the study of animals to survey research—that trained introspection was not essential to study psychological processes. Substantively, Wundt's and Titchener's theories began to undergo substantial revision or abandonment after Titchener's death. Many of the criticisms were focused on a point Wundt and Titchener acknowledged but never studied in earnest—that the whole of experience cannot be dissected and still retain its meaning. Even Titchener's students, unswervingly loyal to him in his life, began efforts to reconcile and integrate after his death. As Watson (1978) concluded, "Titchener's attempt to transfer Wundtian psychology in its entirety proved to be a failure. But it was a magnificent failure" (p. 424).

Despite the ultimate failures of structuralism, Titchener's emphasis on the scientific basis of psychology, his pioneering and prolific study and teaching of experimental psychology in America, and the spawning of important opposition movements by his promotion of structuralism, make him one of the most consequential psychologists in the history of the discipline. As Boring (1927) wrote in his biography of Titchener shortly after Titchener's death at the age of 60, "The death of no other psychologist could so alter the psychological picture in America" (p. 377). Two years later, he wrote, "Titchener was very important in the history of American

---

Titchener resigned from APA (Stanley Hall and Hugo Münsterberg tried to talk him out of it). Another, perhaps more important, factor in Titchener's decision to avoid APA was his desire to found a different type of society. Titchener founded the Society of Experimental Psychologists, and its first meeting was held in 1904. Many of the luminaries of psychology attended these meetings, including Watson, Angell, Witmer, Judd, Hall, Münsterberg, Pillsbury, Yerkes, Cattell, Seashore, and even Allport.

psychology because he represented this older conservative tradition against overwhelming numbers. West of the Atlantic in psychology there was 'America' and there was Titchener" (Boring, 1929, p. 412). Throughout his scientific career, Titchener remained "Moses on the Mount" (or, in Cronbach's words, the "High Priest"), the commandments of structuralism firmly in hand while others danced around the "maypole" of American functionalism.

Madison Bentley

The relationship of Madison Bentley to Titchener stood in stark contrast to the relationship between Titchener and Wundt. After earning his undergraduate degree in psychology from the University of Nebraska, Bentley completed his dissertation (on memory image) under the supervision of Titchener. However, Dallenbach (1956) noted that Bentley viewed Titchener more as a colleague than a mentor, perhaps due to the similarity in their ages. Bentley accepted an appointment at Cornell in 1897 after completing his PhD. Eventually, Titchener was given sole responsibility for the graduate program and Bentley was given responsibility for the undergraduate program. Soon thereafter, tensions developed between the two men, so much so that Titchener vigorously supported Bentley's candidacy for a professorship at Illinois, apparently to be rid of him. In 1912, Bentley moved to Illinois as head of psychology. After Titchener' death in 1927, Bentley returned to Cornell as chairman of the psychology department.

The contrasts in Bentley's and Titchener's careers are striking. Titchener made his name through his dogged pursuit of structuralism and the scientific method of experimental psychology. Bentley made his name through his gifts as editor (he was editor of the *Journal of Experimental Psychology*, the *American Journal of Psychology*, and the *Psychological Index*), critic (he provided critiques of research in virtually all areas of psychology, including behaviorism, and industrial, social, and clinical psychology, as well as writing annual reviews of research on perception for the *Psychological Bulletin*), and administrator (most notably, as president of the American Psychological Association, but also as department chair at Illinois and Cornell, and in various government capacities).

Bentley appeared to be as diffuse and flexible in his views of psychology as Titchener was restrictive and unbending. After his move to Illinois, Bentley delved into many areas in psychology, and even into peripheral topics outside of psychology. Bentley's interests included phrenology, psychiatric disorders and abnormal psychology, otology, animal psychology, and even anthropology. Functional psychology occupied Bentley during the middle part of his career. Even Titchener's opposition to applied psychology did not influence Bentley. Toward the end of his research career,

Bentley's writings were dominated by applied problems, most notably works on the profession and science of psychology, and on psychiatric disorders. He wrote in his autobiography, "Much that was marginal in the subject in the later twenties has since become fairly central; especially in the applications to business and industry, to delinquency and disorder, to vocation and character" (cited in Murchison, 1936, p. 57).

In contemporary parlance, Bentley was a "big tent" thinker—his interests were broad, and he had an inclusive view of the discipline of psychology (though he argued strongly against what he saw as attempts to compromise scientific integrity in the interests of application; Bentley, 1948a, 1948b). He described his own leadership at Cornell as an attempt "artificially but officially to unite the heterogeneous enterprises of many men professing a variety, or an application, of psychology . . ." (Bentley, 1948b, p. 279). Although that effort never succeeded, it did provide an environment that proved to be fertile ground for future pioneers of applied psychology who were to follow shortly.

Harry Helson

Helson obtained his PhD from Harvard in 1924, studying under E. G. Boring.[3] After obtaining his PhD, Helson served on a number of faculties: Cornell (1924 to 1925), Illinois (1925 to 1926), Kansas (1926 to 1928), Bryn Mawr (1928 to 1949; the last 16 years as chairman of the department), Brooklyn College (1949 to 1951), Texas (1951 to 1961), and Kansas State (1961 through retirement).

Most of Helson's attention early in his career was on sensation—vision in particular—and on mostly conceptual analyses of Gestalt psychology. His research on vision led to his most important contribution, adaptation level theory (Helson, 1964). Adaptation level may be explained simply (though its quantification is considerably more complex; see Helson, 1948). For example, we may see colors perfectly well in a gray room illuminated with a broad spectrum light. If the room is flooded with light

---

[3]Edwin Garrigues (E. G. or Garry) Boring was perhaps the most prominent biographer in the history of psychology. Boring studied under Titchener and Bentley, completing his PhD under Titchener's supervision. Boring and Titchener were devoted to each other. Indeed, according to Stevens (1968), Titchener once commented, "Boring is my best student" (p. 592). After Boring completed his studies at Cornell, G. Stanley Hall hired him as an instructor at Clark University. Boring was lured to Harvard in 1922, where he remained for the rest of his career. Boring (1929) was perhaps best known for his *History of Experimental Psychology*. He was also well known for his research on sensation. For the most part, his work as an historian supplanted his earlier work on sensations, which, according to Helson, had played itself out as had much of Titchener's work on structuralism. Boring became president of the American Psychological Association in 1928 and was elected to the National Academy of Sciences in 1932.

from a narrow band of visible color, our perception of gray objects becomes distorted toward or away from the dominant color as a function of
the shade of gray of the object. Adaptation-level theory explains this problem—the point of equilibrium shifts with changes in the presentation of
stimuli, but not so far as to completely counteract extreme stimuli. Thus,
in order to understand adaptation, one must determine the point of reference—the adaptation, or neutral, point. The same adaptation level operates not only with respect to many aspects of vision, but to other sensations
as well. As Helson noted, "The same sound may be loud or soft, the same
light bright or dim, depending on its relation to prevailing levels of stimulation" (cited in Lindzey, 1974, pp. 210–211). Subsequently, Helson extended adaptation-level theory to psychophysical judgments, such as perceptions of weight.

Although it is of note that roughly half of Helson's nearly 100 publications were in the area of psychophysiological processes of vision, he always
will be associated mainly with adaptation-level theory. The theory has
been generalized to anchor effects, series effects, shifts in indifference
points, effects of subliminal stimulation, effects of context on judgment,
influence of expectancies in judgment, reaction time, motivation and
learning, personality, clinical judgment, and intelligence, among others
(see Bevan, 1964). Helson foresaw the application of adaptation-level theory to applied settings, noting, "In attitude studies, if statements denoted
degrees of agreement and disagreement toward an issue are employed,
those that elicit a neutral or indifferent response are indicative of the adaptation level for that universe of discourse" (cited in Lindzey, 1974, p.
211). Similarly, in the area of personality, Helson argued that adaptation
level was relevant, commenting, "A generalized trait of honesty would
mean the neutral point for acceptance of acts as honest is so high that the
slightest semblance of dishonesty is rejected; conversely, dishonesty could
be gauged by the extent to which certain acts are accepted. An individual's
neutral point can thus furnish the clue to attitudes, traits, and personality
structure" (Helson, 1948, p. 311).

Helson was respected in the research community. He served as editor
of the *Psychological Bulletin* from 1959 through 1964. In 1962, Helson won
the Distinguished Scientific Contribution Award from the American Psychological Association.

J. P. Guilford

After completing his undergraduate degree in psychology at the University of Nebraska, J. P. Guilford was offered an assistantship at Cornell to
study under Titchener. Almost immediately at Cornell, Guilford struck up
a close friendship with Helson. Guilford also was influenced by a course

from Dallenbach,[4] which led him to minor in mathematics. Titchener gave Guilford the choice of two topics for his dissertation; Guilford chose to study fluctuation of attention (skin sensations was the other topic). After completing his dissertation and instructing at Illinois, in 1927 Guilford moved to the University of Kansas where he taught a course of abnormal and social psychology. The next year, Guilford accepted an offer from the University of Nebraska and taught there for 12 years. In 1935 and 1936, Guilford served as visiting professor at Northwestern, and had numerous interactions with L. L. Thurstone, Charles Spearman at Chicago, and Spearman's assistant, Ledyard Tucker. In 1940, Guilford accepted a position at the University of Southern California, with a position free of administrative responsibilities, where he remained until his retirement in 1962. He remained active in the field for long thereafter.

Guilford's research contributions are diverse. He is perhaps best known for his work, and especially his books, in the area of psychological methods. His book, *Psychometric Methods*, through two editions (1936, 1954), has been used to instruct countless graduate students in psychology and continues to serve as a standard reference book in the art and science of scaling and measurement. Beyond his textbooks, however, Guilford made several important contributions in this area, most notably in the area of factor analysis. As reviewed in Michael, Comrey, and Fruchter (1963), these contributions took two principal forms: factor analysis in relation to test theory and development, and factor analysis as a psychometric method. In his various papers on factor analysis, Guilford expressed much faith in the technique, although he issued a cautionary note about its inappropriate uses (Guilford, 1952).

Guilford made important contributions in several other areas, including experimental psychology, studying such topics as attention, visual perception, learning and memory, and experimental esthetics. Most of Guilford's studies on attention and visual senses, in particular, are Titchnerian in orientation. His work in the area of experimental esthetics bore a similar Cornell mark, but this time from Bentley, whose work in this area seemed to eschew Titchener in favor of Gestalt psychology (see Bentley, 1938). There were areas in which Guilford's experimental work diverged from the Cornell school. For example, Guilford published experimental studies in the areas of learning and memory, showing in one influential study that subjects' ability to memorize number series depended on the presence of a pattern in the series (Guilford, 1927).

---

[4]Karl M. Dallenbach (1887–1971) was Titchener's most loyal student. Dallenbach received his PhD under Titchener in 1913 and returned in 1916 as a fellow. At Cornell he remained until he moved to Texas in 1948. Dallenbach influenced Ryan (A. T. Ryan, 1982), and his friend, Boring (Boring, 1958). Perhaps his most important influence was to represent Titchenerian psychology and to ensure that the many criticisms resulted from careful tests.

Second, Guilford contributed much to the area of intellectual abilities. Most of his early contributions were associated with World War II and the Army Air Force Aviation Psychology Program. Guilford chaired this program, which made major advances in selection during World War II and set the stage for later advances to come. When Guilford returned to the University of Southern California after the war, he continued to study mental abilities; the culmination of these efforts was Guilford's Structure of Intellect (SOI) model.

Third, and perhaps second in impact only to his work on psychometric methods, Guilford devoted much of his career to personality theory and measurement. He conducted perhaps the first systematic research on extraversion (Guilford, 1934) and, along with Eysenck, has conducted the most important research on this personality trait. The Guilford–Zimmerman Temperament Schedule was the first important factorially derived personality inventory (Michael et al., 1963), and planted the seeds of the current crop of factorially derived measures.

What is most noteworthy about Guilford's career is the impact he had on many diverse areas of psychology. His work ranged from visual sensation to personnel testing. He was an experimentalist, a psychometrician, and a differential psychologist. His work on psychological methods spanned across all areas of psychology and he informed undergraduates and distinguished faculty alike from all areas of psychology. Guilford was president of the American Psychological Association (1949 to 1950) and was elected to the National Academy of Sciences. He wrote or edited 28 books.

Thomas Arthur Ryan

Thomas Arthur ("Art") Ryan was as tied to Cornell as any man ever was. He earned his undergraduate degree in 1933, his PhD under Bentley in 1937, and served on the faculty of the psychology department at Cornell (including as chairman for a time) his entire career.

Ryan was trained as an experimental psychologist and although he conducted much research in the area, his most important research contribution to psychology was his work on goals and intentions. His 1970 book on intentional behavior was the crowning achievement in his research career, and is the work that is most often identified with him. The book continues to be widely cited today. Ryan (1970) noted in his book, "The systematic study of intention as a potent controlling factor in behavior has been neglected—at least in comparison with that of other factors such as learning, conditioning, and 'unconscious motives' " (p. v). Today, of course, this seems obvious. But in the 1960s, cognitive psychology was in its infancy. As Ryan (1970) noted, ". . . intentions have been ignored in general moti-

vational theory primarily because of mistaken belief that it is philosophi-
cally unsound to use explanatory concepts which refer to conscious experiences" (p. 21). Ryan (1970) summed up his premise—and the forerunner
to modern goal-setting theory—with the statement, "There is strong evidence that level of performance is closely related to the specified goals of
an individual as controlled by instructions from the experimenter, or
when they are adopted spontaneously by the subject" (p. 150). His research on intentions and goals influenced the more recognized work done
by others—most notably the seminal contributions of Dulany, Fishbein,
and Locke.

Despite the importance of Ryan's book, and the influence of goals and
intentions in psychology, his career had less acclaim than the careers of
others in the family tree, all of whom were either editors or winners of career achievement awards. It is easy to underestimate Ryan's contributions
because, in many ways, they were indirect—through Smith to Hulin, and
Locke. Ryan also taught a very heavy load at Cornell. For an extended period of time, he taught 5 to 6 courses per year—at one point teaching two
courses in mathematics, two in psychology and one or two courses out of
town. In terms of the influences on Ryan, Bentley is the most important.
Ryan greatly admired his advisor. Bentley's strong influence Ryan is evident in *Intentional Behavior* (Ryan, 1970). Ryan clearly felt inspired by
Bentley's focus on mental processes. Ryan was prescient in his focus on the
soon to be dominant latent perspective of psychology, a focus that Smith
and Hulin noted was laid out to his and other students well before the
1970 publication date of his book.

Because of his experience at Cornell, Ryan was in a unique position to
describe the two Cornellians who preceded him in the family tree. Ryan
(1982) noted that one of the main Titchener influences was that

> Cornell went its own way and was independent of the changing theories and
> fads prevalent in the rest of American psychology . . . Most of the main-
> stream we found not worth emulating. We would have viewed with horror
> the present situation in which promotions depend primarily upon how well
> a person's work is regarded by the "establishment" outside. (p. 352)

In comparing the influence of Titchener and Bentley on Cornell, Ryan
(1982) commented:

> I was spurred to write this account by the fact that some very excellent psy-
> chologists are now almost completely forgotten even in the department
> where they taught. I was particularly concerned that Bentley is so little
> known, even though he was a far better psychologist than Titchener, and
> Bentley's psychology is much more relevant to present-day research and
> thinking. Titchener dramatized himself well and had a powerful effect upon

his students, even upon his critics. Yet he was not really a very original thinker, and the psychology that he espoused has been largely discredited. Bentley, by contrast, was not good at dramatizing himself and selling his views, depending instead on the purely intellectual impact of his critical views and theories, an approach that does not lead to immortality. (p. 368)

Although numerous aspects of what Ryan wrote have been confirmed by others, the aforementioned statement, clearly shows Ryan's sentiments toward Bentley.

CONTEMPORARY FIGURES: PATRICIA CAIN SMITH AND CHARLES L. HULIN

Having described the early influences in the Hulin family tree, I turn to the contemporary figures: Patricia Cain (Pat) Smith and Charles (Chuck) Hulin.

Patricia Cain Smith

Research Areas. As Smith noted in her partially autobiographical article (Smith & Stanton, 1999; see also Smith, 1988), her research interests have been broad. Like many scholars, over the course of her nearly 60-year research career, some of these areas attracted relatively ephemeral research attention. I count 10 separate areas of inquiry, including participation in groups, interviewer decision making, training performance, measurement of work values, job involvement, various aspects of research methodology, and the effect of background music on purchasing behavior. Although her research contributions in these areas should not be discounted, there are four areas where Smith has made major contributions.

One of these four areas is, broadly construed, the motivation and attitudes of workers, usually blue-collar workers, in industrial environments. In the post-World War II era, despite the Hawthorne studies, little thematic study of industrial monotony had occurred. In a qualitative study, Smith (1953) showed that production curves did not show a uniform association with boredom. Smith's results revealed not only interindividual differences in production curves, but also intraindividual differences from day to day. This ran counter to the then-prevailing view that boredom with industrial work followed a predictable pattern leading to reduced production. In a natural extension, Smith (1955) found that individuals prone to poor emotional adjustment were more susceptible to feelings of monotony. This study, along with others (e.g., Weitz, 1952), became forerunners to the dispositional source of job satisfaction that plays such a prominent role in current thinking and theories about job satisfaction. In her other research in this area, Smith investigated the effect of work processes (size of batches or lots in which the work was performed) on motivation and the learning curve for work in a clothing factory (an industry where she was to complete most of her studies in this area).

The second area of research is in the area of performance ratings. Her work (Smith & Kendall, 1963) resulted in the development of Behaviorally Anchored Ratings Scales (BARS). BARS represent one of the most important contributions to the measurement of job performance. BARS were an attempt to reduce some of the subjectivity and biases of trait graphic scales. Although many of the studies investigating BARS have not been supportive, Bernardin and Smith (1981) noted, "The emphasis by subsequent researchers and writers on the BARS approach apparently disregarded the important issues of observations and interpretation . . . BARS was designed to standardize not only the rating process but also the observation process" (pp. 458–459). Although BARS is no longer an active area of research, it has had a lasting effect on the field of performance evaluation (any book failing to discuss BARS would be negligent) and on performance measurement in organizations, where BARS continue to be used.

Smith's third area of research, one often unknown to I-O psychologists, is her work in experimental psychology. Smith's studies in this stream are in the area of visual perception, ranging from frames of reference and adaptation level to depth perception and the illusion of parallelism. For example, several studies examined the effect of the visual field on perception of objects (e.g., investigating the impact of restricting the field of view on subjects' perceptions of the relative distance of objects; Smith & Smith, 1961).

The substantive contributions of these studies would be difficult to judge by those trained in I-O Psychology. However, they are remarkable to this author for two reasons. First, especially today, it is rare for a researcher to establish streams in both experimental and applied psychology. A second noteworthy aspect of these studies is the degree to which they appear to reflect the Cornell influence. Guilford surely influenced Smith's interest in color, as apparently did Helson's and Boring's work on vision.

The fourth area of research, and that for which Smith is most famous, is job satisfaction. Smith, Kendall, and Hulin's (1969) *Measurement of Satisfaction in Work and Retirement* is one of the most important books in job satisfaction research. As Lyman Porter wrote in the forward, "This book has been eagerly awaited by those who have known of it and of the research—commonly known as the Cornell Studies of Satisfactions—on which it was based" (p. v). The most tangible outcome of the book was the description of the development of the Job Descriptive Index (JDI), the most carefully developed and validated measure of job satisfaction. The JDI continues to be the gold standard against which other measures are judged, and is the most widely used measure of job satisfaction. The book describes in great detail the development of validation of the measure. Unfortunately, the other major contribution of the book—the Cornell model of job satisfaction (see Hulin, 1991) and the frames of reference concept that was a central part of the model—has received much less attention by researchers.[5] In recognition of her accomplishments, Smith won the Distinguished Career Achievement Award from the American Psychological Association in 1984, the second year of such an award given by the division.

Influences in Family Tree.   I asked Pat Smith to reflect on the individuals in her family tree. On four different occasions, Smith wrote to me about her predecessors. In reflecting on her comments, I felt it would be most informative to leave the descriptions in her own words. Thus, what follows in this section is, with minor editing on my part, taken directly from Pat Smith's notes to me:

Edward Bradford Titchener. The ghost of Morrill Hall, who had influenced Guilford, Helson, and Dallenbach (of whom I saw a lot). Terrible autocrat. Wore full academic robes when he lectured, and forced all graduate students to precede him into lecture hall and stand as he marched in—so rumor said. I learned a lot of sensory psychology "willy nilly." As a result of Titchener, generations believed that analysis of complex experience into its constituent elements would build a scientific psychology. Too bad he was wrong.

Madison Bentley. Influenced Art Ryan greatly. I frankly did not understand how he clarified anything. Met him once; he evaluated me as too applied. I hope he was wrong.

J. P. Guilford. My undergraduate teacher, role model, and mentor. He was gentle, kind, hard-working, and always available to students, with sought-after reference immediately at hand. He was a youngish man then (1935 to 1939), but colorless. His World War II colleagues called him the "good gray Guilford." Students generally found him boring. I didn't. I had, as a senior in high school, determined that I wanted to be a "psychometric statistician," and Guilford was right up my alley. I double-majored in psychology and math.

His interests were very broad, and he managed to have projects across the range. I remember lie detectors, Hull's postulates, color preferences, psychophysics, intelligence, and personality testing. He believed that psychologists actually would learn enough to be able to help people. One motto was, "milk your data dry." I learned that research can be exciting and that an anomaly in your data is not a snag but a door cracked open.

---

[5]Numerous articles on job satisfaction by Smith and colleagues proceeded and followed the 1969 book, including refutation of Herzberg's two-factor theory, development of the Job in General (JIG) scale, and demonstration of linear relationships of various personal and job variables to job satisfaction.

When I mentioned Guilford the other day, a young colleague said, "Who?" But whole generations of graduate students used his texts. He preached—before Cronbach's "two disciplines of scientific psychology"—that measurement in individual differences paralleled measurement in experimental psychology. I do not see much progress in interdisciplinary research, nor—for that matter—in improving our ability to help people. He reinforced my interest in measurement, in applications of research findings, and encouraged me to do graduate work.[6] Possibly Guilford was the most important influence because my undergraduate years represented a standard against which others were judged (became central in my adaptation level).

Harry Helson. He was the first Cornell psychology faculty member who had presented a nonexperimental dissertation, a study of Gestalt psychology, to which we devoted an entire year's seminar. We went to all original sources. (I rode in to Philly to read Harvey on circulation of the blood—fascinating, but I now remember neither the relevance nor the name of the library.) Besides assisting or teaching several courses under Helson's supervision at Bryn Mawr, I built a light–tight viewing booth and ran subjects on adaptation level's relation to perceived color of illuminated sources. I was heavily overloaded and discouraged. Another graduate student, Marian Kadel, convinced me that I should apply at her alma mater, Cornell, where she planned to return that fall. They offered me a fellowship.

Adaptation level theory handles a lot of judgments better than frame of reference or their latter day substitutes in its weighting of central comparisons. I find conceptual uses here and there as I think about satisfactions—community characteristics (Kendall dissertation, Hulin & Blood, 1968), or Weitz's (1952) and your (Judge's) neutral objects, for two.

T. A. (Art) Ryan. A very kind, supportive, and wise person. I'm biased. Art and Mary (his PhD wife who side-stepped Cornell's antinepotism rule by teaching and writing about the psychology of clothing, in the College of Home Economics) were only 7 years older than us (Pat and Olie Smith), and good friends. Art and I played in a string quartet together for years. Art and Guilford were alike in many ways. Quiet, not showy, lectured in a highly structured way, wrote for the experts in the field, bored the undergraduates. Also, like Guilford, Art was very broad in his interests. Trained in experimental, interested in "business" psychology because of teaching in the College of Engineering during the war. When I came back to Cornell to teach after my internship at Aetna and my building a personnel psychology consulting division, we co-authored a text and collaborated on numerous committees. I considered him a mentor until he died. He influenced my think-

---

[6]Smith finished her undergraduate degree from Nebraska at midterm of her senior year (1939), went directly to Northwestern for one semester, where she found no one interested in psychometrics, and then went to Bryn Mawr for what she describes as a "dreadful, overworked, narrowly focussed year." After Bryn Mawr, Smith transferred to Cornell, completing her PhD in 1942. With her degree in hand, Smith went to Aetna for an internship under Marion Bills.

ing throughout. He took off from my dissertation findings about goal-setting, first in his book *Work and Effort* (Ryan, 1947) and later in *Intentional Behavior* (Ryan, 1970) to build an entire theoretical framework. Ed Locke and Gary Latham built a whole program of research on Art's theoretical structure—with modifications, of course. I intended that BES (modified to be BARS) would represent a feedback/goal setting system.

Art's work on multiple comparisons formed the basis for my half-formulated principles of validity generalization. Art made a big deal out of the importance of considering the entire efficiency equation: $E = O/I$, where E = human efficiency, O = output, including not only production but also satisfaction and other outcomes, and I = input, including effort, fatigue, stress, dissatisfactions, and other costs—Hello Herzberg! I took off from that in postulating an S curve relating presence of an aspect of the situation and the satisfaction with that aspect. Chuck was exposed to that stuff both directly from Art and Art's book and indirectly through me. I got into measuring satisfactions from my dissertation on monotony on the one hand and contacts with real, live, workers in my consulting on the other.

Art, as department chairman, fought for me several times. For example, the Dean wanted to limit faculty consulting, and Art saved the day, arguing for the relevance to teaching and research. More spectacularly, he pushed through my promotion, making me the first woman with tenure, and on the graduate faculty, in the endowed colleges. Cornell did not appreciate Art. He was an undergraduate *and* graduate student at the university in which he taught, always a bad career plan. And he did not seek outside offers. He felt at the end that no one was reading what he wrote. I hope that was not true. (P. C. Smith, personal communication, 1999)

Other Influences Not in Family Tree. In addition to the influence of individuals in her family tree, Smith described the influence of other individuals in her career, including Marion Bills (for whom Smith worked during her internship at Aetna), Kurt Salmon (who was president of the engineering firm for which Smith formed a personnel psychology consulting division), the other creative graduate students who helped shape the JDI project, Lorne Kendall and Ed Locke, Olin W. ("Olie") Smith (Smith's husband, with whom Smith collaborated on numerous experimental projects),[7] and employees in various organizations in which she consulted or did research.

---

[7]Olin W. ("Olie") Smith received his PhD from Cornell, also under Ryan (but, unlike Pat Smith, in I-O Psychology). The research they carried out in the visual perception area was done together. Most of Olin Smith's other research was applied, largely sponsored by the military interested in landing aircraft on carriers. In reflecting on Olin Smith, Hulin noted:

> He was a very strong influence on me. I thought a great deal of him, admired him. He was a good scientist and researcher in very difficult circumstances. He could not have a faculty appointment because of the antinepotism rules in place at the time. He was very smart, cared about us as Pat's students, gave us time, etc.

Relative Importance of the Influences.   When I asked Smith which influences on her were the most important, she had the following reply:

> Who influenced me the most? Depends on the dimension. Olie and the employees for decisions concerning importance of topics. Helson for forcing me to formulate theory, especially about the neutral point. Guilford for career guidance, and my approach to the structure of abilities and attitudes. Ryan on the necessity of my writing up the studies I had done, on dogged persistence, and on academic survival. My students on intellectual stimulation and moral support. Titchener because ghosts always win. And all because they earned my gratitude (well, not Titchener). (P. C. Smith, personal communication, 1999)

Charles L. Hulin

As I suspect is the case with any Hulin student, I could have devoted this entire chapter to describing Hulin's influence on me and my fellow students. However, the focus of this chapter—on Hulin's lineage—does not allow me to go into as much detail in describing Hulin's influence on others as much as others' influence on him. However, to gain a clear perspective on the tree, it is important to highlight Hulin's research contributions and influences.

Research Areas and Influence.   The following citation was read regarding Hulin's receipt of the Distinguished Scientific Contributions Award from the Society for Industrial and Organizational Psychology:

> The 1997 Distinguished Scientific Contributions Award was given to Dr. Charles Hulin, Department of Psychology and Institute of Aviation, University of Illinois. Chuck Hulin received his PhD in 1963 in Psychology from Cornell University. He has been on the faculty of the University of Illinois since 1962, with visiting positions at the University of California–Berkeley and the University of Washington. Chuck's contributions to the science of I-O Psychology are numerous. Apart from his contributions to and development of several major topic areas, he has also contributed through his training of many other I-O Psychologists who have gone on to further the science of our field.
>   Chuck has published over 65 papers in top journals, 25 in the *Journal of Applied Psychology* alone, 4 books, and numerous book chapters (including 2 in the 1992 edition *Handbook of Industrial and Organizational Psychology*). While the quantity of publications in high quality journals speaks to the degree of his contribution to the science of our field, the importance of that work makes that contribution even more striking. Chuck has written seminal work in several areas, including: Item Response Theory (e.g., Hulin, Drasgow, & Komocar, 1982), levels of analysis (e.g., Roberts, Hulin, & Rousseau, 1978); job characteristics theory (e.g., Hulin & Blood, 1968), the im-

pact of time on predictive relationships (e.g., Hulin, Henry, & Noon, 1990), and the measurement and theory of job satisfaction, turnover, and other withdrawal behaviors (e.g., Smith et al., 1969; Hulin, Roznowski, & Hachiya, 1985; Hulin, 1991). All of this work advanced theory, changed the way the field conceptualized various issues central to the field (e.g., reactions to jobs, predictive relationships, and measurement issues), and serve as classics and "must" reading for students of I-O Psychology.

Several themes consistently ran through Chuck's nomination letters. Of particular note, was the influence Chuck has had on the field by mentoring and training so many students and junior colleagues, many who have gone on to be active contributors to the field of I-O Psychology. Another theme concerned Chuck's breadth of contribution, as evidenced by the above list of seminal work. Finally, everyone noted Chuck's continued contribution over four decades. Of greatest note is his work on job satisfaction which has evolved into work on withdrawal behaviors. Indeed, Chuck's 1963 dissertation was entitled "Linear Model of Job Satisfaction" and, well . . . just take a look at the winners for the Ghiselli award.

There is no doubt that Chuck Hulin deserves the recognition afforded him as the recipient of this year's Scientific Contributions Award.

Although the aforementioned statement does a good job of describing Chuck's contributions to psychology, as a former student of Hulin's, I wish to briefly describe his influence on me as I believe it is typical of his influence on his other students. Most fundamentally, Hulin taught me a respect for the science of psychology. He would emphasize the importance of research for the advancement of understanding. In his classes, I can recall almost no time being spent on practical implications, business applications, and the like. It was not that Hulin objected to the practice of I-O psychological research. Rather, it was that Hulin did not seem particularly interested in practical implications of research if practical implications meant business concerns. Furthermore, Hulin communicated deep suspicions about the Boulder scientist–practitioner model, arguing that such a confounding of motives is likely to lead to a diluted or compromised science.

Hulin taught me a love for research and for working with doctoral students. Hulin was always animated when discussing research, especially with his students. I remember in class he once commented, "Don't tell the provost, but I'd do this job even if I weren't paid." As Hulin had comments about Smith (see later), doing research with him was fun. It was fun because Hulin appreciated humor in all its forms, both as a sender and as a recipient. Most classes and meetings with Hulin were an interspersion of serious (often philosophical) discussions with jibes, puns, ironies, derogations (self and other), stories, and jokes. Equally important to the joy, however, was the fact that research was interesting. It was interesting, we learned (more by example and observation than by statement), because it mattered and because research was to be done for discovery. As Smith commented to me, "The joy in discovery seems correlated with productivity among my students, I'm reasonably sure." I would argue this association is even more true *across* mentors.

Another great influence of Hulin was in his training. Hulin emphasized the importance of rigorous research methods, but he emphasized writing even more. His comments on papers were virtual tutorials on academic writing. I saved his hand-written comments on my papers for years. I have always felt he is one of the best writers in our field. I believe much of his appreciation for writing, and editing, came from Smith.

Another influence of Hulin on me was the concern that he expressed for workers. To the extent Hulin was interested in the practical application of research, his interests and values were in terms of the implications for employees. Oftentimes, after attending a class by Hulin, I remembering feeling inspired with a belief that research could better the world. Although good research can and does lead to greater organizational effectiveness, Hulin encouraged me to believe that research that might improve the lives of workers was the most worthy application.

Finally, on a substantive level, Hulin influenced me in two distinct ways. First, he encouraged my interest in dispositional sources of job satisfaction. When I entered graduate school, I had wanted to study the dispositional source of job satisfaction, but had been actively discouraged by two different professors in my first semester. When I took my first class with Hulin, his animated discussion of Weitz's (1952) article on a "gripe index" influenced me so much I later focused on this index in my dissertation, leading to one publication on its relevance to job satisfaction and another on its relevance to turnover. If not for Hulin, I believe I would have abandoned my original (and continuing) interest in personality and studied something else, as had been the advice of others. Second, Hulin's interest in general (as opposed to specific) attitudinal and behavioral constructs influenced me to be interested in general constructs as well, an interest that remains to this day (see Judge, Bono, Erez, Locke, & Thoresen, chap. 3, this volume).

Hulin is one of the two or three greatest influences on my life. He has been an invaluable and inspirational source of professional and, at times, personal advice. I believe his other students feel the same. Hulin's students are listed in Table 2.1.

Influences in Family Tree. As was the case with Pat Smith, I asked Hulin to describe the individuals in his family tree, paying particular attention to those who influenced him most. What follows are Hulin's de-

TABLE 2.1
Students of Charles Hulin

Name	Year of PhD	Current Employment
Milton Blood	1968	AACSB[a]
Arthur Carlson	1969	Retired (Educational Testing Service)
H. Peter Dachler	1969	St. Gallen (Switzerland)
Daniel Ilgen[b]	1969	Michigan State University
Kenneth Alvares	1971	Retired (Sun Microsystems)
Jeanne Brett	1972	Northwestern University
Tom Taber	1972	State University of New York at Albany
Peter Bates	1973	Deceased
John Newman	1974	Private consulting
Randall Dunham	1975	University of Wisconsin
Andres Inn	1976	Unknown
Peter Hom	1979	Arizona State University
Ralph Katerberg	1979	University of Cincinnati
Edward Adams	1980	Enterprise Rent-A-Car
Charles Parsons	1980	Georgia Institute of Technology
Mary Zalesny	1980	Pacific Northwest National Laboratory
Howard E. Miller	1981	Mankato State University
Joseph Rossé	1983	University of Colorado
Dennis Laker	1984	Widener University
Maria DeVera	1985	World Bank
Edwin Wagner	1985	St. Francie College (Pennsylvania)
John Komocar	1986	Unknown
Guy Cornelius	1988	Private consulting
Mary Roznowski	1988	Ohio State University
Hyeon Lee	1988	Lucent Technologies
Mary McLaughlin	1988	Pennsylvania State University
Kathy Hanisch	1990	Iowa State University
Timothy Judge	1990	University of Florida
Kim Schneider	1997	Illinois State University
Theresa Glomb	1998	University of Minnesota
Taihira Probst	1998	Washington State University
Wendy Richman	1998	Mercer Consulting
Joselito Lualhati	1999	Lucent Technologies
Liberty Munson	2000	Boeing

Note. [a]AACSB = American Association of Collegiate Schools of Business. [b]James Davis supervised Ilgen's dissertation while Hulin was a visitor at the University of California–Berkeley.

scriptions of his predecessors and their influence on him. These descriptions are from his notes to me, again with minor editing on my part:

Edward Bradford Titchener. I knew about Titchener mainly through his large and imposing portrait that hung in the fourth floor of Morrill Hall when I was there. It was also said that his ghost still prowled the building at night. His influence, if any, was very indirect being filtered through Madison

Bentley. American psychology had abandoned structuralism by then (1960–1962) for functionalism, behaviorism, and Freud. However, at Cornell, inspired by Ryan and Smith, what became cognitive psychology, goals and intentions, a general acceptance of the usefulness of verbal utterances and cognitive functions, was strong. When I got to Illinois and found Dulany, Fishbein, Erickson, and others talking about the importance of cognitive factors and rejecting such things as learning without awareness, I wondered what all the excitement was about. We had been reading chapters of Ryan's book on goals and intentions, and meeting weekly with him for quite some time.

Titchener was a very large man (not fat) but short. It was said that he had the lab/lecture table in the front of the room in Goldwyn Smith Hall that he lectured in built very short so he would appear to be taller when he lectured from behind it. That may be an "urban" legend. But I do know that the lecture tables that were built *were* very short and when I taught there I (a) felt like a giant and (b) had trouble reading my lecture notes because they were so low and far away from me. One of his students, Elsie Murray, was still there—I knew her only through hearing her walk to the phone in the hall, call a cab company, and announce "This is Elsie Murray, send a cab for me" with no other information . . . and the cab would shortly arrive outside Morrill Hall.

Madison Bentley. We had read Bentley in conjunction with an informal, meet-at-the-house seminar conducted by Ryan on the various chapters of his book on goals and intentions. I remember when I read the original stuff that I was struck by how current some of his thinking about Acte Psychologie was for goals and intentions. His influence would have been one person removed and filtered through Art . . . and perhaps Pat herself.

Harry Helson and J. P. Guilford. Helson and Guilford were Pat's professors at Bryn Mawr and the University of Nebraska. I met both of them at one time or another at Cornell. Guilford was an exceptionally nice man, very willing to talk to us about scaling, psychometric methods in general, and his emerging structure of the intellect. Factor analysis was still a new research tool then for emerging psychologists and it was being badly used by many to "discover" new factors of whatever they were studying. This does not negate his positive influence through his books on psychometric methods and scaling and his strong influence on Pat. I clearly remember him saying that he thought he would be the last non-clinician elected as president of the APA. He was wrong in the specifics but correct in his general assessment of where APA was going . . . rapidly.

T. A. (Art) Ryan. Art was a true scholar and intellectual. His book on goals and intentions was pretty well done in draft form in 1960 or 1961 though it did not get published until 1970. He was a genuinely nice man. Head of the department for some of the time I was there. He made it acceptable for them (Cornell being unnaturally proud of its Ivy League status) to teach I-O Psychology because he had done much experimental work and his work was so good. As Art's interests and teaching duties shifted to general methodology, Pat [Smith] did not have a colleague, her research was as good but did not have the strong experimental cachet his did, and she left. The I-O tradition at Cornell Psychology died about the time she left. To show you how short a time it flowered, I was her first PhD candidate. (See Table 2.2 for a listing of Pat Smith's students.) Lorne Kendall, Ed Locke, Jim Maas, and a couple of others, and then she left for Bowling Green.

Patricia Cain Smith. Pat was a outstanding graduate professor. I learned more in the hallways, her office, our lab (the Satisfactorium—so named because it had been the Olafactorium funded by Seagrams and set up for smell research, never used by the time I was there, and we hijacked it one weekend and moved out the unused equipment and moved in our desks and were set up for business (including the hand lettered "Satisfactorium" sign covering the Seagrams sign) when the "poohbahs" showed up Monday morning), in the cars driving to various research sites, and in her home at dinners and parties than I ever learned from her formal classes. Seminars were an exception. They were exciting. She was/is a warm supportive and intellectually demanding person. I loved her then and still do.

One thing Pat must have said to us 50 times was that we had to take what we did seriously but if we started to take ourselves seriously, she would take us to the woodshed . . . or words to that effect. Research with her was fun. About 16 hours a day of fun. If we were not having fun, we were doing something wrong. But what we were doing was important and serious and, if we did it right, it would have an impact on the lives of many workers. We drove one of the professors (MacLeod) nuts because we laughed "too much" and we must not be serious students. Pat almost required CPR when she reported that he had actually said that in a faculty meeting.

TABLE 2.2
Students of Patricia Cain Smith

Student	University	Year of PhD
Charles Hulin	Cornell	1963
Lorne Kendall[a]	Cornell	1964
Edwin Locke	Cornell	1964
James B. Maas	Cornell	1966
Eugene Ketchum	Cornell	1967
Stephen Wollack	Bowling Green	1969
Sheldon Zedeck	Bowling Green	1969
J. Nicholas Imparato	Bowling Green	1970
Jan Wijting	Bowling Green	1970
Michael L. White	Bowling Green	1970
James Goodale	Bowling Green	1971
David J. Hazard	Bowling Green	1971
Reginald Goodfellow	Bowling Green	1973
Joseph Weintraub	Bowling Green	1973
Julius Scheffers	Bowling Green	1976
Clyde Stutts	Bowling Green	1977
Bonnie Sandman	Bowling Green	1978
Barry Seeskin	Bowling Green	1981

Note. [a]Lorne Kendall completed his PhD under the supervision of Thomas A. Ryan.

Pat also influenced me in her beliefs about the nearly overwhelming importance of individual differences. One of the things she used to do was to make us convert t-ratios to biserial correlations to demonstrate that "significant" effects that were being trumpeted by the authors, while revealing differences between or among groups, also simultaneously revealed that these group differences were trivial in comparison to the unaccounted for individual differences. Pat was a midwestern and western small town girl in her formative years. She worked at summer jobs most of her school years. She had a respect for work and blue-collar workers that she conveyed to me. I hope I still have that belief. She believed that if we did everything we possibly could to make a study rigorous, fates and random glitches would add unwanted noise. But the harder we worked to impose rigor on what we did, the less impact these random forces would have. She was meticulous in her research. I recommend her study of the effects of music in grocery stores on the behaviors of shoppers as an example of this. I hope I assimilated this and still believe it. We had to listen to our research participants . . . not just interview them. When we debriefed them after a study, we really had to listen. They were important. What they thought and felt was both important and informative.

One very important thing that Pat taught us, by statement and practice, was that organizations are excellent laboratories. They control many environmental characteristics that potentially influence means, variances, and the structure of behaviors and constructs of our theories. Research developed in these controlled settings provides an excellent empirical basis for generalizations. Indeed, research conducted in these settings may provide a better basis for generalizations to behaviors in general than generalizations from lab settings to behaviors in general. I don't know how many, if indeed any, believe this except for Pat and me. I try to teach it to my students but . . . (C. L. Hulin, personal communication, 1999–2000)

CONCLUSIONS AND LESSONS LEARNED

In reflecting on Hulin's family tree and what it tells us about intergenerational influences, if this family tree is representative of others, there does appear to be a strong influence from one generation to the next. For example, Titchener was a devoted student of Wundt's, Ryan idolized his advisor, Bentley, and Smith was a strong influence on Hulin, as he has been on his students. It is true that the relationship between Titchener and Bentley did not follow this pattern. Although Titchener had other devoted students (most notably, Dallenbach), Bentley and Titchener were close only in age. However, this is the singular exception in this family tree.

Despite the strong influence advisors had on their students, the nature of this influence varied. In some cases, in addition to being intellectual, the ties were personal (Smith and Ryan were close friends). In other cases, they were not (Titchener was not personally close to Wundt). Another source of variance was in the singularity of the advisors' influences. Some individuals, such as Titchener, appeared to be mainly influenced by their advisor, whereas others, such as Smith and Guilford, were influenced by several individuals beyond their advisor. Finally, it is interesting to note that although the ties from advisor to student were strong, rarely did the advisor and student publish together. In the more than 1,000 articles published by individuals in this family tree, I count fewer than 10 that were authored by two individuals in the tree.

As compared to the direct relationship from advisor to student, the relationship one generation removed exhibits much more variance. Most Hulin students would consider themselves to be heavily influenced by Smith, in part because Hulin was heavily influenced by her. I suspect Hulin's encouragement of my interest in dispositions was due, at least in part, to Smith's interest in this area and her effect on him. Similarly, Hulin considers Ryan to be a strong influence on his career. On the other hand, in Ryan's review of psychology at Cornell (Ryan, 1982), he seemed to perceive little positive influence of Titchener. Similarly, Smith perceived little influence from Bentley (at least direct). Finally, going back two generations say, from Hulin to Bentley, in general the influences are weaker and less consistent, but they do not disappear. The emphasis on cognitive factors, beginning with Bentley, ran through Ryan, Smith, her students (mostly notably Ed Locke), and her students' students (e.g., Hulin and his students' views on attitudes and attitude–behavior linkages; Hulin et al., 1985). Although this emphasis is hardly controversial today, at the time, as Hulin noted to me, "It bucked some very well entrenched notions about what was valid evidence for scientific analysis." Similarly, Ryan impressed on Hulin the importance of verbal utterances and feelings.

In examining the Hulin family tree as a "Gestalt," is there any common theme? One commonality is the steadfast belief in the science of psychology. Perhaps Wundt's and Titchener's most important contributions were their efforts to establish psychology as a science. Bentley, although disagreeing with his predecessors in many ways, agreed on this one. As he noted in his book on psychology:

> Now the sciences are simply the result of man's most steady and most persistent attempt to encompass the world in a coherent and impersonal way by the fixed assumption of the attitude of knowing . . . Psychology belongs to this group . . . There is no choice. The attitude of knowing must be steadily and consistently preserved. (Bentley, 1934, pp. 5–6)

In their industrial psychology textbook, Ryan and Smith (1954) articulated several beliefs about the field, the first of which was the belief that industrial psychologists are to report the facts, not draw conclusions that are influenced by "whoever pays for the research" (p. 6). Thus, scientific objectivity and impartiality are paramount to the industrial psychologist. No student of Hulin would question his scientific orientation; he is the least applied I-O psychologist I know.

In comparison to other I-O family trees (Landy, 1992, 1997), this tree seems less applied. More than the others, it is strong in experimental psychology, from Wundt through Smith. (All trained as experimental psychologists, all conducted a great deal of research in experimental psychology.) Other family trees also had earlier prominent influences on I-O Psychology (Bingham, Cattell, Münsterberg, Scott). Furthermore, although Guilford, Ryan, and Smith all dealt with issues directly in the I-O area, only Smith would be commonly recognized as an I-O psychologist per se (and even this describes only part of Smith's career). Furthermore, even Hulin and his students might consider themselves less strongly tied to I-O Psychology than they would describe themselves as psychologists.

This chapter was written to contribute to our collective memory of the Hulin lineage. It is a lineage and legacy well worth remembering, containing some of the central figures in the history of psychology. In opening his autobiography, Guilford asked, "What is a life—a sequence of personal events, of birth, school, marriage and parenthood, work, retirement, and death?" (Lindzey, 1974, p. 169). Although Guilford—like the others above and alongside him on the family tree—has passed through this sequence, he and they live on through the direct and indirect impacts of their lives' work.

ACKNOWLEDGMENTS

I wish to thank Chuck Hulin and Pat Smith for their contributions to this chapter. The writing in the sections on their influences is essentially theirs.

REFERENCES

Angell, J. R. (1895). Review of E. W. Scripture, *Thinking, Feeling, Doing. Psychological Review, 2,* 606–609.

Bentley, M. (1938). Cornell studies in dynasomatic psychology. *American Journal of Psychology, 51,* 203–224.

Bentley, M. (1948a). Advancement of understanding and advancement of professional service. *American Journal of Psychology, 61,* 111–118.

Bentley, M. (1948b). The Harvard case for psychology. *American Journal of Psychology, 61,* 275–282.

Bernardin, H. J., & Smith, P. C. (1981). A clarification of some issues regarding the development and use of behaviorally anchored ratings scales (BARS). *Journal of Applied Psychology, 66,* 458–463.

Bevan, W. (1964). Contemporary problems in adaptation-level theory. *Psychological Bulletin,* *61,* 161–162.

Boring, E. G. (1927). Edward Bradford Titchener, 1867–1927. *American Journal of Psychology,* *38,* 489–506.

Boring, E. G. (1929). *The history of experimental psychology.* New York: Century.

Boring, E. G. (1950). *A history of experimental psychology* (2nd ed.). New York: Appleton-Century-Crofts.

Boring, E. G. (1958). Karl M. Dallenbach. *American Journal of Psychology, 71,* 1–40.

Boring, E. G. (1967). Titchener's experimentalists. *Journal of the History of the Behavioral Sciences, 3,* 315–325.

Dallenbach, K. M. (1956). Madison Bentley: 1870-1955. *American Journal of Psychology, 69,* 169–186.

Guilford, J. P. (1927). The role of form in learning. *Journal of Experimental Psychology, 10,* 415–423.

Guilford, J. P. (1934). Introversion–extroversion. *Psychological Bulletin, 31,* 331–354.

Guilford, J. P. (1936). *Psychometric methods.* New York: McGraw-Hill.

Guilford, J. P. (1952). When not to factor analyze. *Psychological Bulletin, 49,* 26–37.

Guilford, J. P. (1954). *Psychometric methods* (2nd ed.). New York: McGraw-Hill.

Helson, H. (1948). Adaptation-level as a basis for a quantitative theory of frames of reference. *Psychological Review, 55,* 297–313.

Helson, H. (1964). *Adaptation-level theory.* New York: Harper & Row.

Hulin, C. L. (1991). Adaptation, persistence, and commitment in organizations. In M. D. Dunnette & L. M. Hough (Eds.), *Handbook of industrial and organizational psychology* (Vol. 2, 2nd ed., pp. 445–505). Palo Alto, CA: Consulting Psychologist Press.

Hulin, C. L., & Blood, M. R. (1968). Job enlargement, individual differences, and worker responses. *Psychological Bulletin, 69,* 41–55.

Hulin, C. L., Drasgow, F., & Komocar, J. (1982). Applications of item response theory to analysis of attitude scale translations. *Journal of Applied Psychology, 67,* 818–825.

Hulin, C. L., Henry, R. A., & Noon, S. L. (1990). Adding a dimension: Time as a factor in the generalizability of predictive relationships. *Psychological Bulletin, 107,* 328–340.

Hulin, C. L., Roznowski, M., & Hachiya, D. (1985). Alternative opportunities and withdrawal decisions: Empirical and theoretical discrepancies and an integration. *Psychological Bulletin, 97,* 233–250.

Landy, F. J. (1992). Hugo Münsterberg: Victim or visionary? *Journal of Applied Psychology, 77,* 787–802.

Landy, F. J. (1997). Early influences on the development of industrial and organizational psychology. *Journal of Applied Psychology, 82,* 467–477.

Lindzey, G. (1974). *A history of psychology in autobiography: VI.* Englewood Cliffs, NJ: Prentice-Hall.

Michael, W. B., Comrey, A. L., & Fruchter, B. (1963). J. P. Guilford: Psychologist and teacher. *Psychological Bulletin, 60,* 1–34.

Murchison, C. (1936). *A history of psychology in autobiography.* Worcester, MA: Clark University Press.

Murphy, G. (1949). *Historical introduction to modern psychology* (Rev. ed.). New York: Harcourt, Brace, & Company.

Roberts, K. H., Hulin, C. L., & Rousseau, D. M. (1978). *Developing an interdisciplinary science of organizations.* San Francisco: Jossey-Bass.

Ryan, T. A. (1947). *Work and effort: the psychology of production.* New York: Ronald Press.

Ryan, T. A. (1970). *Intentional behavior: An approach to human motivation.* New York: Ronald Press.

Ryan, T. A. (1982). Psychology at Cornell after Titchener: Madison Bentley to Robert MacLeod, 1928–1948. *Journal of the History of the Behavioral Sciences, 18,* 347–369.

Ryan, T. A., & Smith, P. C. (1954). *Principles of industrial psychology.* New York: Ronald Press.

Smith, P. C. (1953). The curve of output as a criterion of boredom. *Journal of Applied Psychology, 37,* 69–74.

Smith, P. C. (1955). The prediction of individual differences in susceptibility to industrial monotony. *Journal of Applied Psychology, 39,* 322–329.

Smith, P. C. (1988). Patricia Cain Smith. In A. N. O'Connell & N. P. Russo (Eds.), *Models of achievement: Reflections of eminent women in psychology.* Hillsdale, NJ: Lawrence Erlbaum Associates.

Smith, P. C., & Smith, O. W. (1961). Veridical perceptions of cylindricality: A problem of depth discrimination and object identification. *Journal of Experimental Psychology, 62,* 145–152.

Smith, P. C., & Kendall, L. M. (1963). Retranslation of expectations: An approach to the construction of unambiguous anchors for rating scales. *Journal of Applied Psychology, 47,* 149–155.

Smith, P. C., Kendall, L. M., & Hulin, C. L. (1969). *The measurement of satisfaction in work and retirement: A strategy for the study of attitudes.* Chicago: Rand McNally.

Smith, P. C., & Stanton, J. M. (1999). Perspectives on the measurement of job attitudes: The long view. *Human Resource Management Review, 8,* 367–386.

Stevens, S. S. (1968). *American Journal of Psychology, 81,* 589–606.

Titchener, E. B. (1905). *Experimental psychology.* New York and London: Macmillan.

Watson, R. I. (1978). *The great psychologists* (4th ed.). Philadelphia: J. B. Lippincott.

Weitz, J. (1952). A neglected concept in the study of job satisfaction. *Personnel Psychology, 5,* 201–205.

Yik, M. S. M., Russell, J. A., & Barrett, L. F. (1999). Structure of self-reported current affect: Integration and beyond. *Journal of Personality and Social Psychology, 77,* 600–619.

Part II

RESEARCH ON THE PSYCHOLOGY OF WORK

Conceptualization
of Psychological Constructs

The Scientific Merit of Valid Measures of General Concepts: Personality Research and Core Self-Evaluations

Timothy A. Judge
University of Florida

Joyce E. Bono
University of Minnesota

Amir Erez
University of Florida

Edwin A. Locke
University of Maryland

Carl J. Thoresen
Tulane University

Cronbach indicated that psychologists are one of two types: those who seek to make fine distinctions among psychological concepts by splitting them into constituent elements, and those who seek to aggregate concepts by combining narrow concepts into broader ones. Titchener, the pioneer of American experimental psychology, might be classified as the former for his effort to document 40,000 human sensations. In contrast, Spearman's research on a general factor of intelligence would classify him as the latter. In most areas of individual differences, personality factors being the current Zeitgeist, the war between the two types rages on.

Which group is right? Despite decades of attempts to answer this question definitively, there is no single answer. The principle of correspondence (Ajzen & Fishbein, 1977) suggests that psychological concepts must be matched in terms of their generality or specificity if maximum empirical validity and theoretical understanding is to be gained. Specific concepts do have their advantages. Because there is no such thing as an "action in general," compared to general concepts, situationally specific concepts better predict action on a particular task or in a particular situation.[1] Despite the potential advantages of such concepts, however, most psychologists are not entirely content with looking only at narrowly defined, specific variables. From a practical standpoint, it is costly and inefficient to gather such information. For example, in the context of personnel selection, the narrow approach would call for a unique set of predictors of each job. Furthermore, when the job changed, a new set of predictors would be necessary. In addition to practical concerns, it is theoretically misleading to view individuals as bundles of disconnected habits and skills. Because we know from our everyday experiences that there is much in people that endures across time, tasks, and situations, psychologists have been concerned with broad traits that predict action across tasks, situations, and time. Furthermore, from a measurement perspective, specific attitudes and behaviors are often unreliable. As Epstein (1979) commented, "Single items of behavior, no matter how carefully measured, like single items in a test, normally have too high a component of error of measurement to permit demonstration of high degrees of stability" (p. 1121). Unfortunately, despite the many advantages of broad concepts, and even though they have shown their usefulness in many areas of psychology, their superiority is often ignored outside of the ability arena (Rushton, Brainerd, & Pressley, 1983).

In part, broad psychological concepts have been overlooked in nonability areas, such as personality, due to beliefs that the issues are more complex than in the case of intelligence. For example, there is worry about circularity: If we measure traits by combining observations across situations, then are we not simply predicting behavior from behavior? The usual answer is that we are assuming that there are underlying premises, values, and beliefs that cause the behavior. This is a reasonable argument, though labeling these underlying factors "latent variables" does not in itself make the underlying causes real. Another problem in the case of personality traits is that the situations most people encounter differ radically, and, this side of psychopathy, most people take account of situational factors when deciding how to act. For example, a man who is aggressive at

---

[1]Indeed, the superiority of specific attitudes (behavioral intentions) over general attitudes in predicting specific behaviors is well documented. Researchers have linked behavioral intentions and specific attitudes toward a wide range of behaviors—ranging from condom use (Sheeran & Taylor, 1999) to recycling behavior (Boldero, 1995). Thus, if you want to predict whether someone will compost their vegetable garden, whether a woman will elect to have a mammogram, if a person will attend work tomorrow, or whether a particular consumer is likely to buy Velveeta or Camembert, it is hard to do better than behavior intentions. Yet, as Roznowski and Hulin (1992) noted, behavioral intentions are the idiot savants of psychology—they predict specific, proximate behaviors quite well, but that is the limit of their usefulness. Behavioral intentions are not well suited to predict general or broad behaviors, nor do they do much to inform us about the psychological processes underlying the behavior.

work may not be with his family, because he views what is appropriate in the two situations to be quite different. Because situations differ so, actions or attitudes in these situations are difficult to predict on the basis of generalized personality tendencies.

Despite these presumed greater challenges in the personality area, it should be stressed that the case of personality is not really so different from the case of intelligence when it comes to the situational specificity issue. Intelligence tests predict better in situations where cognitive ability (conceptual thinking) is most required (highly complex jobs), and predict less well in situations where thinking is less critical (Ones, Viswesvaran, & Schmidt, 1993). With respect to personality, it is known that certain of the Big Five measures predict best in certain situations as well. For example, conscientiousness is particularly important in autonomous jobs (Mount & Barrick, 1995). Thus, both in the case of intelligence and of personality, there are trait–situation interactions. Although these interactions exist, in both cases, general individual differences predict, at a nonzero level, across situations. Thus, despite controversies and misconceptions, broad concepts have been shown to be quite useful, often more useful than specific measures in industrial psychology.

Within the realm of organizational psychology, individual differences have a shorter and sketchier tradition of research interest. This does not mean, however, that general concepts have failed to demonstrate their value here as well. Much of Charles Hulin's career (especially in the last 20 years) has been focused on correspondence in terms of attitude–behavior relations. As Hulin noted, with few exceptions,[2] most researchers typically have examined antecedents of specific withdrawal behaviors such as absenteeism and turnover in isolation, ignoring the possibility that these behaviors may be manifestations of an underlying concept. Such an approach is both empirically limiting (results of investigations linking job satisfaction to specific withdrawal behaviors are inconsistent and disappointing) and theoretically vacuous (such investigations provide little basis for developing general theoretical concepts that allow generalizations to other, related job behaviors). In response, Hulin (e.g., Hulin, 1991; Hulin, Roznowski, & Hachiya, 1985) argued that researchers should consider the possibility that the communality among specific withdrawal behaviors may indicate a common concept. According to Hulin, these withdrawal behaviors range from the traditionally studied behaviors such as absence, turnover, and lateness, to other behaviors such as wasting time chatting with co-workers, stealing, and substance abuse. An accumulating body of evidence supports the dual claims that the specific behaviors are related, and

---

[2]Fisher (Fisher, 1980; Fisher & Locke, 1992) and Jenkins and Gupta (e.g., Mitra, Jenkins, & Gupta, 1992) are exceptions.

that when the behaviors are aggregated, the ability of job satisfaction to predict these behaviors improves markedly (Fisher & Locke, 1992; Hanisch & Hulin, 1990, 1991; Henne & Locke, 1985; Judge, 1990; Judge & Locke, 1993; Rosse, 1989; Roznowski & Hanisch, 1990; Roznowski & Hulin, 1992).

Hulin's research has specifically concerned criterion aggregation. However, the same logic works with respect to predictor aggregation, whether the predictors are attitudinal[3] or dispositional. The focus of this chapter is on the value of aggregation and breadth in the personality domain. The genesis, nature, and implications of this concept are discussed here.

CORE SELF-EVALUATIONS

Core self-evaluations is a higher order concept representing the fundamental evaluations that people make about themselves, their environments, and the relationship between themselves and their environment. We argue that people tend to appraise events in a consistent and stable manner across situations. Because this evaluation style is fundamental, represented in many situational-specific evaluations, and is directly related to the self and the self-concept, we name it core self-evaluations. We also argue that the core self-evaluations concept is manifested by four traits: self-esteem, locus of control, neuroticism, and generalized self-efficacy. As such, these four traits can be combined to represent the broader core self-evaluations concept.

Self-Esteem, Locus of Control, and Neuroticism

Self-esteem, locus of control, and neuroticism (also known as emotional stability or emotional adjustment) are the most widely studied personality concepts in psychology. In a recent (April 17, 2000) search of the Psyc-INFO database, 1967 to present, we investigated the degree to which these traits, along with two other traits that we thought might have been as widely investigated, appeared as keywords in articles in the database. Our search revealed the following:

- 18,264 articles with self-esteem as a keyword;
- 15,636 articles with neuroticism and/or emotional stability as a keyword;

---

[3]In a meta-analysis of 311 correlations, Judge, Thoresen, Bono, and Patton (2001) showed that when job satisfaction is treated as a general factor, its correlation with job performance is .30, a figure dramatically higher than the often cited .17 correlation by Iaffaldano and Muchinsky (1985), which focused on facet correlations.

- 12,247 articles with locus of control as a keyword;
- 6,293 articles with extraversion or introversion as a keyword;
- 5,432 articles with need for achievement or achievement motivation in its keywords.

Thus, self-esteem, neuroticism, and locus of control do appear to be the most widely investigated traits in psychology. These three traits have been the subject of more than 45,000 studies!

Despite the prominence of these traits, and some rather obvious connections between them, few investigations have included more than a single core trait. Thus, in the vast majority of cases, these traits are studied in isolation. In the rare article when two or more of the traits are included in the same study, they usually are treated as entirely separate variables (e.g., Abouserie, 1994; Hojat, 1983; Horner, 1996). In an even rarer situation, one trait is modeled as an influence on the other, often with bewildering results. For example, Wambach and Panackal (1979) investigated the main effect of neuroticism on locus of control, whereas Morelli, Krotinger, and Moore (1979) investigated locus of a control as a cause of neuroticism. In Industrial and Organizational (I-O) Psychology, the situation is just as confusing. Typically, when two of these traits are included in the same study, they are treated as causally unrelated variables (e.g., Hesketh, 1984; Tiggemann & Winefield, 1984).[4]

In sum, self-esteem, locus of control, and neuroticism have been studied extensively in both personality and I-O Psychology. Curiously, however, the quest of the last 10 years to find broad personality factors within the five-factor model has ignored these traits. Although neuroticism has been considered a broad trait even by those researchers who do not endorse the five-factor model (Eysenck, 1990), self-esteem and locus of control continue to be studied as individual, isolated traits. We argue shortly that this need not—indeed should not—be the case.

Core Self-Evaluations Theory

In seeking to advance research on the dispositional source of job satisfaction, Judge, Locke, and Durham (1997) developed a theory of traits they

---

[4]A number of studies have explicitly investigated relations among pairs of the core traits (e.g., Francis, 1996; Morrison, 1997). However, despite finding strong relations, none of these studies explicitly consider the possibility that these traits may indicate a common higher order trait, despite some evidence that they do. For example, Hunter et al. (1982) concluded that self-esteem and locus of control "act like proxies for a second-order factor, which was named self-concept" (p. 1302). Similarly, Hojat's (1982) results revealed that self-esteem, locus of control, and neuroticism loaded on a common factor.

termed *core evaluations*. The core self-evaluations concept refers to basic conclusions or bottom-line evaluations that represent one's appraisal of people, events, and things in relation to one's self. According to Judge et al. (1997), because core self-evaluations are fundamental appraisals, they are implicated in situationally specific evaluations, such as judgments of job satisfaction or motivational decisions. Based on three criteria (see Judge et al., 1997, for a description of these criteria), Judge and colleagues (Erez & Judge, in press; Judge, Erez, & Bono, 1998; Judge et al., 1997) included four traits as indicators of the core self-evaluations concept—self-esteem, neuroticism, locus of control, and generalized self-efficacy.

Higher order psychological concepts like core self-evaluations can be considered to be latent concepts, which are unobservable and cause the dimensions (indicators) to be positively related; or as aggregate concepts, which are formed from or composed of their dimensions. Judge and Bono (2001a) argued that core self-evaluations is a latent concept. As they note:

> Clearly, the position Judge and colleagues have taken, despite some inconsistency in their treatment of the construct, is that core self-evaluations is a latent multidimensional construct. We agree with this viewpoint. The implication of this perspective is that self-esteem, generalized self-efficacy, locus of control, and neuroticism are measures (rather than components or causes) of the core self-evaluations construct, and it is the latent core construct that causes the individual traits to be intercorrelated. (Judge & Bono, 2001a, pp. 99–100)

Implications of Core Self-Evaluations for Job Satisfaction and Job Performance

Judge et al. (1997) argued that core self-evaluations would be related to job satisfaction, and the evidence appears to support their hypothesis. Judge and Bono (2001b) conducted a meta-analysis of the relationship of the four individual core traits to job satisfaction. Although the specific estimates reported in that paper will be reviewed shortly, it is possible to use their results to estimate the relationship of the overall trait to job satisfaction. Following procedures recommended by Viswesvaran and Ones (1995) with respect to using covariance structure modeling with meta-analytic data, using Judge and Bono's (2001b) data, we estimated the true correlation between the core self-evaluations latent factor and job satisfaction be to .41. Thus, the core self-evaluations concept is perhaps the best dispositional predictor of job satisfaction.

Why is the core self-evaluations concept consistently related to job satisfaction? Two studies conducted by our research team have suggested one explanation: Intrinsic job characteristics mediate the relationship between and job satisfaction. By *intrinsic job characteristics*, we mean the Hackman and Oldham's (1980) core job dimensions (task identity, skill variety, task significance, autonomy, and feedback). In three studies and across various specifications, Judge, Locke, Durham, and Kluger (1998) showed that roughly 37% of the influence of core self-evaluations on job satisfaction was mediated by perceptions of intrinsic job characteristics. Although the Judge, Locke, et al. (1998) study helped to illuminate the process by which core self-evaluations influenced job satisfaction, the studies used only a perceptual measure of job characteristics. It is not clear from Judge, Locke, et al.'s (1998) findings to what degree the core self-evaluations concept is related to increased job complexity as opposed (or in addition) to enhanced perceptions of work characteristics. Accordingly, Judge, Bono, and Locke (2000) tested the mediating role of job characteristics using both objective (coding job titles using the Dictionary Occupational Titles job complexity scoring) and perceptual measures of job characteristics. In two studies, their results indicated that core self-evaluations was related to the actual attainment of complex jobs as well as to the perceptual measures of job characteristics (holding objective complexity constant). Thus, it appears that core self-evaluations influences job satisfaction, in part, because positive individuals actually obtain more challenging jobs, and also because they perceive jobs of equal complexity as more intrinsically fulfilling. In another study, Judge, Thoresen, Pucik, and Welbourne (1999) examined coping with change as the process by which core self-evaluations lead to job satisfaction. In this study, more than half of the influence of core self-evaluations on job satisfaction was mediated by coping, indicating that individuals with positive self-evaluations are more satisfied with their jobs because they cope more effectively with change.

The core self-evaluations concept also appears to matter in terms of job performance. Again following Viswesvaran and Ones (1995) and using Judge and Bono's (2001b) meta-analytic results, we estimated a correlation between the core self-evaluations latent factor and job performance of .30. This level of validity is impressive. As is shown in Fig. 3.1, the validity of the individual core traits is comparable to the validity of conscientiousness. When composite correlations are computed (an alternative means of estimating correlations at the factor level; see Mount & Barrick, 1995), the validities of core self-evaluations and conscientiousness are essentially the same. Much has been made of the validity of conscientiousness as a predictor of job performance. These results suggest that another trait, core self-evaluations, should be placed alongside conscientiousness as a valid personality predictor of job performance.

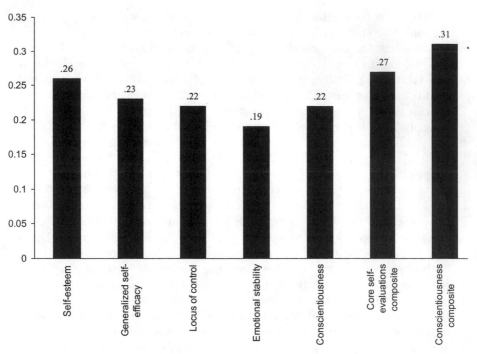

FIG. 3.1. Comparison of the validity of core self-evaluations and conscientiousness as predictors of job performance.

If the core self-evaluations concept is an important predictor of job performance, how is it so? Judge, Erez, et al. (1998) argued that the core self-evaluations concept should influence performance mainly through its effect on motivation. According to these authors, several theories of motivation might explain the effect of core self-evaluations on performance. Erez and Judge (in press) conducted two studies to investigate the degree to which motivation mediated the relationship between core self-evaluations and performance. In a laboratory study, Erez and Judge found that the core self-evaluations factor was positively related to self-reported task motivation ($r = .39, p < .01$), an objective measure of task persistence ($r = .24, p < .05$), and task performance ($r = .35, p < .01$). In a second study, a field study of insurance agents, Erez and Judge found that the core self-evaluations factor was positively related to sales goal level ($r = .42, p < .01$), goal commitment ($r = .59, p < .01$), and both objective (sales volume; $r = .35, p < .01$) and supervisory ratings ($r = .44, p < .01$) of job performance. In both studies, Erez and Judge found that motivation mediated about half of the relationship between core self-evaluations and performance. Thus, it appears that core self-evaluations is a motivational trait, and this explains much of its effect on job performance.

VALIDITY OF CORE SELF-EVALUATIONS CONCEPT[5]

Because core self-evaluations is a relatively new concept in both the personality and I-O Psychology literatures, it is important to examine carefully the validity of the concept. As noted by Schwab (1980), establishing the validity of a psychological concept involves both conceptual issues (definition and theoretical relationships with other variables) and empirical considerations (convergent validity and location of the concept within its nomological network). In ascertaining the validity of the core self-evaluations concept, at least four questions need to be addressed:

1. Do the core traits display convergent validity? In other words, does it appear that the four core self-evaluations traits (self-esteem, locus of control, neuroticism, and generalized self-efficacy) indicate a common concept?
2. Do the core traits display discriminant validity? If the traits display differential patterns of associations with other variables, this would argue against them being interchangeable indicators of a common concept.
3. What is the relative predictive validity of the isolated core traits as opposed to the core concept? If there is value in the broad concept, it must predict better than the isolated core traits.
4. What is the nature of the core self-evaluations concept relative to more established frameworks? Specifically, how—if at all—does core self-evaluations fit into the five-factor model of personality?

We deal with each of these issues in turn.

Covergent Validity of Core Traits

Convergent validity refers to whether different measures of the same concept show sufficient interrelationships to demonstrate that they indicate the same concept. In terms of core self-evaluations theory, the question of convergent validity can be answered by examining the correlations among the four core traits. Table 3.1 provides the correlations among the core self-evaluations traits based on metaanalytic data reported in Judge and Bono (2001b). As the table shows, the correlations are substantial. The average correlation among the traits (.64) is at least as high as the correla-

---

[5]We use the term *concept* in place of *construct* because the latter term has the unfortunate Kantian connotation of being a fictional entity with no basis in reality.

TABLE 3.1
Relationships Among Core Self-Evaluations Traits

Core Trait	Self-Esteem	Generalized Self-Efficacy	Internal Locus of Control
Generalized self-efficacy	.85		
Internal locus of control	.59	.63	
Emotional stability	.66	.59	.51

Note. Correlations are estimated true score correlations corrected for measurement error.

tions among alternative measures of traits in the five-factor model (see Ones, 1993). Another piece of evidence in favor of the core concept is factor analytic research, which consistently suggests that the four core traits identify a common concept (Erez & Judge, in press; Judge et al., 2000; Judge, Locke, et al., 1998). Thus, it appears that the four core traits can be treated as measures of the core self-evaluations concept.[6]

Discriminant Validity of Core Traits

Discriminant validity refers to differential patterns of correlations of the concepts in question with other variables. In the case of core self-evaluations, this is an issue of whether the four core traits display differential associations with other, theoretically relevant, variables. Because we are using the core traits as measures of the core self-evaluations concept, if the traits showed discriminant validity with other variables, it would weigh against the argument that the traits simply are equivalent measures of the same (core self-evaluations) concept. There are at least three theoretically relevant variables that may be used to test if differential relationships exist: subjective well-being, job satisfaction, and job performance. DeNeve and Cooper's (1998) meta-analytic results reveal the following with respect to the uncorrected correlation between three of the core traits and subjective well-being: neuroticism, average $r = -.27$, locus of control, average $r = .25$; efficacy, average $r = .23$. With respect to job satisfaction and job performance, Judge and Bono (2001b) provided a meta-analysis of the relationship of these variables to the four core traits. The correlations are provided in Table 3.2. Although the correlations are not identical, the variability is fairly low. Indeed, with the exception of the correlation between generalized self-efficacy and job satisfaction (which was boosted by a

---

[6]Judge et al. (2000) reported results on the stability of the core self-evaluations concept. They found that the stability of core self-evaluations was .46 (.62 when corrected for measurement error) over a 20-year period.

TABLE 3.2
Relationship of Core Self-Evaluations Traits
to Job Satisfaction and Job Performance

	Job Satisfaction	*Job Performance*
Self-esteem	.26	.26
Generalized self-efficacy	.45	.23
Locus of control	.32	.22
Neuroticism	.24	.19

Note. From Judge and Bono (2001b). Correlations are meta-analytic "true score" correlations corrected for measurement error.

single strong correlation in one large sample study), the credibility intervals all overlap. Thus, it appears that the core traits do not display much discriminant validity in terms of their correlations with the three outcomes, again supporting the argument that they are indicators of a common concept. It should be noted that the results in Table 3.2 represent incomplete evidence of discriminant validity, as we examine relationships with only three dependent variables and do not consider the full nomological network.

Relative Predictive Validity of Individual Core Traits Versus the Core Concept

If the arguments presented earlier in the chapter regarding correspondence are correct and applicable to core self-evaluations, then the broad core trait should predict broad criteria better than the individual traits. We should note that the bandwidth-fidelity issue is currently being debated in both the personality and the personnel selection literatures, with advocates on all sides of the issue (see Costa & McCrae, 1992a; Eysenck, 1992; John, Hampson, & Goldberg, 1991; Ones & Viswesvaran, 1996; Schneider, Hough, & Dunnette, 1996). Although addressing this issue is beyond the scope of this chapter, our concern is the relative predictive validity of the broad core self-evaluations concept versus the four specific traits. Erez and Judge (in press) addressed this issue explicitly in terms of the relationship of core self-evaluations to motivation and job performance. They found that the overall core concept always predicted motivation and performance, whereas the individual traits did so inconsistently. Thus, it appears that the overall concept is a more consistent predictor of outcomes than are the individual traits. This is only one study, however. Further evidence is needed.

Core Self-Evaluations and the Five-Factor Model

Because core self-evaluations theory posited that neuroticism is an indicator of the broader concept, and neuroticism is one of the most established traits in personality research, it is relevant to ask whether core self-evaluations is simply another label for neuroticism. A separate but related question is: How does the core self-evaluations concept fits into the five-factor model of personality? As for the first question, at a conceptual level, it appears that neuroticism may be as broad as core self-evaluations. Eysenck's (1990) conceptualization of neuroticism considers self-esteem to be one of the lower order indicators of the concept, and Watson and Clark's (1984) conceptualization of negative affectivity, which the authors have subsequently argued is neuroticism (Watson, 2000), also includes self-esteem as one of its indicators. Thus, from a conceptual standpoint, core self-evaluations does not appear to be more broad than neuroticism and, on this basis alone, one might argue that core self-evaluations should be subsumed under the neuroticism concept, because the latter has a much more extensive tradition of research. However, the relationships among the other core traits are less studied and, accordingly, the nature of the relationships is less clear. There are a few studies that have investigated the relationship among other pairs of the core traits (e.g., self-esteem and locus of control [Francis, 1996]; locus of control and neuroticism [Morrison, 1997]), but none of these studies explicitly consider the possibility that these traits may indicate a common higher order concept. A few studies have investigated the possibility that the traits may indicate a higher order factor. Specifically, Hunter, Gerbing, and Boster (1982), in a study of Machiavellianism, concluded that self-esteem and locus of control "act like proxies for a second-order factor, which was named self-concept" (p. 1302). Similarly, Hojat (1982) found that self-esteem, locus of control, and neuroticism had their highest loadings on a common factor.

Examining this issue from a measurement perspective is also informative. Typically, measures of neuroticism, perhaps owing to its psychopathological origins, assess dysphoria, hostility, stress, and anxiety. As Judge and Bono (2001a) noted, most measures of neuroticism do not explicitly assess beliefs about one's capabilities or control over one's environment. For example, there are no items in the neuroticism scales of the NEO–FFI (Costa & McCrae, 1992b), the International Personality Item Pool (IPIP; Goldberg, 1999), or the Eysenck Personality Inventory (EPI; H. J. Eysenck & S. B. G. Eysenck, 1968) that explicitly reference control or capability. Thus, although core self-evaluations may be no broader than the theoretical concept of neuroticism, we believe that existing measures of neuroticism are too narrow to fully capture self-evaluations.

Another possibility is that the core self-evaluations concept is a broad trait that represents a composite of several Big Five traits (or facets of sev-

TABLE 3.3
Relationship of Core Traits to Five-Factor Model of Personality

	Neuroticism	Extraversion	Openness	Agreeableness	Conscientiousness
Neuroticism	—	−.30	−.02	−.29	−.49
Self-esteem	−.66	.42	.23	.20	.46
Locus of control	−.51	.36	.03	.16	.47
Generalized self-efficacy	−.59	.54	.25	.20	.46

Note. Correlations are meta-analytic "true score" correlations. Correlations between neuroticism and the other core traits are from Judge and Bono (2001b).

eral traits). In order to explore the relationship of the core traits to the five-factor model, we cumulated correlations between the core traits and the Big Five traits in the studies that were able to access. We then meta-analyzed these correlations to provide an estimate of the correlations among the traits, corrected for measurement error. The estimates were corrected for unreliability using reliability estimates reported in Judge, Bono, Ilies, and Werner (in press). Correlations are based on data we have collected, as well as several articles that have reported correlations between one of the core traits and the Big Five (Jackson & Gerard, 1996; Kwan, Bond, & Singelis, 1997; Morrison, 1997). We caution the reader that this is an incomplete meta-analysis, based on a cursory search of the literature and a relatively small number of correlations. However, pending a more thorough quantitative review, these incomplete results are superior to reporting results study by study.

The correlations of the core traits with the Big Five traits are provided in Table 3.3. As the table shows, each of the core traits correlates the most strongly with neuroticism. Furthermore, these correlations are slightly higher than the average intercorrelation among different measures of the Big Five traits.[7] Yet Table 3.3 also reveals that the core traits correlate moderately strongly with extraversion and conscientiousness. Openness and agreeableness also display nontrivial correlations with the core traits, but in general these correlations are considerably weaker and less consistent than those involving extraversion and conscientiousness. Setting aside neuroticism for the moment, the three core traits display an average correlation of .44 with extraversion and .46 with conscientiousness. These

[7]Ones's (1993) meta-analysis revealed that the average intercorrelation among different measures of the Big Five traits is .49, compared to the average correlation of between neuroticism and the other three core traits of .59 (see Table 3.3). The average intercorrelation between different measures of neuroticism in Ones's (1993) meta-analysis was .63, compared to the .64 average intercorrelation among the core self-evaluations traits reported by Judge and Bono (2001b).

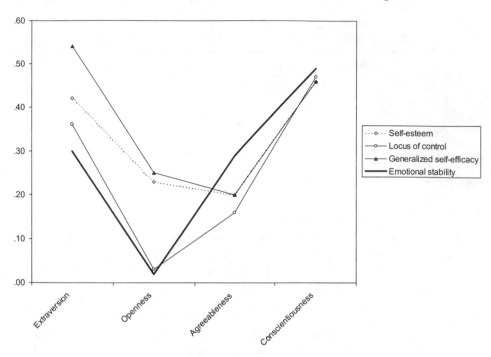

FIG. 3.2. Comparison of correlation of core self-evaluations traits with Big Five. (*Note*. To enhance graphical display, neuroticism is reverse coded and labeled *emotional stability*.)

are substantial correlations and support the argument that core self-evaluations is a broader concept indicated by (or a composite of) three Big Five traits—neuroticism, conscientiousness, and extraversion.

However, it is important to note that the correlations of the three core traits (self-esteem, locus of control, generalized self-efficacy) with the Big Five traits tend to be similar to the correlations of neuroticism with the other Big Five traits.[8] Indeed, an examination of Table 3.3 reveals that whereas the three core traits display stronger correlations with extraversion than neuroticism, the correlations are nearly identical for conscientiousness and actually slightly smaller for agreeableness. Figure 3.2 provides a graphical illustration of these results, and shows that neuroticism (labeled *emotional stability* for ease of interpretation in the figure) tends to display a similar pattern of correlations to the other Big Five traits when

---

[8]Digman (1997) presented 14 intercorrelation matrices among the Big Five factors. Assuming a reliability of .80 in both measures, the average corrected correlation between neuroticism and extraversion in Digman's matrices is −.28 and the average correlation between neuroticism and conscientiousness is −.53. These are quite similar to the averages (−.30 and −.49, respectively) reported in Table 3.3.

compared to the other three core traits. On one hand, core self-evaluations cannot be argued to be independent of extraversion and conscientiousness. On the other hand, although theoretically the Big Five represent five orthogonal personality traits, measures of neuroticism are correlated with measures of conscientiousness and extraversion. Thus, empirically, neither neuroticism nor other three core traits are independent of extraversion and conscientiousness.

FUTURE CORE SELF-EVALUATIONS RESEARCH

Research to date on the validity of the core self-evaluations concept has been generally supportive of the theory. Specifically, the core self-evaluations concept is related to the most central variables in I-O Psychology—job performance and job satisfaction. Furthermore, correlations among the core traits strongly suggest that they are manifestations of a higher order concept. Despite this support, numerous questions remain unanswered. Thus, further investigation is needed in several areas. These are now reviewed.

Further Validity Evidence

Perhaps the most pressing need is further research into the validity of the core self-evaluations concept. It seems clear that there is benefit to the broad concept of core self-evaluations. However, the exact nature of the concept, and its relationship to the five-factor model, remains unclear. Is the core self-evaluations factor the same as neuroticism? Is it a composite of several Big Five traits, including neuroticism, conscientiousness, and extraversion? Or, alternatively, is the core self-evaluations concept a higher order trait indicated by these Big Five traits?[9] It is even possible that the core trait does not belong in the five-factor model at all. Despite evidence presented in this chapter, the answers to these questions are far from clear.

How should future research investigate the validity of core self-evaluations? One useful method is through *hierarchical confirmatory factor analysis*, wherein multiple measures of the core traits are related to the Big Five traits. This would allow researchers to partition variance in the measures to one of the three sources: (a) variance due to the common core concept; (b) variance due to each specific trait (e.g., self-esteem, generalized self-efficacy, etc.); (c) variance idiosyncratic to each measure of the specific

---

[9] We should note that if core self-evaluations is a higher order trait, it does not match up particularly well with Digman's (1997) two meta-traits—α (indicated by agreeableness, conscientiousness, and neuroticism), and β (indicated by extraversion and openness).

trait. The larger the proportion of variance attributable to the core concept, the more valid the core concept. A further step is to determine the nature of the relationship shared between the specific traits and measures of extraversion and conscientiousness. If the shared variance is significant, it suggests that core self-evaluations cannot be subsumed under neuroticism. In general, more evidence is needed to address each of the four questions posed earlier in this chapter.

Development of Overall Measure

It appears that the core self-evaluations concept has predictive validity in terms of job satisfaction and job performance. Thus, researchers interested in predicting these outcomes should strongly consider including the concept in future models of satisfaction and performance. From an operational perspective, though, how should core self-evaluations be measured? In the Appendix are the items we have used in past research to measure core self-evaluations. As the reader can see, our approach has been to measure the four core traits and combine them, generally using a latent variable approach. Although these measures are valid (and nonproprietary), this approach may not be the most efficient, in several ways. First, the number of items is more than in most measures of personality traits, creating some potential inefficiency (perhaps a reliable and valid measure can be formed from fewer items). Second, if core self-evaluations can be accurately predicted by five-factor model traits, it might make more sense to simply use the Big Five traits to measure the concept, at least for predictive purposes. Finally, it is possible the items that we have used to measure core self-evaluations are not the best items; it is possible that other items that directly assess self-evaluations might have higher validity in predicting job satisfaction, job performance, or other concepts. Thus, exploratory work on the merits of a direct measure of the core self-evaluations concept is needed.

Investigation of Other Mediating Processes

Although we have been able to explain some of the reasons individuals with positive core self-evaluations are happier in their jobs and better performers, there is considerable room for further explanation. Across two studies (Judge et al., 2000; Judge, Locke, et al., 1998) utilizing multiple samples, we have been able to explain 45% of variance in the relationship between core self-evaluations and job satisfaction using intrinsic job characteristics. This suggests that other theoretical mechanisms will need to be studied to more fully understand the nature of the relationship between core self-evaluations and job satisfaction. Recently, Judge and Larsen

(2001) developed a stimulus–organism–response (S–O–R) model that describes ways in which personality may moderate the effect of stimuli (the environment) on individuals' responses, as well as ways in which personality processes might govern individuals' responses to the stimuli. There are numerous testable propositions in this chapter, including the hypothesis that individuals with positive core self-evaluations are more satisfied with their jobs because they are more likely to evoke and pursue approach (identified, intrinsic) work goals, whereas negative individuals are more likely to evoke and pursue avoidance (extrinsic, introjected) goals.

With respect to performance, Erez and Judge's (in press) results suggested that motivation accounted for half the relationship of core self-evaluations with performance. That the figure was not higher may be because goal-setting theory was used as the motivational framework. Although goal-setting theory has ample support in the literature, it is not the only theory of motivation and does not exhaust the motivation variance. Thus, it is possible that other motivational theories might play a mediating role. Judge, Erez, et al. (1998) discussed several theories of work motivation that they expect to be related to core self-evaluations. Future research should investigate the link between core self-evaluations and the other theories of work motivation.

Finally, we wish to note that although we have indicated our belief in broad psychological concepts, this does not mean that specific concepts such as goals, attitudes, intentions, or even specific "midrange" traits, are not useful. Indeed, specific concepts have proven to be valuable in many areas of inquiry. We suggest, however, that if maximum psychological understanding is to be gained, and if causal models are to be properly specified, investigations of specific concepts must include theoretically relevant general concepts. There are many such models that could be specified and tested in this area. Ideally, such models would integrate general and specific concepts, using the specific concepts as mediators.

Other Ways to Achieve Breadth

Aggregation across traits—the perspective taken here with respect to core self-evaluations theory—is not the only means to achieve broad measures of valid concepts. Epstein (1983) discussed four principle ways in which aggregation could occur: aggregation over stimuli, aggregation over occasions, aggregation over judges, and aggregation over modes of measurement. With respect to aggregation over stimuli, observer ratings of personality are likely to be more valid when people are observed in different situations (at ease, under stress, when faced with success, and failure, etc.). Alternatively, Epstein (1979) showed convincingly that the reliability and validity of psychological measurements increased monotonically with temporal aggregation (aggregation over occasions). Thus, one means of obtaining a broad assessment of personality is to collect personality information over several time periods and temporally aggregate the responses. Aggregation can also occur by collecting multiple ratings of personality (aggregation over judges), as is sometimes done with "significant other" surveys in personality research, and averaging across these ratings. Finally, aggregation over modes of measurement refers to the pooling of measures of personality obtained by different methods, such as survey and projective measures of personality.

A study we recently completed clearly shows the benefits of aggregation. In this study (Judge, Higgins, Thoresen, & Barrick, 1999), we used existing personality data in which individuals' personalities were evaluated by multiple clinical psychologists over a 50-year period (twice in childhood, three times in adulthood). Thus, personality measures were aggregated over time and across judges. When the two childhood ratings of personality were pooled, we found that the multiple correlation between childhood personality and career success was .54 for extrinsic success and .42 for intrinsic success. When the personality ratings were pooled across all five time periods, these multiple correlations increased to .62 and .64, respectively. These results show that the benefits of aggregation are considerable.

Yet our typical measure of personality remains a "one-shot" survey. It is relatively uncommon for personality researchers to use any of these methods of aggregation and more unusual still for I-O psychologists to use any of these methods. Researchers (present company included) have been remiss in their failure to aggregate more often, and the reliability (and thus validity) of the ratings has suffered.

SUMMARY

We opened this chapter by discussing the merits of broad measures of psychological concepts, and in particular noted Hulin's contribution to this literature with respect to criterion aggregation. His research on this topic made its mark on the first author of this chapter. However, our research team has extended this research to focus on *predictor* aggregation, in the personality area in particular. Results presented here show that predictor aggregation achieves the same positive results as criterion aggregation. Specifically, as is the case with specific withdrawal behaviors sharing sufficient covariance to indicate a higher order factor, we demonstrate that four specific personality traits share sufficient covariance to indicate a underlying, broader concept. We have termed this concept core self-evaluations, although we note that it may be equivalent to neuroticism in the five-factor model of personality (or even a combination of neuroticism, conscientiousness, and extraversion). There are numerous areas for future research that we have suggested in this chapter. For now, however, we wish to conclude by noting that one of the hallmarks of Hulin's career—the benefits of behavioral aggregation—seems to have born fruit in our research as well.

APPENDIX: CORE SELF-EVALUATIONS MEASURE

Self-Esteem (Rosenberg, 1965)

1. I feel that I am a person of worth, at least on an equal basis with others.
2. I feel that I have a number of good qualities.
3. All in all, I am inclined to feel that I am a failure. (r)
4. I am able to do things as well as most other people.
5. I feel that I do not have much to be proud of. (r)
6. I take a positive attitude toward myself.
7. On the whole, I am satisfied with myself.
8. I wish I could have more respect for myself. (r)
9. I certainly feel useless at times. (r)
10. At times I think I am no good at all. (r)

Generalized Self-Efficacy (Judge, Locke, et al. 1998)

1. I am strong enough to overcome life's struggles.
2. At root, I am a weak person. (r)
3. I can handle the situations that life brings.
4. I usually feel that I am an unsuccessful person. (r)
5. I often feel that there is nothing that I can do well. (r)
6. I feel competent to deal effectively with the real world.
7. I often feel like a failure. (r)
8. I usually feel I can handle the typical problems that come up in life.

Locus of Control (from Levenson, 1981)

1. Whether or not I get to be a leader depends mostly on my ability.
2. When I make plans, I am almost certain to make them work.

3. When I get what I want, it's usually because I'm lucky. (r)

4. I have often found that what is going to happen will happen. (r)

5. I can pretty much determine what will happen in my life.

6. I am usually able to protect my personal interests.

7. When I get what I want, it's usually because I worked hard for it.

8. My life is determined by my own actions.

Neuroticism (H. J. Eysenck & S. B. G. Eysenck, 1968)

1. My feelings are easily hurt.

2. I'm a nervous person.

3. I'm a worrier.

4. I am often tense or "high strung."

5. I often suffer from "nerves."

6. I am often troubled by feelings of guilt.

7. My mood often goes up and down.

8. Sometimes I feel miserable for no reason.

9. I am an irritable person.

10. I often feel fed up.

11. I often worry too long after an embarrassing experience.

12. I often feel lonely.

Note. r = reverse-scored item.

REFERENCES

Abouserie, R. (1994). Sources and levels of stress in relation to locus of control and self-esteem in university students. *Educational Psychology, 14*, 323–330.

Ajzen, I., & Fishbein, M. (1977). Attitude-behavior relations: A theoretical analysis and review of empirical research. *Psychological Bulletin, 84*, 888–918.

Boldero, J. (1995). The prediction of household recycling of newspapers: The role of attitudes, intentions, and situational factors. *Journal of Applied Social Psychology, 25*, 440–462.

Costa, P. T., Jr., & McCrae, R. R. (1992a). Four ways five factors are basic. *Personality and Individual Differences, 13*, 653–665.

Costa, P. T., Jr., & McCrae, R. (1992b). *NEO-PI-R and NEO-FFI professional manual.* Odessa, FL: Psychological Assessment Resources.

DeNeve, K. M., & Cooper, H. (1998). The happy personality: A meta-analysis of 137 personality traits and subjective well-being. *Psychological Bulletin, 124*, 197–229.

Digman, J. M. (1997). Higher-order factors of the Big Five. *Journal of Personality and Social Psychology, 73*, 1246–1256.

Epstein, S. (1979). The stability of behavior: I. On predicting most of the people much of the time. *Journal of Personality and Social Psychology, 37*, 1097–1126.

Epstein, S. (1983). Aggregation and beyond: Some basic issues on the prediction of behavior. *Journal of Personality, 51,* 360–392.

Erez, A., & Judge, T. A. (in press). Influence of core self-evaluations on goal commitment, goal setting, task activity, and performance. *Journal of Applied Psychology.*

Eysenck, H. J. (1990). Biological dimensions of personality. In L. A. Pervin (Ed.), *Handbook of personality* (pp. 244–276). New York: Guilford.

Eysenck, H. J. (1992). Four ways five factors are *not* basic. *Personality and Individual Differences, 13,* 667–673.

Eysenck, H. J., & Eysenck, S. B. G. (1968). *Manual for the Eysenck Personality Inventory.* San Diego, CA: Educational and Industrial Testing Service.

Fisher, C. D. (1980). On the dubious wisdom of expecting job satisfaction to correlate with performance. *Academy of Management Review, 5,* 607–612.

Fisher, C. D., & Locke, E. A. (1992). The new look in job satisfaction research and theory. In C. J. Cranny, P. C. Smith, & E. F. Stone (Eds.), *Job satisfaction* (pp. 165–194). New York: Lexington.

Francis, L. J. (1996). The relationship between Rosenberg's construct of self-esteem and Eysenck's two-dimensional model of personality. *Personality and Individual Differences, 21,* 483–488.

Goldberg, L. R. (1999). A broad-bandwidth, public-domain, personality inventory measuring the lower-level facets of several five-factor models. In I. Mervielde, I. J. Deary, F. De Fruyt, & F. Ostendorf (Eds.), *Personality psychology in Europe* (Vol. 7, pp. 7–28). Tilburg, The Netherlands: Tilburg University Press.

Hackman, J., & Oldham, G. (1980). *Work redesign.* Reading, MA: Addison-Wesley.

Hanisch, K. A., & Hulin, C. L. (1990). Retirement as a voluntary organizational withdrawal behavior. *Journal of Vocational Behavior, 37,* 60–78.

Hanisch, K. A., & Hulin, C. L. (1991). General attitudes and organizational withdrawal: An evaluation of a causal model. *Journal of Vocational Behavior, 39,* 110–128.

Henne, D. L., & Locke, E. A. (1985). Job dissatisfaction: What are the consequences? *International Journal of Psychology, 20,* 221–240.

Hesketh, B. (1984). Attribution theory and unemployment: Kelley's covariation model, self-esteem, and locus of control. *Journal of Vocational Behavior, 24,* 94–109.

Hojat, M. (1982). Loneliness as a function of selected personality variables. *Journal of Clinical Psychology, 38,* 137–141.

Hojat, M. (1983). Comparison of transitory and chronic loners on selected personality variables. *British Journal of Psychology, 74,* 199–202.

Horner, K. L. (1996). Locus of control, neuroticism, and stressors: Combined influences on reported physical illness. *Personality and Individual Differences, 21,* 195–204.

Hulin, C. L. (1991). Adaptation, persistence, and commitment in organizations. In M. D. Dunnette & L. M. Hough (Eds.), *Handbook of industrial and organizational psychology* (2nd ed., Vol. 2, pp. 445–505). Palo Alto, CA: Consulting Psychologist Press.

Hulin, C. L., Roznowski, M., & Hachiya, D. (1985). Alternative opportunities and withdrawal decisions: Empirical and theoretical discrepancies and an integration. *Psychological Bulletin, 97,* 233–250.

Hunter, J. E., & Gerbing, D. W., & Boster, F. J. (1982). Machiavellian beliefs and personality: Construct validity of the Machiavellianism dimension. *Journal of Personality and Social Psychology, 43,* 1293–1305.

Iaffaldano, M. T., & Muchinsky, P. M. (1985). Job satisfaction and job performance: A meta-analysis. *Psychological Bulletin, 97,* 251–273.

Jackson, L. A., Gerard, D. A. (1996). Diurnal types, the "Big Five" personality factors, and other personal characteristics. *Journal of Social Behavior and Personality, 11,* 273–283.

John, O. P., Hampson, S. E., & Goldberg, L. R. (1991). The basic level in personality-trait hierarchies: Studies of trait use and accessibility in different contexts. *Journal of Personality and Social Psychology, 60,* 348–361.

Judge, T. A. (1990). *Job satisfaction as a reflection of disposition: Investigating the relationship and its effect on employee adaptive behaviors.* Unpublished doctoral dissertation, University of Illinois at Urbana-Champaign.

Judge, T. A., & Bono, J. E. (2001a). A rose by any other name . . . Are neuroticism, self-esteem, locus of control, and generalized self-efficacy indicators of a common construct? In B. W. Roberts & R. T. Hogan (Eds.), *Personality psychology in the workplace* (pp. 93–118). Washington, DC: American Psychological Association.

Judge, T. A., & Bono, J. E. (2001b). Relationship of core self-evaluations traits—self-esteem, generalized self-efficacy, locus of control, and emotional stability—with job satisfaction and job performance: A meta-analysis. *Journal of Applied Psychology, 86,* 80–92.

Judge, T. A., Bono, J. E., Ilies, R., & Werner, M. (in press). Personality and leadership: A review. *Journal of Applied Psychology.*

Judge, T. A., Bono, J. E., & Locke, E. A. (2000). Personality and job satisfaction: The mediating role of job characteristics. *Journal of Applied Psychology, 85,* 237–249.

Judge, T. A., Erez, A., & Bono, J. E. (1998). The power of being positive: The relationship between positive self-concept and job performance. *Human Performance, 11,* 167–187.

Judge, T. A., Higgins, C., Thoresen, C. J., & Barrick, M. R. (1999). The Big Five personality traits, general mental ability, and career success across the life span. *Personnel Psychology, 52,* 621–652.

Judge, T. A., & Larsen, R. J. (2001). Dispositional source of job satisfaction: A review and theoretical extension. *Organizational Behavior and Human Decision Processes, 86,* 67–98.

Judge, T. A., & Locke, E. A. (1993). Effect of dysfunctional thought processes on subjective well-being and job satisfaction. *Journal of Applied Psychology, 78,* 475–490.

Judge, T. A., Locke, E. A., & Durham, C. C. (1997). The dispositional causes of job satisfaction: A core evaluations approach. *Research in Organizational Behavior, 19,* 151–188.

Judge, T. A., Locke, E. A., Durham, C. C., & Kluger, A. N. (1998). Dispositional effects on job and life satisfaction: The role of core evaluations. *Journal of Applied Psychology, 83,* 17–34.

Judge, T. A., Thoresen, C. J., Bono, J. E., & Patton, G. K. (2001). The job satisfaction–job performance relationship: A qualitative and quantitative review. *Psychological Bulletin, 127,* 376–407.

Judge, T. A., Thoresen, C. J., Pucik, V., & Welbourne, T. M. (1999). Managerial coping with organizational change: A dispositional perspective. *Journal of Applied Psychology, 84,* 107–122.

Kwan, V. S. Y., Bond, M. H., & Singelis, T. M. (1997). Pancultural explanations for life satisfaction: Adding relationship harmony to self-esteem. *Journal of Personality and Social Psychology, 73,* 1038–1051.

Levenson, H. (1981). Differentiating between internality, powerful others, and chance. In H. M. Lefcourt (Ed.), *Research with the locus of control construct* (Vol. 1, pp. 15–63). New York: Academic Press.

Mitra, A., Jenkins, G. D., & Gupta, N. (1992). A meta-analytic review of the relationship between absence and turnover. *Journal of Applied Psychology, 77,* 879–889.

Morelli, G., Krotinger, H., & Moore, S. (1979). Neuroticism and Levenson's locus of control scale. *Psychological Reports, 44,* 153–154.

Morrison, K. A. (1997). Personality correlates of the five-factor model for a sample of business owners/managers: Associations with scores on self-monitoring, Type A behavior, locus of control, and subjective well-being. *Psychological Reports, 80,* 255–272.

Mount, M. K., & Barrick, M. R. (1995). The Big Five personality dimensions: Implications for research and practice in human resources management. *Research in Personnel and Human Resources Management, 13,* 153–200.

Ones, D. S. (1993). *The construct validity of integrity tests*. Unpublished doctoral dissertation, University of Iowa.

Ones, D. S., & Viswesvaran, C. (1996). Bandwidth-fidelity dilemma in personality measurement for personnel selection. *Journal of Organizational Behavior, 17,* 609–626.

Ones, D. S., Viswesvaran, C., & Schmidt, F. L. (1993). Comprehensive meta-analysis of integrity test validities: Findings and implications for personnel selection and theories of job performance [Monograph]. *Journal of Applied Psychology, 78,* 531–537.

Rosenberg, M. (1965). *Society and the adolescent self-image*. Princeton, NJ: Princeton University Press.

Rosse, J. G. (1989). Relations among lateness, absence, and turnover: Is there a progression of withdrawal? *Human Relations, 41,* 517–531.

Roznowski, M., & Hanisch, K. A. (1990). Building systematic heterogeneity into work attitudes and behavior measures. *Journal of Vocational Behavior, 36,* 361–375.

Roznowski, M., & Hulin, C. (1992). The scientific merit of valid measures of general constructs with special reference to job satisfaction and job withdrawal. In C. J. Cranny, P. C. Smith, & E. F. Stone (Eds.), *Job satisfaction* (pp. 123–163). New York: Lexington.

Rushton, J. P., Brainerd, C. J., & Pressley, M. (1983). Behavioral development and construct validity: The principle of aggregation. *Psychological Bulletin, 94,* 18–38.

Schneider, R. J., Hough, L. M., & Dunnette, M. D. (1996). Broadsided by broad traits: How to sink science in five dimensions or less. *Journal of Organizational Behavior, 17,* 639–655.

Schwab, D. P. (1980). Construct validity in organizational behavior. *Research in Organizational Behavior, 2,* 3–43.

Sheeran, P., & Taylor, S. (1999). Predicting intentions to use condoms: A meta-analysis and comparison of the theories of reasoned action and planned behavior. *Journal of Applied Social Psychology, 29,* 1624–1675.

Tiggemann, M., & Winefield, A. H. (1984). The effects of unemployment on the mood, self-esteem, locus of control, and depressive affect of school-leavers. *Journal of Occupational Psychology, 57,* 33–42.

Viswesvaran, C., & Ones, D. S. (1995). Theory testing: Combining psychometric meta-analysis and structural equations modeling. *Personnel Psychology, 48,* 865–885.

Wambach, R. L., & Panackal, A. A. (1979). Age, sex, neuroticism, and locus of control. *Psychological Reports, 44,* 1055–1058.

Watson, D. (2000). *Mood and temperament*. New York: Guilford.

Watson, D., & Clark, L. A. (1984). Negative affectivity: The disposition to experience aversive emotional states. *Psychological Bulletin, 96,* 465–490.

Chapter 4

The Ubiquity of Evaluation:
A Hulinesque Essay

Howard M. Weiss
Purdue University

Daniel R. Ilgen
Michigan State University

Allow us to state the premise of our chapter right at its beginning. We believe that a number of seemingly disparate constructs studied by organizational psychologists are essentially the same construct, requiring the same theoretical framework for explanation. Too often, these essentially identical latent constructs are regarded as different, are studied independent of each other by different sets of researchers, and are enmeshed in different explanatory systems. We believe this situation exists because the organizational "constructs" studied are described and defined by the way organizational phenomena are experienced by organizational members, or by the way they are identified by organizations, rather than by their underlying psychological meaning. Expressed in terms of manifest variables and latent constructs, too often, theory construction in the organizational sciences begins and ends with organizational members' manifest experiences of organizational phenomena. Artificial boundaries are then formed that lead to the development of inappropriately narrow, phenomena-driven theories, and prevent us from recognizing that our separate phenomena are really alternative manifestations of the same underlying construct.

Alternatively, because these manifest variables are overdetermined, treating them as if they were theoretical variables overloads them with excess meaning. Manifest variables thought to represent a single construct are really manifestations of multiple constructs. Just as, apparently, different manifest variables may radiate from the same latent construct, a single manifest variable may be linked to different latent constructs.

Our chapter is an attempt to flesh out this argument and illustrate it by focusing on one example: how the latent construct of evaluation is the underlying explanatory framework for two seemingly disparate constructs, job satisfaction, and performance appraisal. We begin with a discussion of phenomena-driven organizational research, follow this with a general discussion of the nature of evaluation, and then show how both job satisfaction and performance appraisal are different manifestations of the latent process of evaluation, and therefore demand similar theoretical explanations. We use this example to make our general point, not to focus attention on these two phenomena.

OUR POSITION

We contend that current explanations of work variables exist at a surface or phenomenal level. At a deeper level, these surface level phenomena that are believed to be quite different often turn out to be alternative contextual manifestations of the same construct. What do we mean by surface level and deeper level? For us, *surface level variables* have their definitions close to their operations. They focus on the construct as it is manifested and experienced in a particular setting—in this case, the work setting. Turnover, absenteeism, job satisfaction, and performance evaluations are surface level variables. *Deeper level variables* are defined in ways that are more independent of situations even though their existence is, of course, manifested in particular situations. Consider, for example, escape. Escape is a situation-free construct manifested in work contexts as turnover, absenteeism, daydreaming, or other behaviors that remove persons from the work setting, either physically or psychologically. Consider, also, *evaluation*. It is a deeper level construct that shows up as job satisfaction in some situations, performance appraisals in others, or interviewer judgments in still others.

Our ideas are not original. We are making the well-established distinction between theoretical variables, our deep level constructs, and their operations, our surface level constructs. However, too often this distinction is seen as relevant only in the context of experimental design, as the seeming arbitrariness of experimental manipulation is justified by demonstrations of construct validity. Although every organizational researcher knows, or should know, about the nature of theoretical constructs, the evidence does not suggest that the lesson has been learned very well. Also, too often, organizational researchers think they are building theories at the construct level but are really building theories with constructs defined in the context in which they are experienced. Theories of turnover, theories of performance appraisal, and theories of interviewer judgments all illustrate our point. Certainly, at that level, empirical regularities can be reliably observed. But the context dependence hides underlying deep structure and important equivalencies. It also reduces generality, the main advantage of theory.

Perhaps an analogy will help us make our point more effectively. Historically, medical specialties (with some exceptions) have been organized around organ systems: kidney specialists, blood specialists, heart specialists, and so on. These specialties derive from the disease site (the situation), not from the underlying disease process. Modern medicine is moving away from this organization. Medicine is focusing on fundamental disease processes independent of site. Specialties will reorganize to reflect underlying processes across sites. Specialists in genetic medicine or auto-immunity may replace cardiologists and hematologists in the not-too-distant future.

Do not misunderstand. We are not saying that theories of work phenomena cannot or should not be developed. We understand that Industrial and Organizational (I-O) Psychology is a context-focused field. We seek to explain a certain class of situation defined behaviors and attitudes and also to explain the implications of those explanations to people who populate work organizations. So, yes, we need theories of job satisfaction and turnover and performance appraisals. These variables are at the core of our field. But, saying we need theories that explain these phenomena is not the same as saying that these exploratory systems should consist of phenomena level regularities.

How then should our theories be structured? What should they look like? We believe they should be structured to show connections among relevant deeper level constructs and connections between the deeper latent constructs and the surface/manifest variables of interest. Our theories should describe how surface variables are manifestations of deeper underlying constructs and the relationships among these constructs. They should not be structured as relationships among variables at the phenomenal level, at the level of the variable of applied interest. To do so would suggest a conceptual meaning for these phenomena that they do not deserve and hide commonalties that cross seemingly independent variables identified at that level.

A basic task of our science is, therefore, *construct translation*. That is, an important part of our theoretical task is to translate latent constructs into work-relevant manifestations and to describe variables defined in the work context as manifestations of their appropriate theoretical constructs. When this occurs, when we look at the connections between context free constructs and their contextual manifestations, we begin to see underlying equivalencies hidden by our contextual blinders.

Charles Hulin has often said that work settings are a great place to test, even develop, general theories of behavior. He has expressed his disappointment at our inability to export our theories and findings (see chap. 1, this volume). We agree entirely, and we think we know one of the reasons for this disappointing state. If our "theories" are expressed primarily in terms of regularities among context specific variables, their general relevance is limited. If, however, the translation is made more explicit, so too are the general implications of the findings.

I-O Psychology as a field has both its basic and applied objectives. To some, our discussion may seem relevant only to the basic component. We do not think this is the case. Focusing on the deeper level can have practical advantages as well as theoretical ones. If when confronted with a practical problem to solve, we stay only within the phenomenal domain, we may never recognize that we (or someone else) have confronted this same problem before in another domain. If we think at the deeper level, we start to ask questions that we did not ask before. We discover solutions that are novel for one domain but are routinely accepted in another.

This "Hulinfest" is a particularly appropriate place to make this point because his own work illustrates it so well. His extensive research showing that withdrawal is an underlying psychological construct (e.g., Hulin, 1991) that ties together different situational manifestations is a fine example of our theme. However, Hulin's ideas on the withdrawal construct are generally broader than most researchers recognize. By showing that turnover and absenteeism should be considered situational manifestations of the latent withdrawal construct, Hulin was, perhaps, describing something that many I-O psychologists already recognized. Researchers who study one manifestation of withdrawal (e.g., turnover) often study the others (absenteeism, lateness). Even when treated as separate variables, the theoretical explanations are very similar in structure. Witness theories of turnover and absenteeism. Certainly there are differences in models, but when we step back, they seem very similar in overall approach. However, Hulin also told us that there is more to withdrawal than its most typical manifestations. When he also described work withdrawal, he was describing an entirely different kind of phenomenal variable as a manifestation of the latent withdrawal construct. Now we had a theoretical package that brought turnover or absenteeism together with performance.

To make our case, we focus on a different deep structure variable, one that manifests itself as many different work phenomena, often studied quite separately by different people from different research traditions, producing different explanatory frameworks. That deep concept is *evaluation*. It shows up as job satisfaction when employees are asked to evaluate their jobs. It shows up as performance appraisal when supervisors are asked to evaluate those who work for them. It shows up as interviewer ratings when interviewers are asked to evaluate job applicants. It shows up as goal preferences when people evaluate alternative future courses of action. At the core, all of these processes are the same, people evaluating objects. Of course, the objects of evaluation differ, but, from a theoretical perspective, these differences are relatively trivial. Instead, the commonality of the underlying construct suggests that at the construct level, one general explanatory framework should suffice to explain how people come to evaluate their jobs as satisfying or dissatisfying, how supervisors come to evaluate their subordinates as effective or ineffective, how interviewers come to evaluate job candidates as worthy or unworthy of hire, and how preferences for courses of action develop. We make our case by focusing on two seemingly distinct organizational variables, job satisfaction and performance appraisal, but before we do, we look more closely at evaluation.

The Nature of Evaluation

A useful way to begin this discussion of evaluation is to try to differentiate it from some of the other constructs that coinhabit the same conceptual space. We are referring to such constructs as attitudes, affect, and beliefs.

Evaluation involves placing an object on a dimension ranging from good to bad (Eagly & Chaiken, 1993; Smith, Kendall, & Hulin, 1969; Tesser & Martin, 1996). Evaluations, as Eagly and Chaiken (1993) told us, are always made with respect to entities or things, although those entities can be of various types. Any element of experience that is at all discriminable is an object that can become the subject of evaluation. These elements of experience can be concrete entities (my car, your car, my spouse, your spouse, a co-worker), abstractions (my career, democracy, affirmative action), or future states (obtaining a college degree, having my own business). Although these differences can make some difference, for now it only needs to be said that different kinds of entities can be the objects of evaluation and that evaluation involves placing an object along a dimension ranging from good to bad. It should be apparent that many different organizational activities are actually context specific manifestations of evaluation.

Osgood, Suci, and Tannenbaum (1957) showed that evaluation is a central element of meaning. Their factor analyses of semantic space identified three underlying elements of meaning—evaluation, potency and activity (a dimensional structure that had also been identified many years earlier by Wundt; see Boring, 1950). Of these three dimensions, evaluation consistently accounted for the bulk of the variance in ratings. The ubiquity of evaluation is well established.

An *attitude*, it is now understood, is equivalent to an evaluation. Eagly and Chaiken (1993) noted, "Attitude is a psychological tendency that is expressed by evaluating a particular entity with some degree of favor or disfavor" (p. 1). Similarly, Petty, Wegener, and Fabrigar (1997) stated that attitudes are "summary evaluations of objects (oneself, other people, issues, etc.) along a dimension ranging from positive to negative" (p. 611).

Where does affect lie in this conceptual space? The classic tripartite model of attitudes suggested that attitudes are composed of affective, belief, and behavior components. In some way, these elements coexisted as part of the attitude construct. Current thinking reconfigures this relationship. It appears more useful to say that attitudes are summary evaluations that are formed by affective experiences with the attitude object, beliefs about the object, and behaviors directed toward the object. Each of these former elements of attitude is now seen as a different piece of information that helps form the attitude (Crites, Fabrigar, & Petty, 1994; Olson & Zanna, 1993). Attitude operations are consistent with this structure. Basic attitude measures ask respondents to place the attitude object along a scale of evaluation. That evaluation is the attitude.

Traditional arguments would have it that evaluations/attitudes are manifested as affect, behavior and or beliefs, the components of the attitude. A more appropriate conception would be that evaluation is contained in each of these domains. Things we do, ways we feel, beliefs we have, all have an evaluative component. At the same time, each has surplus elements in addition to the evaluative component. An affective experience has an evaluative component, but it is not the only part; evaluation does not capture all there is to affect. Likewise, to say a person cheats on his or her taxes is to express a belief that has an evaluative element, but evaluation does not capture all there is to this belief.

It is understood that affect is not attitude and attitude is not affect. They are conceptually distinct (Eagly & Chaiken, 1993; Tesser & Martin, 1996). Affect has an evaluative component but much more. The distinctiveness of attitudes, affect and beliefs is not just a verbal parsing of constructs. Weiss (in press) reviewed the evidence for the importance of these distinctions. We will not go into the details of the evidence here, but some of its elements include data showing factor structures separating the three constructs and data showing that affective experiences with attitudinal objects have causal influences on overall evaluations separate from the effects of beliefs. Generally, none of the evidence is consistent with affect and beliefs being components of attitudinal evaluations and all is consistent with affective experiences and beliefs being separate, if related, causes of the evaluations. Our point is that attitude and evaluation are equivalent constructs that are distinct from affect, and affect, along with beliefs and behaviors, help determine the evaluation. But, at the same time, the three coexist and overlap in a domain of associations linked to the object.

Some other important aspects of evaluation can be mentioned. They are often formed automatically (Pratto, 1994). They vary in strength, or more properly, the association between the evaluation and the mental representation of the object can vary in strength (Fazio, 1989). They can sometimes be made without conscious awareness (Zajonc, 1980). We are able to develop quite reasonable post hoc explanations for evaluations made for reasons we are unaware of (Tesser & Martin, 1996). They help organize our thoughts about the object and serve as heuristic devices for making judgments about other aspects of the object (Pratkanis & Turner, 1994).

Why Job Satisfaction Is Evaluation?

Some researchers define job satisfaction as an emotional or affective reaction to one's job (Cranny, Smith, & Stone, 1992; Locke, 1976). Others define it as the attitude one holds toward one's job (Brief, 1998; Miner, 1992). Still others hold both points of view, accepting the classic idea that attitudes are partly affective responses (Smith et al., 1969).

Our preference, which we think is well supported by the literature, is to accept job satisfaction as the attitude one holds toward one's job. However, we want to make clear that consistent with the basic literature on attitudes, to say that job satisfaction is an attitude is to say that it is the evaluation we make with our job as the object of evaluation. Accepting job satisfaction as an attitude is to also say, simultaneously, that it is not an affective reaction even though it is likely to be related to affect. This latter position runs counter to much that has been and is written on job satisfaction.

Overall job satisfaction is, from our position, the evaluative judgment we make about the overall experience of a job. When job facet satisfaction is considered, the evaluations are specific elements of the work environment. There is no special relationship between overall satisfaction and facet satisfaction. The part–whole conceptualization that has become lore in our field, in the absence of good supportive data, we should add, is unnecessarily distracting. The difference between overall satisfaction and facet satisfaction is simply a difference in the object of evaluation.

Why do we believe that the best way to conceptualize satisfaction is as an evaluative judgment and why are we so adamant in making the case that satisfaction is not affect? Our argument has two elements. First, most operations of satisfaction require evaluative judgments. When they do not, for example, when people are asked whether or not a particular condition does or does not describe their job, the descriptor was selected because of its evaluative connotation. Second, just as in the social psychological literature, there is evidence that beliefs about the object and affective experiences with the object independently predict people's overall evaluations of their jobs, each contributing unique variance to the prediction of job satisfaction.

Brayfield and Crockett (1955) reviewed the literature on the relationship between satisfaction and performance. As they did, they struggled with the problem of how to define satisfaction. In the end, they concluded that any attempt to define satisfaction must stick close to the operations. "We have not attempted to define such terms as job satisfaction and morale. Instead we have found it necessary to assume that the measuring operations define the variables involved" (p. 397). In our opinion, this was not some extreme form of operationalism. We take this to mean that we can get a good picture of the construct by paying close attention to what is actually being done instead of what the researchers believe is being done.

What is being done when it comes to job satisfaction? Clearly, job satisfaction measures, like attitude measures in other domains, ask respondents to place the attitude object along some scale of evaluation. Sometimes the evaluative scale is presented to the person to locate his or her response on it. Other times, people are presented with descriptive items already scaled for evaluative meaning by subject matter experts. Scales sometimes may be phrased in ways that make them seem like they are tapping affective states, but make no mistake, evaluation is what is being tapped.

Some might suggest that we are being too operational, that we are falling into the same trap that we started off criticizing. That trap is to forget the difference between operations or phenomenal variables and latent constructs. Operationally, the argument goes, we have measures of job satisfaction that tap into the latent construct of affect. We respond in two ways. First, we are aware of a latent construct in job satisfaction and that construct is *evaluation*. Second, if one looks at the history of job satisfaction, and particularly the history of job satisfaction measurement, there have been no attempts to develop scales tapping true affective experiences. Said another way, there have been no real attempts to gather construct validity evidence that these measures are tapping true affect, affect as it is defined in the literature as such experiences as moods and emotions. As rigorous as was the development of the Job Descriptive Index (JDI; Smith et al., 1969), and make no mistake, it was a model for measurement research, moods and emotions were not part of the data collected to demonstrate construct validity. Nor were they part of the construct validity evidence for the Minnesota Satisfaction Questionnaire (MSQ; Lofquist & Dawis, 1969). The reason is obvious. When attitude and affect were viewed as synonymous, there was no real need for such evidence.

The research of Weiss, Nicholas, and Daus (1999) showed the usefulness of conceptualizing satisfaction as evaluation. Using an Experience

Sampling Method (ESM), Weiss et al. (1999) collected online affective experiences at work. They also collected beliefs about the job. Together the affective experiences and the beliefs had independent and significant influences on the overall job satisfaction responses. These data are consistent with similar results in the social psychology literature and attest to the usefulness of keeping affect separate from evaluation and defining satisfaction as evaluation.

Our contention is that by understanding satisfaction to be evaluation (and not affect), certain questions will arise that would not otherwise. What might some of these be? One possible line of research is already underway and that research studies the way emotional experiences on the job and beliefs about the job jointly contribute to satisfaction and/or evaluation (Weiss et al., 1999). As part of this general inquiry, one can also ask about the relative influence of beliefs and affective experience on evaluations of different kinds of work objects or the relative influence of these same factors for different kinds of people.

The concept of *attitude strength* as the strength of the link between the mental representation of the object and the evaluation also becomes an important topic of inquiry. How do work attitudes vary in strength? What causes strength differences? What consequences result from these differences? These questions are being studied extensively in the basic literature on evaluations but receive no systematic treatment in the study of job satisfaction.

One can also ask about the functions of satisfaction as evaluation in a way that goes well beyond the traditional treatment of satisfaction–performance relationships. How do our job attitudes help us organize our work experiences? How do we manage to keep our evaluations consistent? Again, what are the implications of these processes?

Making a cleaner distinction between evaluation and affect also produces advantages for how we study the behavioral outcomes of these variables. Weiss and Cropanzano (1996) distinguished between those behaviors that are driven directly by current affective states, unmediated by overall evaluations, and those that are driven by evaluative judgments. Evidence is developing that supports this distinction (see chap. 7 by Probst; chap. 6 by Richman-Hirsch & Glomb; chap. 11 by Glomb & Miner, this volume). No one would even consider gathering such data if satisfaction as evaluation was not seen as different from an affective state.

Defining satisfaction as evaluation and as something different from affect in no way diminishes the importance of evaluations; it does, however, change how we regard evaluation and job satisfaction. It requires us to be more precise about the role of evaluations, their behavioral and cognitive implications, and clearly tells us that the role is going to be something quite distinct from affect. It also allows us to bring all of the wide-ranging

knowledge about evaluations in the abstract to bear on the study of job satisfaction, and this is a critical advantage. It is an advantage that accrues for
all phenomena that are evaluations at the deeper level.

Here, however, we simply conclude that at its core, satisfaction is evaluation. It is one of many ways in which evaluation is expressed in work contexts.

Performance and Evaluation

Work role performance is and has been a dominant concern of I-O Psychology. Personnel selection, placement and classification strive to improve the match between characteristics of people and those of work settings, based on the assumption that job performance is a positive function
of the match. Task performance is the primary criterion of almost all
training efforts. For millennia before Frederick Taylor impressed the
business community with his ability to get Schmidt to load his wheelbarrow with more pig iron per hour (and enjoy it, according to Taylor) people
tried to motivate workers, soldiers, bakers, and scribes to do more in less
time—to maintain or increase performance. For many, understanding,
predicting and measuring performance is the *raison d'être* of industrial and
organizational psychology.

Hundreds, if not thousands, of measures of individual performance exist that involve one person judging the performance of another. But, in
spite of the vast array of appraisals and the long history of attempts to develop good measures, satisfaction with them has not improved much over
time. Certainly improvement in their quality is not proportionate to the
amount of effort devoted to their development. Some convergence does
exist across sources of evaluations, as evidenced by a meta-analysis of
interrater agreement among supervisors and peers in the low .50s for supervisors and low .40s for peers (Viswesvaran, Ones, & Schmidt, 1996).
Convergence among measures varies depending on the nature of performance being addressed and the setting, but, in general, validities are
moderate. We are confident that, regardless of the measures in vogue today, they will lose their luster and be replaced by something we have yet to
consider.

Why, after so much research, is there not more convergence? We suggest it is likely due to where the solutions to the problem are sought. Attention is focused on the measure and the construct itself is loaded with
contextual elements. There is, among investigators, high agreement on
four criteria for evaluating performance measures. These are validity, reliability, freedom from bias, and the adequacy with which a measure represents the performance domain of interest. Measures can be compared and
relative judgments about the strengths and weaknesses of each identified.

Gottfredson (1991) provided an excellent example of such comparisons among measures suggesting that questions of measure equivalence consider the four criteria along with issues that arise out of the use of the measures in organizations, for example, costs, changes over time, and the acceptability of the measures to those affected by them.

The criteria just listed arise from measurement theory and social and work contexts in which the appraisals are obtained. Rating errors (leniency, halo, similar-to-me), unfair biases against women or minorities, ease of implementation, and training demands created by their use are just a few of the many performance appraisal criteria studied extensively. All these exist in a space bounded by the nature of measures or of the workplace, in a phenomenal rather than a psychological domain.

We suggest that dissatisfaction with the psychometric quality of performance appraisals may be due to the failure to consider the nature of the underlying latent construct of performance appraisals. The deep level construct in our framework is evaluation. The fact that we call it "performance appraisal" attests to the centrality of evaluation. Yet, approaches to appraisal are primarily phenomenological and mask the usefulness of understanding appraisals as conceptually equivalent to attitudes.

The fact that performance measures are evaluations provides one way to look more deeply at the nature of performance measurement. Consider just two issues that we have already established in our discussion of job satisfaction. First is the position that an attitude is an evaluation. If attitudes are evaluative judgments and performance appraisals are also evaluative judgments, then perhaps performance appraisals are simply attitudes about the person being evaluated. Before the logicians among you take us to task for the flaws in our syllogism, let us suggest that even though the two are not necessarily equivalent, assuming that they are similar deep level constructs is instructive. We consider a few of the potential implications, recognizing that there are many more that could be addressed.

In our earlier discussion of job satisfaction, much effort was devoted to unpacking attitudes, affect, and beliefs. The challenge was to establish the need for stripping job satisfaction of the excesses of affect and beliefs that have been bundled with it. For performance appraisals, the nature of the problem is just the opposite. Interest is and always has been on the evaluation—only evaluation. From attitude research, in which attitudes are defined only as evaluations, we know that affect and beliefs coexist with evaluations and, in a predictive sense, contribute independently to evaluations of attitude objects (Crites et al., 1994; Eagly, Mladinic, & Otto, 1994). Thus, we conclude that it should not be assumed evaluations are sufficiently captured by affect or beliefs to represent evaluations. Neither is it likely that beliefs and affect can be controlled to the point that they do not influence evaluations. Yet, performance appraisals often attempt to do one or the other or both. Worse yet, affect or beliefs, particularly affect, is ignored. We now illustrate these problems and some potential implications of both.

Beliefs as Evaluations. The Behaviorally Anchored Rating Scale (BARS) was introduced as a method for constructing a performance appraisal instrument that would validly and reliably capture the evaluation of employees' performance in context for which the scale was designed and would, once they existed, provide a guide for observing behaviors of those who were to be rated. From its introduction in the early 1960s by Smith and Kendall (1963), BARS scales and modifications of the process spawned from the general model have possessed reasonable levels of validity and reliability as performance measures. The scales present raters with descriptions of a specific dimension of performance relevant on the job held by the persons to be rated (e.g., technical competence), and a number or alternative descriptions of behaviors that represent the dimension and are scaled along a continuum from good to bad. The behaviors presented for a dimension are identified by subject matter experts who are job incumbents or know the job well. The final set of behaviors are selected through a scaling process that requires agreement among the experts on both the behavior representing the dimension and the evaluative implications of the behavior—its location along the goodness–badness dimension. In general, the data show that, when scales use behavioral anchors that have been carefully scaled on jobs for which they are appropriate, the effects are positive on several psychometric criteria and rating errors are reduced.

If we assume that performance evaluations are attitude ratings and that attitudes are closely associated with affect and beliefs, BARS scales attempt to capture evaluative judgments by measuring beliefs. Raters are presented with a carefully selected set of beliefs in the form of expectations about likely behaviors. The rater selects the belief statement from the set that best represents his belief about what the ratee will do. The alternatives presented to the rater were selected because of their evaluative implications. However, if, as we know from the attitude literature, beliefs are not synonymous with evaluation, the beliefs alone are likely to provide only a limited view of the evaluative domain they are assumed to represent. Furthermore, the stringent criteria for acceptance of a belief as representative of the performance domain further constrains the performance domain. Only those beliefs for which a majority of the experts agree on both the dimension and the evaluative level it represents survive to be placed on the scale. In sum, BARS scales purchase improved psychometric properties, reflected particularly in interrater agreement or convergence over time, by constraining the evaluative domain represented by them. The constraint is in terms of the content of performance represented by the scale.

Affect Free Evaluations?   The objective of performance evaluations is to obtain a measure of performance that captures the underlying performance construct independent of any affective relationship between the person who provides a rating of the performer. Measuring instruments, policies, and practices in the use of scales attempt to remove the possibility of affect entering into the rating. BARS does this by focusing on observable and verifiable behaviors. The uses to which performance evaluations are put in organizations assume that they represent evaluated states of the person measured uncontaminated by the attitudes of the rater.

To see a performance rating as an attitude immediately makes salient the fact that evaluations and affect share the same space. When the rater is rating a person with whom he or she has had opportunities interact over time, it is unlikely that the rater does not possess some feelings about the person that may or may not have anything to do with performance. Furthermore, temporary events independent of job performance often occur around the time of appraisals that create affect. The ratee may disappoint the rater by not inviting him or her to some off task activity; he or she may have acted in a way that embarrassed the rater in some way not associated with job performance, and so on. Considering an appraisal measurement as an attitude will not solve the problem that affect creeps into ratings but may prevent the users of such measures from the dilution that the measure is affect free. This perspective will also encourage us to look to the attitude literature for effects that might be expected in evaluations.

Research on attitude formation finds that frequently asking persons to provide attitude ratings of an attitude object leads to forming general attitudes that converge on a stable attitude toward that object that is less likely to be influenced by external events over time. In the performance appraisal area, recommendations for frequent observations of a person's performance are often suggested under the assumption that these observations pick up "actual" performance incidents and thus are more valid indicators of performance behaviors. Yet, the attitude literature suggests just the opposite. The frequent ratings should converge on the internally held attitude of the evaluator rather than capture behavioral events more accurately. Combining the needs of appraisal processes with knowledge of attitude research leads to approaching the observation issue not as one of behavior sampling alone but as a tension or dilemma balancing opportunity to observe changing behaviors with the tendency of the observer to form general impressions.

Evaluative Judgments and the Nature of Performance. Performance
appraisals are natural extensions to evaluative judgments and attitudes
due to the high degree of overlap in measurement procedures. Stepping
back to the underlying theory, specific consideration of the underlying
evaluative judgment process can also be useful. In the text that follows, we
suggest that understanding performance would be well served by looking
to general principles, latent processes if you like, that underlie behavior
more broadly defined than performance but central to it. In particular, we
suggest that evaluative judgments comprise much of what defines the domain of performance and its measurement. Weiss and colleagues (Weiss,
in press; Weiss & Cropanzano, 1996) made a convincing case for the value
of recognizing the role of evaluative judgments in job satisfaction and iso-
lating their effects from those of other constructs with which evaluative
judgments are often confused, specifically affect and beliefs. In like manner, we argue that evaluative judgments permeate the nature and measurement of performance but the failure to recognize explicitly where
evaluative judgments interject themselves in the process limits our common understanding of performance. Furthermore, considering the extent
to which we look for common latent processes that cross content domains
typically considered in isolation (e.g., job satisfaction or performance), the
greater the possibility of unifying the field and advancing toward common
theories of behavior that link the field with other behavioral, social, and
physical science constructs. Without a search for commonality we spin toward more and more idiosyncratic contingency theories wrapped in security blankets of boundary conditions.

Although, in general, the field of industrial and organizational psychology has failed to systematically and carefully address the nature of performance at work, the work of Campbell is a notable exception to the general state of affairs. We begin our discussion of performance with his
model and use it to address the role of evaluative judgments in performance and performance measurement.

For Campbell, "*Performance* is synonymous with *behavior*" (Campbell,
Gasser, & Oswald, 1996, p. 261, emphasis in original). Furthermore, by
definition, to be performance behaviors, they must only be behaviors that
are relevant to the organization's goals, and they must be scaleable in
terms of contribution to such goals. They must also be able to be mapped
onto individuals. That is, variance in the behaviors has to be able to be isolated from the influence of contextual factors, social or physical, present
in the job. Campbell argues performance is not to be confused with its outcome. *Performance behaviors* are the observable behaviors people do and
not the results of their behaviors. To Campbell, the debate in the performance measurement arena about whether to use performance behaviors or
performance outcomes as performance is a nonissue; the latter are simply

not performance. Accepting only behaviors as performance frees performance from the influence of factors that may be beyond the control of the individual so that such factors do not get mapped back into individual performance.

Consider the case of a nurse who attends a bedridden geriatric patient and forgets to pull up the bed rail. In practice, the nurse's performance is likely to be seen quite differently depending on whether the patient remains in bed or rolls out. Similarly, we evaluate the performance of the armed intruder who is a good shot much differently than the one who misses the intended victim. Performance, as a behavior, is what people actually do and can be observed doing (Campbell, McCloy, Oppler, & Sager, 1993).[1]

Campbell defines the set of performance behaviors in terms of usefulness across a number of jobs. Theoretically, every job could have its own unique set of behaviors that constituted performance. However, the utility of any taxonomic system is expanded as the number of cases to which it applies expands. Thus, in the work domain, Campbell argued that the number of jobs to which the performance behaviors apply must be sufficiently large to be worth the effort to construct measures of the domain. The actual behaviors comprising the performance domain of his model are listed in Table 4.1. The behaviors were identified by (a) carefully considering the nature of human behaviors from an individual difference perspective; (b) the nature of a large number of jobs; (c) and measures of the behaviors collected from several large samples, including military personnel as part of Project Alpha (Campbell, McHenry, & Wise, 1990).

Evaluative Judgments and the Campbell Model. It is easy to look at the Campbell model and see the performance components of Table 2.1 as "objective" behavioral dimensions. To do so overlooks the role of evaluative judgments in the model.[2] Four evaluative judgments in the Campbell model place boundaries on the domain of behaviors defining performance. One is the judgment about the number of jobs in which the behavior is likely to play a critical role. This is a practical judgment. Behaviors idiosyncratic to a small number of jobs are excluded because, from the overall performance system point of view, they apply to too few jobs to be retained. Second, behaviors for inclusion in the set are judged against the

---

[1]Campbell (1990) recognized that some behaviors, such as solving a mathematics problem, are not observable and clearly does not intend to exclude such behaviors from performance. Observation is to be treated in the sense that some measuring system can detect the behavior and do so in a reliable and valid manner.

[2]Campbell's discussion of the model (e.g., Campbell et al., 1996) clearly makes the reader aware of where evaluative judgments are made, but the emphasis is more on the content of components than on the judgments.

TABLE 4.1
Campbell's Taxonomy of Performance Components[a]

Component	Description
Job-specific task proficiency	Level of performance of the core substances or technical elements central to the job.
Nonjob-specific task proficiency	Performance on tasks that are part of the job but not central to the primary task.
Written and oral communication	Level of performance of written and oral communication that usually cross many elements of the job.
Demonstration of effort	The extent to which the person expends effort continuously in the job, and the frequency he or she expends extra effort when asked or under adverse conditions (e.g., tight deadlines or bad weather).
Maintenance of personal discipline	Degree to which negative behaviors, such as substance abuse, rule infractions, excessive absences, and so on are avoided.
Facilitation of peer and team performance	Facilitates the performance of co-workers, helps others out, trains and advises others, is a good model for others, and so on.

[a]Adapted from Campbell (1999).

criterion of their importance to the goals and objectives of the organization. Because the behaviors of Table 4.1 are meant to be relevant to a large number of jobs found in many organizations, goal importance or relevance was referenced to organizations in general not to one specific organization. Importance is an evaluative judgment. A third judgment addressed whether or not the behaviors could be scaled at least ordinally along some quantitative dimension reflecting the amount of the behavior in question and that the quantitative evaluation reflected a level of performance. In addition, as mentioned earlier, the model included only performance behaviors and excluded performance outcomes. Thus, a dichotomous inclusion/exclusion judgment was made.

When viewed from within the performance domain, the Campbell model of performance is viewed as one of domain specification. The process it represents tends to be described as criterion specification. As such, its implications with respect to evaluative processes are easily overlooked. The model requires a number of evaluative judgments leading up to the creation of the set of dimensions and pushes off a key evaluative judgment to later. When the components of performance listed in Table 4.1 are brought to bear with respect to the performance of particular individuals, some evaluative judgment process is necessary to map a level of performance on the dimension onto each person. The nature of the mapping algorithm and the way in which behaviors are "observed" is left to the measurement process and is not part of the performance definition.

NPI and Performance.   Naylor, Pritchard, and Ilgen (NPI; 1980) offered a definition of performance from an entirely different perspective.
They developed a theory of behavior in organizations and anchored their
theory in the psychological process of decision and choice. Whereas the
framework of Campbell's model is built around the concrete constructs of
personal characteristics and organizational conditions, NPI is structured
around cognitive and affective processes. Their model is a resource alloca-
tion one, with effort as the resource is invested in activities (behaviors) at
work. To NPI, performance is not behavior; it is an evaluation of the results of behavior. Specifically, the theory proposes that people behave
(act). Their actions are converted into outcomes (called products). These
outcomes can be scaled in terms of their value to the organization. If they
are so scaled, the sum of the outcome evaluations is performance. In other
words, performance is only an evaluative judgment where the evaluation is
based on the outcomes of behaviors. For NPI, performance was not central to the theory but is simply one of the constructs at work incorporated
in the theory. As a result, the theory provides only a metatheoretic framework for performance lacking the specificity needed to address particular
performance issues in work settings.

At first glance, Campbell (1990; Campbell, McHenry, & Wise, 1990)
and Naylor et al. (1980) offer what appear to be disparate views of performance. But, when the role of evaluative judgments in each is explored,
some of the disparity disappears or, at least, points of similarity and dis-
similarity appear.

In the Campbell model, behavior is performance, and every effort is
made to give the appearance that evaluation is controlled or removed.
Campbell says the outcomes of behaviors are excluded from performance.
But are they? Recall that a necessary condition for the inclusion of a behavior in the domain of performance is that the behavior be considered
relevant for meeting organizational goals. Thus, in a very real sense, the
evaluative judgment is made by the scientist as the performance domain is
defined by the elements (dimensions) that are included in it. Evaluative
judgment is a primary underpinning of the performance model and is in-
terjected by the scientist in the construction of the behavioral taxonomy
that represents the performance domain by scaling the behavioral elements within any behavioral performance component in terms of the degree to which these elements represent the component.

For NPI, products of effort are quite similar to behaviors in the Campbell sense. These products are the result of effort and are generated by the
individual. Also, it is assumed that there exists an evaluative system that
identifies these products as part of the domain of relevant products. Thus,
although the NPI do not specify the products that will be in the pool of

products, the model is dealing with elements quite similar to those of Campbell's model.

If one assumes that products and behaviors are elements of performance processes that are reasonably similar, then the models can be compared on how they address evaluative judgments. As mentioned earlier, Campbell's model relies on the evaluative judgments of the behavioral scientist to define the domain of performance behaviors. The judgments consider issues both between and within behavioral components described in Table 4.1. Between-components judgments relate to the content of the performance dimensions such that the domain is adequately represented. Within-component judgments involve the scalability of performance incidents on each component with respect to performance. Outcomes resulting from the behaviors are not considered part of performance, at least not directly. Indirectly, judgments about the outcomes affect judgments about whether or not a component is considered part of the performance domain. Thus, we argue, even though Campbell denies that outcomes of performance are part of performance, they are part of it in the sense that they influence the inclusion of components in the performance domain. They do not, however, contribute variance to differences among individuals in performance, so they are, in that sense, not part of performance. Finally, when it comes to mapping performance onto a particular individual, a single judgment process is passed from the scientist to a judge (where the judge could be a human or an algorithm mechanically applied) who uses the scaled component levels within in each performance component to reach a judgment.

NPI shifts the primary burden of the judgment processes from the behavioral scientist to the end user. The content of the effort/product domain (analogous to behavior in the Campbell model) is idiosyncratic to the performance setting. This is best seen in the work of Pritchard and colleagues (Pritchard, Jones, Roth, Stuebing, & Ekeberg, 1988), who adopted the theory to a performance measurement process.[3] Job incumbents use their work as a referent and make an evaluative judgment about the products over which they have some control that are most important in their work setting. The result is a set of components that are linked to an undifferentiated behavior—effort in an unspecified way. It is a process that serves the same function if not conducted in the same way as that used by the behavioral scientists who place behavioral components into the domain. Next, the same or other individuals in the immediate job environment scale the products in terms of their contribution to effectiveness.

---

[3]Pritchard, despite my best advice, calls performance productivity. To him the terms are synonymous in spite of the fact that, to the rest of the world, productivity is a ratio concept—the ratio of some measure of output to volume or total capacity usually framed by time.

We raise these two models because, on the surface, the two models appear very different. One claims performance is behavior stripped of behavior and the other states performance is only evaluated behavior. Both would distance themselves from job satisfaction. Yet, if one looks for deeper processes, it is clear that evaluation is playing a major role at many junctures in both models as it is in job satisfaction.

CONCLUSION

In this chapter, we tried to show that both job satisfaction and performance appraisal are contextual manifestations of the deep structure construct of evaluation. We also tried to show the advantages that accrue from focusing on this deep structure. Those advantages result from the ability to bring both contextual variables under the broader nomological network of evaluation. This context-free network of constructs allows us to ask new questions, see new relationships, make new predictions, and generally refocus our study of these very traditional variables.

In the main body of the chapter, we illustrated this advantage by suggesting new research questions that develop when satisfaction and performance appraisal are treated as attitudes/evaluations. By design, we gave more attention to new areas of performance appraisal research because the satisfaction–evaluation connection is more apparent to readers than is the idea that a performance appraisal is (simply) an attitude measure.

Nonetheless, new ideas can be developed in both areas, as can ideas for other contextual variables that are also evaluations. These include goal preferences, interviewer judgments, self-esteem, and so on. Eventually, a general research strategy that demonstrates that all of these contextual variables show similar relationships with a common set of theoretical variables will make our point empirically.

So far, we have spent a great deal of time discussing the role of evaluative judgments with respect to two literatures that play a dominant role in I-O Psychology. We believe that evaluative judgments are extremely important deep level constructs that are manifested across a number of behavioral domains. However, the primary point that we want to leave with you is not the ubiquity of evaluative judgments. It is in the need for I-O Psychology to look to deep level constructs as the building blocks of its theory and to avoid being hoodwinked by our infatuation with phenomenal constructs. The latter lead us astray in many ways. We have already mentioned the limits, thinking that we are building theory, when we observe correlations among phenomenal variables that are so confounded with specific situational conditions to be of little interest in any sense but descriptive in the narrowest of senses. The distinction between phenomenal level variables and deeper level constructs goes beyond the way crite-rion variables are organized or work experiences are studied. We see the same problems frequently exhibited in the domain of individual differ-ences. Too frequently, industrial and organizationalist psychologists cre-ate individual difference variables that are essentially preferences for dif-ferent organizational phenomena. Examples include the Growth Needs Strength measure of the Job Characteristics Model or the Importance component of the Theory of Work Adjustment. When these measures turn out to moderate situation–outcome relationships, that is all they do. Be-cause they are defined in terms of phenomenal preferences, they bring lit-tle or no extra information to bear on the underlying theoretical problem.

Certainly, the moderation may have practical significance, but most of-ten these variables are presented as theoretically important constructs. Yet, their theoretical importance is negligible, because no context-free in-formation is added.

Consider the difference between two results. In the first instance, we find that the effects of job characteristics are moderated by preferences for job characteristics. In the second we find, hypothetically, that they are moderated by differences in need for achievement. The second finding brings all the information from the nomological network associated with need for achievement to bear on the issue of job design. The first simply accounts for more variance.

These two illustrations point out failures to look to underlying con-structs. The search for deeper level constructs as guides for structuring theory and research is well represented in Hulin's (1991) withdrawal work. By modeling that work, advances are likely in the future. Ignoring the model is to continue to develop literatures in separate domains with little cumulative learning. The alternatives are clear to us and we hope to you.

ACKNOWLEDGMENTS

This chapter has benefited greatly from continued conversations with Art Brief. We may not always come to the same conclusions, but our discus-sions have been very helpful and immensely enjoyable. I also want to thank Rebecca Henry, Carolyn Jagacinski, Eliot Smith, and Duane Wege-ner for their comments.

REFERENCES

Boring, E. G. (1950). *A history of experimental psychology*. Englewood Cliffs, NJ: Prentice-Hall.
Brayfield, A. H., & Crockett, W. H. (1955). Employee attitudes and employee performance. *Psychological Bulletin, 52*, 396–424.

Brief, A. P. (1998). *Attitudes in and around organizations*. Thousand Oaks, CA: Sage.

Campbell, J. P. (1990). Modeling the performance prediction problem in industrial and organizational psychology. In M. D. Dunnette & L. M. Hough (Eds.), *Handbook of industrial and organizational psychology* (2nd ed., Vol. 1, pp. 687–732). Palo Alto, CA: Consulting Psychologist Press.

Campbell, J. P. (1999). The definition and measurement of performance in the new age. In D. R. Ilgen & E. D. Pulakos (Eds.), *The changing nature of performance* (pp. 399–431). San Francisco: Jossey-Bass.

Campbell, J. P., Gasser, M. B., & Oswald, F. L. (1996). The substantive nature of job performance variability. In K. R. Murphy (Ed.), *Individual differences and behavior in organizations* (pp. 258–299). San Francisco: Jossey-Bass.

Campbell, J. P., McCloy, R. A., Oppler, S. H., & Sager, C. E. (1993). A theory of performance. In N. Schmitt & W. Borman (Eds.), *Personnel selection in organizations*. San Francisco: Jossey-Bass.

Campbell, J. P., McHenry, J. J., & Wise, L. L. (1990). Modeling job performance in a population of jobs. *Personnel Psychology, 43*, 313–333.

Cranny, C. J., Smith, P. C., & Stone, E. F. (1992). The construct of job satisfaction. In C. J. Cranny, P. C. Smith, & E. F. Stone (Eds.), *Job satisfaction: How people feel about their jobs and how it affects their performance* (pp. 1–3). New York: Lexington Press.

Crites, S. L., Jr., Fabrigar, L. R., & Petty, R. (1994). Measuring affective and cognitive properties of attitudes: Conceptual and methodological issues. *Personality and Social Psychology Bulletin, 20*, 619–634.

Eagly, A. H., & Chaiken, S. (1993). *The psychology of attitudes*. Fort Worth, TX: Harcourt, Brace & Janovich.

Eagly, A. H., Mladinic, A., & Otto, S. (1994). Cognitive and affective bases of attitudes toward social groups and social policies. *Journal of Experimental Social Psychology, 30*, 113–137.

Fazio, R. H. (1989). On the power and functionality of attitudes: The role of attitude accessibility. In A. R. Pratkanis & S. J. Breckler (Eds.), *Attitude structure and function* (pp. 153–179). Hillsdale, NJ: Lawrence Erlbaum Associates.

Gottfredson, G. (1991). Position classification inventory (PCI). *Psychological Assessment Resources, 5*, 54.

Hulin, C. L. (1991). Adaptation, persistence, and commitment in organizations. In M. D. Dunnette & L. M. Hough (Eds.), *Handbook of industrial and organizational psychology* (Vol. 2, pp. 445–505). Palo Alto, CA: Consulting Psychologists Press.

Locke, E. A. (1976). The nature and causes of job satisfaction. In M. D. Dunnette (Ed.), *Handbook of industrial and organizational psychology* (pp. 1297–1349). Chicago: Rand McNally.

Lofquist, L. H., & Dawis, R. V. (1969). *Adjustment to work: A psychological view of man's problems in a work-oriented society*. New York: Appleton-Century-Crofts.

Miner, J. B. (1992). *Industrial-organizational psychology*. New York: McGraw-Hill.

Naylor, J. P., Pritchard, R. D., & Ilgen, D. R. (1980). *A theory of behavior in organizations*. New York: Academic Press.

Olson, J. M., & Zanna, M. P. (1993). Attitudes and attitude change. *Annual Review of Psychology, 44*, 117–154.

Osgood, C. E., Suci, G. J., & Tannenbaum, P. H. (1957). The nature and theory of meaning. *The measurement of meaning*. Urbana, IL: Illinois Press.

Petty, R. E., Wegener, D. T., & Fabrigar, L. R. (1997). Attitudes and attitude change. *Annual Review of Psychology, 48*, 609–647.

Pratkanis, A. R., & Turner, M. E. (1994). Of what value is a job attitude? *Human Relations, 47*, 1545–1576.

Pratto, F. (1994). Consciousness and automatic evaluation. In P. M. Niedenthal & S. Kitayama (Eds.), *The heart's eye: Emotional influences in perception and attention* (pp. 115–143). San Diego: Academic Press.

Pritchard, R. D., Jones, S. D., Roth, P. L., Stuebing, K. K., & Ekeberg, S. E. (1988). Effects of group feedback, goal setting, and incentives on organizational productivity. *Journal of Applied Psychology, 73*, 337–358.

Smith, P. C., & Kendall, L. M. (1963). Retranslation of expectations: An approach to construction of unambiguous anchors for rating scales. *Journal of Applied Psychology, 47*, 149–155.

Smith, P. C., Kendall, L. M., & Hulin, C. L. (1969). *The measurement of satisfaction in work & retirement: A strategy for the study of attitudes.* Chicago: Rand McNally.

Tesser, A., & Martin, L. (1996). *The psychology of evaluation.* New York: Guilford Press.

Viswesvaran, C., Ones, D. S., & Schmidt, F. L. (1996). Comparative analysis of the reliability of performance ratings. *Journal of Applied Psychology, 81*, 557–574.

Weiss, H. M. (in press). Deconstructing job satisfaction: Separating evaluations, beliefs and affective experiences. *Human Resource Management Review.*

Weiss, H. M., & Cropanzano, R. (1996). Affective events theory: A theoretical discussion of the structure, causes, and consequences of affective experiences at work. In B. M. Staw & L. L. Cummings (Eds.), *Research in organizational behavior* (Vol. 18, pp. 1–74). Greenwich, CT: JAI Press.

Weiss, H. M., Nicholas, J. P., & Daus, C. S. (1999). An examination of the joint effects of affective experiences and job beliefs on job satisfaction and variations in affective experiences over time. *Organizational Behavior and Human Decision Processes, 78*, 1–24.

Zajonc, R. B. (1980). Feeling and thinking: Preferences need no inferences. *American Psychologist, 35*(2), 151–175.

Chapter 5

Motivation to Work in Cross-Cultural Perspective

Harry C. Triandis
University of Illinois

In 1981, Hulin and I (Hulin & Triandis, 1981) published a chapter on work motivation in which we discussed the design of organizations. We argued that in designing an organization, managers need to take a close look at the culture, subculture, demographic background, and personality of their employees. When discussing culture, we considered the contrast between cultures that emphasize independence versus conformity and interdependence, but we did not elaborate on that contrast.

This chapter updates the 1981 chapter by first giving an in-depth review of the cultural characteristics of individualism and collectivism, which have been called the "deep structure of cultural differences" (Greenfield, 1999). It then reviews the corresponding personality contrasts between idiocentrics and allocentrics. Finally, the chapter examines the implications of these attributes for work motivation and the meaning of work.

THEORY

One way of conceptualizing *culture* is in terms of the patterns of information that people sample from their environment (Triandis, 1989). In collectivist cultures, such as those found in most of Asia, Africa, and Latin America, people are likely to sample information that relates to their interdependence (Markus & Kitayama, 1991) with their in-groups (family, co-workers, tribe, country, etc.) They are more likely than in individualist cultures to give priority to the goals of their in-groups than to their personal goals (Triandis, 1990); they are more likely to rely on in-group norms than on personal likes and dislikes (Abrams, Ando, & Hinkle, 1998) as factors shaping their behavior; and they usually conceive of social relationships as communal (Mills & Clark, 1982) rather than instrumental.

Collectivist cultures generally have languages that do not require the use of "I" and "you" (E. S. Kashima & Y. Kashima, 1998). People in collectivist cultures feel more positively about "us" and negatively about "them" than do people in individualist cultures (Iyengar, Lepper, & Ross, 1999).

In individualist cultures, such as those of Northern and Western Europe and most of North America, the sampling of the individual self is very common. In such cultures the self is conceived as independent of in-groups, personal goals are given priority, attitudes determine much of social behavior, and interpersonal relationships are well accounted by exchange theory. Individualist cultures have languages that require the use of "I" and "you." (E. S. Kashima & Y. Kashima, 1998). English is a good example. It would be difficult to write a letter in English without the use of these words.

The Self in Collectivist Cultures

People from collectivist and individualist cultures vary in the kind of responses they give when they are asked to complete 20 statements that start with "I am. . . ." People from collectivist cultures give responses that have more social content (Triandis, McCusker, & Hui, 1990). When introducing themselves to others, people in individualist cultures are most likely to mention an individual attribute, such as their profession (e.g., I am an engineer), whereas people in collectivist cultures are most likely to mention a group, such as their corporation (e.g., I work for Sony Corporation).

Parkes, Schneider, and Bochner (1999) identified *autonomous abstract* responses (I am kind, I am busy, I am pretty, I am worried), *autonomous contextual* responses (I am kind at work, I am interested in the future more than in the past, I am good at my work, I am feeling ill today), *social abstract* responses (I am kind to others, I am interested in other people, I am frustrated by incompetent people), and *social contextual* responses (I am a warm person toward my friends, I am a father, I am a student, I am a person depended on by my relatives). They found that Australians (people from an individualist culture) and Asians (people from collectivist cultures) had the percentages of the four types of responses shown in Table 5.1.

Personal and Ingroup Goals

Yamaguchi (1994) presented situations where what the individual wanted to do was incompatible with what the group wanted done. He showed that in collectivist cultures, the group wins; in individualist cultures, the individual wins.

TABLE 5.1
Percentages of Responses to "I am . . ." Task

By	Autonomous		Social	
	Contextual	Abstract	Contextual	Abstract
Australians	10%	67%	18%	5%
Asians	7%	47%	37%	9%

Kinds of Individualism and Collectivism

Nations are collectives that include many cultures and subcultures. In some situations (e.g., of sexual harassment) men and women have different cultures. Occupations (nurses and physicians) have distinct cultures; religions, political systems, ideologies, and kingship systems also correspond to different cultures. Thus, in discussing cross-national differences, we are oversimplifying. Nevertheless, there are some ways in which we can characterize nations as emphasizing one or another of the cultural patterns reflected in individualism and collectivism.

There are many kinds of collectivist cultures. For example, Korea and the Israeli kibbutz are both collectivist cultures, but they are different from one another. Thus, we need to use additional attributes to distinguish between the different kinds of collectivist and individualist cultures (Triandis, 1995). One of the major ways in which cultures differ is the vertical–horizontal dimension. People who emphasize the vertical dimension are especially concerned with hierarchy; those who emphasize the horizontal are concerned with equality (e.g., one person, one vote).

In Horizontal Individualist (HI) cultures people want to be unique and do their own thing. In Vertical Individualist (VI) cultures, people want to be unique but also to be "the best." They get upset when somebody tells them that they are "just average" (Weldon, 1984). American student samples exhibit self-enhancement. That is, when they are asked to compare themselves to the average student on some desirable trait, they see themselves as much better than the average student (Markus & Kitayama, 1991). Because it is impossible for everyone to be better than average that shows self-enhancement.

In Horizontal Collectivist (HC) cultures, people think of themselves as members of their groups rather than as autonomous individuals but they do not emphasize the hierarchy within the group. In Vertical Collectivist (VC) cultures, people accept their insignificance in relation to their group and its authorities, and are willing to submit to the group and sacrifice themselves for the benefit of the group. Vertical Collectivism is correlated about .40 with Right Wing Authoritarianism (Triandis & Gelfand, 1998).

Parkes et al. (1999) found that VC was significantly correlated with giving social–contextual responses in describing oneself, and negatively correlated with giving autonomous responses. Conversely, VI was positively correlated with giving autonomous responses and negatively correlated with giving social responses.

Triandis, Chen, and Chan (1998) used scenarios followed by responses that had been pretested to be HI, VI, HC, or VC. Then they computed the percent of the time that a cultural sample selected one of these four types of responses to be the best course of action across 16 different scenarios. This provided an individual differences measure of these four attributes. By summing the responses of the individuals within each culture to the four types of responses, they obtained a profile of the culture. Triandis et al. (2001), for instance, obtained such data from 8 cultures. As an example, the profiles of the German and Hong Kong samples are shown in Table 5.2.

In short, people are not "stamped" with a collectivism or individualism label. Rather, depending on the situation, they are sometimes VI, VC, HI or HC. But in collectivist cultures, they are more likely to be HC and VC, and in individualist cultures people are more likely to be HI or VI.

Individualism and Collectivism and Behavior

Cultural information predicts diverse behaviors, but the correlations are low (around .2 to .3). For instance, collectivism predicts high levels of conformity (Bond & Smith, 1996); preference for situations with few choices (Iyengar & Lepper, 1999); emphasis on heroes doing their duties in novels (Hsu, 1983); changing the self to fit into the situation (Diaz-Guerrero, 1979); and little or no social loafing when working with in-group members (Early, 1989), and so on. Individual differences information can result in higher correlations, but the prediction is about a specific behavior in a particular situation.

The Importance of the Situation

A number of factors increase the probability that people will sample the collective self. Triandis (1995) hypothesized that the following situational factors predict whether or not a person will sample the collective self:

TABLE 5.2
Percent of Responses That Were HI, HC, VI, and VC

Sample	HI	HC	VI	VC
German	43%	27%	20%	10%
Hong Kong	25	36	20	19

Note. Any difference of 2% or greater is significant at $p < .001$.

1. *Small in-groups.* For most behaviors, smaller in-groups, such as the family, influence the probability of sampling of the collective self more than larger in-groups such as tribe, co-religionists, members of the same political unit, the state, and so on. For one thing surveillance can be more dependable, and thus sanctions for not behaving according to the norms of the in-group can be imposed more surely in small in-groups. Furthermore, the emotional involvement of the individual with the group is likely to be greater in small than in very large in-groups.

2. *Homogeneous in-groups.* People in homogeneous in-groups can agree about the proper norms of behavior, and thus can be more effective when they pressure individuals to follow the in-group's norms.

3. *Tight situations.* Situations differ in their *tightness*, that is, the extent to which they impose the norms of the in-group. At a church or mosque, there is much tightness; at a party, there is less tightness.

In tight situations, there are rules that specify what one is supposed to do, where, when, and how. When rules are ignored, there are sanctions that range from raised eyebrows to the execution of the individual.

By contrast, at a party or a bar there is considerable looseness. One has many options about how, when, and where to act. If one does not behave according to the prevailing norms, it is much less likely that the person will receive severe sanctions. All situations can be rated on a looseness-tightness dimension.

The *tightness* of the situation is also reflected in the number of rules, regulations, laws, review panels and so on found in a social environment. The more tightness there is, the greater is the sampling of the collective self.

4. *Philosophical monism* (as opposed to philosophical pluralism), which views the person as made up "of the same substance as the rest of nature" (Markus & Kitayama, 1991, p. 227) results in emphasis on interdependence, and thus in the sampling of the collective self.

5. *Membership in an in-group.* If one is in an in-group, one is more likely to sample the collective self; if one is alone, for example, abroad, one is more likely to sample the individual self. Sampling the collective self results in people conforming to group norms (Bond & Smith, 1996), and many other behaviors; sampling the individual self results in acting according to one's attitudes rather than according to a combination of attitudes and in-group norms.

6. *The in-group is under attack.* If the in-group is under attack, regardless of culture, people will sample the collective self. If survival depends on doing what the in-group requires, the collective self is likely to be sampled. If the individual cannot survive without the help of the in-group, then the collective self is sampled. If material advancement can be achieved better

by advancing the status of the in-group than through personal advancement, there is a tendency to sample the collective self. If most members of the in-group are sampling the collective self (e.g., conforming to in-group norms) the probability of sampling it increases; if most members of the in-group sample the individual self (e.g., people act in idiocentric ways), the probability of sampling the individual self increases.

7. *Interdependent task.* If one has to write a book as a sole author, one is more likely to sample the individual self. Cooperative tasks, and situations of intergroup competition, increase the sampling of the collective self; individually competitive tasks increase the sampling of the individual self. Tasks that require joint action for success result in sampling the collective self; tasks that allow for individual solutions increases the sampling of the individual self (Breer & Locke, 1965).

8. *Collectivist primes.* Individuals who are primed to think of what they have in common with their family and friends are likely to sample the collective self. Individuals primed to think of what makes them different from their family and friends sample the individual self (Trafimow, Triandis, & Goto, 1991).

9. *Situations that offer few choices.* The more choices are offered in a situation, the more likely it is that the individual will sample the individual self. Because it is the individual who must choose, the focus becomes a private matter. People from collectivist cultures are uncomfortable in such situations and avoid them.

People in individualist cultures value choice more than those in collectivist cultures do and perform better when they are offered a choice, whereas people from collectivist cultures are quite happy to do what is suggested to them by trusted in-group authorities (Iyengar & Lepper, 1999). However, the number of choices that people want is not very large. Although people perform well when they have four or five choices, they do not perform as well when they have 25 or 30 choices (Iyengar & Lepper, 2001).

One of the important differences among cultures is in the number of choices that people have. The richer cultures provide more choices than poorer cultures, and within a culture the poor have fewer choices than the rich. People develop a level of adaptation for the number of choices they find ideal. If they have been socialized to have access to 30 kinds of mustard, they feel that something is lacking if they only have access to 10 kinds of mustard. But if they have been socialized to have one kind of mustard, having two kinds feels most desirable; 10 kinds is overwhelming.

For example, in the USSR, there were very few choices for many products. Russians who came to the USA in the 1970s where overwhelmed by the number of choices available to them, and sometimes mentioned that they preferred life in the USSR because they did not have so many choices.

Similarly, people have levels of adaptation for the number of choices available in a job. When people have autonomy, unstructured supervision, or jobs without job descriptions, they are left to determine on their own what they are supposed to do, when, where, with whom, and so on. People from collectivist cultures often feel more comfortable when supervision is structured, or assignments are given to the group who then decides, through intragroup interaction, who is to do what, when, and where.

Personality Affects the Frequency With Which People Sample Different Selves

1. *Idiocentrism–allocentrism.* In every culture, there are individual differences in the extent to which people have allocentric personalities (i.e., they sample the collective self most of the time) or idiocentric personalities (i.e., they sample the individual self most of the time; Triandis, Leung, Villareal, & Clack, 1985). People feel more comfortable when they interact with others who are like them than when they work with others who are very different from them. Thus, allocentrics feel more comfortable in collectivist cultures whereas idiocentrics feel more comfortable in individualist cultures. When the match between personality and culture is poor, people try to move, if they can, to another culture that fits them better. This means that when there is freedom of movement, people will find themselves in cultures and situations that require sampling of either the individual or the collective self, depending on their personality. Personality is shaped by socialization, for example, parental emphasis on exploration, creativity, and independence results in idiocentrism; parental emphasis on conformity, reliability, and dependence results in allocentrism.

2. *People choose situations to fit their personalities.* For example, consider the situation "to buy a carpet." Other things being equal, such as the price of the carpet, the idiocentric is most likely to go to a fixed price department store, pay the price, and buy the carpet. The transaction may take a few minutes. The allocentric is more likely to go to a store, where one can negotiate the price after establishing a social relationship, for example, in a Middle-Eastern bazaar. He may go more than once to that store, be offered coffee, discuss current events, and then discuss the price of the carpet. The transaction may take a couple of days.

3. *Primary or secondary control.* In general, allocentrics change themselves to fit into the situation. That is called secondary control. Idiocentrics change the situation to fit their needs (Diaz-Guerrero, 1979); that is called primary control (Weisz, Rothbaum, & Blackburn, 1984). For example, if the job requires spending a lot of time away from the family, the allocentric is likely to accept it, and the idiocentric is likely to protest, and

try to change the job. Allocentrics get a lot of training in "fitting in," which means changing themselves to fit into situations.

In individualist cultures, parents tell their children that that they must be independent and shape the environment to fit their needs.

Miscellaneous Factors That Affect Sampling

There are also a number of other factors that may be both individual and situational that affect the frequency with which people sample their individual and collective selves.

1. *Affluence.* Affluence is the strongest correlate of cultural individualism (Hofstede, 1980). The relationship may be reciprocal, that is, affluence leads to individualism, but also individualism may increase affluence (Triandis, 1990). In collectivist cultures, financial decisions are made by the group, and there is also a high need for security (Schwartz, 1994). That combination is likely to lead to very conservative financial decisions that usually do not result in high levels of affluence. Furthermore, in very collectivist cultures, the extended family often has access to all the assets of all individuals. Thus, individuals do not have an incentive to get rich, because their money would be shared by many others, and they do not need much money because they will be taken care of by the family.

The upper classes around the world sample the individual self more than the lower classes; the lower classes sample the collective self more than they sample the individual self.

2. *Economic independence.* Individuals who are economically independent are more likely to sample the individual self than individuals who depend financially on in-group members.

3. *Leadership roles.* In all cultures, those who have leadership roles are more likely to sample the individual self than are those who have subordinate roles (Kohn, 1969). Historical analysis shows that emperors and kings, even in very collectivist cultures, act idiocentrically. Freeman (2001) found that among Sri Lankans, low socioeconomic status was the best predictor of allocentrism.

4. *Migration, social mobility.* Those who leave their in-group and join other groups are more idiocentric than those who stay in their in-groups. Gerganov, Dilova, Petkova, and Paspalanova (1996) developed a Bulgarian scale for the measurement of allocentrism and idiocentrism, and showed that it had high reliability and validity. They then asked a number of questions, such as "Are you ready to leave Bulgaria for a long period of time?" The length of time that one was ready to live abroad (i.e., only one

item of low reliability) correlated .18 ($p < .001$) with the Bulgarian measure of idiocentrism.

5. *Mass media.* Those who spend much time looking at television, films, and other Western-made mass media are more idiocentric than those who are rarely exposed to the Western mass media. McBride (1998) did a content analysis of American-made television programs and found that they use extremely individualistic themes (what the hero likes rather than what the hero must do for the good of the group). Hsu (1983) pointed out that in Western novels, love conquers all; in novels from East Asian cultures, the heroes do their duty at great personal sacrifice. By contrast, American-made television soap operas rarely emphasize such themes as doing your duty, obligations, and the like, that are common in films made in collectivist cultures.

6. *Traditional and religious people.* Traditional and religious people tend to sample the collective self (e.g., the tribe, the co-religionists) more than the individual self (Triandis & Singelis, 1998).

7. *Bilateral family structure.* When kinship through the mother's or the father's side is about equally important, the individual may confront two equally "valid but different" normative systems. Then the individual has to decide which set of norms to follow. That increases the sampling of the individual self. On the other hand, in the case of either a patrilineal or a matrilineal family structure, there is likely to be only one normative system, and thus the individual is more likely to be pushed toward tightness and hence allocentrism. Thus bilateral family structure is associated with individualism.

8. *Availability of resources.* The more resources there are in an environment (e.g., minerals, food) the greater is the probability of affluence and individualism. The lack of resources is sometimes associated with rationing, which is a collectivist outcome. However, extreme lack of resources results in rejection of all norms, which is associated with extreme individualism, as in the case of the Ik, the mountain people of Uganda (Turnbull, 1972). The Ik were hunters deprived of their hunting grounds and suffered from extreme lack of food. Thus, resource availability is curvilinearly related to individualism.

9. *Age.* There is some evidence that older members of a society are more collectivist than younger members of that society. For example, Noricks et al. (1987) studied a large sample in California and examined the extent the individuals used context in describing other persons. Previous studies (Shweder & Bourne, 1982) found that a Chicago sample used context 28% of the time, and Indians in Orissa used context 50% of the time. For instance, in individualist cultures, people may say "She is intelligent." In collectivist cultures they may say "she is intelligent in the market place; she is stupid when dealing with her mother-in-law." In general,

people in collectivist cultures use more context in their thinking and talking, whereas those in individualist cultures use more abstractions (Choi, Nisbett, & Naranzayan, 1999).

Noricks et al. (1987) found that those who were less than 50 years old used context 32% of the time, whereas those who were more than 50 years old used it 43% of the time. Older individuals are more embedded (in context) in their in-groups, including family, neighborhood, city, and so forth, than younger individuals who are more mobile.

Triandis, Bontempo, Villareal, Asai, and Lucca (1988) studied Japanese students and their parents. The parents were more collectivist than the students; this may be a cohort effect. However, Schwartz (1994, and in numerous presentations at international conferences) presented data from samples of students and teachers from some 60 countries, and in all cases, the teachers are located toward the collectivist side of his multidimensional scaling map relative to the students. Gudykunst (1993) found that in some studies, age differences were more important than national differences as correlates of collectivism.

10. *Acculturation.* Berry and Sam (1997) argued that when two cultures (A and B) come in contact, members of the less dominant culture (B) have four options: They might adopt the new culture (use only A, assimilation), they may reject the new culture (use only B, segregation), they may choose elements of both cultures (A + B, biculturalism), or they may reject both cultures (marginalization, anomie). Yamada and Singelis (1999) found that bicultural individuals in situations where collectivist and individualist cultures meet, are high in both idiocentrism and allocentrism, and are especially well adjusted.

CULTURE, WORK MOTIVATION, AND THE MEANING OF WORK

Culture and Goals

Individualism and collectivism are reflected in the goals of members of the culture. People in individualist cultures tend to have self-actualizing goals; those from collectivist cultures are oriented in achieving for the sake of others. As goals have important implications for work motivation, culture too has implications for work motivation. The motive structure of allocentrics reflects receptivity to others, adjustment to the needs of others, and restraint of own needs and desires. The basic motive structure of idiocentrics reflects their internal needs, rights, and capacities, including the ability to withstand social pressures (Markus & Kitayama, 1991). Erez (1997) suggested that when people select goals, in horizontal individualist cultures, they use goals that maximize their personal involvement, whereas in vertical individualist cultures, they tolerate assigned goals. In horizontal collectivist cultures, people use group goals, whereas in vertical collectivist cultures, they accept assigned goals without discussion. Thus verticality leads to the acceptance of assigned goals.

Collectivism and power distance are highly correlated (Hofstede, 1980) and thus people in collectivist cultures generally accept assigned goals. In this context, it is interesting to note again the study by Iyengar and Lepper (1999). Working with 11-year-olds, they found greater performance among children from collectivist cultures if the task had been chosen by their mother than if it had been chosen by themselves. Conversely, children from individualist cultures were most motivated when they chose their own task. The generalization can be made that, in the case of people in collectivist cultures, if an in-group member chooses the task, it is just as satisfying and motivating as it would have been if they themselves had chosen the task.

Achievement motivation is socially oriented among people from collectivist cultures, and individually oriented among those from individualist cultures. Yu and Yang (1994) discussed achievement motivation in collectivist cultures. People from collectivist cultures achieve for others more often than they achieve to self-actualize. Yu and Yang (1994) constructed a social-oriented achievement motivation (SOAM) scale that they compared with an individual-oriented achievement motivation (IOAM) scale. A typical item in SOAM is "The major goal in my life is to work hard to achieve something which will make my parents feel proud of me"(p. 247). A typical item of the IOAM scale is "No matter how many times I fail, I'll keep on trying even without others' encouragement" (p. 247). After item analyses, they achieved alphas of .89 for both scales. Yu and Yang administered these two scales to 400 Taiwanese, and after factor analysis obtained two factors: SOAM and IOAM. They found that when choosing a job, people with high SOAM scores focused on family benefits and welfare. They desired high salaries so their family would have enough income. Those high in IOAM were especially interested in an enjoyable activity and self-development. They looked for jobs that were challenging and responsible. Incidentally, the Taiwan sample was quite high in both SOAM and IOAM. Similarly, Yu (1996) argued that the Chinese collective representations include both individual achievement and familial glorification.

Yang (1998) presented a theory of motivation that is more complex than Maslow's (1954). Yang argues that physiological and safety needs are universal. However, after these needs are satisfied, there are three hierarchies: one is based on genetic transmission, and includes, in ascending form, sexual needs, offspring-bearing needs, and finally parenting needs. The other two are based on genetic expression and include, in ascending form, individualist interpersonal belonginess needs, individualist esteem needs, and individualistic self-actualization needs. In collectivist cultures, one finds the corresponding collectivist needs. For example the collectivist self-actualization need, according to Yang, is defined as service to the community, or more generally to the collective. The individual is an aspect of the group, and reaches the highest self-fulfillment when the group reaches its goals. The self-actualized Chinese is a *junzi*, that is, a highly competent social being with a Confucian self, who is the center of relationships. To sacrifice the individual for the preservation of the group is the ultimate ideal.

In vertical collectivist cultures, such as in East Asia, the welfare of the in-group is paramount, even if the individual members must suffer. In East Asian cultures, individuals are expected to value education and self-improvement, obey rules, practice discipline, and respect authority. These values lead to diligence and achievement that will please the in-group.

The application of some of these points to the work place is clear: People in horizontal cultures are more likely to favor small salary differentials, whereas people in vertical cultures will tolerate large salary differentials. People from collectivist cultures will be motivated by goals that are widely accepted by the in-group, even when they did not have much say in how the goals were developed. People in individualist cultures will be more motivated if they had a hand in shaping the goals.

In evaluating these points, however, it must be remembered that culture, personality, the situation, and other factors are likely to be important in determining which goals will be most salient for an individual. For example, Chatman and Barsade (1995) randomly assigned allocentrics and idiocentrics to simulated industrial situations that were either individualist or collectivist. They measured the degree of cooperation of the individuals in those situations. They found that the most cooperation occurred among allocentrics assigned to the collectivist situation. Allocentrics assigned to the individualist situation or idiocentrics assigned to any situation were not especially cooperative.

The Meaning of Work

The meaning of work is different in collectivist and individualist cultures. Individuals from collectivist cultures emphasize cooperation, endurance, persistence, obedience, duty, in-group harmony, personalized relationships, order, and self-control, whereas people from individualist cultures emphasize self-realization, self-glory, pleasure, competition, and fair exchange (Hui & Villareal, 1989). The goals of those from collectivist cultures tend to be role relevant, long term, and consistent with in-group goals. The goals of those from individualist cultures tend to be specific to their personal needs and relatively short term. Those from collectivist cultures tend to be lower in self-efficacy than those from individualist cultures (Oettingen, Little, Lindenberger, & Baltes, 1994), but see the self as higher in self-efficacy when they work with the in-group than when they work alone (Earley, 1993). Also, they do not show as much social loafing (Earley, 1989) when working with in-group members, as do people from individualist cultures, and they have lower decisional self-esteem than people in individualist cultures (Radford, Mann, Ohta, & Nakane, 1993). Success among people from collectivist cultures tends to be associated with external factors (e.g., help from others), whereas failure is usually attributed to internal factors (e.g., I did not try hard enough). Conversely, among people from individualist cultures, success is attributed to internal factors (e.g., my ability) and failure to external factors (e.g., task difficulty).

People in collectivist cultures do not pay as much attention to cognitive consistency as do people in individualist cultures. For example, they do not think that attitudes are consistent with behavior (Y. Kashima, Siegel, Tanaka & E. S. Kashima, 1992), and judge most attributes of individuals in context. For instance, they use concepts such as "a meat-eating vegetarian" (i.e., a person who usually eats vegetables, but when others eat meat, eats meat). Individuals from collectivist cultures see performance as due to ability + effort. This contrasts with those from individualist cultures who see performance as ability × effort (Singh, 1981). This difference can be understood if we take into account that people from collectivist cultures think of group performance, and a group can perform well if some members are able and others are highly motivated.

In work settings, people in collectivist cultures like most those co-workers who are humble and self-effacing, whereas people in individualist cultures are used to self-enhancing co-workers (Markus & Kitayama, 1991; Yoshida, Kojo, & Kaku, 1982). People from collectivist cultures do not like to be praised in public; for example, they do not want to be used as "good examples for others" (Jones, Rozelle, & Chang, 1990). Effective rewards in individualist cultures are individual, whereas in collectivist cultures, both individual and group rewards are used (Wang, 1994). Performance appraisal should compare teams rather than individuals in collectivist cultures. Erez and Earley (1993) provided an extensive discussion of the way the two types of cultures differ and the implication of these differences for work behavior. For example, they recognize that one of the limitations of collectivism is that people keep valuable information within the in-group, even if the information would benefit the whole organization. Leadership theories (House, Wright, & Aditya, 1997) in collectivist cultures emphasize the importance of the nurturance of the leader (Misumi, 1985; Sinha, 1980). Paternalism is acceptable in collectivist cultures; for example, 80%

of the Japanese accepted it, but only 51% of the American samples accepted paternalism (Hayashi, 1992).

CONCLUSIONS

People in collectivist cultures sample the collective self and people in individualist cultures are more likely to sample the individual self. That has implications for many aspects of work motivation and the meaning of work.

Thus, the contrast between collectivism and individualism is an important dimension of cultural differences that needs to be included in discussions of the meaning of work in different environments. The Hulin and Triandis (1981) chapter provided a beginning of an analysis of the way culture influences the meaning of work. This chapter provides an up-to-date picture of the effect of an aspect of culture on work motivation and the meaning of work.

ACKNOWLEDGMENTS

I thank J. Brett and C. Hulin for excellent comments on previous drafts of this chapter.

REFERENCES

Abrams, D., Ando, K., & Hinkle, S. (1998). Psychological attachment to groups: Cross-cultural differences in organizational identification and subjective norms as predictors of workers' turnover intentions. *Personality and Social Psychology Bulletin, 24,* 1027–1039.

Berry, J. W., & Sam, D. (1997). Acculturation and adaptation. In J. W. Berry, M. H. Segall, & C. Kagitcibasi (Eds.), *Handbook of cross-cultural psychology* (Vol. 3., 2nd ed., pp. 291–326). Boston, MA: Allyn & Bacon.

Bond, R. A., & Smith, P. B. (1996). Culture and conformity: A meta-analysis of studies using Asch's line judgment task. *Psychological Bulletin, 119,* 111–137.

Breer, P. E., & Locke, E. A. (1965). *Task experience as a source of attitudes.* Homewood, IL: Dorsey Press.

Chatman, J. A., & Barsade, S. G. (1995). Personality, organizational culture, and cooperation: Evidence from a business simulation. *Administrative Science Quarterly, 40,* 423–443.

Choi, I., Nisbett, R. & Norenzayan, A. (1999). Causal attribution across cultures: Variation and universality. *Psychological Bulletin, 125,* 47–63.

Diaz-Guerrero, R. (1979). The development of coping style. *Human Development, 22,* 320–331.

Earley, P. C. (1989). Social loafing and collectivism. A comparison of the U.S. and the People's Republic of China. *Administrative Science Quarterly, 34,* 565–581.

Earley, P. C. (1993). East meets West meets Mideast: Further explorations of collectivist and individualist workgroups. *Academy of Management Journal, 36,* 319–348.

Erez, M. (1997). A culture based model of work motivation. In P. C. Earley & M. Erez (Eds.), *New perspectives on international industrial and organizational psychology* (pp. 193–242). San Francisco: Lexington Press.

Erez, M., & Earley, P. C. (1993). *Culture, self-identity, and work.* New York: Oxford University Press.

Freeman, M. A. (2001). *Demographic correlates of individualism and collectivism: A study of social values in Sri Lanka.* Manuscript submitted for publication.

Gerganov, E. N., Dilova, M. L., Petkova, K. G., & Paspalanova, E. P. (1996). Culture-specific approach to the study of individualism/collectivism. *European Journal of Social Psychology, 26,* 277–297.

Greenfield, P. (1999, August). *Three approaches to the psychology of culture: Where do they come from? Where can they go?* Paper presented at the 3rd Conference of the Asian Association of Social Psychology, Taiwan.

Gudykunst, W. (Ed.). (1993). *Communication in Japan and the United States.* Albany, NY: State University of New York Press.

Hayashi, C. (1992). Quantitative social research: Belief systems, the way of thinking, and sentiments of five nations. *Behaviormetrika, 19,* 127–170.

Hofstede, G. (1980). *Culture's consequences.* Beverly Hills, CA: Sage.

House, R. J., Wright, N. S., & Aditya, R. N. (1997). Cross-cultural research on organizational leadership: A critical analysis and a proposed theory. In P. C. Earley & M. Erez (Eds.), *New perspectives on international industrial and organizational psychology* (pp. 535–625). San Francisco: Lexington Press.

Hsu, F. L. K. (1983). *Rugged individualism reconsidered.* Knoxville: University of Tennessee Press.

Hui, C. H., & Villareal, M. (1989). Individualism–collectivism and psychological needs: Their relationship in two cultures. *Journal of Cross-Cultural Psychology, 24,* 428–444.

Hulin C. L., & Triandis, H. C. (1981). Meaning of work in different organizational environments. In P. C. Nystrom & W. H. Starbuck (Eds.), *Handbook of organizational design* (pp. 336–357). New York: Oxford University Press.

Iyengar, S. S., & Lepper, M. R. (1999). Rethinking the value of choice: A cultural perspective on intrinsic motivation. *Journal of Personality and Social Psychology, 76,* 349–366.

Iyengar, S. S., & Lepper, M. R. (2001). *When choice is demotivating: Can one desire too much of a good thing?* Manuscript submitted for publication.

Iyengar, S. S., Lepper, M. R., & Ross, L. (1999). Independence from whom? Interdependence from whom? Cultural perspectives on ingroups versus outgroups. In D. A. Prentice & D. T. Miller (Eds.), *Cultural divides: Understanding and overcoming group conflict* (pp. 273–301). New York: Russell Sage Foundation.

Jones, A. P., Rozelle, R. M., & Chang, M. (1990). Perceived punishment and reward values of superior's actions in a Chinese sample. *Psychological Studies, 35,* 1–10.

Kashima, E. S., & Kashima, Y. (1998). Culture and language: The case of cultural dimensions and personal pronoun use. *Journal of Cross-Cultural Psychology, 29,* 461–486.

Kashima, Y., Siegel, M., Tanaka, K., & Kashima, E. S. (1992). Do people believe behaviors are consistent with attitudes? Toward a cultural psychology of attribution processes. *British Journal of Social Psychology, 331,* 111–124.

Kohn, M. K. (1969). *Class & conformity.* Homewood, IL: Dorsey Press.

Markus, H., & Kitayama, S. (1991). Culture and self: Implications for cognition, emotion and motivation. *Psychological Review, 98,* 224–253.

Maslow, A. H. (1954). *Motivation and personality.* New York: Harper & Row.

McBride, A. (1998) Television, individualism, and social capital. *Political Science and Politics, 31,* 542–555.

Mills, J., & Clark, M. S. (1982). Exchange and communal relationships. In L. Wheeler (Ed.), *Review of personality and social psychology* (Vol. 3, pp. 121–144). Beverly Hills, CA: Sage.

Misumi, J. (1985). *The behavioral science of leadership: An interdisciplinary Japanese research program.* Ann Arbor: University of Michigan Press.

Noricks, J. S., Agler, L. H., Bartholomew, M., Howard-Smith, S., Martin, D., Pyles, S., & Shapiro, W. (1987) Age, abstract things and the American concept of person. *American Anthropologist, 89,* 667–675.

Oettingen, G., Little, T., Lindenberger, U., & Baltes, P. (1994). Causality, agency, and control beliefs in East vs. West Berlin children: A natural experiment in the role of context. *Journal of Personality and Social Psychology, 66,* 579–595.

Parkes, L. P., Schneider, S. K., & Bochner, S. (1999). Individualism–collectivism and self-concept: Social or contextual? *Asian Journal of Social Psychology, 2,* 367–383.

Radford, M. H., Mann, L., Ohta, Y., & Nakane, Y. (1993). Differences between Australian and Japanese students in decision self-esteem, decision stress, and coping styles. *Journal of Cross-Cultural Psychology, 24,* 284–297.

Schwartz, S. H. (1994). Beyond individualism and collectivism: New cultural dimensions of values. In U. Kim, H. C. Triandis, C. Kagitcibasi, S.-C. Choi, & G. Yoon (Eds.), *Individualism and collectivism: Theory, method, and applications* (pp. 85–122). Newbury Park, CA: Sage.

Shweder, R. A., & Bourne, E. J. (1982). Does the concept of person vary cross-culturally? In A. J. Marsella & G. M. White (Eds.), *Cultural conceptions of mental health and therapy* (pp. 97–137). London: Reidel.

Singh, R. (1981). Prediction of performance from motivation and ability: An appraisal of the cultural difference hypothesis. In J. Pandey (Ed.), *Perspectives on experimental social psychology in India* (pp. 21–53). New Delhi, India: Concept.

Sinha, J. B. P. (1980). *The nurturant task leader.* New Delhi, India: Concept.

Trafimow, D., Triandis, H. C., & Goto, S. (1991). Some tests of the distinction between the private and collective self. *Journal of Personality and Social Psychology, 60,* 649–655.

Triandis, H. C. (1989). The self and social behavior in differing cultural contexts. *Psychological Review, 96,* 506–520.

Triandis, H. C. (1990). Cross-cultural studies of individualism and collectivism. In J. Berman (Ed.), *Nebraska Symposium on Motivation, 1989* (pp. 41–133). Lincoln: University of Nebraska Press.

Triandis, H. C. (1995). *Individualism & collectivism.* Boulder, CO: Westview Press.

Triandis, H. C., Bontempto, R., Villareal, M. J., Asai, M., & Lucca, N. (1988). Individualism and collectivism: Cross-cultural perspectives on self-in-group relationships. *Journal of Personality and Social Psychology, 54,* 323–338.

Triandis, H. C., Carnevale, P., Gelfand, M., Robert, C., Wasti, S. A., Probst, T., Kashima, E., Dragonas, T., Chan, D., Chen X. P., Kim U., Kim, K., de Dreu, C., van de Vliert, E., Iwao, S., Ohbuchi, K.-I., & Schmitz, P. (2001). *Culture, personality, and deception.* Manuscript submitted for publication.

Triandis, H. C., Chen, X. P., & Chan, D. K.-S. (1998). Scenarios for the measurement of collectivism and individualism. *Journal of Cross-Cultural Psychology, 29,* 275–289.

Triandis, H. C., & Gelfand, M., (1998). Converging measurement of horizontal and vertical individualism and collectivism. *Journal of Personality and Social Psychology, 74,* 118–128.

Triandis, H. C., Leung, K., Villareal, M., & Clack, F. L. (1985). Allocentric vs. idiocentric tendencies: Convergent and discriminant validation. *Journal of Research in Personality, 19,* 395–415.

Triandis, H. C., McCusker, C., & Hui, C. H. (1990). Multimethod measurement of individualism and collectivism. *Journal of Personality and Social Psychology, 59,* 1006–1020.

Triandis, H. C., & Singelis, T. M. (1998). Training to recognize individual differences in collectivism and individualism within culture. *International Journal of Intercultural Relations, 22,* 35–48.

Turnbull, C. M. (1972). *The mountain people*. New York: Simon & Schuster.

Wang, Z.-M. (1994). Culture, economic reform, and the role of industrial and organizational psychology in China. In H. C. Triandis, M. Dunnette, & L. Hough (Eds.), *Handbook of industrial and organizational psychology* (2nd ed., pp. 689–726). Palo Alto, CA: Consulting Psychologists Press.

Weisz, J. R., Rothbaum, F. M., & Blackburn, T. C. (1984). Standing out and standing in: The psychology of control in America and Japan. *American Psychologist, 39,* 955–969.

Weldon, E. (1984). Deindividuation, Interpersonal affect, and productivity in laboratory task groups. *Journal of Applied Social Psychology, 14,* 469–485.

Yamada, A.-M., & Singelis, T. M. (1999). Biculturalism and self-construal. *International Journal of Intercultural Relations, 23,* 697–710.

Yamaguchi, S. (1994). Empirical evidence on collectivism among the Japanese. In U. Kim, H. C. Triandis, C. Kagitcibasi, S.-C. Choi, & G. Yoon (Eds.), *Individualism and collectivism: Theory, method, and applications* (pp. 175–188). Newbury Park, CA: Sage.

Yang, K.-S. (1998, August). *Beyond Maslow's culture-bound, linear theory: A preliminary statement of the double-Y model of basic human needs*. Invited address at the 24th International Congress of Applied Psychology, San Francisco.

Yoshida, T., Kojo, K., Kaku, H. (1982). A study of the development of self-presentation in children. *Japanese Journal of Educational Psychology, 30,* 30–37.

Yu, A.-B. (1996). Ultimate life concerns, self, and Chinese achievement motivation. In M. H. Bond (Ed.), *The handbook of Chinese psychology* (pp. 227–246). Hong Kong: Oxford University Press.

Yu, A.-B., & Yang, K.-S. (1994). The nature of achievement motivation in collectivist societies. In U. Kim, H. C. Triandis, C. Kagitcibasi, S.-C. Choi, & G. Yoon (Eds.), *Individualism and collectivism: Theory, method, and applications* (pp. 235–239). Newbury Park, CA: Sage.

Antecedents and Outcomes of Satisfaction

Are Men Affected by the Sexual Harassment of Women? Effects of Ambient Sexual Harassment on Men

Wendy L. Richman-Hirsch
William M. Mercer, Inc., New York

Theresa M. Glomb
University of Minnesota

Research linking organizational antecedents and job-related outcomes of sexual harassment has focused mainly on the person who is the direct target of sexual harassment (e.g., Fitzgerald, Drasgow, Hulin, Gelfand, & Magley, 1997; Fitzgerald, Hulin, & Drasgow, 1995). Recent research reports that effects of sexual harassment may reach beyond the target to co-workers and others in the organization (e.g., Glomb et al., 1997; Schneider, 1996; Sorenson, Luzio, & Mangione-Lambie, 1994). The study described here tests whether the effects of ambient sexual harassment extend to men in work groups where women have experienced sexual harassment. *Ambient sexual harassment* is defined as the general level of sexual harassment of women in a work group as measured by the frequency of sexually harassing behaviors experienced by women in a man's work group. This study extends the framework developed by Fitzgerald et al. (1997) by examining indirect exposure to sexual harassment, that is, ambient sexual harassment, as an additional workplace stressor.

DIRECT EFFECTS OF SEXUAL HARASSMENT ON WOMEN

Evidence that between 40% (United States Merit Systems Protection Board, 1981, 1987) and 68% (Schneider, Swan, & Fitzgerald, 1997) of female employees experience sexually harassing behaviors in their workplaces has stimulated research that treats sexual harassment as one of several job-related stressors within comprehensive models of organizational behavior (Hulin, 1993). For example, Fitzgerald et al. (1995) developed an integrated model of sexual harassment that treats the organizational antecedents and consequences of sexual harassment in the context of other job-related stressors. This model suggests two organizational-level antecedents of sexual harassment of women: (a) perceived organizational tolerance for harassment, and (b) the gendered nature of the individual's work environment, including the gender ratio, the gender of one's supervisor, and work traditionality (Fitzgerald et al., 1997). In addition, the model suggests negative relations between workplace stressors (i.e., sexual harassment and general job stress) and job-related, psychological, and health outcomes (Fitzgerald et al., 1997; Glomb et al., 1997).

DIRECT EFFECTS OF SEXUAL HARASSMENT
ON MEN

Research on the sexual harassment of men is limited. Measures of the frequency of men's experienced harassment are problematic because of the reliance on methods developed for women rather than men (e.g., United States Merit Systems Protection Board, 1981, 1987; Waldo, Berdahl, & Fitzgerald, 1998). Recent research suggests that (a) Men and women differ with respect to what behaviors they consider potentially harassing; (b) unlike women, who experience harassment primarily from members of the opposite gender, men experience harassment from both genders about equally; and (c) men report relatively fewer negative outcomes from direct harassment than women (Berdahl, Magley, & Waldo, 1996; Waldo et al., 1998). These findings are supported by work on gender differences in perceptions of harassment behaviors that indicate that, overall, women are more likely to perceive behaviors as harassing than men (Blumenthal, 1998; Rotundo, Nguyen, & Sackett, 2001). Because the evidence suggests that direct sexual harassment functions differently for men and women, it seems reasonable to explore whether men and women's experience of ambient sexual harassment is different as well.

INDIRECT EFFECTS OF SEXUAL HARASSMENT

Evidence of Indirect Effects

Employees are often aware of the sexual harassment of their co-workers. Some co-workers of a sexual harassment victim may witness the harassment and others may hear about the harassment experience from the victim or other co-workers (Bond, 1990; Salisbury, in press). For example, women know which male co-workers harass other women (Gutek, 1985), further evidence that sexual harassment incidents are often well known among co-workers. Employees are also frequently aware of sexual harassment complaints and organizational investigations into such complaints, sometimes because they are interviewed about these situations, but also because they share information in the workplace. These findings suggest that there is indirect exposure to sexual harassment.

Ambient or indirect sexual harassment can cause negative outcomes similar to those of the victim. For example, in a laboratory assuming the role of a witness to a hypothetical sexual harassment incident involving sexual coercion or unwanted sexual attention can lead to negative affect, increased depression, and decreased motivation (Sorenson et al., 1994). Field research indicates that women who experience bystander stress when observing or hearing about co-workers being sexually harassed reported lower satisfaction with their co-workers and supervision, decreased life satisfaction, and lower levels of psychological well-being compared to others in their organization (Schneider, 1995, 1996).

In another field study, ambient sexual harassment had the same exogenous antecedents as direct sexual harassment (i.e., organizational tolerance) as well as similar job-related, psychological, and health outcomes (Glomb et al., 1997). See Fig. 6.1 for the model and path coefficients. Even after accounting for a woman's direct exposure to sexual harassment, women who were members of work groups with high levels of ambient sexual harassment reported lower job satisfaction and greater psychological distress. Glomb et al. (1997) argued that for those women who themselves were never the targets of direct sexual harassment, "just being exposed to ambient sexual harassment in their work group results in negative outcomes" (p. 323).

Women who are aware of the harassment of their co-workers may experience negative consequences because of concerns about what might happen if they themselves became a target of sexual harassment, about the negative or unsupportive response from the victim's co-workers or the organization, or about feeling powerless to curb the harassment of a co-worker. Men may experience negative outcomes of indirect exposure to sexual harassment from observing what they interpret as an unsupportive work environment or feeling unable to stop the harassment. Men may also feel stress from slightly different sources, such as fear of being blamed as a party to the harassing environment or fear that their behaviors and actions might be misinterpreted as harassment (Berdhal et al., 1996). Despite these possibilities, there is no research on the negative effects of indirect harassment on men.

The present study examines whether the negative job-related, health, and psychological outcomes associated with sexual harassment will extend

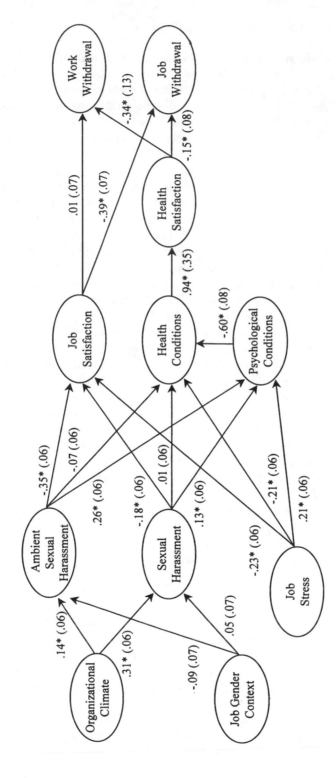

FIG. 6.1. LISREL estimates of structural model coefficients and their standard errors in testing the model for women (Glomb et al., 1997).

to men in the workgroup. The goal of this study was to examine the generalizability of the ambient sexual harassment framework to men. Using the Glomb et al.'s (1997) conceptualization of ambient sexual harassment and their extension of the Fitzgerald et al. (1997) framework, the current study examines the effects on men of indirect exposure to the harassment of their female co-workers (see Fig. 6.2).

METHOD

Participants and Procedures

We collected survey data from 455 women and 687 men employed at a large utility company and 295 women and 299 men working for a food-processing company. Of the men's answers, 789 were sufficiently complete to be included in the analyses (questionnaires with more than 50% missing data were not analyzed). After creation of the work group level variable (see upcoming text) and listwise deletion of cases with missing values, the resulting sample size was 161.

Questionnaires were administered in mixed-sex group sessions ranging in size from 1 to 78. All measures were completed by both men and women with the exception of the Sexual Experiences Questionnaire (SEQ; Fitzgerald, Drasgow, Hulin, & Gelfand, 1993; Fitzgerald, Gelfand, & Drasgow, 1995) which was only completed by women. The study was conducted as part of the organizations' efforts to create harassment-free workplaces and was described as a survey of the quality of organizational life. Participation in these sessions was voluntary, but was strongly encouraged by the human resource department.

Measures

Organizational Antecedents. The organizational antecedents of ambient sexual harassment were assessed via two scales: organizational tolerance of sexual harassment and job gender context. The Organizational Tolerance of Sexual Harassment Inventory (OTSHI) measures organizational climate for sexual harassment (Hulin, Fitzgerald, & Drasgow, 1996; Zickar, Matt, & Hulin, 1997). Participants reported perceptions of organizational sanctions that would occur contingent on various forms of harassing behavior. The OTSHI presents vignettes in which the organizational role of a male harasser (supervisor or co-worker) is crossed with a type of harassing behavior (gender harassment, unwanted sexual attention, or sexual coercion) resulting in six vignettes. Using a 5-point Likert scale, participants respond to three questions for each vignette. The questions

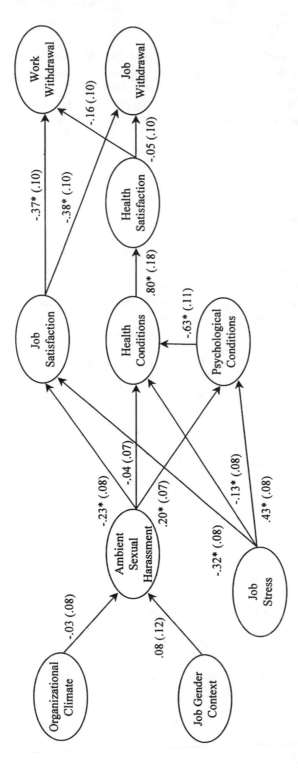

FIG. 6.2. LISREL estimates of structural model coefficients and their standard errors in testing the model for men.

assess: (a) perceived risk to a female victim of reporting the harasser, (b) the likelihood that her allegations would be taken seriously by the organization, and (c) the likelihood that the harasser would be punished. Individuals' responses to all 18 items are combined to create an individual level assessment of climate. For a discussion of climate as a group level variable, see Zickar et al. (1997).

Job gender context, the degree to which a participant's job context is considered masculine or feminine, was determined by three items; each item was treated as a separate indicator of the job gender context construct in the LISREL measurement model. Participants were asked whether or not they were the first of their sex to do their job, whether their immediate supervisor was male or female, and the gender ratio of their work group. The gender ratio was measured on a 5-point scale, ranging from *almost all men* to *almost all women*. A work group numerically dominated by men with a male supervisor would be considered to be a masculine job context.

Ambient Sexual Harassment. *Ambient sexual harassment* (ASH) is an estimate of the (ambient) level of sexual harassment of women in a work group. The self-report, SEQ, developed by Fitzgerald et al. (1993, 1995) was used to assess ASH. The SEQ assesses the frequency with which women are exposed to three categories of offensive sex-related behaviors: *gender harassment, unwanted sexual attention*, and *coercion*. Gender harassment comprises offensive, misogynist, degrading remarks and behavior. Unwanted sexual attention is characterized by unwelcome sexual behaviors that are unwanted and unreciprocated by the target; these behaviors are not tied to any job-related outcomes. Behaviors in the sexual coercion category, however, consist of implicit or explicit efforts to make job-related outcomes conditional on sexual cooperation. Using a 5-point scale ranging from *never* to *most of the time*, women report whether they have experienced offensive sex-related behaviors from male co-workers or supervisors in the previous 2 years. The words sexual harassment do not appear until the last item in the scale. For an account of the theoretical and empirical development of the SEQ, see Fitzgerald et al. (1995).

Consistent with Glomb et al. (1997), we conceptualized a man's exposure to ambient sexual harassment as a work group-level variable, and determined his degree of exposure by computing the mean SEQ score for all female employees in his work group. This procedure provides an estimate of the ambient level of harassment of women occurring in a man's work group. By using a measure of ambient sexual harassment assessed from the women in a work group and examining its relationship to antecedents and outcomes assessed from men, we avoid the common method variance problem inherent in using strictly self-report or single-source data.

Individuals were classified into work groups based on common job information, specifically work location, department, area, job title, and shift.

Participants who did not provide this information could not be placed into work groups, and were eliminated from all analyses. Those work groups identified as having fewer than three female employees were also eliminated from the analyses due to unreliability in computing a mean work group SEQ score for small work groups. The aforementioned elimination of participants accounts for a considerable amount of reduction in sample size. For the resulting 161 men included in the analysis, a total of 38 work group ambient harassment scores were created, aggregating scores from between 3 to 33 women.

Job Outcomes. Job outcomes were assessed via measures of job satisfaction and organizational withdrawal. Job satisfaction was measured using shortened versions of the work, supervisor, and co-worker scales of the Job Descriptive Index (JDI; Smith, Kendall, & Hulin, 1969), as revised by Roznowski (1989). Participants responded *yes, no,* and *?* to a series of adjectives describing relevant characteristics of their work, supervisor, and co-workers.

Organizational withdrawal was assessed using measures of *work withdrawal*, defined as attempts to avoid the tasks of one's work role, and *job withdrawal*, defined as partial or complete withdrawal from one's job in an organization (Hanisch, 1990; Hanisch & Hulin, 1990, 1991). The work withdrawal scale assesses the frequency with which employees engage in work withdrawal behaviors (i.e., taking long breaks, leaving work early, and missing meetings) on an 8-point scale ranging from *never* to *more than once a week*. The job withdrawal scale assesses the extent to which employees engage in job withdrawal behaviors such as intentions to quit, perceived difficulty in securing alternative employment, and thinking about quitting.

Psychological Outcomes. The Mental Health Index (MHI; Veit & Ware, 1983), Satisfaction With Life Scale (SWLS; Diener, 1984; Diener, Emmons, Larsen, & Griffin, 1985), and Faces Scale (Kunin, 1955) were used to assess the psychological outcomes of ambient sexual harassment. The MHI was constructed specifically to assess the more prevalent symptoms of psychological distress (e.g., anxiety and depression). Participants respond to items describing these symptoms using a 6-point Likert scale ranging from *none of the time* to *all of the time*. The SWLS is a global assessment of well-being with respect to all aspects of a person's life. Using a 7-point response scale ranging from *strongly disagree* to *strongly agree,* the SWLS asks respondents to indicate the extent to which they are satisfied with their life. Kunin's (1955) one-item Faces Scale presents respondents with seven faces depicting various levels of happiness. Respondents select the face that best represents their general life satisfaction. All psychological outcome measures described were coded so that higher scores indicate higher levels of psychological distress.

Health Outcomes. Health outcomes were assessed via measures of health conditions and health satisfaction. The Health Conditions Index (HCI) is a *yes/no* checklist of health and physical symptoms adapted from the Cornell Medical Checklist (Brodman, Erdman, Lorge, & Wolff, 1949). Participants are asked to indicate the presence or absence of specific health symptoms such as severe headaches, shortness of breath on exertion, and difficulty falling asleep. Lower scores on the HCI indicate poorer physical health. Health satisfaction was assessed via a subscale of the Retirement Descriptive Index (RDI; Smith et al., 1969), in which participants respond *yes, no,* and *?* to short descriptive phrases reflecting feelings and perceptions of one's health.

Control Variable. The Stress in General (SIG; Smith, Sandeman, & McCrary, 1992) assessed the global occupational stress using a *yes, no,* and *?* format. The SIG provides a baseline measure against which ambient sexual harassment can be evaluated and was included in the structured equations model to ensure that covarying effects due to quotidian job stress were not erroneously attributed to ambient sexual harassment.

Additional Measures. Because this study was conducted as part of a larger academic research project, there were additional scales completed by participants that were not included in the present analyses. These measures assessed participants' attitudes toward sexual harassment, characteristics of the specific harassing incident, and potential coping responses to sexual harassment.

Analyses

To test the model shown in Fig. 6.2, we used LISREL VIII (Jöreskog & Sörbom, 1993) structural equations modeling software. A measurement model was analyzed to determine the factor loadings of the observed indicators on each of the latent constructs. Analysis of the structural model assessed the proposed relationships among the latent constructs.

Consistent with Fitzgerald et al. (1997) and Glomb et al. (1997), we created three manifest indicators for each latent construct. Items were distributed among the indicators in an attempt to balance them with respect to classical test theory item statistics and item content; this procedure "maximizes the extent to which the indicators of each construct share variance" (Fitzgerald et al., 1997, p. 13).

To determine the extent to which the data conformed to our predictions, we examined a variety of goodness-of-fit indices, such as the χ^2 to degrees of freedom ratio, the goodness-of-fit index (GFI), the adjusted goodness-of-fit index (AGFI), the root mean square residual (RMSR), and the non-normed fit index (NNFI). We examined standardized path coefficients to determine the degree of relatedness among the constructs.

RESULTS

Table 6.1 presents the scale means divided by the number of items in the scale, standard deviations, scale reliabilities, and intercorrelations for the variables in the study. As would be expected, ASH is negatively correlated with measures of job, health, and life satisfaction as well as work withdrawal. The significant correlations between ASH and these outcome measures cannot be attributed to single source method bias; a measure solicited from women (i.e., ASH) is significantly correlated with several measures solicited from men (i.e., the outcome measures) in their work group.

Measurement Model. As evident from the goodness-of-fit indices in Table 6.2, the measurement model provided a satisfactory fit to the data. The χ^2 to degrees of freedom ratio was 1.31, the GFI was .86, the AGFI was .81, the RMSR was .05, and the NNFI was .95. The factor loadings from the measurement model for each set of three manifest indicators on their latent variable (Table 6.3) were large and significant at the .001 level. Together, these results suggest a good fit to the data.

Structural Model. The second stage of analysis involved estimating the relationships among the latent constructs shown in Fig. 6.2. As shown in Table 6.2, the fit indices for the structural model included a χ^2 to degrees of freedom ratio of 1.46, a GFI of .83, an AGFI of .79, a RMSR of .09, and an NNFI of .93. These statistics suggest a reasonable fit to the data.

The estimated paths and their standard errors are shown in Fig. 6.2. Inspection of these coefficients indicates that 13 of the 14 predicted relationships were in the hypothesized direction and 9 of the 14 were statistically significant; the remaining 5 paths were not significantly different than zero.

The paths from organizational climate and job gender context to ambient sexual harassment indicate that these antecedents are not significantly related to the level of ambient sexual harassment in a man's work group. The lack of a significant relationship from organizational climate to ambient sexual harassment is not surprising given that men may perceive the work environment differently than woman (Hulin, 1993; Zickar, 1994). A man may not perceive the climate as one that is tolerant of sexual harassment even though women are experiencing sexually harassing behaviors; this is supported by the fact that the set of behaviors viewed as potentially

TABLE 6.1

Means, Standard Deviations, Scale Reliabilities, and Intercorrelations Among Variables

	#Items	M^a	SD	α	OTSHI	ASH	WKSAT	COWSAT	SUPSAT	JWITH	WWITH	HELCOND	LIFESAT	MHI	HELSAT	JOBSTRESS
OTSHI	18	1.94	0.74	.94	1.00											
ASH	1	1.31	0.18	—^b	-.03	1.00										
WKSAT	9	1.80	0.92	.88	-.31**	-.18**	1.00									
COWSAT	12	2.11	0.72	.86	-.09	-.22**	.28**	1.00								
SUPSAT	18	1.91	0.81	.92	-.27**	-.21**	.45**	.42**	1.00							
JWITH	7	2.37	0.99	.71	.25**	-.13	-.28**	.04	-.11	1.00						
WWITH	12	2.52	1.41	.79	.28**	-.27**	-.10	-.02	-.08	.43**	1.00					
HELCOND	13	1.78	0.20	.77	-.07	-.03	.10	.21**	.10	-.15*	-.33**	1.00				
LIFESAT	5	4.17	1.49	.90	-.14*	-.22**	.31**	.25**	.26**	-.10	-.11	.40**	1.00			
MHI	30	3.66	0.60	.95	.04	.02	-.07	-.14	-.08	-.13	-.21**	.13	.22**	1.00		
HELSAT	9	2.45	0.51	.71	.05	-.14*	.27**	.27**	.17*	.10	.06	.50**	.44**	.05	1.00	
JOBSTRESS	9	1.45	0.92	.87	.03	-.09	-.14	-.22**	-.26**	.06	.02	-.36**	-.27**	-.01	-.20**	1.00

Note. OTSHI, Organizational Tolerance of Sexual Harassment Inventory; ASH, Ambient Sexual Harassment; WKSAT, JDI Satisfaction with Work; COWSAT, JDI Satisfaction with Co-workers; SUPSAT, JDI Satisfaction with Supervision; JWITH, Job Withdrawal; WWITH, Work Withdrawal; HELCOND, Health Conditions Index; LIFESAT, Satisfaction with Life Scale; MHI, MHI Stress and Well-Being; HELSAT, RDI Health Satisfaction; JOBSTRESS, Stress in General.

^aMeans shown are the scale means divided by the number of items in the scale.

^bDash indicates that this particular statistic is not applicable.

*p < .05, ** p < .01.

131

TABLE 6.2
Goodness-of-Fit Indices for Measurement and Structural Model

Model	χ^2	df	χ^2/df	GFI	AFGI	RMSR	NNFI
Measurement	402.33	306	1.31	.86	.81	.05	.95
Structural	487.71	334	1.46	.83	.79	.09	.93

Note. GFI = goodness-of-fit index; AFGI = adjusted goodness-of-fit index; RMSR = root mean square residual; NNFI = non-normed fit index.

TABLE 6.3
Measurement Model Factor Loadings

Construct	Loadings		
	1	2	3
Organizational tolerance of sexual harassment	.88	.86	.95
Job context	.27	−.35	−.61
Job stress	.90	.84	.78
Ambient sexual harassment	1.00	—[a]	—[a]
Job satisfaction	.89	.94	.93
Health conditions	.81	.58	.67
Psychological conditions	.96	.96	.94
Health satisfaction	.58	.27	.87
Job withdrawal	.56	.66	.84
Work withdrawal	.81	.65	.60

[a]A dash indicates that this particular statistic is not applicable.

harassing differs for men and women (Berdhal et al., 1996; Waldo et al., 1998).

The lack of a significant relationship between job gender context and ASH may be the result of range restriction. Men who work in highly masculinized workgroups may not have been included in the analyses due to the requirement that a man's workgroup had to contain three or more women (i.e., to compute an ASH score).

Relationships between ambient sexual harassment and the job and psychological outcomes were in the hypothesized direction. The path from ambient sexual harassment to job satisfaction was −.23, indicating that men who are members of work groups where women are being harassed are less satisfied with their jobs. Although the path from ambient sexual harassment to health conditions was not significant, this result is consistent with the findings of both Fitzgerald et al. (1997) and Glomb et al. (1997). It has been suggested that, for women, ambient sexual harassment affects health conditions through its effect on psychological conditions; this same effect was found for men. There was a significant positive relationship (a standardized path coefficient of .20) between ambient sexual harassment and psychological conditions, indicating that men who are in work groups where the sexual harassment of women is prevalent experience higher psychological distress.

The paths from job stress to job satisfaction, health conditions, and psychological conditions were −.32, −.13, and .43 respectively. Thus, men who report higher levels of job stress also reported being less satisfied with their jobs and having more health and psychological problems. It is important to note that after accounting for the effects due to ordinary job stress, ambient sexual harassment also had an independent effect on job and psychological outcomes.

Several job stressors have been hypothesized to affect health conditions through their effects on psychological conditions (Fitzgerald et al., 1997). In our model, there was a significant negative path of −.63 between psychological conditions and health conditions; men who experienced psychological distress reported more health problems. As expected, experiencing health conditions was significantly related to health satisfaction; the path coefficient was estimated as .80. These findings are consistent with those found for women (see Fitzgerald et al., 1997; Glomb et al., 1997).

The significant negative paths from job satisfaction to both work withdrawal and job withdrawal were −.37 and −.38 respectively. The less satisfied a man was with his job, the more likely he was to report engaging in work withdrawal behaviors (i.e., taking long breaks, leaving work early, and missing meetings) and job withdrawal behaviors (i.e., intentions to quit, perceived difficulty in securing alternative employment, and thinking about quitting).

Significant relationships were not found between health satisfaction and either work or job withdrawal. These findings are not that surprising given that men may not engage in organizational withdrawal behaviors as a result of health dissatisfaction. To the extent that men are the primary breadwinners of their households, their financial responsibilities may make withdrawing from their jobs impossible. Sole fiscal responsibility may be less common among women and thus engaging in withdrawal behaviors may not be as constrained and therefore more likely to be related to health conditions (as has been shown by both Fitzgerald et al., 1997, and Glomb et al., 1997).

DISCUSSION

The phenomena of ambient sexual harassment can be detrimental to men, just as it is to women. Tests of a structural equation model of male ambient sexual harassment indicate that ambient sexual harassment has severe negative effects on job-related outcomes and psychological conditions for men. Men who are members of work groups where women are being harassed report lower job satisfaction, greater psychological distress, and they engage in more organizational withdrawal behaviors (e.g., absenteeism, intentions to quit, missing meetings, etc.). Although men are less likely than women to be the victims of harassment (Waldo et al., 1998), they still experience negative outcomes due to indirect exposure to ambient sexual harassment in their work group.

These negative effects of ambient sexual harassment occurred even after accounting for general job stress. The significant paths from job stress to the outcome measures, as well as from ambient sexual harassment to the outcome measures, illustrate that indirect exposure to sexually harassing behaviors results in detrimental effects over and above that accounted for by traditional job stressors.

The antecedents of job gender context and organizational tolerance for harassment, as perceived by men who experience negative outcomes of ambient sexual harassment, are not significantly related to the level of ambient sexual harassment in a man's work group. These findings, although inconsistent with the results for women (Glomb et al., 1997), are not surprising given that men may perceive the organization's tolerance for sexual harassment differently than woman (Hulin, 1993; Zickar, 1994). In general, women perceive their organization as more tolerant of harassment than men—behaviors viewed as harassing differ for men and women (Berdhal et al., 1996; Waldo et al., 1998). Job gender context may also be a problematic variable in testing this model for men. Typically, a masculine job gender context is related to sexual harassment (Fitzgerald et al., 1997). However, an extremely masculine context is likely to have too few women to compute an ambient harassment score, thus deleting them from our sample. This restriction of range may be responsible for the lack of significant results. Similar nonsignificant relations between job gender context and ambient sexual harassment were found for women (Glomb et al., 1997).

Strengths of the Study

Our study design refutes the "whiner hypothesis." Ambient sexual harassment contributes to male employees' negative outcomes when controlling for other organizational stressors and when measured indirectly from reports of women in the work group. The findings, therefore, cannot be due to self-consistency, negative affectivity, or whining about quotidian, minor events by the respondents.

Limitations

Our findings were significant despite what we must presume was substantial error in the definition of work groups. Defining work groups by such variables as work location, department, area, job title, and shift may not capture the fuzzily defined groups and interpersonal networks that exist in organizational reality. A man who is a boundary spanner or a liaison with another work group may be indirectly exposed to the harassment of women who are not in his work group as defined by the structured organizational categories, but may still experience negative effects. Conversely, a man may be a member of a work group in which ambient sexual harassment is prevalent, but if he is in some way isolated or buffered from this indirect exposure, for example, if he is an isolate within his work group, he may not experience the same negative outcomes. Utilization of group-level data requires substantial efforts to define work groups that are meaningful to the participants to ensure an accurate depiction of the operation of the phenomena.

Further refinement of methods of identifying meaningful work groups should reduce error and increase validity coefficients. We limited our study to groups in which there were three or more women but we did not restrict the group size in other ways. Work group size may influence the effects of ambient sexual harassment. Although one might predict stronger effects of ambient sexual harassment in small, tightly networked work groups, a measure of ambient sexual harassment would be based on fewer women and would be less reliable in small work groups. Consequently, it should not be surprising to find larger effects for the ambient sexual harassment variable when larger work groups are used in the analysis. This methodological question needs to be addressed in future research seeking to compare the effects of ambient sexual harassment in large and small work groups.

Directions for Future Research

Even though ambient sexual harassment has substantial negative effects for men, just as it does for women, the experience of ambient sexual harassment may be quite different for men and women. A woman who is indirectly exposed to sexual harassment may experience stress because she is worried about being the next target of the harassment or is upset by the lack of support provided by the organization in harassment incidents. However, a man "may experience stress from feeling unable to do anything about it or from fear of being perceived as similar to the harasser and a contributor to the sexually harassing environment" (Glomb et al., 1997, p. 326).

Although in this chapter we do not specifically identify the underlying process leading to the relations observed in the model, there are relatively few mechanisms by which ambient sexual harassment of women in a man's work group might get translated into negative outcomes for men. These mechanisms may likely differ from those by which ambient sexual harassment results in negative outcomes for women. Possible explanations are now presented as a guide to future research in this area. These explanations fall into three broad categories of hypotheses: a sympathetic stress hypothesis, a perpetrator stress hypothesis, and a disrespectful work environment hypothesis.

Sympathetic Stress. The sympathetic stress hypothesis focuses on feelings due to witnessing the harassment of others. Men may experience stress because they know that their co-workers are being harassed or because they see little support for women in attempting to deal with sexual harassment. Men may feel similarly powerless to do anything about the objectionable behavior.

The sympathetic stress hypothesis is akin to a phenomena known as emotional contagion. Research on emotional contagion suggests that, like flu sufferers who spread their illness to others, individuals' emotional states can "spread" so that others experience a similar emotion or similar levels of anxiety (Gump & Kulik, 1997; Hatfield, Cacioppo, & Rapson, 1994; Joiner, 1994). Emotional contagion may result because (a) people seek to establish a common social reality and attempt to influence one another's emotions (Schachter, 1959), or (b) people mimic other's emotional expressions (e.g., frowning or smiling; Hatfield, Cacioppo, & Rapson, 1992). Therefore, the negative emotions experienced by a target of sexual harassment may diffuse to members of the target's work group through the process of emotional contagion. Men (and women for that matter) may experience negative outcomes of indirect exposure to sexual harassment simply because they observe the harassment and or because the negative emotional state of the victim spreads to other work group members.

Acting on this sympathetic stress by reporting the harassment, however, may also result in negative outcomes. Men may feel anxieties about being a "whistle-blower" to sexual harassment. "Whistle-blowers suffer severe retaliation from management, especially when their information proves significant" (Rothschild & Miethe, 1999, p. 107). People fear that management will ignore the whistle-blower's complaints or allegations, attempt to silence or intimidate the whistle-blower by transferring him to another job, destroy any paper trail revealing the wrongdoing, threaten and actually discredit the employee, or attempt to ruin the whistle-blower's reputation (Baucus, 1998). Management has been known to even fire whistle-blowers for "complaining," "causing trouble," or being "disloyal" (Baucus, 1998). The fear of retaliation if a man reports (i.e., blows the whistle on) the sexual harassment may be what ultimately leads to lower job satisfaction and greater psychological conditions among men in work groups where sexual harassment is prevalent.

Perpetrator Stress. The perpetrator stress explanation for the relations between ambient sexual harassment and negative outcomes is unique to male employees. Men may experience stress from being afraid of being accused as a party to the harassment or from being overly cautious about their words and actions so that they might not be interpreted as harassment. Men report a "backlash" effect whereby they feel burdened by oversensitivity to harassment complaints and the need to watch what they say (Berdhal et al., 1996).

It is also possible that the negative outcomes found in the model are because men may be perpetrators of sexual harassment. Men who perpetrate harassment may engage in a host of dysfunctional job behaviors such as work and job withdrawal and have poor relations with their supervisors and co-workers (i.e., report lower co-worker and supervisor satisfaction). Presumably the women in the perpetrators' work groups would report experiencing harassment and the ambient sexual harassment score would be elevated. Causal inferences are particularly problematic in the perpetrator stress hypothesis, as one could argue that job dissatisfaction might result in a pattern of dysfunctional work behaviors, including harassment.

Disrespectful Work Environment. A third potential explanation of the effects of ambient sexual harassment on men is that sexual harassment experienced by women may be a reflection of a broader disrespectful or poor work environment. Thus, men may be experiencing other stressors from a negative work climate, such as workplace aggression or other forms of harassment, that result in negative job outcomes. However, a pervasive negative work environment should be reflected in general job stress and controlled for in our model. The presence of an overarching negative work environment remains a possibility but the path coefficient from job stress to the negative outcome variables would be expected to reflect this general, pervasive, negative work environment without a negative path from ambient sexual harassment if this were the explanation for the observed effects.

There are many more avenues to pursue in the quest to understand the effect of ambient sexual harassment on men. Qualitative data (such as interview data) would be valuable in the exploration of these alternative hypotheses. This is an inchoate research area and the process underlying ambient sexual harassment is likely to be complex, particularly for men who are not exposed to or threatened by a harassing environment in the same way as are women. Interviews that address these different hypotheses may shed light on the mechanisms by which ambient sexual harassment results in negative outcomes for men. Future research should also consider additional survey studies that address other workplace stressors that may have pervasive effects beyond the target.

Implications

A primary contribution of this research is that the negative outcomes of sexual harassment extend beyond the target of the harassment, beyond the other women in the target's work group to men in that group, even when these men do not perceive the organization as tolerant of sexual harassment. Men experience similar detrimental indirect effects as women.

With this research, organizations cannot avoid the fact that ambient sexual harassment has important implications for men and women in work groups. Ambient sexual harassment is an organizational and group problem rather than an individual problem. Sexual harassment and its potent effects on individuals other than the target are embedded in an organizational context; the negative outcomes of sexual harassment diffuse well beyond the target to others in the organization.

REFERENCES

Baucus, M. S. (1998). Internal vs. external whistleblowers: A comparison of whistleblowing processes. *Journal of Business Ethics, 17,* 1281–1298.

Berdahl, J. L., Magley, V. J., & Waldo, C. R. (1996). The sexual harassment of men?: Exploring the concept with theory. *Psychology of Women Quarterly, 20,* 527–547.

Blumenthal, J. A. (1998). The reasonable woman standard: A meta-analytic review of gender differences in perceptions of sexual harassment. *Law and Human Behavior, 22,* 33–57.

Bond, M. (1990). Division 27 sexual harassment survey: Definitions, impact and environmental context. In M. Paludi & R. B. Barickman (Eds.), *Academic and workplace sexual harassment* (pp. 189–197). Albany: State University of New York.

Brodman, K. A., Erdman, J., Jr., Lorge, I., & Wolff, H. G. (1949). The Cornell Medical Index. *Journal of the American Medical Association, 140,* 530–534.

Diener, E. (1984). Subjective well-being. *Psychological Bulletin, 95,* 542–575.

Diener, E., Emmons, R. A., Larsen, R. J., & Griffin, S. (1985). The satisfaction with life scale. *Journal of Personality Assessment, 49,* 71–75.

Fitzgerald, L. F., Drasgow, F., Hulin, C., & Gelfand, M. (1993). *The Sexual Experiences Questionnaire: Revised edition.* Unpublished research scale, Department of Psychology, University of Illinois.

Fitzgerald, L. F., Drasgow, F., Hulin, C. L., Gelfand, M. J., & Magley, V. J. (1997). The antecedents and consequences of sexual harassment in organizations: A test of an integrated model. *Journal of Applied Psychology, 82,* 578–589.

Fitzgerald, L. F., Gelfand, M. J., & Drasgow, F. (1995). Measuring sexual harassment: Theoretical and psychometric advances. *Basic and Applied Social Psychology, 17,* 425–427.

Fitzgerald, L. F., Hulin, C. L., & Drasgow, F. (1995). The antecedents and consequences of sexual harassment in organizations. In G. Keita & J. Hurrell, Jr. (Eds.), *Job stress in a changing workforce. Investigating gender, diversity, and family issues* (pp. 55–73). Washington, DC: American Psychological Association.

Glomb, T. M., Richman, W. L., Hulin, C. L., Drasgow, F., Schneider, K. T., & Fitzgerald, L. F. (1997). Ambient sexual harassment: An integrated model of antecedents and consequences. *Organizational Behavior and Human Decision Processes, 71,* 309–328.

Gump, B. B., & Kulik, J. A. (1997). Stress, affiliation, and emotional contagion. *Journal of Personality and Social Psychology, 72,* 305–319.

Gutek, B. A. (1985). *Sex and the workplace: Impact of sexual behavior and harassment on women, men and organizations.* San Francisco: Jossey-Bass.

Hanisch, K. A. (1990). *A causal model of general attitudes, work withdrawal, and job withdrawal, including retirement.* Unpublished doctoral dissertation, University of Illinois at Urbana-Champaign.

Hanisch, K. A., & Hulin, C. L. (1990). Job attitudes and organizational withdrawal: An examination of retirement and other voluntary withdrawal behaviors. *Journal of Vocational Behavior, 37,* 60–78.

Hanisch, K. A., & Hulin, C. L. (1991). General attitudes and organizational withdrawal: An evaluation of a causal model. *Journal of Vocational Behavior, 39,* 110–128.

Hatfield, E., Cacioppo, J. T., & Rapson, R. L. (1992). Primitive emotional contagion. In M. S. Clark (Ed.), *Review of personality and social psychology: Vol. 14. Emotions and social behavior* (pp. 151–177). Newbury Park, CA: Sage.

Hatfield, E., Cacioppo, J. T., & Rapson, R. L. (1994). *Emotional contagion.* Cambridge, England: Cambridge University Press.

Hulin, C. L. (1993, May). *A framework for the study of sexual harassment in organizations: Climate, stressors, and patterned responses.* Paper presented at the meeting of the Society of Industrial Organizational Psychology, San Francisco.

Hulin, C. L., Fitzgerald, L. F., & Drasgow, F. (1996). Organizational influences on sexual harassment. In M. Stockdale (Ed.), *Sexual harassment in the workplace* (Vol. 5, pp. 127–150). Thousand Oaks, CA: Sage.

Joiner, T. E. (1994). Contagious depression: Existence, specificity to depressed symptoms, and the role of assurance seeking. *Journal of Personality and Social Psychology, 67,* 287–296.

Jöreskog, K. G., & Sörbom, D. (1993). *New features in LISREL 8.* Chicago, IL: Scientific Software, Inc.

Kunin, T. (1955). The construction of a new type of attitude measure. *Personnel Psychology, 8,* 65–78.

Rothschild, J., & Miethe, T. D. (1999). Whistle-blower and management retaliation: The battle to control information about organization corruption. *Work & Occupations, 26,* 107–128.

Rotundo, M., Nguyen, D. H., & Sackett, P. R. (2001). *A meta-analytic review of gender differences in the perceptions of sexual harassment.* Manuscript under review.

Roznowski, M. (1989). An examination of the measurement properties of the Job Descriptive Index with experimental items. *Journal of Applied Psychology, 74,* 805–814.

Salisbury, J. (in press). Healing the aftermath of sexual harassment complaints: The final challenge. In M. Paludi (Ed.), *9 to 5: Women, men, sex and power.* Albany: State University of New York Press.

Schachter, S. (1959). *The psychology of affiliation.* Stanford, CA: Stanford University Press.

Schneider, K. T. (1995). *Bystander stress: The effect of organizational tolerance of sexual harassment on victims' coworkers.* Unpublished doctoral dissertation, University of Illinois, Urbana-Champaign.

Schneider, K. T. (1996, August). *Bystander stress: The effect of organizational tolerance of sexual harassment on victims coworkers.* Paper presented to the Convention of the American Psychological Association, Toronto.

Schneider, K. T., Swan, S., & Fitzgerald, L. F. (1997). Job related and psychological effects of sexual harassment in the workplace: Empirical evidence from two organizations. *Journal of Applied Psychology, 82,* 401–415.

Smith, P. C., Kendall, L., & Hulin, C. L. (1969). *The measurement of satisfaction in work and retirement.* Chicago: Rand McNally.

Smith, P. C., Sandeman, B., & McCrary, L. (1992, May). *Development and validation of the Stress in General (SIG) scale.* Paper presented at Society for Industrial and Organizational Psychology, Montreal, Canada.

Sorenson, R. C., Luzio, R. C., & Mangione-Lambie, M. G. (1994, July). *Perceived seriousness, recommended and expected organizational response, and effects of bystander and direct sexual harassment.* Paper presented at the 23rd International Congress of Applied Psychology, Madrid, Spain.

United States Merit Systems Protection Board. (1981). *Sexual harassment of federal workers: Is it a problem?* Washington, DC: United States Government Printing Office.

United States Merit Systems Protection Board. (1987). *Sexual harassment of federal workers: An update.* Washington, DC: United States Government Printing Office.

Veit, C. T., & Ware, J. E., Jr. (1983). The structure of psychological distress and well-being in general populations. *Journal of Counseling and Clinical Psychology, 51,* 730–742.

Waldo, C. R., Berdahl, J. L., & Fitzgerald, L. F. (1998). Are men sexually harassed? If so by whom? *Law and Human Behavior, 22,* 59–79.

Zickar, M. (1994, April). Organizational antecedents of sexual harassment. In C. L. Hulin (Chair), *Symposium of sexual harassment in organizations.* Annual Meeting of Society of Industrial/Organizational Psychology, Nashville, TN.

Zickar, M., Matt, L. J., & Hulin, C. L. (1997). *Consequences of psychological and work group climate toward sexual harassment in two organizations.* Manuscript submitted for publication.

Chapter 7

The Impact of Job Insecurity on Employee Work Attitudes, Job Adaptation, and Organizational Withdrawal Behaviors

Tahira M. Probst
Washington State University at Vancouver

Virtually every sector of the American economy is experiencing financial pressures due to commercial rivalries around the globe, government deregulation of industry, and the increasing pace of organizational technology change. As a result, massive layoffs, conversion of full-time jobs to part-time positions, and the increase of temporary workers are but a few of the realities facing organizations and workers today. In 1998 alone, U.S. corporations announced a record 570,000 layoffs (Jacoby, 1998). These are impressive numbers. However, they do not capture the number of employees who might be concerned that their job may be the next slated for "right-sizing." Ultimately, what is perhaps most critical to consider is that in the United States, a person's job is one of the most important mechanisms through which one gains a sense of identity. As Judge and Hulin (1993) noted, "To do nothing may be to be nothing for many Americans" (p. 413). Therefore, as organizations continue to downsize, merge with other organizations, and otherwise restructure, several questions become significant:

1. What impact do such organizational changes have on the job security of individual workers?
2. What other factors might alter perceptions of job security?
3. Is it meaningful to distinguish between *perceptions* of job security, *satisfaction* with job security, and *affective reactions* to events that might alter job security?

141

4. What are the cognitive, affective, physical, and behavioral consequences of heightened job insecurity?

The purpose of this chapter is to develop and conduct a systematic exploration of these questions. Previous research on job insecurity, although
abundant, is rather fragmented. Research on job insecurity has typically
examined single variables of interest in relative isolation from other theoretically and empirically pertinent organizational variables. The current
research endeavors to demonstrate that perceptions of job insecurity are
derived from multiple antecedents and result in the experience of a myriad of outcomes—even after integrating these variables into the larger organizational framework.

A THEORETICAL FRAMEWORK
FOR STUDYING JOB SECURITY

The developing of a theoretical framework for studying the antecedents
and consequences of job security benefited from considering several relevant literatures—in particular, person–environment fit theories of stress
(e.g., Beehr & Newman, 1978; Everly & Sobelman, 1987; Lazarus, 1966),
Weiss and Cropanzano's Affective Events Theory (AET; 1996), and theories of adaptation, commitment, and withdrawal in organizations (Hulin,
1991; Hulin, Roznowski, & Hachiya, 1985; Roznowski & Hulin, 1992).
Using these theories as a general framework, I developed an integrated
model of job security.

Person–Environment Fit Theory of Stress

According to McCabe and Schneiderman (1985), stress occurs as a result
of change or threat of change that demands adaptation by the organism.
In a similar vein, Lazarus (1966) defined stress as a "relationship between
the person and environment that is appraised by the person as taxing or ex-
ceeding his or her resources and endangering his or her well-being" (p. 19).
McGrath (1976) asserted that stress is a "perceived substantial imbalance
between demands and response capabilities under conditions where failure
to meet demands has important perceived consequences" (p. 1352).

Common among these definitions of stress is the emphasis on the
match between person and environment characteristics. Person–environment fit theories of stress (Everly & Sobelman, 1987; French, Caplan, &
Van Harrison, 1982) suggested that environmental events are not universal stressors. Rather, the stress value depends on the perceived imbalance
between (a) an individual's perceptions of the demands being made by the

environment (i.e., the potential stressor), and (b) the individual's perceived ability and motivation to cope with those demands (Landy, 1989). I propose that job insecurity is perceived by an employee as change or a precursor to change demanding adaptation that may be difficult to meet. Further, failure to cope with potential future unemployment or loss of desired job features may have significant consequences. Thus, consistent with Ironson (1992), I view job insecurity as a job stressor (Beehr & Newman, 1978; Roskies & Louis-Guerin, 1990; Roskies, Louis-Guerin, & Fournier, 1993).

Affective Events Theory

According to Weiss and Cropanzano (1996), work environment features and events are subject to a cognitive appraisal of whether and to what extent these work events and features facilitate or obstruct goal attainment. If goal obstruction is apparent and there is a perceived imbalance between the environmental demands and the individual's ability to cope with those demands (based on dispositions and available resources), stress results.

Job-related stress results in an experienced strain, or response, by the person. The resultant strain can be physiological (e.g., elevated blood pressure), psychological (e.g., more negative job attitudes), behavioral (e.g., increased propensity to withdraw), or any combination thereof (Kavanaugh, Hurst, & Rose, 1981). Therefore, when stress exists, work attitudes and affective reactions are anticipated to be negative. Negative affective reactions are expected to lead to negative work attitudes and affect-driven behaviors in the form of work withdrawal (Hulin, 1991; Weiss & Cropanzano, 1996). Negative work attitudes are predicted to trigger judgment-driven behaviors in the form of job withdrawal (Hulin, 1991; Hulin et al., 1985; Roznowski & Hulin, 1992). Finally, two additional strains that can result from stress are physical and mental health outcomes. These are expected to be mediated by work attitudes and affective reactions, although direct effects may occur as well.

DEVELOPMENT OF AN INTEGRATED MODEL OF JOB SECURITY

Antecedents

Figure 7.1 shows an integrated model of the antecedents and consequences of job insecurity. Much of the past research on job security has conceived of job insecurity as resulting from organizational decline (e.g., Greenhalgh, 1983) or as a result of being a layoff survivor (e.g., Brockner & Greenberg, 1992; Davy, Kinicki, & Scheck, 1991). However, I propose and illustrate in Fig. 7.1 that job insecurity occurs as a result of multiple

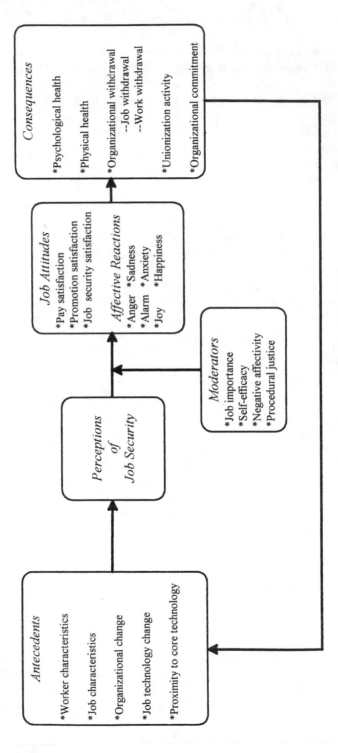

FIG. 7.1.   An integrated model of job security.

antecedents that may serve to stimulate the perception that the future of one's job is endangered.

Worker Characteristics.   Worker characteristics refer to a variety of individual differences variables that might objectively cause an individual to be more or less secure in his or her position. These variables include absenteeism, grievance filing, organizational tenure, and education level. It seems likely that workers who are frequently absent are less likely to be secure in their position than workers who do not absent themselves as often. In addition, research has shown that workers who file grievances are less likely to be promoted, receive lower performance evaluations following the grievance activity, and have higher voluntary and involuntary turnover rates (Carnevale, Olson, & O'Connor, 1992; Lewin, 1987). The frequent implementation of "last hired, first fired" lends credence to the suggestion that job longevity or organizational seniority may provoke feelings of security . Finally, individuals with more education tend to hold positions of greater power within organizations. Thus, individuals with more education might perceive their job to be more secure than individuals with little education (Roskies & Louis-Guerin, 1990).

Job Characteristics.   Job characteristics refer to those aspects of a job that might serve to increase or decrease one's job security. This could include what type of contract the worker has with the organization (e.g., binding vs. nonbinding, temporary vs. permanent, part-time vs. full-time) and whether the job falls under union jurisdiction. Nonbinding, temporary, or part-time contracts are expected to result in lower job security because these characteristics implicitly suggest a briefer tenure with the organization than a binding, permanent, full-time contract would suggest. In addition, union affiliation might be expected to result in higher perceptions of job security because union employees have some formal recourse when they perceive their jobs to be threatened.

Organizational Change Characteristics.   Organizational change characteristics include those characteristics typically examined in studies of job insecurity (e.g., Ashford, Lee, & Bobko, 1989; Buessing, 1986; Davy et al., 1991; Greenhalgh, 1983; Greenhalgh & Rosenblatt, 1984). Formal announcement of layoffs, upcoming merger or acquisition, organizational restructuring, and downsizing are all potential change characteristics that may serve to decrease the job security of employees (Ashford et al., 1989; Roskies & Louis-Guerin, 1990).

Characteristics Pertaining to Organizational Technology.   Two characteristics pertaining to organizational technology (i.e., those factors that aid in the transformation of organizational input into organizational output; Hulin & Roznowski, 1985) can be conceived of as antecedents of job security. First, the *proximity* of one's job in relation to the organizational technology can often be more important than the job itself in determining the security of that position. Positions located in the buffering or peripheral systems of an organization are more likely to be seen as unnecessary or easily replaced than those found in the core organizational systems. According to Hulin and Roznowski (1985), all components other than the core technology systems exist solely to support the core activities. Thus, proximity to core organizational technology is predicted to be positively related to perceptions of job security. Second, a *change* in the technological systems of an organization can also have a profound effect on the security of positions experiencing the technology change. According to Hulin and Roznowski (1985), as the level of technological complexity required in an organization changes, so do the worker requirements, which can in turn affect the security of those individuals who cannot adapt to the change or whose skills are no longer required (i.e., obsolescence).

Perceived Job Security

According to the model, worker characteristics, job characteristics, organizational change characteristics, proximity to organizational technology, and job technology change are all subject to cognitive appraisal. This involves an assessment of the relevance and importance of these factors to one's well-being, particularly with respect to one's job security. *Job security* is defined here as the perceived stability and continuance of one's job as one knows it. In contrast to other definitions of job security (e.g., Ashford et al., 1989; Greenhalgh & Rosenblatt, 1984), this definition does not include any attitudinal or affective reactions to perceived job insecurity. The resulting perceptions of job security are then predicted to generate an emotional or affective response to the work events as well as influence evaluative judgments regarding one's job (i.e., job attitudes).

Job Attitudes

Although an imbalance between desired and actual work conditions results in low job satisfaction (Locke, 1969), it is important to note that job insecurity is unlikely to influence equally all facets of job satisfaction. Focusing primarily on those aspects of one's job that would be threatened by a loss of job security, two frequent outcomes of workplace restructuring are pay decreases, lack of promotion opportunities, or even demotions. Often, organizations will resort to these measures to avoid laying off workers (Luthans & Sommer, 1999). Therefore, it is expected that employees with low job security will be less satisfied with their pay and promotion opportunities than individuals with high job security. However, job security perceptions are not predicted to influence satisfaction with work, co-workers, or supervision because these latter facets are not likely to change as a direct result of higher or lower job security.

Affective Reactions

According to the AET (Weiss & Cropanzano, 1996), if an antecedent event is appraised as obstructing goal attainment (in this case, retaining a valued job), it is predicted that such events will lead to the experience of negative emotions. Therefore, if the cognitive appraisal stage results in a perceived decrease in job security, such job insecurity should lead to an increase in negative affective reactions to the antecedent events. Thus, affective reactions are mediated by the cognitive appraisal stage and not predicted by the events themselves.

Individual and Organizational Consequences of Job Insecurity

Figure 7.1 summarizes the predicted individual and organizational consequences of job insecurity into four general categories: organizational withdrawal, organizational commitment, psychological health, and physical health.

Organizational Withdrawal. Organizational withdrawal (Hanisch & Hulin, 1990, 1991) can be broken down into work withdrawal and job withdrawal behaviors. *Work withdrawal* constitutes those behaviors that reflect attempts to avoid performing one's tasks (e.g., missing meetings, tardiness, taking extended or frequent breaks), whereas *job withdrawal* behaviors reflect intentions to leave the organization (e.g., turnover and retirement intentions, accepting layoffs and buyouts).

Although past research on the relationship between job security and organizational withdrawal has mainly focused on intentions to leave (Ashford et al., 1989; Davy et al., 1991), one might infer that related organizational withdrawal behaviors would similarly increase as job security decreases. According to Weiss and Cropanzano's (1996) AET, work withdrawal behaviors are more spontaneous and less well-reasoned, whereas turnover intentions are more thoughtful and considered. Therefore, job attitudes (i.e., one's cognitive appraisal of one's job) are expected to influence job withdrawal intentions (e.g., intentions to quit). However, it is one's affective reactions to workplace events that are expected to lead to the enactment of work withdrawal behaviors. Thus, one would expect that, rationally, employees would be on their "best behavior" during times of organizational transition. However, based on AET, one would predict that increasingly negative affective reactions to the workplace reorganization will lead to greater numbers of the more spontaneous work withdrawal behaviors.

Finally, another result of increased job security satisfaction is proposed to be increased ease of quitting (not to be confused with intentions to quit). Individuals who are very satisfied with their job security are predicted to perceive that they could quit their jobs easily, if they wanted to. This prediction is less a result of theory and more a consequence of today's booming economy. In the current tight labor market, individuals who are secure in their value to a company may also perceive that other companies would equally value their skills. Thus, if they were to desire to seek employment elsewhere, they are predicted to perceive the move to be a relatively easy one to make.

Organizational Commitment. Organizational commitment has also been demonstrated to be an important consequent of job security (Ashford et al., 1989), the effects of which are mediated through job satisfaction (Davy et al., 1991). Therefore, it is predicted that decreased job security satisfaction, lower job attitudes, and negative affective reactions will all lead to decreased organizational commitment.

Psychological Distress and Physical Health. Job insecurity has repeatedly been shown to be related to decreased mental and physical health (Brenner et al., 1983; Cottington, Matthews, Talbot, & Kuller, 1986; Dooley, Rook, & Catalano, 1987; Kuhnert, Sims, & Lahey, 1989; Roskies & Louis-Guerin, 1990). Although evidence for a direct link between job security and psychological and physical health is abundant, there is also evidence that job attitudes directly influence these outcomes as well (e.g., Caplan, Cobb, French, Van Harrison, & Pinneau, 1975; Fitzgerald, Drasgow, Hulin, Gelfand, & Magley, 1997; Kavanaugh et al., 1981; Weintraub, 1973). Based on these findings, it was anticipated that the less satisfied individuals are with their job and the more negative their affective reactions to workplace events are, the more psychological distress and the greater number of health conditions they will report.

METHOD

Participants

In July 1997, it was announced that five state agencies involved in providing human services to the public were to be merged in an effort to consolidate their operations and reduce redundancy and duplication of services.

Shortly thereafter, a task force was appointed to design and implement the merger. Following this announcement, agency employees were gradually notified about how these changes were going to affect them. For some employees, the changes would be minimal. For others, the restructuring would involve moving offices, changing supervisors, being demoted, learning new job-related technologies, a reduction in job status, and/or new work tasks. Layoffs were not specifically mentioned during the announcement of the merger. However, rumors were rampant that they would occur. Within the same agency, some employees were in danger of losing key features of their job, their current position, or employment with the state, whereas others remained essentially unaffected by the reorganization.

A stratified random sample of 500 employees from these agencies was selected. The basis of stratification was the employee's objective level of job security as judged by the assistant to the director of each agency. In addition, individuals were selected from all levels within the organizational hierarchy. Surveys were administered in person at each data site where 10 or more individuals had been sampled. Any sites with fewer than 10 sampled individuals were mailed the surveys. A total of 313 individuals responded to the survey—a response rate of 63%. However, a turnover and retirement rate of 9.6% since time of initial sampling resulted in an effective response rate of 69%. Examination of sample demographics did not reveal significant departures from the overall makeup of the organization's workforce suggesting the sample was demographically representative of the organization from which it was selected.

Data were collected from this sample at two different points in time. The first was immediately on announcement of the reorganization. A total of 126 employees participated in this data collection. The second data collection was 6 months following the merger announcement; 283 employees participated at this time. At Time II, many changes had begun to take effect; however, there was still much uncertainty regarding possible future layoffs, changing policies, changing job technology, and so on. Layoffs had not occurred at that point; however, after the data were collected, a number of layoffs were announced, thus supporting the veracity of the rumors that employees were reporting at the time of both data collections. A small subset of participants completed surveys at both Time I and Time II sessions ($n = 96$).

Measures

A survey assessing the antecedents and consequences of job insecurity as outlined in the model just proposed was administered immediately following the merger announcement and 6 months into the reorganization. The scales are now described. Unless otherwise noted, each variable was measured at both data collection points. In addition to collecting survey data, several constructs were assessed with the aid of contact personnel within each of the agencies for the purpose of avoiding single-source method bias and spurious overinflation of the predicted relationships.

Job Security Index (JSI).   The 18-item Job Security Index (JSI; Probst, 1998) was written for the purpose of this study to assess an individual's cognitive appraisal of the future of his or her job with respect to the perceived level of stability and continuance of that job. The scale consists of a series of adjectives or short phrases describing the future of an employee's job, for example, *my job is almost guaranteed* and *permanent position if I want it.* If the phrase applies to the future of their job, respondents would circle *yes*; if the word does not apply to the future of their job, respondents would circle *no*. If the respondent cannot decide, a ? is circled. Positive and negative items were intermixed in equal numbers on the page to minimize any response set. Responses were scored such that higher numbers reflected more job security.

General Job Stress.   Ten items from Matteson and Ivancevich's (1982) Stress Diagnostic Survey were used to measure the degree of general job stress experienced by the respondents at Time II. Five items were taken from the job stress subscale; 5 were taken from the organizational stress subscale. These items tap the constructs of role ambiguity, role conflict, work overload, and time pressure. The subscales were collapsed to form a single measure of general job stress. This scale was included in the survey in order to test for the effects of job insecurity on the outcome variables of interest independent of the effects of these five commonly studied job stressors.

Job Satisfaction.   Nine-item versions of the five subscales of the JDI (Smith, Kendall, & Hulin, 1969), as revised by Roznowski (1989), were used to measure satisfaction with co-workers, pay and promotions, supervision, and the work itself. Respondents indicated using the 3-point (*yes, no, ?*) response scale the extent to which each adjective or phrase described that aspect of their job.

Job Security Satisfaction (JSS).   Whereas the JSI was designed to assess perceptions of job security, the JSS scale (Probst, 1998) was designed to capture an individual's attitudes regarding that level of job security. The scale consists of a series of adjectives or short phrases describing the various evaluative responses one might have to a perceived level of job security. Although the evaluative response was targeted, 20 adjectives or short phrases such as *sufficient amount of security* and *makes me anxious* were cho-sen to span the descriptive–evaluative continuum in the attempt to avoid any general affectivity bias. The response format is identical to that of the JSI.

Affective Reactions to the Workplace Reorganization.

In order to as-sess affective reactions to the organizational restructuring, individuals were asked to rate on a 5-point scale the extent to which they experienced nine emotions as a result of the workplace reorganization. Responses were scaled such that higher scores reflect more negative affective reactions to the organizational restructuring. Sample emotions assessed were anger, alarm, sadness, happiness, and contentment. These were chosen based on the typology of emotions presented in Shaver, Schwartz, Kirson, and O'Conner (1987). Affective reactions to the workplace restructuring were assessed only at Time II.

Organizational Commitment.

The nine-item Organizational Commit-ment Questionnaire (OCQ) developed by Mowday, Steers, and Porter (1979) was used to measure the relative strength of an individual's identifi-cation with and involvement in a particular organization.

Physical Health.

Physical health of respondents was measured using Hanisch's (1992) Health Conditions Index (HCI). This scale lists 12 health conditions, such as severe headaches and high blood pressure, and asks respondents to indicate whether or not they experience the condition us-ing a simple *yes–no* checklist response format.

Psychological Well-Being.

Psychological well-being was measured us-ing 15 items from the MHI (Veit & Ware, 1983). The index measures emo-tional ties, general positive affect, anxiety, depression, and loss of behav-ioral control, emotional control, or both. Three items from each of these facets were used.

Organizational Withdrawal.

The job and work withdrawal measures used in this survey were the scales reported in Hanisch and Hulin (1990, 1991). Seven job withdrawal items reflected employees' efforts at and ease of removing themselves from their organization and work role (e.g., How likely is it that you will quit your job in the next several months? How easy or difficult would it be for you to leave your job?). Eleven work withdrawal items measure attempts to avoid completion of specific work tasks (e.g., missing meetings, being late for work).

Grievance Filing.   Grievance filing was assessed by a single item asking the respondent if he or she had filed a workplace grievance within the past year. This was assessed at Time II only.

Absenteeism.   Absenteeism was measured at Time II with a single item asking respondents the number of days they had been absent from work in the past year. The response scale was 0 = none, 1 = 1–2 days, 3 = 3–5 days, 4 = 6–10 days, 5 = more than 10 days.

Organizational Change.   Organizational change was assessed by means of four indicators. First, before the Time I data collection, the assistant to the director of each agency dichotomously categorized each sampled employee as being either extremely affected by the reorganization or not affected by the reorganization (0 = not affected; 1 = extremely affected). Second, during the Time II data collection, individuals were asked to rate on a scale from 1 to 7 (a) how much their position had changed as a result of the workplace reorganization, and (b) overall, how much their job had been affected by the reorganization. Finally, using a checklist format, respondents indicated the number of organizational changes they experienced as a result of the workplace reorganization (e.g., changed supervisors, changed offices, new policies, etc.). Each indicator was standardized and equally weighted.

Job Technology Change.   Job technology change was assessed by the assistant to the director of each of the five agencies. Each job class was rated on a scale from 1 to 13 in terms of how much job technology change had occurred as a result of the reorganization. This was assessed at Time II.

Proximity to Core Technology.   Each job class was ranked by the assistant to the director of each of the five agencies from 1 to 10 according to how proximal that position was to the organization's core technology. The organization's core technology was defined by the contact personnel as "providing and managing human services programs to the public." Jobs involved in policy and planning, program management, and working in the local field offices were ranked as closest to the organizations core technology, whereas individuals in the accounting, legal, and legislative departments were rated as furthest from the core technology.

Structural Equation Modeling Analyses

The first test of the hypothesized model of job insecurity was conducted by means of structural equation modeling of the Time II data. The two-step approach recommended by Anderson and Gerbing (1988) was used. First, the measurement model was assessed in order to discriminate empirically the theoretical constructs of the job security model and to validate the operational measures thereof. Second, the structural equation model, specifying the causal relationships among the latent variables, was tested. Models were tested using LISREL 8 (Jöreskog & Sörbom, 1993).

Measurement Model. The test of the measurement model in structural equation modeling can be likened to a confirmatory factor analysis where each factor represents a hypothesized independent construct. The measurement model specifies how the latent variables are indicated by the observed variables. In the current study, grievance filing, absenteeism, organizational tenure, education, job technology change, and proximity to core technology were manifest variables with one indicator each. Organizational change, perceptions of job security, job stress, job security satisfaction, work attitudes, affective reactions, ease of quitting, turnover intentions, organizational commitment, health conditions, psychological distress, and work withdrawal behaviors were latent variables. Three parallel indicators were formed for each of the latent constructs based on confirmatory factor loadings, item-total correlations, and item content (Fitzgerald et al., 1997). Before proceeded with the tests of the structural models, the goodness-of-fit indices were examined to determine if the measurement model adequately empirically discriminated the theoretical constructs of interest.

Structural Model of Job Security. Once the measurement model was assessed, the proposed structural model of job security was tested (see Fig. 7.2). The proposed model consisted of grievance filing, education level, organizational tenure, job technology change, proximity to core technology, organizational change, absenteeism, and job stress as exogenous variables. All exogenous variables (excluding general job stress) were predicted to influence job security perceptions, which in turn were expected to influence job security satisfaction, work attitudes, and affective reactions to the organizational events.

In order to estimate the relative impact of job insecurity on the hypothesized outcome variables, general job stress was modeled as an exogenous variable with direct influences on job security satisfaction, job attitudes, and affective reactions. In this way, one could assess if perceptions of job security have separate, independent, and significant effects on these variables while taking into account other commonly experienced workplace stressors.

Paths were then estimated from job security satisfaction to ease of quitting, turnover intentions, organizational commitment, health conditions, and psychological distress. Paths were also estimated from job attitudes to

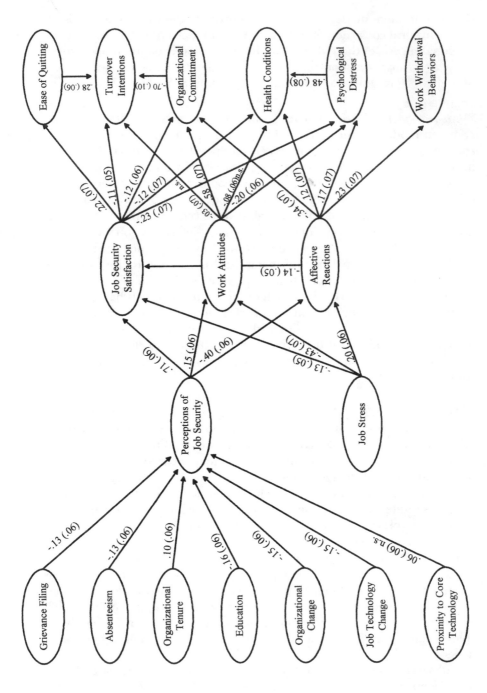

FIG. 7.2. Structural model of proposed job security.

turnover intentions, organizational commitment, health conditions, and psychological distress. In addition, paths were estimated from affective reactions to organizational commitment, health conditions, psychological distress, and work withdrawal behaviors. Based on research demonstrating the impact of psychological health on physical health (Fitzgerald et al., 1997; Fuller, Edwards, Sermsri, & Vorakitphokatorn, 1993), a path was estimated from psychological distress to physical health. In addition, paths from organizational commitment and ease of quitting to turnover intentions were estimated. Finally, in accordance with the Affective Events Theory, a path was also hypothesized from affective reactions to job security satisfaction.

Longitudinal Analyses

For a small subsample of the data set ($n = 96$), there were longitudinal data collected on the majority of the relevant constructs. Thus, although structural equation modeling allows for a simultaneous test of the set of interconnected hypotheses regarding the causes and effects of job security, the longitudinal analyses allow for a better test of the causality of the effects of job insecurity.

Because the sample size of 96 was too small for SEM analyses, simple regression analyses were used. In order to test whether the proposed causal model would be supported with longitudinal data, the first regression analysis assessed whether Time I job security perceptions (i.e., the cognitive appraisal regarding one's level of job security) would predict Time II job attitudes, affective reactions to the organizational restructuring, and job security satisfaction. The second analysis examined the predictive validity of job security satisfaction at Time I in accounting for Time II outcome variability with respect to mental and physical health outcomes, organizational commitment, work withdrawal behaviors, and turnover intentions.

STRUCTURAL EQUATION MODELING RESULTS: CROSS-SECTIONAL TIME II ANALYSES

Table 7.1 presents the means and standard deviations for each of the variables examined in this study. Table 7.2 contains the scale reliabilities and zero-order product-moment correlations among the variables.

Measurement Model

Table 7.3 contains the goodness-of-fit statistics obtained from analyses of the parallel indicators. As is evident from the indices, the measurement model provided a very good fit to the data. Table 7.3 shows that the χ^2 / df

TABLE 7.1
Descriptive Statistics for Each Time II Variable

Variable	No. Items	Mean	SD	Potential Range
1. Grievance filing	1	.07	.26	0–1
2. Absenteeism	1	3.16	1.20	1–5
3. Organizational tenure	1	13.06	8.08	1–39
4. Education level	1	4.81	1.53	1–7
5. Organizational change (standardized variable)	4	.00	1.00	–3–+3
6. Job technology change	1	9.38	3.68	1–13
7. Proximity to core technology	1	4.53	1.23	1–10
8. Perceptions of job security	18	1.51	1.05	0–3
9. Job stress	10	2.63	.66	1–5
10. Job security satisfaction	20	1.71	.95	0–3
11. Co-worker satisfaction	9	2.32	.77	0–3
12. Pay satisfaction	8	1.61	.86	0–3
13. Promotions satisfaction	9	.87	.88	0–3
14. Supervisor satisfaction	9	2.25	.83	0–3
15. Work satisfaction	9	1.83	.98	0–3
16. Overall job satisfaction	44	1.78	.56	0–3
17. Affective reactions	9	2.42	1.03	1–5
18. Ease of quitting	3	2.00	.80	1–5
19. Turnover intentions	4	2.03	1.00	1–5
20. Organizational commitment	9	4.58	1.19	1–7
21. Health conditions	12	2.39	2.42	0–12
22. Psychological distress	15	2.32	.76	1–6
23. Work withdrawal	11	1.94	.70	1–8

ratio was 1.40, which is quite good. The GFI was .87; the AGFI was .83, both of which are satisfactory. The NNFI was .95; and the RMSEA and RMSR were both .04, which is excellent. The PFI was .69. Finally, all factor loadings obtained from fitting the measurement model to the parallel indicators were large and statistically significant. Together, these results suggest a good fit of the measurement model to the data.

The next phase in the analysis was the structural modeling procedure. Elements of the β and Γ matrices were either fixed at zero or freed (i.e., estimated) according to the proposed model of job security presented in Fig. 7.2. Maximum likelihood estimation was used to estimate parameters.

Proposed Model

The goodness-of-fit indices for the proposed structural model are presented in Table 7.3. In general, the fit of this model to the data is quite satisfactory. The χ^2 / df ratio was 1.65, which is very good in light of the sample size of 283. Other indices included a GFI of .83, an AGFI of .80, and a

TABLE 7.2
Scale Reliabilities and Interscale Correlations of Variables Measured for SEM Analyses

Variable	1	2	3	4	5	6	7	8	9	10	11	12	13	14	15	16	17	18	19	20	21	22	23
1. GRIEV	na																						
2. ABSENT	.28	na																					
3. TENURE	-.01	-.05	na																				
4. EDUC	-.12	-.36	-.05	na																			
5. OCHANGE	.15	-.03	-.04	-.01	.78																		
6. TCHANGE	.14	.18	-.04	.04	.18	na																	
7. CORE	.07	-.03	.08	.03	.09	-.29	na																
8. JSI	-.19	-.11	.16	-.09	-.24	-.23	.09	.97															
9. STRESS	.22	.14	.08	.03	.19	.10	-.09	-.20	.76														
10. JSS	-.24	-.19	-.00	.00	-.19	-.26	-.01	.73	-.27	.96													
11. COWSAT	-.10	-.18	.10	.04	-.07	-.05	.11	.16	-.28	.19	.87												
12. PAYSAT	-.13	-.31	.14	.16	.00	-.11	.20	.18	-.13	.28	.23	.84											
13. PROMSAT	-.17	-.16	.01	-.04	.12	-.16	.20	.27	-.35	.38	.22	.24	.89										
14. SUPSAT	-.06	-.04	-.08	-.07	.00	-.04	.10	.06	-.47	.20	.26	.12	.24	.88									
15. WORKSAT	-.04	-.21	.11	.15	.05	.03	.28	.12	-.26	.25	.37	.27	.34	.24	.90								
16. AFFECT	.10	.00	.03	.09	.34	.17	-.15	-.39	.23	-.44	-.04	-.05	-.13	-.20	-.09	.82							
17. JWEASE	-.02	-.00	-.11	.11	.08	.02	.14	.10	.10	.21	-.02	.11	.13	.03	.17	.01	.71						
18. JWTO	.08	.07	-.09	.08	.09	.05	.01	-.13	.42	-.21	-.30	-.11	-.26	-.39	-.31	.27	.28	.81					
19. ORGCOMT	-.12	-.10	.13	-.11	-.05	-.05	.13	.23	-.43	-.23	.38	.18	.43	.43	.50	-.18	-.07	-.58	.82				
20. HCOND	.25	.34	-.05	-.12	.17	.11	-.06	-.20	.35	-.33	-.14	-.18	-.21	-.27	-.20	.28	-.13	.30	-.20	.75			
21. DISTRESS	.28	.16	-.02	.05	.06	.11	-.13	-.19	.34	-.37	-.22	-.10	-.24	-.26	-.29	.29	-.16	.34	-.27	.53	.93		
22. WW	.05	.02	-.00	.10	-.05	.02	-.20	-.24	.25	-.06	-.11	.03	-.21	-.18	-.26	.13	.05	.37	-.31	.19	.34	.62	
23. SATALL	-.15	-.29	.08	.08	.04	-.11	.23	.24	-.47	.41	.62	.57	.66	.58	.73	-.16	.13	-.43	.60	-.32	-.36	-.23	.91

Note. Scale reliabilities are on the diagonal; *na* denotes 1-item measures.

*r*s > .12 are significant at *p* < .05; *r*s > .15 are significant at *p* < .01; *r*s > .19 are significant at *p* < .001.

GRIEV = Grievance Filing; ABSENT = Absenteeism; TENURE = Organizational Tenure; EDUC = Education Level; OCHANGE = Amount of Organizational Change; TCHANGE = Amount of Job Technology Change; CORE = Proximity of Job Position to Organization's Core Technology; JSI = Job Security Perceptions; STRESS = Job Stress; JSS = Job Security Satisfaction; COWSAT = Co-worker Satisfaction; PAYSAT = Pay Satisfaction; PROMSAT = Promotions Satisfaction; SUPSAT = Supervisor Satisfaction; WORKSAT = Work Satisfaction; AFFECT = Affective Reactions; JWEASE = Ease of Quitting; JWTO = Turnover Intentions; ORGCOMT = Organizational Commitment; HCOND = Health Conditions; DISTRESS = Psychological Distress; WW = Work Withdrawal; SATALL = Overall Job Satisfaction.

TABLE 7.3
Goodness-of-Fit Indices for Measurement and Structural Models

Model	χ^2	df	χ^2/df	GFI	AGFI	NNFI	RMSEA	RMSR	PFI
Measurement	943.98	672	1.40	.87	.83	.95	.04	.04	.69
Proposed structural	1264.93	767	1.65	.83	.80	.94	.05	.08	.78

Note. GFI = goodness-of-fit index; AGFI = adjusted goodness-of-fit index; NNFI = nonnormed fit index; RMSEA = root mean square error of approximation; RMSR = root mean square residual; PFI = parsimony fit index.

NNFI of .94. Each of these goodness-of-fit statistics suggest a reasonable fit of the model to the data, particularly given the complex nature of the model and the relatively few paths that were freed. The lack-of-fit statistics, root mean square error of approximation (RMSEA) and root mean square residual (RMSR), were .05 and .08, respectively. These residuals are also good, considering that the covariation among the 18 constructs was constrained to a model freeing only 26 paths (e.g., estimating only those 26 relationships while fixing each of the remaining 127 paths at zero). Finally, the parsimony normed fit index (PFI) was .78, which is quite good, because PFI values above .70 are considered acceptable. This indicates that not only does the model fit the data well, but it does so in a parsimonious fashion. Given that the model appeared to fit the data reasonably well, an examination of the path coefficients was undertaken.

Twenty-three of the 26 paths were significant beyond the traditional significance level of $p < .05$. Of these, 21 are in the expected direction, providing support for many of the hypotheses outlined earlier. As anticipated, grievance filing (–.13), absenteeism (–.13), organizational change (–.15), and job technology change (–.15) were significantly negatively related to perceptions of security, whereas organizational tenure was positively related to perceptions of job security (.10). Thus, individuals who were more frequently absent from their job perceived their job to be less secure than individuals who had missed fewer days of work. In addition, individuals filing grievances were more likely to feel they had less job security. As predicted, the longer an employee had worked for the organization, the more security that individual perceived. Further, the more organizational changes employees experienced as a result of the workplace restructuring, the less secure they perceived their jobs to be. Finally, the more an employee's job technology changed as a result of the workplace reorganization, the less secure that employee perceived the job to be.

Contrary to expectations, proximity to the organization's core technology did not predict an individual's perceptions of job security. In addition, education level was negatively (not positively, as anticipated) related to perceptions of job security, such that more educated individuals perceived their jobs to be less secure. On consultation with state government employees, an interesting explanation was generated. They suggested that the more educated individuals in this organization are likely to hold managerial positions and, thus, not be affiliated with the union that operates within the organization. Post hoc analyses suggest this to be true. Managers had a mean education level of 5.47 ($s = 1.44$), whereas nonmanagers had a mean education level of 4.44 ($s = 1.46$), $F(1, 276) = 31.98, p < .01$. Therefore, perhaps education was functioning as a proxy for union membership that was not explicitly measured in this study. The job security model predicts that union membership should result in higher perceptions of job security than nonunion membership.

Perceptions of job security were strongly positively related to job security satisfaction, as evidenced by a path coefficient of .71. This is consistent with the contention that higher job security is strongly (but not perfectly) related to job security satisfaction. In addition, job security perceptions were also significantly related to work attitudes (.15), such that the more employees perceived their jobs to be secure, the more positive their work attitudes were. Consistent with expectations, the path coefficient from perceptions of security to affective reactions was −.40, indicating that the less secure individuals perceived their job to be, the more negative their affective reactions were to the organizational restructuring. Finally, the path from affective reactions to job security satisfaction was significant (−.14), indicating that, after controlling for job attitudes, the more negatively an individual reacted affectively to the workplace reorganization, the more dissatisfied the individual was with his or her job security.

It was argued previously that one must examine the effects of job insecurity while simultaneously taking into account other job stressors that may influence attitudes and affect. This is particularly relevant here. There are many aspects of a workplace reorganization that may result in negative job attitudes and negative affective reactions that have little to do with job insecurity. Perhaps role ambiguity increases or role conflict arises. These job stressors may lead to negative reactions to the reorganization or more negative job attitudes independent of job security perceptions. Therefore, paths were estimated from general job stress to job security satisfaction, work attitudes, and affective reactions. The standardized path coefficients for these relationships were −.13, −.43, and .20, respectively. Controlling for these effects, the negative effects of job insecurity were still significant.

Turning to the outcomes of job security satisfaction, the path from job security satisfaction to ease of quitting was .22, indicating that individuals whose evaluation of their job security was positive thought it would be easier to leave the organization with respect to their finances and finding another job. However, as anticipated, the path from job security satisfaction to turnover intentions was significant and negative at −.11. Thus, the more satisfied individuals were with their job security, the less they intended to quit their job. In addition, the more satisfied employees were with their job security, the fewer health conditions (−.12) and lower levels of psychological distress (−.23) they reported.

Contrary to prediction, the path from job security satisfaction to organizational commitment was −.12, suggesting that the more satisfied an individual is with his or her job security, the less committed that individual is to the organization. This was somewhat surprising given that the zero-order correlation between the two variables was +.23, $p < .001$. However, this illustrates the importance of examining job insecurity within the larger organizational context by taking into account other variables that also influence the outcome variables of interest—in this case, the impact of work attitudes and affective reactions on organizational commitment. Thus, previous research, which has largely examined zero-order correlations between job insecurity and organizational commitment, may have been missing the effects of the larger organizational picture.

Next, the results show that job attitudes were significantly related to organizational commitment (.58) and psychological distress (−.20), indicating that individuals who were satisfied with their job were more committed to their organization and had lower levels of psychological distress. Contrary to expectations, work attitudes were not directly related to turnover intentions. Rather, the relationship appears to be mediated through organizational commitment. Similarly, work attitudes do not directly influence health conditions, but appear to be mediated through psychological distress.

Finally, the paths from negative affective reactions to work withdrawal (.23), organizational commitment (−.34), psychological distress (.17), and health conditions (.12) were significant and in the expected direction. Thus, the more negative employees' affective reactions to the workplace reorganization were, the less committed they were to the organization. In addition, these workers reported greater numbers of health-related problems and higher levels of psychological distress. Finally, they also engaged in more work withdrawal behaviors than individuals whose reactions to the workplace reorganization were less negative.

Taken together, these results indicate that not only does this model fit the data well, but also the majority of the paths (23 of 26) are significant, in the expected direction, and large enough to be of interest.

REGRESSION RESULTS: TIME I AND TIME II LONGITUDINAL ANALYSES

Descriptive Statistics

Table 7.4 presents descriptive statistics, reliabilities, and zero-order product-moment correlations among the study variables for the participants at Time I and Time II. As expected, job security perceptions at Time I are

TABLE 7.4

Descriptive Statistics, Scale Reliabilities, and Interscale
Correlations of Variables Measured for Longitudinal Analyses

Variable	M	SD	1	2	3	4	5	6	7	8	9	10	11
1. JSI—Time I	1.26	1.05	.98										
2. JSS—Time I	1.57	.85	.66	.99									
3. SATALL—Time I	1.84	.50	.50	.39	.96								
4. JSS—Time II	1.67	1.03	.55	.49	.41	.96							
5. SATALL—Time II	1.84	.56	.44	.37	.76	.58	.93						
6. AFFECT—Time II	2.50	1.11	-.25	-.35	-.04	-.37	-.11	.85					
7. ORGCOMT—Time II	4.72	1.27	.21	.17	.51	.28	.56	-.15	.85				
8. HCOND—Time II	2.71	2.76	-.26	-.36	-.30	-.31	-.35	.30	-.28	.79			
9. JWTO—Time II	2.03	1.05	-.24	-.34	-.44	-.32	-.47	.30	-.53	.41	.84		
10. DISTRESS—Time II	1.83	1.00	-.23	-.26	-.13	-.39	-.29	.20	-.07	.54	.30	.95	
11. WW—Time II	1.92	.76	-.01	-.03	-.26	-.12	-.27	.11	-.36	.30	.48	.22	.66

Note. Scale reliabilities are on the diagonal; $N = 96$.
$rs > .20$ are significant at $p < .05$; $rs > .26$ are significant at $p < .01$; $rs > .35$ are significant at $p < .001$.
JSI = Job Security Perceptions; JSS = Job Security Satisfaction; SATALL = Overall Job Satisfaction; AFFECT = Affective Reactions; ORGCOMT = Organizational Commitment; HCOND = Health Conditions; JWTO = Turnover Intentions; DISTRESS = Psychological Distress; WW = Work Withdrawal.

positively related to Time II levels of job satisfaction. In accordance with Weiss and Cropanzano's (1996) Affective Events Theory, job security perceptions at Time I are negatively related to Time II negative affective reactions regarding the workplace reorganization, such that employees who initially perceive their jobs to be less secure report more negative affective reactions 6 months into the reorganization. Finally, Time I satisfaction with job security is negatively related to Time II mental and physical health problems and turnover intentions, such that lower job security satisfaction at Time I is associated with more negative outcomes at Time II.

Regression Analyses

Job Attitudes and Affective Reactions. Regression analyses indicate that Time I perceptions of job security are significantly related to Time II overall job satisfaction (a composite of the five JDI measures), job security satisfaction, and affective reactions to the workplace reorganization, $F(3, 86) = 13.86, p < .001$. Twenty-nine percent of the variance in Time II job security satisfaction scores is accounted for by Time I job security perceptions, $F(1, 88) = 37.35, p < .001$, whereas 16% of the Time II overall job satisfaction scores, $F(1, 88) = 18.26, p < .001$, and 6% of the Time II affective reaction scores, $F(1, 88) = 6.88, p < .01$, are accounted for by the Time I job security perceptions.

Health Conditions, Commitment, and Turnover Intentions. Regression analyses indicate that Time I job security satisfaction is significantly related to Time II outcome variables, $F(5, 81) = 4.00, p < .005$. Univariate analyses revealed that, as with the cross-sectional data, job security satisfaction is significantly related to mental health ($R^2_{adj} = .05; F(1, 85) = 5.85, p < .05$), physical health ($R^2_{adj} = .11; F(1, 85) = 11.49, p < .001$), and turnover intentions ($R^2_{adj} = .06; F(1, 85) = 6.91, p < .001$). Also consistent with the cross-sectional analyses, job security satisfaction at Time I was not shown to predict Time II work withdrawal behaviors, $F(1, 85) = .01, ns$, nor Time II organizational commitment, $F(1, 85) = 2.14, ns$.

DISCUSSION

This study was designed to test an integrated model of the antecedents and consequences of job insecurity. A model delineating the process by which multiple antecedents influences several classes of outcome variables was based on theories of job stress, job adaptation, and affective events. Both cross-sectional and longitudinal data provided good support for the model and hypotheses. Although a small number of specific hypotheses were not supported, the entire model provides a great deal of information and reduces much uncertainty about the causes and consequences of job insecurity.

The first finding of this study confirms prior research findings that organizational change such as workplace restructuring affects perceptions of job security. However, this study extends prior research by showing that grievance filing, absenteeism, organizational tenure, education level, and job technology change are related to these perceptions as well.

The second contribution of this study is the confirmation of the hypothesized links between job security perceptions and job security satisfaction, work attitudes, and affective reactions to the organizational restructuring. As hypothesized, cognitive appraisal regarding one's level of job security strongly predicted satisfaction with job security. Job security perceptions predicted work attitudes to a lesser extent. Finally, perceptions of job security predicted affective reactions to organizational restructuring. It is important to note that these relationships were found while taking into account quotidian work stressors such as role ambiguity, time pressure, and role conflict. In addition, the relationships were apparent in both the cross-sectional and longitudinal data sets.

The third contribution of this study showed that multiple consequences of job insecurity were mediated by job attitudes and affective reactions. As anticipated, job insecurity had major negative consequences at both the individual and organizational levels, resulting in increased organizational withdrawal, greater incidence of reported health conditions, more psychological distress, and lower organizational commitment.

Strengths and Limitations

In these studies, the precision of the definition and measurement of job security allowed for an exploration of the antecedents and consequences of job insecurity, as well as potential mediators of those relationships. Thus, the integrated approach to studying job insecurity allowed for a detailed conceptual development of the process by which several classes of antecedents led to the experience of job insecurity and the eventual incidence of negative affective, attitudinal, behavioral, physical, and psychological outcomes.

In a related fashion, the current study of job security did not follow the more traditional research approach of examining single variables in relation to job insecurity in isolation from other potentially pertinent variables. Rather, the use of structural equation modeling allowed for a simultaneous test of a set of interconnected hypotheses regarding a network of causes and effects of job security. Further, the structural model embedded the primary variables of interest within a larger organizational framework by including other workplace stressors that might reasonably impact the outcome variables of interest. In this way, I discovered that although these traditional workplace stressors have significant effects on the outcome variables of interest, perceptions of job security have independent and strong influences as well. The longitudinal analyses lent further support to the model by showing that job insecurity at Time I is not only related to the predicted outcomes at Time I but also predicts outcomes at Time $I + 6$ months.

A final strength of the study is the evidence that job security is a rather complex phenomenon. There are many variables influencing perceptions of job security; few, however, are typically measured. For example, this is the first study to test empirically the proximity and change propositions related to organizational technology suggested by Hulin and Roznowski (1985). In addition, this study distinguished between perceptions of, attitudes about, and affective reactions to job security—and found this distinction to be fruitful. Finally, this study acknowledged that there are multiple possible reactions one might have to job insecurity, and that individual reactions will vary as a function of individual and organizational contingencies and constraints (Hulin, 1991), thus necessitating the measurement of many possible outcome variables.

Although it is agreeable to discuss the strengths of any study, there are a number of limitations to this study that should be addressed. First, because of the nature of the reorganization, the sensitivity of certain variables, and organizational constraints, not all features of the proposed model could be measured and tested at both points in time. In addition, only some of the potential organizational change characteristics were occurring within the organization at the time the data were collected. A further criticism of this study might be that the majority of the variables being assessed were self-reported. Therefore, there was the potential for method variance associated with the use of a single-source, self-report methodology of data collection. To counter this threat, measures for three of the exogenous variables were obtained from upper management. Given that two of the three independent-source measures significantly predicted perceptions of job security, and were of similar strength to self-report variables, tentative conclusions can be drawn in favor of rejecting the method-bias argument. Nevertheless, future research should gather data on each portion of the proposed model across multiple organizations and from multiple sources.

Implications and Directions for Future Research

The development of an integrated model of job security represents a theoretical improvement over the seemingly atheoretical analysis of the antecedents and consequences of job security that has been conducted in the past. By specifying multiple causes for similar effects (in particular by taking into account other traditional work stressors), this research was less likely to overestimate or underestimate the importance of job insecurity as an influence on individual and organizational outcomes (Guion, 1991). In addition, the process by which job insecurity influences behavior, attitudes, and physical and mental health was less likely to be misspecified. Finally, by acknowledging that there are multiple responses to job insecurity and measuring several of these possibilities, this set of studies was less likely to overlook important compensatory and substitute behaviors in response to job insecurity than if single variables in isolation had been examined.

Despite these advancements, opportunities for conceptual development and empirical testing remain. The search for additional theoretically and conceptually meaningful antecedents of job security should continue. Although the majority of the predicted antecedent variables were significant and in the expected direction, none had very large relationships with perceptions of security. This suggests that only a portion of the variance in job security perceptions was being accounted for. One set of antecedents that was not measured in this study—job characteristics—might account for some additional variance. In addition, research should extend these findings from the public sector to the more volatile private sector. Government employees may have unique perspectives on and attitudes toward job security that could restrict the generalizability of the current findings.

Once the process of job insecurity is understood, future research might focus on developing organizational interventions for the purpose of attenuating the more negative individual and organizational effects. Organizational restructuring is a reality. Layoffs, acquisitions, mergers, and their ilk will continue. This set of studies was an important step toward delineating the process by which such organizational changes impact employees. The next essential step is to use that information to assist organizations make these transitions easier for the organization and its most valuable human resources. Conducting research on the multiple antecedents and consequences of job insecurity may inform an organization as to what it can do to compensate for higher job insecurity. For example, agreeing to provide workers with skills for dealing with organizational change or acquiring a new job may reduce the stress of job insecurity, thereby reducing the strain manifested in negative individual and organizational outcomes of job insecurity.

REFERENCES

Anderson, J., & Gerbing, D. (1988). Structural equation modeling in practice: A review and recommended two-step approach. *Psychological Bulletin, 103*, 411–423.

Ashford, S., Lee, C., & Bobko, P. (1989). Content, causes, and consequences of job insecurity: A theory-based measure and substantive test. *Academy of Management Journal, 32,* 803–829.

Beehr, T., & Newman, J. (1978). Job stress, employee health and organizational effectiveness: A facet analysis model and literature review. *Personnel Psychology, 31,* 665–669.

Brenner, S., Arnetz, B., Levi, L., Hall, E., Hjelm, R., Petterson, I., Salovarra, H., Soerbom, D., Tellenback, S., & Akerstedt, T. (1983, December). *The effects of insecurity at work, job loss, and unemployment: Project description and preliminary findings.* Paper presented at the WHO conference on unemployment and health, Stockholm, Sweden.

Brockner, J., & Greenberg, J. (1992). The impact of layoffs on survivors: An organizational perspective. In J. S. Carville (Ed.), *Applied psychology and organizational settings.* Hillsdale, NJ: Lawrence Erlbaum Associates.

Buessing, A. (1986). Worker responses to job insecurity: A quasi-experimental field investigation. In G. Debus & H. W. Schroiff (Eds.), *The psychology of work and organization* (pp. 137–144). North Holland: Elsevier.

Caplan, R. D., Cobb, S., French, J. R. P., Jr., Van Harrison, R. V., & Pinneau, S. R., Jr. (1975). *Job demands and worker health: Main effects and occupational differences.* Washington, DC: U.S. Department of Health, Education, and Welfare.

Carnevale, P. J., Olson, J. B., & O'Connor, K. M. (1992, June). *Reciprocity and informality in a laboratory grievance system.* Paper presented at the International Association of Conflict Management: Minneapolis, MN.

Cottington, E. M., Matthews, K. A., Talbot, E., & Kuller, L. H. (1986). Occupational stress, suppressed anger, and hypertension. *Psychosomatic Medicine, 48,* 249–260.

Davy, J., Kinicki, A., & Scheck, C. (1991). Developing and testing a model of survivor responses to layoffs. *Journal of Vocational Behavior, 38,* 302–317.

Dooley, D., Rook, K., & Catalano, R. (1987). Job and non-job stressors and their moderators. *Journal of Occupational Psychology, 60,* 115–132.

Everly, G. S., & Sobelman, S. A. (1987). *Assessment of the human stress response: Neurological, biochemical, and psychological foundations.* New York: AMS Press.

Fitzgerald, L. F., Drasgow, F., Hulin, C. L., Gelfand, M. J., & Magley, V. J. (1997). Antecedents and consequences of sexual harassment in organizations: A test of an integrated model. *Journal of Applied Psychology, 82,* 578–589.

French, J. R. P., Jr., Caplan, R. D., & Van Harrison, R. (1982). *The mechanisms of job stress and strain.* New York: Wiley.

Fuller, T., Edwards, J., Sermsri, S., & Vorakitphokatorn, S. (1993). Housing, stress, and physical well-being: Evidence from Thailand. *Social Science and Medicine, 36,* 1417–1428.

Greenhalgh, L. (1983). Managing the job insecurity crisis. *Human Resource Management, 22,* 431–444.

Greenhalgh, L., & Rosenblatt, Z. (1984). Job insecurity: Towards conceptual clarity. *Academy of Management Review, 9,* 438–448.

Guion, R. (1991). Personnel assessment, selection, and placement. In M. Dunnette & L. Hough (Eds.), *Handbook of industrial and organizational psychology* (Vol. 2, pp. 327–398). Palo Alto, CA: Consulting Psychologists Press, Inc.

Hanisch, K. A. (1992). *The development of a Health Condition scale and its relations to health satisfaction and retirement valence.* Paper presented at the 2nd APA/NIOSH Conference on Stress and the Workplace, Washington, DC.

Hanisch, K. A., & Hulin, C. L. (1990). Job attitudes and organizational withdrawal: An examination of retirement and other voluntary withdrawal behaviors. *Journal of Vocational Behavior, 37,* 60–78.

Hanisch, K. A., & Hulin, C. L. (1991). General attitudes and organizational withdrawal: An evaluation of a causal model. *Journal of Vocational Behavior, 39,* 110–128.

Hulin, C. L. (1991). Adaptation, persistence, and commitment in organizations. In M. Dunnette & L. M. Hough (Eds.), *Handbook of industrial and organizational psychology* (2nd ed., Vol. 2, pp. 445–505). Palo Alto, CA: Consulting Psychologists Press.

Hulin, C. L., & Roznowski, M. (1985). Organizational technologies: Effects on organizations' characteristics and individuals' responses. *Research in Organizational Behavior, 7,* 39–85.

Hulin, C. L., Roznowski, M., & Hachiya, D. (1985). Alternative opportunities and withdrawal decisions: Empirical and theoretical discrepancies and an integration. *Psychological Bulletin, 97,* 233–250.

Ironson, G. H. (1992). Job stress and health. In C. J. Cranny, P. C. Smith, & E. F. Stone (Eds.), *Job satisfaction: How people feel about their jobs and how it affects their performance* (pp. 219–239). New York: Lexington Books.

Jacoby, N. (1998). *1998 layoffs near record high* [On-line]. Available: http.//cnnfn.cnn.com/1998/12/28/economy/layoffs/

Jöreskog, K. G., & Sörbom, D. (1993). *LISREL 8: User's reference guide*. Mooresville, IN: Scientific Software, Inc.

Judge, T. A., & Hulin, C. L. (1993). Job satisfaction as a reflection of disposition: A multiple source causal analysis. *Organizational Behavior and Human Decision Processes, 56,* 388–421.

Kavanaugh, M. J., Hurst, M. W., & Rose, R. (1981). The relationship between job satisfaction and psychiatric health symptoms for air traffic controllers. *Personnel Psychology, 34,* 691–707.

Kuhnert, K., Sims, R., & Lahey, M. (1989). The relationship between job security and employees health. *Group and Organization Studies, 14,* 399–410.

Landy, F. J. (1989). *Psychology of work behavior*. Pacific Grove, CA: Brooks/Cole.

Lazarus, R. S. (1966). *Psychological stress and the coping process*. New York: McGraw-Hill.

Lewin, D. (1987). Dispute resolution in the non-union firm: A theoretical and empirical analysis. *Journal of Conflict Resolution, 31*(3), 465–502.

Locke, E. A. (1969). What is job satisfaction? *Organizational Behavior and Human Performance, 4,* 309–336.

Luthans, B., & Sommer, S. M. (1999). The impact of downsizing on workplace attitudes: Differing reactions of managers and staff in a health care organization. *Group and Organization Management, 24*(1), 46–70.

Matteson, M. T., & Ivancevich, J. M. (1982). The how, what and why of stress management training. *Personnel Journal, 61*(10), 768–774.

McCabe, P., & Schneiderman, N. (1985). Psychophysiologic reactions to stress. In N. Schneiderman & J. T. Tapp (Eds.), *Behavioral medicine: A biopsychological approach* (pp. 99–131). Hillsdale, NJ: Lawrence Erlbaum Associates.

McGrath, J. E. (1976). Stress and behavior in organizations. In M. D. Dunnette (Ed.), *Handbook of industrial and organizational psychology* (pp. 1351–1395). Chicago: Rand-McNally.

Mowday, R., Steers, R., & Porter, L. (1979). The measurement of organizational commitment. *Journal of Vocational Behavior, 14,* 224–247.

Probst, T. M. (1998). *Antecedents and consequences of job insecurity: Development and test of an integrated model*. Unpublished doctoral dissertation, University of Illinois at Urbana-Champaign.

Roskies, E., & Louis-Guerin, C. (1990). Job insecurity in managers: Antecedents and consequences. *Journal of Organizational Behavior, 11,* 345–359.

Roskies, E., Louis-Guerin, C., & Fournier, C. (1993). Coping with job insecurity: How does personality make a difference? *Journal of Organizational Behavior, 14,* 617–630.

Roznowski, M. (1989). An examination of the measurement properties of the Job Descriptive Index with experimental items. *Journal of Applied Psychology, 74,* 805–814.

Roznowski, M., & Hulin, C. L. (1992). The scientific merit of valid measures of general constructs with special reference to job satisfaction and job withdrawal. In C. J. Cranny, P. C.

Smith, & E. F. Stone (Eds.), *Job satisfaction: How people feel about their jobs and how it affects their performance.* New York: Lexington Books.

Shaver, P., Schwartz, J., Kirson, D., & O'Conner, C. (1987). Emotion knowledge: Further exploration of a prototype approach. *Journal of Personality and Social Psychology, 52,* 1066–1086.

Smith, P. C., Kendall, L., & Hulin, C. L. (1969). *The measurement of satisfaction in work and retirement.* Chicago: Rand McNally.

Veit, C. T., & Ware, J. E. (1983). The structure of psychological distress and well-being in general populations. *Journal of Consulting and Clinical Psychology, 51,* 730–742.

Weintraub, J. (1973). The relationship between job satisfaction and perceived states of health: A multivariate investigation. *Dissertation Abstracts International, 34,* 4111B. (University Microfilms No. 74-1776)

Weiss, H. M., & Cropanzano, R. (1996). Affective events theory: A theoretical discussion of the structure, causes and consequences of affective experiences at work. *Research on Organizational Behavior, 18,* 1–74.

Chapter 8

The Legacy of Charles Hulin's Work on Turnover Thinking and Research

Peter Hom
Arizona State University

Charles Hulin has left an enduring legacy on how we think about and investigate employee turnover. This chapter reviews his influential writings and how they have shaped—and continue to shape—the way researchers study and conceptualize this phenomenon. The sections that follow review Hulin's myriad contributions in chronological order, which roughly parallel the development of turnover research, beginning with his Montreal studies.

MONTREAL STUDIES OF TURNOVER AMONG OFFICE AND CLERICAL WORKERS

Hulin's (1966, 1968; Mikes & Hulin, 1968) earliest contribution to turnover research was a series of studies conducted in Montreal. These studies confirmed early theoretical assumptions that job attitudes induce employees to quit (Brayfield & Crockett, 1955; Herzberg, Mausner, Peterson, & Capwell, 1957; March & Simon, 1957). Pioneering a longitudinal design, Hulin (1966) established that an unweighted sum of the Job Descriptive Index (JDI; Smith, Kendall, & Hulin, 1969) subscales predicted subsequent turnover up to a year after survey assessment ($r = -.27, p < .05$). Mikes and Hulin (1968) replicated this finding with another sample of female office personnel: a sum of the JDI scales predicted subsequent quits ($r = -.46, p < .05$). In a 1968 quasiexperimental test, Hulin resurveyed the first clerical workforce and showed that increases in job satisfaction from 1964 to 1966 (due to workplace improvements in areas of disaffection revealed by the 1964 survey) accompanied an 18% decrease in the turnover rate during this period.

Although present-day scholars take for granted the significance of job attitudes for job behaviors, turnover studies done prior to the Montreal studies reached this conclusion using questionable research methods (cf. Brayfield & Crockett, 1955; Herzberg et al., 1957; Schuh, 1967; Vroom, 1964). Specifically, early investigators often used ad hoc indices of job satisfaction (Porter & Steers, 1973). Some researchers operationalized job satisfaction with an incomplete sentence technique (Friesen, 1952), whereas others used a tear ballot measure (Kerr, 1948). Except for student attrition studies (whose generalizability to terminations from paid employment is questionable), virtually all industrial tests carried out during those years failed to use predictive research designs to document satisfaction–quit relations (cf. Vroom, 1964). Instead, early researchers applied postdictive designs, correlating attitude measures with self-reported duration of employment in current or past jobs (Friesen, 1952; Van Zelst & Kerr, 1953) or inferring attitudinal causes from exit interviews (Wickert, 1951). Quite obviously, strong causal inferences that dissatisfaction prompts quits cannot be drawn from studies measuring attitudes after the behavior (turnover or completed job tenure) has occurred. Other investigations correlated average morale scores in departments or companies with aggregate quit rates (Giese & Ruter, 1949; Kerr, 1948). As we know today from Roberts, Hulin, and Rousseau (1978), extrapolating individual-level relationships between attitudes and terminations from aggregate-level relationships risks the ecological fallacy. Weitz and Nuchols (1953) did use a predictive design to forecast job survival among life insurance agents from measured job attitudes. Yet their turnover criterion was not purely voluntary for unproductive sales agents, paid on a straight commission, were likely dismissed (Hulin, 1966).

In the context of past satisfaction-turnover research, the Montreal studies represent major advances over prevailing methodological approaches. Chuck's early tests set a methodological paradigm for turnover research to follow: Measure individuals' job attitudes with psychometrically sound scales and relate those measures to voluntary, workplace resignations (Hulin, 1966; Mikes & Hulin, 1968). Despite Mobley's (1982) endorsement of Hulin's (1968) work, quasiexperiments remain rare today. Still, Hulin's panel designs inspired subsequent inquiries into the temporal process of withdrawal, which tracked how changes in turnover antecedents underpin quits (Hom & Griffeth, 1991; Porter, Crampon, & Smith, 1976; Porter, Steers, Mowday, & Boulian, 1974; Rusbult & Farrell, 1983; Youngblood, Mobley, & Meglino, 1983).

Hulin's predictive and quasiexperimental designs rigorously established job satisfaction as a central turnover cause, furnishing a basic structure for subsequent literature reviews and theories of attitude–turnover relationships. Thus, three prominent literature reviews in the 1970s highlighted Hulin's striking demonstrations (Locke, 1976; Price, 1977; Porter & Steers, 1973). For example, Locke (1976) remarked,

> *Especially interesting* [italics added] is Hulin's (1968) quasi-experimental field study in which an increase in satisfaction and a reduction in turnover were observed following management-initiated changes designed to increase satisfaction in problem areas uncovered in an earlier, correlational study. (Hulin, 1966, p. 1331)

Similarly, Porter and Steers (1973) wrote, "In two related predictive studies of *particular merit* [italics added], Hulin investigated the impact of job satisfaction on turnover among female clerical workers" (p. 152).

Moreover, the Montreal investigations shaped a host of theoretical models emerging in the 1970s and 1980s (Mobley, 1977; Mobley, Griffeth, Hand, & Meglino, 1979; Porter & Steers, 1973; Price, 1977; Price & Mueller, 1981a; Steers & Mowday, 1981). Given Hulin's evidence, these formulations universally adopted job satisfaction as an essential explanatory construct. To illustrate, Mobley (1977) conceptualized job dissatisfaction as the prime mover of organizational withdrawal, whereas Price and Mueller (1981a) conceived a crucial mediating role for this attitude: Translate how workplace conditions impact quit intentions. Although not directly acknowledging Hulin's work, many turnover theorists based their inclusion of job satisfaction within their frameworks by citing the literature reviews underscoring the Montreal results (Locke, 1976; Porter & Steers, 1973; Price, 1977). Drawing from Porter and Steers (1973) and Locke (1976), Mobley et al. (1979) argued that "previous reviews . . . have documented the consistent and negative . . . relationship between job satisfaction and turnover" (p. 518) to justify satisfaction as an antecedent. Similarly, Price (1977) alluded to Mikes and Hulin (1968) when formulating his earliest model, which positioned satisfaction as directly influencing turnover. In short, the Montreal findings ultimately became styled facts, forming empirical cornerstones for a wide range of turnover perspectives that followed.

INVESTIGATIONS OF NATIONAL GUARD REENLISTMENT

In the late 1970s, Hulin returned to the study of organizational withdrawal in a series of examinations of National Guard reenlistment (Hom & Hulin, 1981; Hom, Katerberg, & Hulin, 1979; Katerberg, Hom, &

Hulin, 1979; Miller, Katerberg, & Hulin, 1979). This line of inquiry pioneered competitive testing of turnover models (Hom & Hulin, 1981; Hom et al., 1979). Adopting Platt's (1964) logic, Hulin and colleagues argued that a model achieves stronger confirmation when it predicts turnover not only accurately but also more accurately than theoretical alternatives. They reasoned that even though a model fits the data, a competing model could provide an even better fit. In several tests, Hulin's research team compared the relative strength of behavioral decision-making models (Fishbein & Ajzen, 1975; Triandis, 1977), organizational commitment (Porter et al., 1976), and job satisfaction for predicting reenlistment decisions. This groundbreaking comparative fit approach has been widely adopted in Industrial and Organizational (I-O) Psychology to validate theories as well as establish unique contributions of new determinants (Aquino, Griffeth, Allen, & Hom, 1997; Dalessio, Silverman, & Schuck, 1986; Hom, Caranikis-Walker, Prussia, & Griffeth, 1992; Jaros, Jermier, Koehler, & Sincich, 1993; Sager, Griffeth, & Hom, 1998).

Apart from generalizing behavioral decision-making theories (Fishbein & Ajzen, 1975; Triandis, 1977), these competitive tests confirmed Mobley's (1977) claim that behavioral intentions represent the most proximal antecedent of turnover and would funnel the effects of all other causes, including job attitudes (Hom et al., 1979; Hom & Hulin, 1981). Although previously examined (Kraut, 1975, Newman, 1974; Waters, Roach, & Waters, 1976), Mobley's (1977) theory of intermediate linkages most advanced withdrawal intentions as an essential intervening construct between dissatisfaction and quits. At the same time, the National Guard tests produced the strongest evidence to date for behavioral intentions (surpassing even Mobley, Horner and Hollingsworth's, 1978, test of the Mobley, 1977, model), showing that intentions can explain as much as 49% of the variance in reenlistment decisions across a 6-month period. Subsequent meta-analyses have reaffirmed their primacy as the foremost turnover precursor (Griffeth, Hom, & Gaertner, 2000; Steel & Ovalle, 1984). In summary, their theoretical prominence in Mobley's (1977) far-reaching model and impressive efficacy for predicting National Guard reenlistment (Hom et al., 1979; Miller et al., 1979) account for why quit intentions became a mainstay construct in nearly all conceptual perspectives (Farrell & Rusbult, 1981; Hulin, Rosnowski, & Hachiya, 1985; Lee & Mitchell, 1994; Price & Mueller, 1981a; Steers & Mowday, 1981).

Despite their strong turnover predictions, Hulin and associates nonetheless called attention to situational and methodological moderators of their predictions (Hom et al., 1979; Hom & Hulin, 1981). Echoing Fishbein and Ajzen (1975), Hulin pointed out that optimal base rates (55% of guardsmen reenlisted) and predictor scales (attitudes, intentions) that match the turnover criterion in measurement specificity enhance predictive accuracy (Hom & Hulin, 1981). Moreover, the preprogrammed nature of reenlistment decisions (guardsmen make explicit stay or leave decisions at some predictable, future date) enhances their temporal stability, and hence predictive validity. Indeed, many first-term enlistees joined the National Guard to escape the draft and thus made up their minds to resign even before enlisting (Hom & Hulin, 1981). Concurrently, Mobley et al. (1979) introduced a comprehensive framework specifying that measurement specificity and time lag between predictor and criterion assessments moderate intention–turnover relationships. The latter moderator operates like temporal stability because predictors change during long time intervals, losing predictive effectiveness (Fishbein & Ajzen, 1975). Because the National Guard studies and Mobley et al.'s (1979) seminal theory underscored moderators, subsequent meta-analyses have routinely tested how turnover base rate, time interval, and measurement specificity affect predictor–turnover correlations (Carsten & Spector, 1987; Griffeth et al., 2000; Hom et al., 1992; McEvoy & Cascio, 1987; Steel & Griffeth, 1989; Steel, Hendrix, & Balogh, 1990; Steel & Ovalle, 1984). Furthermore, Hulin's National Guard work distinguished reenlistment decisions—which are preprogrammed and highly consequential (obligating reenlistees to years of continued service)—from civilian turnover (Hom & Hulin, 1981; Hom et al., 1979). Those early deliberations on the limited generalizability of military data led other researchers to recognize that military and civilian terminations engender different processes and test for occupational variations in withdrawal patterns (Carsten & Spector, 1987; Hom et al., 1992; Steel, 1996; Steel & Griffeth, 1989; Steel & Ovalle, 1984).

The National Guard research also advanced understanding of the process by which dissatisfaction progresses into terminations. Hulin and the research team (Miller et al., 1979) replicated the first test (Mobley, Horner, & Hollingsworth, 1978) of Mobley's (1977) theory of the intermediate steps between dissatisfaction and withdrawal. Using double cross-validation, Miller et al.'s hierarchical regression analyses explained 55% of reenlistment's variance (compared with 26% explained in Mobley et al.'s, 1978, test) as well as corroborate Mobley's (1977) claim that job-seeking and quitting intentions mediate between dissatisfaction and quits. Despite supportive results, Miller et al. (1979) challenged Mobley's far-reaching depiction of the dissatisfaction→turnover sequence. Rather, they advanced (and verified) an alternative intermediate-linkages model, in which withdrawal cognitions (a summary construct reflecting thoughts of quitting, search intentions, and quit intentions) translate the influence of career mobility (a composite of age, tenure, and perceived chances of securing alternatives) and job satisfaction on terminations. Miller et al. (1979) further pointed out that Mobley et al.'s (1978) own test did not fully sustain Mobley's (1977) theory.

The early, and "successful," validations by Miller et al. (1979) and Mobley et al. (1978) of Mobley's (1977) model initiated a series of studies extending over 10 years (Bannister & Griffeth, 1986; Dalessio, Silverman, & Schuck, 1986; Hom et al., 1992; Hom, Griffeth, & Sellaro, 1984; Lee, 1988; Mowday, Koberg, & McArthur, 1984). Empirical tests of Mobley's (1977) theory dominated turnover research during those years (Lee & Mitchell, 1994). All the same, this avenue of research often disputed Mobley's original 1977 formulation, reaffirming Miller et al.'s (1979) preliminary challenge. Prompted by Miller et al. (1979), many researchers developed alternative causal sequences linking dissatisfaction to quitting (cf. Dalessio et al., 1986; Hom et al., 1992).

Apart from stimulating rethinking about intermediate linkages, Miller et al. (1979) introduced an explanatory construct—namely, withdrawal cognitions—that has been validated by confirmatory factor analyses and adopted by modern theories (Hom & Griffeth, 1991; Jaros et al., 1993; Tett & Meyer, 1993). Following Miller et al. (1979), Hom and Griffeth (1991) proposed another intermediate-linkages model in which withdrawal cognitions mediate the dissatisfaction–exit relationship. Lee and Mitchell (1994) submitted a more comprehensive turnover theory, including the Hom-Griffeth model, along with withdrawal cognitions, as a subsystem (i.e., Decision Path 4). Similarly, Jaros et al. (1993) conceptualized a multiple-constituency commitment model, in which withdrawal cognitions translate how various commitment forms affect departures. Finally, Tett and Meyer (1993) combined path analysis and meta-analysis to verify a causal structure in which dissatisfaction→withdrawal cognitions→turnover.

In conclusion, the National Guard studies pioneered various methodological and conceptual advances for turnover theory and research. Hulin's studies popularized competitive testing and underlined the methodological constraints that undermine turnover prediction. This research stream also disputed orthodox thinking about how dissatisfaction evolves into quitting and championed theoretical parsimony even as turnover theories have become increasingly expansive over the years (cf. Hom & Griffeth, 1995).

INTEGRATIVE FRAMEWORK BY HULIN, ROZNOWSKI, AND HACHIYA (1985)

In a seminal article, Hulin et al. (1985) conceived a theory to resolve the long-standing but puzzling contradiction between strong macroeconomic effects of unemployment rates on aggregate quit rates (Forrest, Cummings, & Johnson, 1977; March & Simon, 1958; Price, 1977) and modest effects of perceptions of alternatives on individual exits (Griffeth & Hom, 1988; Steel & Griffeth, 1989; Steers & Mowday, 1981). This thoughtful review systematically documented the frail support for the accepted wisdom that plentiful job opportunities induce individuals to quit (March & Simon, 1958; Mobley, 1977; Mobley et al., 1979; Price, 1977; Price & Mueller, 1981a, 1981b; Steers & Mowday, 1981). Unlike macrolevel data, Hulin et al. (1985) concluded that individual-level data actually did not uphold this central tenet in established withdrawal formulations.

Importantly, Hulin and students identified a flawed logic in dominant schools of thought, which generalized macrolevel unemployment effects on quit rates to individual-level effects (Hulin et al., 1985). That is, prevailing formulations overstated the role job alternatives play in the withdrawal of individual workers, basing its significance on strong labor-market effects (cf. Forrest et al., 1977; Hulin et al., 1985; Mobley, 1982; Price, 1977). In their classic model, March and Simon (1958), for example, hypothesized that "the greater the number of perceived extraorganizational alternatives, the greater the perceived ease of movement" (p. 100). They claimed that "evidence for this proposition is substantial," citing Reynolds (1951) who reported that the average monthly quit rate in 39 firms fell from 3.5% to 1.6% during the 1948–1949 recession. In the same manner, Price and Mueller (1981b) posited a direct effect of "opportunity" (availability of alternative jobs in the organization's environment) on turnover in their provisional structural model. They too derived their assertion from labor–economic findings of aggregate unemployment–turnover relations (Burton & Parker, 1969; March & Simon, 1958). When formulating his model, Mobley (1977) similarly drew from Armknecht and Early's (1972) finding—that changes in new hire rates in preceding quarters foreshadow aggregated quit rates—to support his thesis that job-seeking expected utility underlies job search and turnover.

In addition to rejecting conventional formulations about the centrality of perceived alternatives, Hulin et al. (1985) contended that aggregated labor-market effects represent an entirely different phenomenon. They thus put forth a new model that assigned different roles to job opportunities from those of then current conceptual schemes. Although still untested in its entirety, this innovative theory has yielded a wealth of fresh ideas that sparked considerable research and rethinking. Provocative implications of the Hulin et al. (1985) formulation include the notions of multiple withdrawal paths, extrawork alternatives, direct unemployment effects, and alternative reactions to dissatisfaction.

Multiple Withdrawal Paths

Hulin et al. (1985) argued that traditional thinking assumed a relatively homogeneous workforce and thus inadequately explained the process by which marginal workers (e.g., temporary workers, part-timers, secondary wage earners) and drifters terminated employment. In the Hulin et al. (1985) model, peripheral workers do not engage in the "cognitive processes outlined in current theoretical models" and "labor markets play little role in their turnover decisions" (p. 241). Unlike committed labor force participants, neither dissatisfaction nor work alternatives play much role in their decisions to quit.

This line of thinking foreshadowed later theorizing, explicitly hypothesizing that leavers follow different routes of withdrawal (Lee & Mitchell, 1994). Building on Hulin et al.'s (1985) insights, Lee and Mitchell's (1994) unfolding theory further elaborated different termination paths. Some employees exit via a standard route: dissatisfaction→job search→comparison of alternatives→turnover (Decision Path 4b). Others follow termination patterns not envisioned by conventional perspectives (e.g., Mobley, 1977; Price & Mueller, 1981a, 1986). For instance, Decision Path 1 in the unfolding model posits that some employees resign without jobs in hand if they encounter a shock (a jarring event) that triggers a matching script (a preexisting action plan, such as pregnancies inducing workforce attrition). Leavers taking this path do not engage in prolonged mental deliberations before departing. Years earlier, Hulin et al. (1985) conceptualized a similar withdrawal pattern for marginal workers, especially secondary wage earners, who often intend to resign before starting work. Their action plan might be to terminate employment once they accumulate enough savings to "pursue more pleasurable and less stressful avocations on a full-time basis" (Hulin et al., 1985, p. 240).

What is more, Hulin et al. (1985) proposed that "many individuals simply form behavioral intentions to quit their jobs on the basis of their experienced job dissatisfaction" (p. 246). This withdrawal pattern, too, presaged later viewpoints explicitly acknowledging that dissatisfaction can translate directly into quits without an intervening job search (Hom & Griffeth, 1991; Lee & Mitchell, 1994). To illustrate, Decision Path 2 in the unfolding model proposes that a shock may provoke image violation (e.g., belief that one cannot attain personal values, goals, or behavioral strategies in the current workplace). The ensuing (high) job dissatisfaction can drive some people to quit without first soliciting other positions.

Extrawork Alternatives

Hulin and co-authors cogently reasoned that employees, especially peripheral workers and drifters, may quit to pursue extrawork alternatives (Hulin et al., 1985). As they put it, "some individuals may quit a job to leave the regular work force temporarily, or permanently, to engage in other activities" (p. 246). Later theories and research began to recognize the lure of extrawork alternatives and that leavers who pursue full-time participation in these roles follow a different withdrawal route than those attached to the workforce (i.e., job-to-nonemployment vs. job-to-job quits; Royalty, 1998). To illustrate, research on the unfolding model has documented how nonwork shocks (e.g., pregnancies, graduate school admissions) prompt leavers to take unconventional withdrawal paths (Decision Path 1; Lee, Mitchell, Holtom, McDaniel, & Hill, 1999; Lee, Mitchell, Wise, & Fireman, 1996). In a similar vein, other turnover scholars have focused on interrole conflict—work interference with extraorganizational pursuits (e.g., child-bearing or -rearing)—as motivating job-to-nonemployment turnover (Hom & Griffeth, 1991). Turnover studies increasingly implicate interrole conflict (or anticipated conflict) as a prime cause of departures from both jobs and the labor market (Dalton, Hill & Ramsay, 1997; Greenhaus, Collins, Singh, & Parasuraman, 1997; Netermeyer, Boles, & McMurrian, 1996).

Direct Unemployment Effects

Extending a provisional idea suggested by Michaels and Spector (1982), Hulin et al. (1985) explicitly modeled a direct effect of unemployment rates on individual-level terminations. As they put it, "organizational members do not quit on the basis of probabilities estimated from alternatives available; they quit on the basis of certainties represented by alternative jobs already offered" (p. 244). This unemployment→exit pathway extended traditional viewpoints emphasizing perceived alternatives (Mobley et al., 1979; Price & Mueller, 1981a) and was adopted by subsequent theorists (Gerhart, 1990; Lee et al., 1999). Moreover, later empirical tests have upheld Hulin et al.'s assertion about the primacy of external market conditions. For instance, investigations of the unfolding model have documented how the (improving) labor market can directly trigger departures by exposing incumbents to job-offer or job-inquiry shocks (Lee et al., 1996, 1999). Similarly, other studies have reported that objective unemployment circumstances exert unique (direct) effects on resignations, beyond those of subjective impressions of job alternatives (Gerhart, 1990; Steel, 1996).

Besides inspiring more inquiry into labor-market turnover effects (Dickter, Roznowski, & Harrison, 1996), Hulin et al.'s (1985) review of how worker beliefs about job opportunities did not materially impact the withdrawal process ironically initiated more inquiry into these beliefs. This pessimistic review motivated an influential meta-analysis by Steel and Griffeth (1989), who validated Hulin et al.'s (1985) conclusion with more precise estimates of the weak correlation between perceived alternatives and turnover. They supplemented Hulin et al.'s (1985) conceptual arguments for why subjective impressions of alternatives are so inconsequential with methodological explanations. Common methodological artifacts, such as poor instrumentation and insufficient sampling of diverse occupational and local labor markets, might also be responsible for weak findings. In line with their suggestions, recent tests have detected stronger turnover effects for perceived alternatives when they use more complete, multidimensional measures and broadly sample heterogeneous labor markets (Griffeth & Hom, 1988; Steel, 1996).

Alternative Responses to Dissatisfaction

Though briefly alluded to by Mobley (1977) and Steers and Mowday (1981), Hulin et al. (1985) elaborated on the alternative reactions to dissatisfaction, which may interrupt or short-circuit the termination process. They theorized that dissatisfaction does not inevitably lead to resignations. Instead, some dissatisfied employees may reduce job inputs or attempt to change the work situation. By implication, such actions would reduce the exit propensity. This innovative idea presaged later attempts to integrate responses other than turnover into the termination process (cf. Chen, Hui, & Sego, 1998; Hanisch & Hulin, 1990, 1991; Rusbult, Farrell, Rogers, & Mainous, 1988). Hulin et al.'s (1985) line of thinking clarified why job satisfaction modestly predicts turnover as employees can resolve their disaffection through means other than quitting (Locke, 1976; Mobley, 1977). Further, Hulin et al.'s (1985) portrayal of the multiple ways that dissatisfaction is expressed or managed implied an intriguing prescription: Reducing dissatisfaction decreases not only turnover but also a host of other dysfunctional workplace reactions.

FAMILIES OF WITHDRAWAL BEHAVIORS

According to Hulin (1991; Hanisch & Hulin, 1990, 1991; Hanisch, Hulin, & Roznowski, 1998), turnover is better construed as a member of a broader family of related responses that have the same psychological function. Termed *job withdrawal,* these behaviors distance employees from aversive work situations, thereby alleviating dissatisfaction. Rather than adopt managerial preoccupation with economically costly behaviors, Hulin argued that researchers should investigate a behavioral syndrome rather than a single surface manifestation. Given that dichotomous turnover behaviors often exhibit nonnormal, skewed distributions, conventional statistical analyses (e.g., ordinary least squares regression) may fail to confirm otherwise valid theories. Rather, Hulin (1991) prescribed a multiple-act criterion that includes turnover and other functionally equivalent or related acts. A family of responses is more predictable because combining many job-withdrawal acts (that share a common factor) would rapidly increase the proportion of construct-relevant variance relative to unique variance (Hanisch et al., 1998; Hulin, 1991; Rosse & Hulin, 1985). Importantly, Hulin (1991) argued that theorists should design broader attitudinal models that have greater breadth for predicting a wider range of behaviors (Ajzen & Fishbein, 1980). By contrast, conventional schemes that specialize only in turnover may not account for other, even functionally equivalent, behaviors. Narrow explanations of single-act criteria thus lack parsimony as each withdrawal act warrants its own special model.

Hulin and associates (Fitzgerald, Drasgow, Hulin, Gelfand, & Magley, 1997; Glomb, Munson, Hulin, Bergman, & Drasgow, 1999; Hanisch & Hulin, 1990, 1991; Hanisch et al., 1998) demonstrated that turnover indeed belongs to a family of interrelated behaviors (including retirement plans) and that this multiple-act criterion is better predicted by job attitudes than are separate acts. Hulin (1991) first proposed a family of withdrawal responses that shared the same psychological function: reducing work-role inclusion. Subsequent research divided this family into two families: job withdrawal (which comprises quits and early retirement) and work withdrawal. The latter behavioral repertoire represents all attempts to avoid work tasks (e.g., absences, tardiness) while remaining within the organization. These response families have different (overlapping) antecedents with work withdrawal being less dependent on dissatisfaction.

Following the lead of Rosse and Hulin (1985), Rusbult et al. (1988) also established that turnover belongs to a response family (called *exit*, which includes transfers and job search) that is highly predictable from job satisfaction. Like Hulin's research, they distinguished exit from *neglect* responses—reactions such as chronic lateness and absences—and observed different determinants for these behavioral families. Dissatisfaction increases exit more than neglect, whereas quality of perceived alternatives induces exits but not neglect (cf. Withey & Cooper, 1989).

Hulin's (1991) inception of a broad withdrawal–response family inspired Chen et al. (1998) to add organizational citizenship behavior (OCB) to this family. Chen et al. (1998) theorized that OCB would predict resignations better than do traditional avoidance acts (e.g., absences, tardiness). The latter responses are often constrained by organizations, whereas OCB is discretionary because employment contracts do not formally mandate extrarole behaviors. Dissatisfied employees do not necessarily lower in-role performance or miss workdays, for such actions invoke severe company sanctions. Yet they might express discontent by withholding OCB acts because employers do not ordinarily punish poor citizenship. Consequently, infrequent OCB behaviors may constitute a form of job withdrawal. Extending Rosse and Hulin's (1985) findings, Chen et al.

(1998) found that supervisory ratings of OCB acts of mainland Chinese workers were related inversely to turnover ($r = -.28$, $p < .05$).

Toward a Midlevel Job-Withdrawal Model

Finally, Hulin's research and thinking imply a plausible midlevel model for the job withdrawal behavioral family. An explanatory scheme focused on this response family would not be so broad as to simultaneously explain multiple families (Hanisch et al., 1998; Hulin et al., 1985; Withey & Cooper, 1989) nor so narrow as to focus on a single withdrawal act, the preoccupation of traditional thinkers. Based on preliminary research on this behavioral family (Fitzgerald et al., 1997; Hanisch & Hulin, 1990; Rusbult et al., 1988; Withey & Cooper, 1989), this model postulates that health status, job satisfaction, company commitment, optimism about change, job investment (and sunk costs), quality of alternatives, and work avoidance influence job withdrawal (Hom & Griffeth, 1995). Following Fishbein and Ajzen's (1975) analysis of levels of intentional specificity, this model holds that a global intention measure, such as withdrawal cognitions, is the most direct determinant of this broad behavioral class (Hom & Griffeth, 1991; Miller et al., 1979). In keeping with findings by Jaros et al. (1993) and Tett and Meyer (1993), this model also specifies that organizational commitment and job satisfaction influence withdrawal cognitions. Extending theories by Fishbein and Ajzen (1975) and Hanisch et al. (1998), normative pressures—or demands from others to leave a workplace permanently— might further underlie withdrawal cognitions (Hom & Griffeth, 1995). Further, studies on the progression-of-withdrawal effect suggest that work withdrawal predate, if not reinforce, turnover (Hom & Griffeth, 1995; Griffeth et al., 2000). That is, less extreme forms of withdrawal (e.g., tardiness, absences) may progress into more severe job withdrawal. Finally, Hulin's latest findings reveal how experienced or observed sexual harassment can induce job withdrawal by creating dissatisfaction (see later). Figure 8.1 summarizes this provisional conception of the antecedents of the job-withdrawal family.

SEXUAL HARASSMENT AS JOB STRESSOR AND TURNOVER CAUSE

Hulin and colleagues further contributed to the turnover literature by demonstrating how sexual harassment—whether experienced or observed—can activate withdrawal (Fitzgerald et al., 1997; Glomb et al., 1997; 1999). Although long ignored by turnover researchers, there is

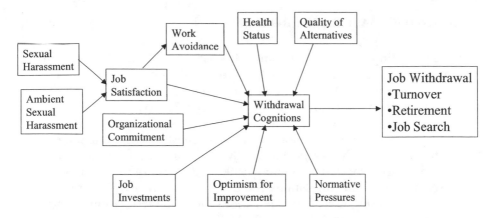

FIG. 8.1.   Provisional model of job-withdrawal family.

growing evidence of the pervasiveness of sexual harassment and its pivotal role in prompting women to leave (Schneider, Swan, & Fitzgerald, 1997). For example, a UCLA poll in 1992 of women executives at 1,500 companies revealed that 59% had been sexually harassed at work and that 5% of them coped with harassment by quitting (Hom & Griffeth, 1995). Similarly, a national survey of lawyers disclosed that two thirds of female lawyers in private practice and nearly one half of those in corporate or public agency settings encountered or witnessed sexual harassment by male superiors, colleagues, or clients (Laband & Lentz, 1998). Such harassment significantly increased quits among women lawyers.

Turnover scholars have overlooked sexual harassment because its alleged turnover effects are primarily suggestive, based on journalistic reports or anecdotal evidence. Adding greater theoretical and scientific rigor to this burgeoning literature, Hulin and research partners developed a more valid operationalization of experienced sexual harassment and rigorously tested its effect on turnover (job withdrawal), using panel studies and causal modeling procedures (Fitzgerald et al., 1997; Glomb et al., 1999). Additionally, Glomb et al. (1997) cleverly assessed a work group's "ambient sexual harassment" by averaging self-reported harassment scores for all women in the group (excepting the focal respondent to avoid method bias). They then showed that women who only witness others being sexually harassed felt job dissatisfaction and psychological distress, much like victims of direct harassment. In sum, Hulin's latest findings persuasively showed that the deleterious effects of sexual harassment are more pervasive than previously thought. Turnover researchers, as a result, can longer dismiss sexual harassment as a minor influence on organizational withdrawal.

TURNOVER BASE RATE PROBLEMS

Finally, Hulin (1984, 1991; Hulin & Rousseau, 1980) inspired methodologists to develop formulas to adjust predictor–quit correlations for extreme base rates and dichotomous turnover data (Bass & Ager, 1991; Kemery, Dunlap, & Griffeth, 1988; Steel, Shane, & Griffeth, 1990). He forcibly argued how extreme behavioral base rates and dichotomous manifestations of (latent) continuous withdrawal constructs can attenuate the predictability of withdrawal behaviors by restricting criterion variance. Although still controversial (Williams, 1990), scholars are thus increasingly correcting turnover correlations for discontinuity or extreme turnover base rates (or both) in structural equations modeling tests (Hom, Griffeth, Palich, & Bracker, 1998; Jaros et al., 1993; Sager et al., 1998) and meta-analyses (Griffeth et al., 2000; Tett & Meyer, 1993; Williams & Livingstone, 1994).

CONCLUSION

No organizational scholar has contributed as much—or in so many varied ways—to turnover thinking and research as Charles Hulin. As this chapter reviews, Hulin and colleagues have introduced many theoretical insights about the termination process (e.g., direct unemployment effects on individual quits, extrawork alternatives, job satisfaction, sexual harassment, multiple withdrawal paths). His methodological contributions are equally remarkable as he pioneered predictive and longitudinal research designs, corrections for turnover correlations, and survival analysis for studying withdrawal behaviors (e.g., Harrison & Hulin, 1989). As we enter the new millennium, future generations of turnover scholars will continue to build on the immense foundation Charles Hulin has built.

REFERENCES

Ajzen, I., & Fishbein, M. (1980). *Understanding attitudes and predicting social behavior*. Englewood Cliffs, NJ: Prentice-Hall.

Aquino, K., Griffeth, R. W., Allen, D. G., & Hom, P. W. (1997). Outcome and supervisory satisfaction as predictors of turnover: A test of a referent cognitions model. *Academy of Management Journal, 40*, 1208–1227.

Armknecht, P. A., & Early, J. F. (1972). Quits in manufacturing: A study of their causes. *Monthly Labor Review, 95*, 31–37.

Bannister, B. D., & Griffeth, R. W. (1986). Applying a causal analytic framework to the Mobley, Horner, and Hollingsworth (1978) turnover model: A useful reexamination. *Journal of Management, 12*, 433–443.

Bass, A., & Ager, J. (1991). Correcting point-biserial turnover correlations for comparative analysis. *Journal of Applied Psychology, 76*, 595–598.

Brayfield, A. H., & Crockett, W. H. (1955). Employee attitudes and employee performance. *Psychological Bulletin, 52*, 396–424.

Burton, J., & Parker, J. (1969). Interindustry variations in voluntary labor mobility. *Industrial and Labor Relations Review, 22*, 199–216.

Carsten, J. M., & Spector, P. E. (1987). Unemployment, job satisfaction, and employee turnover: A meta-analytic test of the Muchinsky model. *Journal of Applied Psychology, 72*, 374–381.

Chen, X.-P., Hui, C., & Sego, D. J. (1998). The role of organizational citizenship behavior in turnover: Conceptualization and preliminary tests of key hypotheses. *Journal of Applied Psychology, 83*, 922–931.

Dalessio, A., Silverman, W. H., & Schuck, J. R. (1986). Paths to turnover: A re–analysis and review of existing data on the Mobley, Horner, and Hollingsworth turnover model. *Human Relations, 39*, 245–263.

Dalton, D. R., Hill, J. W., & Ramsay, R. J. (1997). Women as managers and partners: Context specific predictors of turnover in international public accounting firms. *Auditing: A Journal of Practice & Theory, 16*, 29–50.

Dickter, D., Roznowski, M., & Harrison, D. (1996). Temporal tempering: An event history analysis of the process of voluntary turnover. *Journal of Applied Psychology, 81*, 705–716.

Farrell, D., & Rusbult, C. E. (1981). Exchange variables as predictors of job satisfaction, job commitment, and turnover: The impact of rewards, costs, alternatives, and investments. *Organizational Behavior and Human Performance, 28*, 78–95.

Fishbein, M., & Ajzen, I. (1975). *Belief, attitude, intention and behavior: An introduction to theory and research.* Reading, MA: Addison-Wesley.

Fitzgerald, L., Drasgow, F., Hulin, C., Gelfand, M., & Magley, V. (1997). Antecedents and consequences of sexual harassment in organizations: A test of an integrated model. *Journal of Applied Psychology, 82*, 578–589.

Forrest, C. R., Cummings, L. L., & Johnson, A. C. (1977). Organizational participation: A critique and model. *Academy of Management Review, 2*, 586–601.

Friesen, E. (1952). The incomplete sentences technique as a measure of employee attitudes. *Personnel Psychology, 5*, 329–345.

Gerhart, B. (1990). Voluntary turnover and alternative job opportunities. *Journal of Applied Psychology, 75*, 467–476.

Giese, W., & Ruter, H. (1949). An objective analysis of morale. *Journal of Applied Psychology, 33*, 421–427.

Glomb, T., Munson, L., Hulin, C., Bergman, M., & Drasgow, F. (1999). Structural equation models of sexual harassment: Longitudinal explorations and cross-sectional generalizations. *Journal of Applied Psychology, 84*, 14–28.

Glomb, T., Richman, W., Hulin, C., Drasgow, F., Schneider, K., & Fitzgerald, L. (1997). Ambient sexual harassment: An integrated model of antecedents and consequences. *Organizational Behavior and Human Decision Processes, 71*, 309–328.

Greenhaus, J. H., Collins, K. M., Singh, R., & Parasuraman, S. (1997). Work and family influences on departure from public accounting. *Journal of Vocational Behavior, 50*, 249–270.

Griffeth, R. W., & Hom, P. W. (1988). A comparison of different conceptualizations of perceived alternatives in turnover research. *Journal of Organizational Behavior, 9*, 103–111.

Griffeth, R., Hom, P., & Gaertner, S. (2000). A meta-analytical update of antecedents and correlates of employee turnover: Research in the nineties with research implications for the next millennium. *Journal of Management, 26*, 463–488.

Hanisch, K., & Hulin, C. (1990). Job attitudes and organizational withdrawal: An examination of retirement and other voluntary withdrawal behaviors. *Journal of Vocational Behavior, 37*, 60–78.

Hanisch, K., & Hulin, C. (1991). General attitudes and organizational withdrawal: An evaluation of a causal model. *Journal of Vocational Behavior, 39,* 110–128.

Hanisch, K., Hulin, C., & Roznowski, M. (1998). The importance of individuals' repertoires of behaviors: The scientific appropriateness of studying multiple behaviors and general attitudes. *Journal of Organizational Behavior, 19,* 463–480.

Harrison, D., & Hulin, C. (1989). Investigations of absenteeism: Using event history models to study the absence-taking process. *Journal of Applied Psychology, 74,* 300–316.

Herzberg, F., Mausner, B., Peterson, R., & Capwell, D. (1957). *Job attitudes: Review of research and opinion.* Pittsburgh, PA: Psychological Service of Pittsburgh.

Hom, P. W., Caranikas-Walker, F., Prussia, G., & Griffeth, R. (1992). A meta-analytical structural equations analysis of a model of employee turnover. *Journal of Applied Psychology, 77,* 890–909.

Hom, P. W., & Griffeth, R. (1991). Structural equations modeling test of a turnover theory: Cross-sectional and longitudinal analyses. *Journal of Applied Psychology, 76,* 350–66.

Hom, P., & Griffeth, R. (1995). *Employee turnover.* Cincinnati, OH: South-Western College Publishing.

Hom, P. W., Griffeth, R. W., Palich, L. E., & Bracker, J. S. (1998). An exploratory investigation into theoretical mechanisms underlying realistic job previews. *Personnel Psychology, 51,* 421–451.

Hom, P. W., Griffeth, R. W., & Sellaro, C. L. (1984). The validity of Mobley's 1977 model of employee turnover. *Organizational Behavior and Human Performance, 34,* 141–174.

Hom, P. W., & Hulin, C. L. (1981). A competitive test of the prediction of reenlistment by several models. *Journal of Applied Psychology, 66,* 23–39.

Hom, P. W., Katerberg, R., Jr., & Hulin, C. L. (1979). Comparative examination of three approaches to the prediction of turnover. *Journal of Applied Psychology, 64,* 280–290.

Hulin, C. (1966). Job satisfaction and turnover in a female clerical population. *Journal of Applied Psychology, 50,* 280–285.

Hulin, C. (1968). Effects of changes in job satisfaction levels on employee turnover. *Journal of Applied Psychology, 52,* 122–126.

Hulin, C. (1984). Suggested directions for defining, measuring, and controlling absenteeism. In P. Goodman, R. Atkins, R. Avery, M. Fichman, V. Hotz, C. Hulin, G. Johns, F. Landy, G. Latham, H. Miller, N. Napier, S. Rhodes, J. Rosse, F. Smith, R. Steels, & J. Vassey (Eds.), *Absenteeism* (pp. 391–420). San Francisco: Jossey-Bass.

Hulin, C. L. (1991). Adaptation, persistence, and commitment in organizations. In M. Dunnette & L. Hough (Eds.), *Handbook of industrial and organizational psychology* (pp. 445–505). Palo Alto, CA: Consulting Psychologists Press.

Hulin, C. L., & Rousseau, D. (1980). Analyzing infrequent events: Once you find them, your troubles begin. In K. Roberts & L. Burstein (Eds.), *Issues in aggregation* (pp. 39–52). San Francisco, CA: Jossey-Bass.

Hulin, C. L., Roznowski, M., & Hachiya, D. (1985). Alternative opportunities and withdrawal decisions: Empirical and theoretical discrepancies and an integration. *Psychological Bulletin, 97,* 233–250.

Jaros, S. J., Jermier, J. M., Koehler, J. W., & Sincich, T. (1993). Effects of continuance, affective, and moral commitment on the withdrawal process: An evaluation of eight structural models. *Academy of Management Journal, 36,* 951–995.

Katerberg, R., Hom, P. W., & Hulin, C. L. (1979). Effects of job complexity on the reactions of part–time workers. *Organizational Behavior and Human Performance, 24,* 317–332.

Kemery, E., Dunlap, W., & Griffeth, R. (1988). Corrections for variance restrictions in point-biserial correlations. *Journal of Applied Psychology, 73,* 688–691.

Kerr, W. (1948). On the validity and reliability of the job satisfaction tear ballot. *Journal of Applied Psychology, 32,* 275–281.

Kraut, A. (1975). Predicting turnover of employees from measured job attitudes. *Organizational Behavior and Human Performance, 13*, 233–243.

Laband, D., & Lentz, B. (1998). The effects of sexual harassment on job satisfaction, earnings, and turnover among female lawyers. *Industrial and Labor Relations Review, 51*, 594–607.

Lee, T. W. (1988). How job satisfaction leads to employee turnover. *Journal of Business and Psychology, 2*, 263–271.

Lee, T. W., & Mitchell, T. R. (1994). An alternative approach: The unfolding model of voluntary employee turnover. *Academy of Management Review, 19*, 51–89.

Lee, T. W., Mitchell, T. R., Holtom, B. C., McDaniel, L. S., & Hill, J. W. (1999). The unfolding model of voluntary turnover: A replication and extension. *Academy of Management Journal, 42*, 450–462.

Lee, T. W., Mitchell, T. R., Wise, L., & Fireman, S. (1996). An unfolding model of voluntary employee turnover. *Academy of Management Journal, 39*, 5–36.

Locke, E. A. (1976). The nature and causes of job satisfaction. In M. Dunnette (Ed.), Handbook *of industrial and organizational psychology* (pp. 1297–1350). Chicago: Rand McNally.

March, J. G., & Simon, H. A. (1958). *Organizations.* New York: Wiley.

McEvoy, G. M., & Cascio, W. F. (1987). Do good or poor performers leave? A meta-analysis of the relationship between performance and turnover. *Academy of Management Journal, 30*, 744–762.

Michaels, C. E., & Spector, P. E. (1982). Causes of employee turnover: A test of the Mobley, Griffeth, Hand, and Meglino model. *Journal of Applied Psychology, 67*, 53–59.

Mikes, P. S., & Hulin, C. (1968). Use of importance as a weighting component of job satisfaction. *Journal of Applied Psychology, 52*, 394–398.

Miller, H. E., Katerberg, R., & Hulin, C. L. (1979). Evaluation of the Mobley, Horner, and Hollingsworth model of employee turnover. *Journal of Applied Psychology, 64*, 509–517.

Mobley, W. H. (1977). Intermediate linkages in the relationship between job satisfaction and employee turnover. *Journal of Applied Psychology, 62*, 237–240.

Mobley, W. H. (1982). *Employee turnover: Causes, consequences, and control.* Reading, MA: Addison-Wesley.

Mobley, W. H., Griffeth, R. W., Hand, H. H., & Meglino, B. M. (1979). Review and conceptual analysis of the employee turnover process. *Psychological Bulletin, 86*, 493–522.

Mobley, W. H., Horner, S. O., & Hollingsworth, A. T. (1978). An evaluation of precursors of hospital employee turnover. *Journal of Applied Psychology, 63*, 408–414.

Mowday, R. T., Koberg, C. S., & McArthur, A. W. (1984). The psychology of the withdrawal process: A cross-validation test of Mobley's intermediate linkages model of turnover in two samples. *Academy of Management Journal, 27*, 79–94.

Netermeyer, R. G., Boles, J. S., & McMurrian, R. (1996). Development and validation of work–family conflict and family–work conflict scales. *Journal of Applied Psychology, 81*, 400–410.

Newman, J. (1974). Predicting absenteeism and turnover: A field comparison of Fishbein's model and traditional job attitude measures. *Journal of Applied Psychology, 59*, 610–615.

Platt, J. R. (1964). Strong inference. *Science, 146*, 347–353.

Porter, L. W., Crampon, W. J., & Smith, F. J. (1976). Organizational commitment and managerial turnover: A longitudinal study. *Organizational Behavior and Human Performance, 15*, 87–98.

Porter, L. W., & Steers, R. M. (1973). Organizational, work, and personal factors in employee turnover and absenteeism. *Psychological Bulletin, 80*, 151–176.

Porter, L. W., Steers, R. M., Mowday, R. T., & Boulian, P. V. (1974). Organizational commitment, job satisfaction, and turnover among psychiatric technicians. *Journal of Applied Psychology, 59*, 603–609.

Price, J. L. (1977). *The study of turnover.* Ames: Iowa State University Press.

Price, J. L., & Mueller, C. W. (1981a). A causal model of turnover for nurses. *Academy of Management Journal, 24,* 543–565.

Price, J. L., & Mueller, C. W. (1981b). *Professional turnover: The cases of nurses.* New York: Spectrum Publications.

Price, J. L., & Muller, C. W. (1986). *Absenteeism and turnover of hospital employees.* Greenwich, CT: JAI Press.

Reynolds, L. (1951). *The structure of labor markets.* New York: Macmillan.

Roberts, K., Hulin, C., & Rousseau, D. (1978). *Developing an interdisciplinary science of organizations.* San Francisco: Jossey-Bass.

Rosse, J. G., & Hulin, C. L. (1985). Adaptation to work: An analysis of employee health, withdrawal, and change. *Organizational Behavior and Human Decision Processes, 36,* 324–347.

Royalty, A. B. (1998). Job-to-job and job-to-nonemployment turnover by gender and educational level. *Journal of Labor Economics, 16,* 392–443.

Rusbult, C. E., & Farrell, D. (1983). A longitudinal test of the investment model: The impact of job satisfaction, job commitment, and turnover of variations in rewards, costs, alternatives, and investments. *Journal of Applied Psychology, 68,* 429–438.

Rusbult, C. E., Farrell, D., Rogers, G., & Mainous, A. G. (1988). Impact of exchange variables on exit, voice, loyalty, and neglect: An integrative model of responses to declining job satisfaction. *Academy of Management Journal, 31,* 599–627.

Sager, J., Griffeth, R., & Hom, P. (1998). A comparison of structural models representing turnover cognitions. *Journal of Vocational Behavior, 53,* 254–273.

Schneider, K., Swan, S., & Fitzgerald, L. (1997). Job-related and psychological effects of sexual harassment in the workplace: Empirical evidence from two organizations. *Journal of Applied Psychology, 82,* 401–415.

Schuh, A. (1967). The predictability of employee tenure: A review of the literature. *Personnel Psychology, 20,* 133–152.

Smith, P. C., Kendall, L. M., & Hulin, C. L. (1969). *The measurement of satisfaction in work and retirement.* Chicago: Rand McNally.

Steel, R. P. (1996). Labor market dimensions as predictors of the reenlistment decisions of military personnel. *Journal of Applied Psychology, 81,* 421–428.

Steel, R. P., & Griffeth, R. W. (1989). The elusive relationship between perceived employment opportunity and turnover behavior: A methodological or conceptual artifact? *Journal of Applied Psychology, 74,* 846–854.

Steel, R. P., Hendrix, W. H., & Balogh, S. P. (1990). Confounding effects of the turnover base rate on relations between time lag and turnover study outcomes: An extension of meta-analysis findings and conclusions. *Journal of Organizational Behavior, 11,* 237–242.

Steel, R. P., & Ovalle, N. K., II. (1984). A review and meta-analysis of research on the relationship between behavioral intentions and employee turnover. *Journal of Applied Psychology, 69,* 673–686.

Steel, R. P., Shane, G. S., & Griffeth, R. W. (1990). Correcting turnover statistics for comparative analysis. *Academy of Management Journal, 33,* 179–187.

Steers, R., & Mowday, R. (1981). Employee turnover and post-decision accommodation process. In L. Cummings & B. Staw (Eds.), *Research in organizational behavior* (Vol. 3, pp. 237–249). Greenwich, CT: JAI Press.

Tett, R. P., & Meyer, J. P. (1993). Job satisfaction, organizational commitment, turnover intention, and turnover: Path analyses based on meta-analytic findings. *Personnel Psychology, 46,* 259–293.

Triandis, H. C. (1977). *Interpersonal behavior.* Monterey, CA: Brooks/Cole.

Van Zelst, R., & Kerr, W. (1953). Workers' attitudes toward merit rating. *Personnel Psychology, 6,* 159–172.

Vroom, V. H. (1964). *Work and motivation.* New York: Wiley.

Waters, L. K., Roach, D., & Waters, C. W. (1976). Estimates of future tenure, satisfaction, and biographical variables as predictors of termination. *Personnel Psychology, 29,* 57–60.

Weitz, J., & Nuckols, R. (1953). The validity of direct and indirect questions in measuring job satisfaction. *Personnel Psychology, 5,* 487–494.

Wickert, F. (1951). Turnover, and employees' feelings of ego-involvement in the day-to-day operations of a company. *Personnel Psychology, 4,* 185–197.

Williams, C. (1990). Deciding when, how, and if to correct turnover correlations. *Journal of Applied Psychology, 75,* 732–737.

Williams, C., & Livingstone, L. (1994). Another look at the relationship between performance and voluntary turnover. *Academy of Management Journal, 37,* 269–298.

Withey, M. J., & Cooper, W. H. (1989). Predicting exit, voice, loyalty, and neglect. *Administrative Science Quarterly, 34,* 521–539.

Youngblood, S. A., Mobley, W. H., & Meglino, B. M. (1983). A longitudinal analysis of the turnover process. *Journal of Applied Psychology, 68,* 507–516.

Chapter 9

Turnover: An Integration of Lee and Mitchell's Unfolding Model and Job Embeddedness Construct With Hulin's Withdrawal Construct

Chris J. Sablynski
University of Washington

Thomas W. Lee
University of Washington

Terence R. Mitchell
University of Washington

James P. Burton
University of Washington

Brooks C. Holtom
Marquette University

Two notable approaches toward studying employee withdrawal and voluntary turnover have been developed by Hulin and colleagues (e.g., Hanisch, Hulin, & Roznowski, 1998; Hulin, 1991; Hulin & Ilgen, 2000) and Lee and Mitchell and colleagues (Lee & Mitchell, 1994; Lee, Mitchell, Holtom, McDaniel, & Hill, 1999; Lee, Mitchell, Wise, & Fireman, 1996). Hulin and colleagues have been studying organizational withdrawal as a general construct encompassing turnover, absenteeism, and other behaviors. Lee and Mitchell's unfolding model of turnover (Lec & Mitchell, 1994; Lee et al., 1996, 1999) and their conceptualized job embeddedness construct (Mitchell, Holtom, Lee, Erez, & Sablynski, 1999) focus on understanding why people leave and why they stay with their organizations. In this chapter, we address two questions about these two related streams of research and theorizing. First, how are these two approaches similar and how are they different? Second, what can be learned from each approach that helps us deepen our understanding of employee behavior—specifically that of withdrawal and voluntary turnover? Thus, the goal of this chapter is to expand thinking about employee attachment and withdrawal.

We begin by examining Hulin's contributions with a focus on turnover. This is followed by a review of Lee, Mitchell, and colleagues' work on why people leave and why they stay with their organizations. Finally, we integrate the two approaches and suggest ways to enhance our understanding of turnover and a family of behaviors related to employee "attachment" and "detachment" from organizations.

HULIN'S ADAPTATION–WITHDRAWAL CONSTRUCT

Organizational withdrawal has a rich and long history of research in organizational behavior and Industrial and Organizational (I-O) Psychology. Hanisch and Hulin (1991) defined withdrawal as "a general construct composed of a variety of acts, or surrogate intentions, that reflect both the negativity of the precipitating job attitudes and the target of these negative job attitudes" (p. 111). More recently, Hanisch (1995) defined organizational withdrawal as . . . a construct denoting various behaviors employees engage in to remove themselves from their job or avoid work" (p. 604).

The foundations of Hulin's organizational withdrawal construct can be traced back to early studies interested in exploring the attitude–behavior relationship. Many of these studies examined the relationship between job attitudes such as job satisfaction and work behaviors such as absenteeism, tardiness, and turnover (see Porter & Steers, 1973, for a review). Hulin's (1966, 1968) early work, for example, documented a negative relationship between job satisfaction and turnover. In developing the implications of these findings, Hulin drew upon the theorizing of Doob (1947) and Thurstone (1931), who argued that attitudes are not related to single isolated behaviors but instead to patterns or syndromes of behaviors. In addition, Rice and Trist (1952), Hill and Trist (1955), March and Simon (1958), and Herzberg, Mausner, Peterson, and Capwell (1957) developed models of organizational withdrawal that describe how dissatisfied employees withdraw from their organizations. These researchers proposed that, over time, dissatisfied employees offer some (simple or complex) behavioral or attitudinal indicators of their desire to remove themselves from their jobs or organizations. Building on the ideas of patterns of behaviors, time, and families of behaviors, Hulin's current conceptualization of organizational withdrawal began to emerge in papers published from the mid-1980s through the early 1990s.

Hulin and colleagues' work during this time serves as the cornerstone of our current understanding of the organizational withdrawal process. For example, Hulin (1984) called for researchers to redirect their attention toward behavioral patterns or syndromes representing theoretical constructs and away from specific behaviors. Following Rosse and Miller's (1984) initial model of employee adaptation, Rosse and Hulin (1985) developed a general model of adaptation, which linked work environment dissatisfaction with withdrawal behaviors and attempts to change working conditions. Their data confirmed that adaptation predicted records of tardiness, lateness, and turnover. These studies signaled the need to examine a variety of criteria in the general attitude $\rightarrow$ general behavior equation and the interrelationships among these criteria. During the same period, Hulin, Roznowski, and Hachiya's (1985) labor economic model offered a major new perspective in the attitude–behavior relationship in turnover theory: that the attractiveness of work alternatives directly affect job satisfaction, a reversal of the contention that it is satisfaction that influences the attractiveness of alternatives (Hom & Griffeth, 1995).

In yet another contribution, Hanisch and Hulin (1990) found evidence of two factors of the withdrawal construct in their study of the retirement pattern of university employees. The first factor focused on work withdrawal and was defined by such behaviors as lateness and absenteeism, which represent ways for employees to withdraw from work while maintaining their organizational and work role membership. The second factor represented job withdrawal and was defined by behaviors such as turnover intentions, desire to retire, and intended retirement age. Each of these behaviors represents employees' efforts to remove themselves from their work role or organization. Work withdrawal maintains role and organization membership, whereas job withdrawal does not. Subsequent studies confirmed a causal model of attitudes and these withdrawal behaviors (Hanisch & Hulin, 1991). Work and job withdrawal behaviors are correlated and make up a general organizational withdrawal factor. Employee dissatisfaction is linked to a pattern of work/job/organizational withdrawal activities such as increased absenteeism, lateness, unfavorable job behaviors and (where feasible) retirement (Hanisch & Hulin, 1991).

Hulin (1991) provided an in-depth look at withdrawal, adaptation, and commitment. He offers a modified organizational adaptation–withdrawal model that is drawn from various models of organizational withdrawal including the independent form model, the spillover model, the alternative forms model, the compensatory model, and the progression-of-withdrawal model (see Hom & Griffeth, 1995, for a review of these models). Hulin's model includes several antecedents of job/work role satisfaction including work role inputs (e.g., skills, time, effort), utility of direct and opportunity costs (e.g., local unemployment rates), frames of reference for evaluating job outcomes (e.g., past experience), and work role outcomes (e.g., salary/wages, fringe benefits). The model predicts that dissatisfied employees may exhibit various intention–behavior relationships, including (a) intentions to increase job outcomes that would lead to specific attempts to increase job outcomes (e.g., steal, moonlight); (b) intentions to reduce job inputs that would lead to psychological job withdrawal (e.g., miss meetings, take long coffee breaks); (c) intentions to reduce work role inclusion that would lead to behavioral job withdrawal/avoidance (e.g., tardiness, absenteeism, quitting); and (d) intentions to change one's work role that would lead to specific change behaviors (e.g., unionization activity).

One of the strengths of this model is the broad family of behavioral outcomes including aggression and sabotage that Hulin integrates into the withdrawal construct. This broader focus should lead not just to a greater general understanding of additional withdrawal behaviors (e.g., transfer, absenteeism, sabotage, and turnover) but also offer a glimpse at an underlying psychological mechanism used by employees from a more general psychological approach (Hulin, 1991).

Hulin and associates (Hanisch et al., 1998; Hulin, 1998) continued to argue forcefully for the study of a family of withdrawal behaviors rather than single, often highly visible, isolated behaviors (i.e., absenteeism, lateness, turnover). They emphasize that by examining attitudes and patterns of organizational withdrawal behaviors, we can move closer to understanding the adaptation and withdrawal process from the employee's perspective (Hulin, 1998).

Efforts to refine, clarify, and expand the measurement and modeling of the adaptation–withdrawal construct continue today. Hulin and colleagues continue to expand the set of behavioral indicators subsumed under the withdrawal construct. For example, recent studies have extended the model to study sexual harassment (Fitzgerald, Drasgow, Hulin, Gelfland, & Magley, 1997; Glomb, Munson, Hulin, Bergman, & Drasgow, 1999). In addition, developments in computational modeling now allow the testing of the relationships among various withdrawal behaviors and organizational interventions (Hanisch, 2000).

THE CONTRIBUTIONS OF LEE, MITCHELL, AND ASSOCIATES

In this section we describe Lee and Mitchell's unfolding model of voluntary turnover and the job embeddedness construct. These ideas have developed over the last 10 years and began when Lee, Mitchell, and associates decided to reassess the traditional theories of voluntary turnover.

Why People Leave: The Unfolding Model

Traditional theory and research on employee turnover assumes an underlying model that employees follow an intentionally rational decision-making process (March & Simon, 1958). In particular, employees who are dissatisfied with their jobs or companies are assumed first to identify specific benefits and costs brought on by quitting, and second to calculate the relative values of staying versus leaving. It is also assumed that those people who gain more by leaving will soon do so, whereas those who gain more by staying will continue on their jobs (e.g., Hom & Griffeth, 1995).

Lee and Mitchell (1994) proposed that instead of a single process that involves maximizing returns, turnover occurs via four distinctive paths. In three of the paths, turnover is initiated by a precipitating event, which they call a shock to the system, a stochastic event, (e.g., getting passed over for a promotion) instead of being induced by accumulated job dissatisfaction. In Path 1, a shock triggers a preexisting action plan. That is, an employee already knows what to do based on preexisting action plans; a shock engages the plan. For example, an employee's spouse may retire (the shock), and then, that employee quits in order to travel with the retired spouse (the action plan). In Path 2, the shock elicits such a strong (and usually negative) reaction that quitting occurs almost immediately. For instance, a person may be passed over for promotion and then become so angry that he or she quits without considering job alternatives. In Path 3, the shock causes a more extensive evaluation process that involves the comparison of job alternatives. For example, an unsolicited job opportunity may cause that employee to imagine life with a different company. Instead of leaving because of dissatisfaction with the current job, the employee is attracted away by the promise of a better position. Path 4, which has two "subpaths," involves no shock and is similar to the dissatisfaction-induced ideas from traditional turnover theory. In Path 4a, the employee and organization grow apart, until the employee's felt dissatisfaction becomes too great and the employee leaves regardless of the presence or absence of job alternatives. In Path 4b, accumulated job dissatisfaction leads to searching for alternatives, comparing the costs and benefits of these alternatives relative to the current job and deciding to quit.

To date, there have been two empirical studies on the unfolding model. In the first empirical test, a qualitative study was conducted involving 44 nurses (Lee et al., 1996). Based on in-depth and semistructured interviews, 6, 6, 8, and 13 quitting nurses could be reliably classified into Paths 1–4, respectively (33 of 44, or 75%). In the second empirical test, a survey study involving a random sample of 229 former public accountants, 6, 7, 136 and 63 leavers could be reliably classified into Paths 1–4, respectively, with the modified classification system (212 of 229, or 92.6%). In sum, people who left could be reliably classified into one of the four paths.

Why People Stay: Job Embeddedness

Traditional models of voluntary turnover, Hulin's general model of withdrawal, and Lee and Mitchell's unfolding model, provide a variety of explanations for why employees leave their organizations. However, far less is known about the psychological processes behind remaining with one's organization (Maertz & Campion, 1998). The attachment literature notes that job satisfaction, organizational commitment, and job involvement are important constructs influencing one's decision to leave an organization (Hom & Griffeth, 1995). In addition, other factors involved in the decision to leave or stay are made salient by the unfolding model (Lee et al., 1996). For example, many of the nurses from the Lee et al. (1996) sample who left their jobs described organizational and personal factors (i.e., different types of shocks) that precipitated their decisions. Issues such as work–family balance, attachments to the community, and relationships with co-workers surfaced as reasons precipitating withdrawal in focus groups and interviews with employees. There is empirical evidence that reference group membership influences attachment (Reichers, 1985), that employment rates and opportunities to obtain work influence the turnover process (Hulin et al., 1985), and that marital status and the presence of children at home are related to turnover (Lee & Maurer, 1999).

With the knowledge that organizational factors and off-the-job factors are important factors influencing why people stay and leave organizations, Lee, Mitchell, and colleagues developed the *job embeddedness* construct. In terms of retention, this construct is conceptualized as the extent to which a person has links to other people or activities (both on and off the job), the extent to which a job was similar to, or fit, with the other aspects in their life space, and the ease with which attachments could be broken (i.e., what people would give up if they left). These three dimensions—links, fit, and sacrifice—can be applied to the organization and community.

In the first empirical test of the construct, Mitchell et al. (1999) found job embeddedness predicted both intent to leave and voluntary turnover. Further, job embeddedness predicted significant incremental variance over and above job satisfaction and organizational commitment. In other words, many nonattitudinal factors influence a person to stay on the job.

INTEGRATION OF WITHDRAWAL CONSTRUCT AND UNFOLDING MODEL AND JOB EMBEDDEDNESS CONSTRUCT

As two notable theories of employee turnover (Maertz & Campion, 1998), Hulin's withdrawal model (Hulin, 1991; Rosse & Hulin, 1985) and Lee and Mitchell's unfolding model (Lee & Mitchell, 1994; Lee et al., 1996,

1999) and subsequent job embeddedness construct (Mitchell et al., 1999) represent different approaches toward understanding employee withdrawal. In this section, we investigate whether integrating elements of each model provides greater leverage than each model taken alone in understanding what factors affect an employee's attachment or withdrawal from an organization.

Although there are many aspects of each approach available for discussion, we concentrate only on those areas that may help us understand the processes behind why people leave and why people stay with their organizations. These include the underlying purpose of each model, the notion of behavioral patterns, time, decision making, attitudes, and the antecedents and consequences posited by each approach.

Purpose

The two models clearly differ in their purpose. As previously described, the Hulin approach examines the relationships between dissatisfaction and a broad family of interrelated behaviors indicative of an underlying withdrawal construct (e.g., Hulin, 1998). The behaviors are a variety of "escape" routes for dissatisfied or discontent employees and range from attempts to reduce the stress of a job to actually leaving a job. Although these escape routes or behaviors are often characterized as "negative" by organizational researchers and practitioners, such behavior is merely adaptive from the employee's perspective (Hulin, 1991).

Lee and Mitchell seek to answer why people leave (the unfolding model) and why they stay (job embeddedness) with their organizations. The unfolding model was originally descriptive—it sought to represent the different routes involved in leaving (Lee & Mitchell, 1994; Lee et al., 1996, 1999). They found that leaving happened by many routes (i.e., paths) and only some of those routes reflected an escape from dissatisfaction. Thus, although the unfolding model broadened our view of how people leave organizations, it kept a narrow view of the criterion (turnover). This approach is the exact opposite of Hulin's emphasis on broadening the criteria.

In terms of why people stay, Lee and Mitchell's preliminary findings suggest that job embeddedness may be a dominant force until a shock (Paths 1, 2, or 3) or accumulated job dissatisfaction (Path 4) pushes people out of their embeddedness/inertia. In addition, their current research suggests that job embeddedness may buffer such shocks or dissatisfaction, allowing employees to maintain their attachment with the organization. That is, highly embedded employees may experience and react to a shock very differently from less embedded employees.

Behavioral Patterns

The notion of behavioral patterns is important to examine as well. Hulin sees these as resulting from employee job dissatisfaction (Hanisch et al., 1998; Hanisch, Hulin, & Seitz, 1996). The paths in the Lee and Mitchell unfolding model may be behavioral patterns of decisions related to work withdrawal (Lee & Mitchell, 1994; Lee et al., 1999). A key difference in the two approaches is that in the unfolding model, paths to turnover are not always initiated by accumulated dissatisfaction—a very important component of Hulin's (1991) organizational withdrawal model. Lee and Mitchell find that about one half of their leavers experience shocks before leaving. Among their samples of accountants and nurses, more of them reported leaving because of a shocking event than because of low levels of satisfaction (Lee et al., 1999). In addition, these shocks are often positive or unexpected and many occur outside of the organization. In other words, the shocks are simply not the result of negative affect. The job embeddedness construct is also mostly nonaffective. In other words, people may be dissatisfied (or have a shock) but stay because they are embedded. Borrowing from the Hulin approach, further examination of the relationship between a variety of other withdrawal behaviors (i.e., deviance, sabotage, taking long breaks) and job embeddedness may prove useful in determining if job embeddedness reduces the probability of such behavior. In addition, it may be useful to consider assessing a broader family of variables that operate to embed an employee in an organization as well as the antecedents of job embeddedness.

Time

Time is an important element of the Hulin, Lee, and Mitchell approaches. Organizational withdrawal is, by its very nature, a dynamic construct, and employees presumably cycle through the model repeatedly until job/work role satisfaction is improved in some way (Hulin, 1998). However, as Hulin points out, most of the work done in the area has relied on cross-sectional studies using seemingly arbitrary points for data collection and subsequent analysis (Hulin, 1998). Computational modeling and studies that incorporate time have the potential to capture the dynamic relationships between attitudes and withdrawal behaviors (Hanisch et al., 1998; Hulin & Ilgen, 2000).

Time is also important in the unfolding model and job embeddedness construct. For example, in the unfolding model, there is the time between a shock, thinking about leaving, deciding to leave, and actual leaving. If accumulated job dissatisfaction exists, then there is the time between deciding to leave and actually leaving. The length of this time varies across paths. For example, Lee at al. (1999) found that the time between first thoughts of quitting and the decision to leave occurred significantly more quickly in Path 1 than in Path 3 and Path 4b. This is expected because Paths 3 and 4b include the evaluation of alternatives, whereas Path 1 does not.

In addition, in most empirical work examining withdrawal, increasing the time between the assessment of thoughts or intentions (survey) and the action of withdrawing weakens the association between the variables (Steel & Ovalle, 1984). However, the relationships between variables over time may be different for job embeddedness. We propose that the passage of time will strengthen a person's job embeddedness. Although time may weaken the association between attitudes and behavior, some dimensions of job embeddedness are likely to get stronger with time independent of affect (fit). That is, one may become a member of various work teams, community activities (links), and build up work "credits" of various sorts (sacrifice). Thus, overall job embeddedness probably increases over time, other things being equal. Exploration into the interaction of shocks, the passage of time, and job embeddedness is needed. This concurs with Hulin's (1998) call for research that incorporates the temporal nature of behavioral processes in organizations.

Decision Making

Hulin's withdrawal construct requires decision making in the adaptation process. Hanisch et al. (1996) stated that these decisions are made in bounded rationality with a satisficing framework. Decisions are related to such concepts as attitudes, past reinforcement histories, and local economic conditions (Hulin, 1991). Other factors such as luck, habit, inertia, and labor-market pressures may also affect the level and type of decisions employees make during the withdrawal process (Hulin et al., 1985).

Lee and Mitchell's approach identifies different kinds of decisions. Image theory (i.e., Beach, 1993) is one important component of the unfolding model. Here, individuals filter the constant inflow of information they receive and determine via "screening" whether this incoming information becomes part of the options available in the decision-making process, which could lead to potential changes in behavior. This process occurs quickly, usually requiring little cognitive effort and is a precursor to intended rational decision-making (e.g., maximizing expected utilities). Other types of decisions in the model include (a) script-driven decisions, that is, Path 1; (b) image-driven decisions (do not fit–leave), that is, Paths 2 and 4a; and (c) dissatisfaction–search–compare–leave decisions (i.e., Paths 3 and 4b). From image theory, Paths 2 and 4a are compatibility decisions. Paths 3 and 4b are more rational, expected-value-like choices. Thus, the unfolding model suggests some very different types of decisions that recur in the different paths.

Attitudes

The attitude–behavior link is emphasized by Hulin and associates (i.e., Hanisch et al., 1996). Job affect and job adaptation play important roles in organizational withdrawal (Hulin, 1991).

In the unfolding model, dissatisfaction is the main precipitating construct in Paths 4a and 4b. It is also important in Path 3, as relative satisfaction or dissatisfaction can occur. For example, you could leave a job that you liked for a job even more appealing (the shock) or you could receive a transfer that makes you unhappy thereby beginning the process of judging alternatives and potentially leaving. Although important to the understanding of turnover (Griffeth, Hom, & Gaertner, 2000; Hom & Griffeth, 1995) and withdrawal (Hulin, 1991), satisfaction is clearly not the main focus of the unfolding model nor the job embeddedness construct. For example, in the unfolding model's Paths 2 and 4a, compatibility is a crucial determinant of what happens and compatibility is not an attitude. In addition, Path 1 is script driven. Thus, three of the five possible exit paths include a process that is not completely caused by attitudes.

Antecedents and Consequences

Hulin and colleagues seek to broaden the criteria related to job/work role satisfaction. The withdrawal construct is manifested through a variety of behaviors and cognitions; turnover is merely one of these and its study as an isolated behavioral response has "little scientific merit" (Hulin, 1991, p. 446).

In terms of antecedents, Hulin acknowledges that both work and nonwork factors affect the process of withdrawal. Such factors as local economic conditions (as part of the frames of reference for evaluating job outcomes), local unemployment rates, and available alternatives (as part of the utility of direct and opportunity costs) are considered in the leaving process. Hom and Hulin (1981) suggested that rates of joblessness may indirectly ("spuriously") affect the withdrawal process by impacting the quit base rate. Essentially, high unemployment depresses turnover rates, thereby attenuating relationships between turnover and its antecedents (Steel & Griffeth, 1989). Also, high employment may encourage marginal workers, whose decision processes about leaving jobs may not map onto those of regular, full-time workers, to join the workforce (Hulin et al., 1985).

   Lee and Mitchell and colleagues seek to broaden our understanding of the process leading to the singular behavior of voluntary turnover. For example, antecedents such as "shocks to the system," the psychological decision processes involved in quitting a job, and the paths involved in leaving an organization are key components of the unfolding model. In addition, job embeddedness provides us with a better understanding of employees' organizational and community links, fit, and sacrifice, which are key antecedents of the decision to stay or leave (Mitchell et al., 1999).

   In the spirit of integrating organizational withdrawal and job embeddedness, perhaps the two are on opposite ends of a continuum. As employees immerse themselves in their jobs, organizations, and communities (i.e., become highly embedded), they may be less likely to attempt to withdraw from the organization via changing their job outcomes (e.g., steal), reducing job inputs (e.g., take long coffee breaks), changing their work role (e.g., transfer or actively pursue unionization), or reducing their role inclusion (e.g., quit). We expect that job embeddedness will have a positive relationship with organizationally beneficial outcomes and a negative relationship with organizationally harmful ones. Current research in this area seems to support this proposition.

CONCLUSION

Hulin and colleagues have taken an underlying negative affective construct and suggested how it is played out in a set of withdrawal behaviors. Their study of general attitudes and behaviors and call for examination of the manifest scope of underlying constructs have helped us to view turnover as part of a set of behavioral and cognitive responses to an unsatisfactory work environment. Lee and Mitchell's unfolding model and job embeddedness construct complement Hulin's idea by investigating (a) the ways that nonnegative attitudes or events can precipitate leaving, and (b) how a predominantly nonaffective construct like job embeddedness may deflect negative events or feelings and sustain attachment. In addition, the Lee, Mitchell, and colleagues' approach brings a number of new constructs to the investigation of turnover. We look at shocks as initiating leaving. We describe script-driven exits. We describe how positive events or people who are satisfied may leave. We discuss leaving without searching. We suggest the external, off-the-job aspects of job embeddedness that may keep people in their jobs. Neither the unfolding model nor the job embeddedness construct is a competitive theory to Hulin's conceptualization. Instead, they complement what is known and expand and/or push the existing theory and research in new directions by putting organizational reality and life's complexity back into our thinking.

FUTURE RESEARCH

Our examination of the Hulin withdrawal construct and the Lee and Mitchell unfolding model/job embeddedness construct suggests many areas for further research. To date, job embeddedness has been conceptualized as an aggregate multidimensional construct; the more embedded one is, the more likely he or she will remain in the organization and be productive (Mitchell et. al., 1999). However, future research should address the degree to which the different dimensions of embeddedness influence specific outcomes. For example, the three organizational subdimensions may have a stronger relationship with in-role and extra-role performance than the community subdimensions will.

In addition, studies examining the relationships between the subdimensions of job embeddedness, the unfolding model, and organizational withdrawal may provide valuable insight into voluntary turnover. For example, will dissatisfied, low-embedded employees choose to reduce the number of links they have with the organization and the community? If so, which link would be reduced first? Why? Will dissatisfied employees with high levels of organizational sacrifice be absent frequently? Would dissatisfaction interact with nonaffective shocks to expedite an employee's withdrawal from an organization? What is the interaction between the type of shock and the degree to which one is embedded? What are the antecedents of different levels of job embeddedness? When negative emotions are triggered, will job embeddedness or one of its subdimensions (e.g., links to the community) focus attention away from work, allowing an employee to remain with an organization? Will cultural differences impact organizational withdrawal and job embeddedness? Although Hulin (1991) discussed satisfaction across cultures via the social information modeling approach, there may be important cross-cultural differences that explain variance in withdrawal and/or turnover in the two approaches. If so, at what point do they enter the equation? These and many other questions suggest research opportunities waiting to be explored.

Focusing on the singular withdrawal behavior of turnover, it is fair to say that while we as researchers have come a long way in understanding its processes, we have not yet "hit a home run" in our ability to understand and predict the behavior. Maertz and Campion (1998) noted that despite the multitude of turnover studies, the empirical relationships between models of voluntary turnover behavior have been modest. The question of why this is the case remains. Perhaps, as Hulin suggests, the process of removing oneself from an organization is just too complex to be assessed by a single measure such as turnover. Or, perhaps, as he also suggests, our widely applied approaches and measures (i.e., cross-sectional assessments of job satisfaction and organizational commitment) are not fully capturing the underlying forces at work. Hulin's approach focuses on the former—seeking to expand the study toward a wider set of behaviors, all reflecting the same underlying construct. That is, Hulin seeks to understand the various ways employees "get out" of their organizations. Lee and Mitchell's approach looks at the latter—seeking to expand the study of the antecedents of voluntary turnover to understand why people leave as well as how they "get into" their organizations. Over time, perhaps this research will become symbiotic, benefiting researchers exploring the various processes involved in attachment, organizational withdrawal, and turnover.

REFERENCES

Beach, L. R. (1993). *Making the right decision*. Englewood Cliffs, NJ: Prentice-Hall.

Doob, L. W. (1947). The behavior of attitudes. *Psychological Review, 45*, 135–156.

Fitzgerald, L. F., Drasgow, F., Hulin, C. L., Gelfand, M. J., & Magley, V. J. (1997). Antecedents and consequences of sexual harassment in organizations: A test of an integrated model. *Journal of Applied Psychology, 82*(4), 578–589.

Glomb, T. M., Munson, L. J., Hulin, C. L., Bergman, M. E., & Drasgow, F. (1999). Structural equation models of sexual harassment: Longitudinal explorations and cross-sectional generalizations. *Journal of Applied Psychology, 84*(1), 14–28.

Griffeth, R. W., Hom, P. W., & Gaertner, S. (2000). A meta-analysis of antecedents and correlates of employee turnover: Update, moderator tests, and research implications for the next millenium. *Journal of Management, 26*, 463–488.

Hanisch, K. A. (1995). Organizational withdrawal. In N. Nicholson (Ed.), *The Blackwell encyclopedic dictionary of organizational behavior* (p. 604). Cambridge, MA: Blackwell.

Hanisch, K. A. (2000). The impact of organizational interventions on behaviors: An examination of different models of withdrawal. In D. R. Ilgen & C. L. Hulin (Eds.), *Computational modeling of behavior in organizations: The third scientific discipline* (pp. 33–60). Washington, DC: American Psychological Association.

Hanisch, K. A., & Hulin, C. L. (1990). Job attitudes and employee withdrawal: An examination of retirement and other voluntary organizational behaviors. *Journal of Vocational Behavior, 37*, 60–78.

Hanisch, K. A., & Hulin, C. L. (1991). General attitudes and organizational withdrawal: An evaluation of a causal model. *Journal of Vocational Behavior, 39*, 110–128.

Hanisch, K. A., Hulin, C. L., & Roznowski, M. (1998). The importance of individuals' repertoires of behaviors: The scientific appropriateness of studying multiple behaviors and general attitudes. *Journal of Organizational Behavior, 19*, 463–480.

Hanisch, K. A., Hulin, C. L., & Seitz, S. T. (1996). Mathematical/computational modeling of organizational withdrawal processes: Benefits, methods, and results. In G. R. Ferris (Ed.), *Research in personnel and human resources management* (Vol. 14, pp. 91–142). Greenwich, CT: JAI Press.

Herzberg, F., Mausner, B., Peterson, R., & Capwell, D. (1957). *Job attitudes: Review of research and opinion*. Pittsburgh, PA: Psychological Service of Pittsburgh.

Hill, J. M., & Trist, E. L. (1955). Changes in accidents and other absences with length of service: A further study of their incidence and relation to each other in an iron and steel works. *Human Relations, 8*, 121–152.

Hom, P. W., & Griffeth, R. W. (1995). *Employee turnover*. Cincinnati, OH: South-Western College Publishing.

Hom, P. W., & Hulin, C. L. (1981). A competitive test of prediction of reenlistment by several models. *Journal of Applied Psychology, 66,* 23–39.

Hulin, C. L. (1966). Job satisfaction and turnover in a female clerical population. *Journal of Applied Psychology, 50,* 280–285.

Hulin, C. L. (1968). The effects of changes in job satisfaction levels on turnover. *Journal of Applied Psychology, 52,* 122–126.

Hulin, C. L. (1984). Suggested directions for defining, measuring, and controlling absenteeism. In P. S. Goodman & R. S. Atkin (Eds.), *Absenteeism: New approaches to understanding, measuring and managing employee absence* (pp. 391–420). San Francisco: Jossey-Bass.

Hulin, C. L. (1991). Adaptations, persistence, and commitment in organizations. In M. D. Dunnette & L. M. Hough, *Handbook of industrial and organizational psychology* (Vol. 2, 2nd ed., pp. 445–506). Palo Alto, CA: Consulting Psychologists Press.

Hulin, C. L. (1998, April). *Behaviors, constructs, and time: Potholes on the road well traveled.* Invited address presented at the Society for Industrial and Organizational Psychology, Dallas, TX.

Hulin, C. L., & Ilgen, D. R. (2000). Introduction to computational modeling in organizations: The good that modeling does. In D. R. Ilgen & C. L. Hulin (Eds.), *Computational modeling of behavior in organizations: The third scientific discipline* (pp. 3–18). Washington, DC: American Psychological Association.

Hulin, C. L., Roznowski, M., & Hachiya, D. (1985). Alternative opportunities and withdrawal decisions: Empirical and theoretical discrepancies and an integration. *Psychological Bulletin, 97,* 233–250.

Lee, T. W., & Maurer, S. D. (1999). The effects of family structure on organizational commitment, intention to leave and voluntary turnover. *Journal of Managerial Issues, 11,* 493–513.

Lee, T. W., & Mitchell, T. R. (1994). An alternative approach: The unfolding model of voluntary employee turnover. *Academy of Management Review, 19,* 51–89.

Lee, T. W., Mitchell, T. R., Holtom, B., McDaniel, L., & Hill, J. W. (1999). The unfolding model of turnover: A replication and extension. *Academy of Management Journal, 22*(4), 450–463.

Lee, T. W., Mitchell, T. R., Wise, L., & Fireman, S. (1996). An unfolding model of voluntary employee turnover. *Academy of Management Journal, 39,* 5–36.

Maertz, C. P., Jr., & Campion, M. A. (1998). 25 years of voluntary turnover research: A review and critique. *International Review of IO Psychology, 13,* 49–81.

March, J. G., & Simon, H. A. (1958). *Organizations.* New York: Wiley.

Mitchell, T. R., Holtom, B. C., Lee, T. W., Erez, M., & Sablynski, C. J. (1999, August). *The retention of employees: The role of organizational embeddedness.* Paper presented at the meeting of the Academy of Management, Chicago, IL.

Porter, L. W., & Steers, R. M. (1973). Organizational, work, and personal factors in employee turnover and absenteeism. *Psychological Bulletin, 80*(2), 151–176.

Reichers, A. (1985). A review and reconceptualization of organizational commitment. *Academy of Management Review, 10,* 465–476.

Rice, A. K., & Trist, E. L. (1952). Institutional and subinstitutional determinants of change in labor turnover. *Human Relations, 5,* 347–372.

Rosse, J. G., & Hulin, C. L. (1985). Adaptation to work: An analysis of employee health, withdrawal, and change. *Organizational Behavior and Human Decision Processes, 36,* 324–347.

Rosse, J. G., & Miller, H. E. (1984). Relationship between absenteeism and other employee behaviors. In P. S. Goodman & R. S. Atkins (Eds.), *Absenteeism: New approaches to understanding, measuring, and managing employee absence.* San Francisco, CA: Jossey-Bass.

Steel, R. P., & Griffeth, R. W. (1989). The elusive relationship between perceived employment opportunity and turnover behavior: A methodological or conceptual artifact? *Journal of Applied Psychology, 74,* 846–854.

Steel, R. P., & Ovalle, N. K., II. (1984). A review and meta-analysis of research on the relationship between behavioral intentions and employee turnover. *Journal of Applied Psychology, 69,* 673–686.

Thurstone, L. L. (1931). The measurement of social attitudes. *Journal of Abnormal and Social Psychology, 26,* 249–269.

Chapter 10

Emotional Reserve
and Adaptation to Job Dissatisfaction

Howard E. Miller
Minnesota State University, Mankato

Joseph G. Rosse
University of Colorado

What happens when people are dissatisfied at work? That question has led to thousands of studies of job satisfaction, including investigations of job satisfaction measures in relation to other internal constructs, such as commitment, loyalty, and intentions, as well as with more observable constructs, such as turnover, absence, tardiness, and voice (Locke, 1976; Rosse, 1991). In this chapter, we discuss how people adapt to dissatisfying work conditions, building on a model of employee adaptation (Rosse & Miller, 1984). Our original model had been developed for a conference on absence to help organize our thinking about how people respond to dissatisfaction at work. There have been substantial theoretical and empirical developments reported in the research literature since our work adaptation model was published. We offer an update on our model in this chapter, reflecting key changes in our understanding of adaptation based on recent research developments. We hypothesize that three constructs, *emotional arousability, emotional reserve,* and *emotional control* may play important roles in how low job satisfaction manifests behaviorally in the work place. We also discuss measurement and research design issues for conducting empirical tests of relations among measures of adaptation behaviors and job satisfaction.

ADAPTATION TO JOB DISSATISFACTION

Organizational researchers have long been interested in how employees respond when dissatisfied with work and life. Although many scholars investigated job satisfaction in relation to one behavior or another in isolation (Miller, 1981), there had been suggestions along the way that the varieties of behaviors correlated with low job satisfaction may share a common theme—behavioral withdrawal from work (Herzberg, Mausner, Peterson, & Capwell, 1957; Lyons, 1972).

We used the withdrawal construct as one of four broad behavioral outcomes of dissatisfaction in developing our model for the Carnegie Mellon absenteeism conference (Rosse & Miller, 1984.) We formulated a simple model of employee adaptation in which we proposed that multiple behavioral families (behavioral withdrawal, psychological withdrawal, voice/attempts at constructive change, and retaliation) were all related to employees' dissatisfaction with work. From this perspective, the behavior families represent different strategies for adapting to, or coping with, dissatisfaction. Adaptations were considered positive if they helped reduce the source of dissatisfaction, and negative if they served to exacerbate the source of dissatisfaction. *Neutral adaptations*—those that have no effect on the source of dissatisfaction—were the most challenging to model, as it was unclear how long people would respond similarly when the source of dissatisfaction was unaffected by their behavioral choices. The choice of behavioral family was hypothesized to be affected by personal experience, vicarious learning, social norms, and environmental constraints or facilitators. One important implication from this model is that adaptation need be understood as an interaction over time of the person with her or his work environment (e.g., supervisor, colleagues, clients, etc.), so that understanding job satisfaction as it relates to behavior sets requires data that captures a stream of interactions of the person with others in the work environment, from triggering event to resolution of satisfaction (or exit/leaving the field.)

Rosse and Hulin (1985), using a rich multiwave, but small sample data set, found some support for the model, including the finding that dissatisfied employees who did not choose an adaptive response (i.e., defaulting to the neutral adaptation category) experienced more physical and mental health symptoms than those who successfully adapted. Significant theoretical and empirical research has been conducted since 1984, offering refinements in our understanding both of behavior families (Rosse, 1991) and of job satisfaction (Weiss & Cropanzano, 1996.) We turn to a discussion of these developments.

Behavioral Families

As noted, a plethora of studies have explored the relationship between job satisfaction and turnover (Rosse, 1991). Substantial numbers of those studies investigated the association between job satisfaction and other behaviors, such as absence, lateness, goldbricking, and reduced productivity.

As a result of this research activity, there is substantial agreement that job satisfaction is negatively related, although weakly, to behaviors that represent withdrawal from, or avoidance of, unpleasant work conditions. Satisfaction measures have correlated most strongly with other attitude measures, such as commitment and intent to leave (Locke, 1976); relations with observable behaviors have been strongest with voluntary turnover followed by volitional absenteeism (Rosse, 1991.) The smaller body of evidence regarding job satisfaction–lateness relations suggests a more tentative relationship may also exist with this form of job withdrawal (Blau, 1994.) Some evidence also suggests that there may be a "progression of withdrawal" beginning with employees showing up late, and culminating with resignation from the job (Gupta & Jenkins, 1982; Rosse, 1988.)

An important shift in thinking took place among some researchers in this field in the last 15 or so years, as increasing evidence has shown that behaviors such as these are better understood when considered as manifestations of broad underlying behavioral families. For example, Hanisch and colleagues (Hanisch & Hulin, 1990, 1991; Hanisch, Hulin, & Roznowski, 1998) showed that behaviors such as being late or absent, quitting, thinking about retirement, and reducing work effort fit into two broader families of job withdrawal and work withdrawal. According to this view, *job withdrawal* includes a group of behaviors intended to remove the worker completely from both the organization and the job; examples include quitting or deciding to retire. *Work withdrawal*, on the other hand, comprises behaviors intended to provide more temporary escape from work, such arriving late or leaving work early, or being absent; or, to minimize time spent on task, such as by goofing off while at work, or engaging in escapist drinking and/or substance abuse.

Other researchers have taken a similar "behavioral family" approach to studying other kinds of work behaviors. One well-known school of thought has focused on prosocial or organizational citizenship behaviors—discretionary behaviors that, in the aggregate, are believed to benefit the organization or individuals and groups within the organization (Organ & Ryan, 1995). Enactment of prosocial, organizational citizenship behaviors has consistently been positively linked with employees' perceptions of job satisfaction and organizational justice (Organ & Ryan, 1995). Pulakos, Arad, Donovan, and Plamondon (2000) defined adaptation specifically in relation to job performance, describing *adaptive performance* as a worker characteristic increasingly demanded by employers who operate in rapidly changing organizational environments. Their empirical research confirmed that adaptive performance requirements are components of jobs, that jobs vary in adaptive performance demands, and that an eight-factor model captured the covariance among the performance adaptation survey items, including: handling emergencies, handling work stress, solving problems creatively, dealing with uncertain and unpredictable work situations, learning work tasks/technologies/procedures, demonstrating interpersonal adaptability, demonstrating cultural adaptability, and demonstrating physically oriented adaptability. They mention both the selection and training implications of having established adaptative performance as a job requirement, noting that in either case, the effort must be tied to specific job requirements. Thus, adaptive performance may be a stable individual difference, implying a selection strategy by employers, or a modifiable individual difference, suggesting an employer training intervention. It is clearly not considered a consequence of adaptation to dissatisfaction in their approach.

Of relevance to the question, "Are adaptive behaviors trainable?," Frayne and Geringer (2000) conducted self-management training (learning to structure work environment, self-motivate, and act to achieve performance objectives), showing positive improvements in self-efficacy, outcome expectations, and job performance. The behaviors they label as *self-management* could easily be viewed as adaptive performance or prosocial adaptation, suggesting that positive-oriented adaptations (i.e., those that reduce the source of dissatisfaction) may be changed through training.

Finally, prosocial adaptation may be a function of stable individual differences. Wanberg and Kammeyer-Mueller (2000) showed that two personality traits, extraversion and openness to experience, were correlated with higher levels of proactive socialization behavior (e.g., information seeking, feedback seeking, relationship building, positive framing) among newly socialized employees. They note that successfully socialized employees self-reported that they are more committed, more satisfied, more likely to stay, and also perform better. In their results, higher extraversion among new employees was associated with more feedback seeking and relationship building. Higher openness was associated with higher feedback seeking and positive framing. Wanberg and Kammeyer-Mueller's results would suggest that selection in favor of extraverts and people open to experience would result in a workforce more likely to engage in prosocial behaviors. Thus both selection (from Wanberg & Kammeyer-Mueller, 2000) and training techniques (from Frayne & Geringer, 2000) offer hope for encouraging proactive adaptation behaviors, based on thin but promising evidence.

The behavior family approach can also be seen in studies of negative adaptation behaviors, such as job and work withdrawal (noted earlier), organizational deviance/aggression, and deviance alone, as the focus has shifted from isolated highly visible events (e.g., violence, or sabotage) to patterns of more subtle—but serious in the aggregate—behaviors (Hollinger & Clark, 1982; Robinson & Bennett, 1995; Skarlicki & Folger, 1997). Beehr and Gupta (1978) suggested that withdrawal behaviors could be distinguished as either behavioral or psychological withdrawal. Our own early work (Rosse, 1983; Rosse & Miller, 1984) added the categories of *attempts to make constructive changes* (also mentioned by Mowday, Porter, & Steers, 1982), *retaliatory behavior*, and *cognitive readjustment*. Henne and Locke (1985) suggested a distinction between *action alternatives* (changes in job effort, persuasive protest, aggressive protest, and physical withdrawal) and *psychological alternatives* (changing perceptions of the job, changing one's values, changing reactions via defense mechanisms, and toleration). Farrell, building on Hirschman's political science theory (Hirschman, 1970) of how societies and organizations cope with decline, proposed the categories of *exit, voice, loyalty,* and *neglect* (Farrell, 1983).

Unfortunately the empirical support for complex, multidimensional models has been something short of spectacular. Rosse and Hulin (1985) concluded that their data supported a more limited taxonomy of *avoidance* and *attempts at change*. Using a much larger data set and a variety of factoring techniques, Roznowski, Rosse, and Miller (1992) also found that the date supported a simple model, including a positive (*attempts at change*) versus negative (*withdrawal*) behavior distinction (both of which were distinct empirically from organizational citizenship behaviors). Hanisch and her colleagues have also used numerous samples, some relatively large, as the basis for their two-factor, job versus work withdrawal model. Using a multidimensional scaling approach, Farrell (1983) found support for his *exit–voice–loyalty–neglect* model, although subsequent factor analyses have not always provided support for all four factors, particularly the neglect category (Withey & Cooper, 1989).

Recently, Bennett and Robinson (2000) developed a scale to measure *workplace deviance*, where deviance constituted behaviors directly harmful either to the organization or to individuals in the organization. They found factor analytic support for a two-factor measure of deviance, corresponding to organizational deviance and individual deviance constructs. They found significant correlations of their two scales with measures of property deviance, production deviance, physical withdrawal, psychological withdrawal, antagonistic work behavior, procedural justice, interactional justice, Machiavellianism, and conscientiousness. Weak or nonsignificant relations were observed with measures of voice, exit, loyalty, normlessness, distributive justice, and frustration. Similar results have been found for workplace aggression and organizational aggression (Glomb, 1999; Skarlicki & Folger, 1997). The simpler formulations seem to garner more support empirically, especially among the factor analytic studies.

In each case just mentioned, researchers have looked at groups of behaviors thought to share a common basis in a broader behavioral construct, whether it was labeled *withdrawal, deviance, aggression, adaptation, citizenship, self-management,* or *adaptive performance*. Fifty years of theory and research seems to imply that broadband attitudinal measures (such as job satisfaction) should be much more predictive if matched up to equally broadband measures of behavior, compared to predicting narrow measures of isolated behaviors (Doob, 1947; Rushton, Brainerd, & Pressley, 1983). If we change our view from studying behaviors in isolation to a view that treats discrete behaviors as surface indicators of an underlying construct, we should experience increases in both predictive power and theoretical understanding (Hulin, 1991).

Criticism of Job Satisfaction-Based Behavior Families Models

Recently, however, some significant criticisms have been directed toward behavioral family models of withdrawal and/or adaptation. In particular, Blau (1998) suggested that the job and work withdrawal categories suggested by Hanisch and colleagues (Hanisch & Hulin, 1990, 1991; Hanisch, Hulin, & Roznowski, 1998) are overly simplistic, and the range of behavioral options is likely to be more richly multidimensional. Blau cites work on violence and/or aggression as one example of a set of behaviors that should be incorporated into a comprehensive model of satisfaction-driven behavior. At the same time, important distinctions within behaviors, such as between excused and unexcused absences, avoidable or unavoidable turnover, or among different categories of lateness—such as *increasing chronic, periodic stable*, and *involuntary*—are not part of the two-category withdrawal model. Although Blau appears to accept the idea of aggregating related behaviors, he argues that our theoretical understanding is impaired by the use of only two, extremely heterogeneous, behavioral categories. By contrast, Hanisch and colleagues seem to accept theory complexity to the extent that the complexity is consistent with empirical results.

Other criticisms have focused on the role of job satisfaction as a central driving mechanism of adaptive behavior. Some point out that many of the behaviors we are discussing may have multiple possible causes, of which satisfaction is only one. People may quit, for example, not because they dislike their current job but because they need to relocate (possibly due to a spouse's job change, or to be closer to family). Similarly, people are often absent due to illness or injury, and being late may be the result of traffic, weather, or other conditions not under the control of the employee. Clearly, changes in job content or organizational participation may be driven by factors other than psychological events like job satisfaction. Indeed, Pulakos and colleagues (2000) defined adaptation without reference to satisfaction at all.

On the other hand, we note that job-related psychological reactions, such as satisfaction, can be evoked by externally imposed changes, such as recessions or changing family needs. For example, relocation decisions are arguably affected at least in part by job satisfaction; it may be much easier to decide to move for a spouse's career if you do not like your current job. Such influences were considered triggering events in Rosse and Miller's (1984) model, if they caused the subject to evaluate the work situation, and experience some level of job (dis)satisfaction. Nonwork triggering events provide legitimizing cover for dissatisfied employees to express their dissatisfaction through work withdrawal or other forms of adaptation. One interesting study showed that committed, satisfied employees are more likely to attend work despite environmental constraints (e.g., a major blizzard) that provided an excellent excuse not to come to work (Smith, 1977). Similarly, most of us know of dedicated employees who will come to work despite being sick, and others who use any minor ailment as an excuse not to do so. Judge and Hulin (1991) found that a measure of subjective well-being (a type of life satisfaction construct) accounted for withdrawal behaviors even after accounting for job satisfaction. Similarly, Necowitz and Roznowski (1991) found that negative affectivity (a personal characteristic) influenced withdrawal after job satisfaction was controlled. It seems only reasonable that reactions specific to the job or work environment should explain only a portion of employee withdrawal behavior.

Another criticism of job satisfaction as a causal mechanism in withdrawal behavior modeling is that job satisfaction (and related constructs such as organizational commitment or justice evaluations) provide only one component of how employees react to the workplace. Weiss and Cropanzano (1996) distinguish between satisfaction and affect, suggesting that satisfaction, inherently a cognitive evaluation, should relate to more evaluative behaviors like turnover, whereas affect may relate to less thought-out behaviors such as absence or tardiness. They believe that events trigger affect, which may lead to either affective-driven behaviors, and/or work attitudes (i.e., job satisfaction), which then lead to judgment-driven behaviors. They offer a theoretical framework, Affective Events Theory, which defines job satisfaction as a cognitive evaluation of workplace conditions—different from, and decidedly not, affect (Weiss & Cropanzano, 1996). Because job satisfaction involves a cognitive appraisal, it is more likely to lead to purposive adaptive behaviors, such as deciding to change employers or careers. They contrast this cognitive appraisal process with more purely affective or emotional response processes that are more likely to result in less thought-out reactions, such as impulsively quitting, or punching out a supervisor. Pelled and Xin (1999) provided empirical support for this proposition in showing that negative moods (low positive affect) are more strongly related to absenteeism than to turnover.

An additional concern with withdrawal/adaptation behavioral families has centered on their predictive performance. Although this has been a long-standing question, Blau (1998) provided the most recent criticism of predictive utility. Blau first argues that studies have been inconsistent in showing any statistically significant relations between job satisfaction and either job or work withdrawal; Blau also argues that even when significant associations are found, their magnitude has been modest and rarely exceeds the strongest single-behavior correlations. On the other hand, both Fisher and Locke (1991) and Hanisch and associates (Hanisch et al., 1998) have reviewed contrary evidence.

Limitations Inherent in Research Design and Measurement

One set of reasons for unimpressive predictive results involve statistically difficult artifacts that result when studying behaviors that are hard to measure, that have low base rates, and/or are highly skewed in their distribution (Hulin, 1991), as certainly is the case with many adaptation or withdrawal behaviors. Low base rates and resulting skewed distributions limit the magnitude of statistical relations and, in the case of correlational analyses, violate assumptions underlying the procedure. Although certainly part of the story, we do not, however, believe that these two methodological issues provide a sufficient explanation for disappointing empirical results. Beyond these two points, it may simply be that the research designs and measurement techniques we commonly employ do not capture the environmental, psychological, and behavioral events as they unfold in real time. Covariance structures from data sets that missed measuring the event or the corresponding psychological reactions are not likely to produce impressive prediction.

We suspect, in light of these inconsistent findings, that factor analysis of behavior frequency data may not be the best approach to determining the structure of behavior families. Part of the reason is that behavior self-report data are notoriously messy, due to social desirability biases (employees are often reluctant to report "deviant" behaviors, even on anonymous surveys), along with the two previously noted issues—naturally low base rates (e.g., even habitual absentees usually show up more than they are absent, and by definition you can usually only quit once from a particular organization), and very skewed distributions (e.g., a small number of employees are generally responsible for the majority of absenteeism and, probably, other nonnormative behavior). These artifacts make it very difficult to meet the statistical assumptions underlying factor analysis, or other correlational analysis techniques. The general linear model may be robust to violations of distributional assumptions, but maybe not robust enough for the violations observed in the behaviors of interest here.

More importantly, from a theoretical point of view, it is not at all clear that we should expect the behaviors to strongly co-vary within a family of related behaviors, as would be necessary for a factor analytic approach to reveal behavioral families. If an employee chooses one response alternative from among a set of related options, it typically implies *not* the other behaviors, at least in the short run. In some cases, engaging in one behavior literally places a physical limit on other behaviors. For example, being absent precludes one from being late, leaving early, or goofing off on the job (at least on the particular day one is absent); quitting similarly precludes any subsequent work-related behavior. A set of behaviors could share a common construct basis, but correlate negatively among themselves in a short time frame, preventing loading on common factors.

There is also a question of timing, both in terms of when the psychological and behavioral events actually unfold, and in terms of data collections intended to capture the unfolding of these events. For example, assume the progression of behavioral withdrawal hypothesis holds true—that dissatisfied people will start with tardiness, move toward absence, then ultimately end up quitting altogether. The correlation of tardiness and absence could be negative when measured within a single month (tardiness, or absence, is used to address the dissatisfaction, but unsuccessfully). By contrast the correlation may be positive if tardiness for months prior is correlated with subsequent months of absence data, as the employee moves toward progressively more severe forms of behavioral withdrawal in the face of persistent dissatisfaction.

Attempts to work around this problem raise at least two research design problems: knowing when behavioral substitutions occur (among members of the same behavioral family), and actually measuring attitudes and behaviors prior to and subsequent to a behavior substitution or switch within a behavioral family. Even more basic, if behaviors have positive adaptive value (i.e., they successfully affect the source of dissatisfaction), then compensatory models of behavior imply that engaging in one successful form of adaptation should make it unnecessary to engage in others. If this were to occur, it is perfectly reasonable to find negative correlations among the behaviors described in the model, at least when considered at the level of specific individuals. Note that negative adaptations, such as implied in the withdrawal model, imply positive lagged correlations among behaviors within a family, if the source of satisfaction is unresolved. By contrast, positive adaptations imply negative correlations among behaviors within a family because the source of dissatisfaction is fixed. If you have a heterogeneous employee sample with respect to the use of positive versus negative adaptations (i.e., some are using positive adaptations, others are using negative adaptations) it would be reasonable to expect the weak and inconsistent findings common to job satisfaction–job behavior studies, even though people are all conforming to a common adaptation process.

We believe that the solution to this problem in the long-term is to conduct more in-depth, etic research that explores how employees think, feel, and react as they facing emotionally negative, dissatisfying events and situations. Such work would be highly labor intensive, as numerous observations would be needed for each subject, along the lines of Rosse and Hulin (1985) and Weiss, Nicholas, and Daus (1993.) In addition, measurement reactivity effects would be a source of concern, as the process of eliciting the data may produce a net shift toward more cognitive, deliberate behavioral choices in the employee's approach. Still, such data would have a better chance of measuring important environmental, psychological, and behavioral events closer to their real-time influence.

We believe that greater success will result if we develop models actually consistent with employee psychological processes and actions, and that a behavior families approach will contribute to those models. Even if one were persuaded by Blau's (1998) argument that the predictive power of work and job withdrawal composites is less than it should be, we do not agree with his conclusion that the solution is to move away from behavior family approaches and toward prediction of more discrete behaviors. For one, we think that has been attempted, with even less impressive results. Further, we believe that developing finer grained understanding of discrete behaviors in isolation—such as absenteeism, lateness, or quitting—has been promoted from a practice-driven, but inappropriate approach that we need to predict and control specific problem behaviors. For example, a manager may note a problem with a behavior, such as tardiness, and seek to address that problem, without getting into complicated considerations. Although we are sympathetic to a KISS approach (i.e., keep it simple, stupid), this approach has serious limitations for both theory development and management practice unless the behaviors are truly independent of one another, sharing neither covariance nor common causal roots. If the behaviors are connected, either as members of behavioral families or due to common causal roots (and there is reasonable evidence to suggest both), then treating them as independent and isolated creates two major problems, even from a practice perspective.

The first problem is that it is inefficient to develop separate theories (or control mechanisms) for each problem behavior if the behaviors share—at least to some extent—common causes. This results in an overly complex set of models for managers to grapple with, as well as contradicting the scholar's appreciation for Occam's razor (i.e., parsimonious models). Only after addressing the common variance does it make sense to go further to explore the marginal utility of capturing unique variance in each behavior of concern. The second problem, from a very practical perspective, is that treating one behavior symptomatically (e.g., an absence control system or a retention program) may result in symptom substitution or switching, if behavior families reflect reality. The employee who is sanctioned for being late may adapt by using absence as the outlet for dissatisfaction instead. The computer programmer who considers leaving the firm over a boring work assignment may decide to stay when offered a substantial retention bonus. But if the boring nature of the employee's work is not changed, he or she may decide to take the occasional day off (figuring that the employer who just engaged in a bidding war for her services is not likely to then crack down on some absenteeism), or to engage in some more intellectually stimulating hacking, or jump on the next offer from a firm willing to offer interesting work. In short, it matters if we use a model that captures reality with some fidelity.

Despite these arguments for studying behavioral families—none of which are new—we must acknowledge the criticisms of the behavioral family approach. Empirical associations between job satisfaction and behavior families have not been as strong or consistent as theory would predict. We suspect that advances in both theory and method will be needed to fairly address the criticisms of those who are skeptical about the utility of behavior family models in relation to job satisfaction. We turn next to offer a revised adaptation model to help promote theoretical discussion and development.

A REVISED MODEL OF EMPLOYEE ADAPTATION

The model we are proposing here is an extension of the adaptation model described earlier (Rosse & Miller, 1984), and modified by Rosse and Noel (1996). The current model shares with those earlier models the notion that much employee behavior is motivated by a desire to adapt to dissatisfying working conditions. Our use of the term *adapt* encompasses many of the terms used by scholars in job satisfaction research, including coping, voice, exit, retaliation, withdrawal, aggression, and deviance. Excluded from our adaptation construct are organizational citizenship behaviors and loyalty expressions. Behaviors such as the latter imply a desire for the status quo, as it is a satisfying state. By contrast, adaptation behaviors share in common that the person who engages in them desires a change that results in a more positive emotional state for them at work. We also exclude from this model similar adaptive processes that may occur in nonwork social roles (e.g., family relations, friendships). Although adaptation processes may be parallel across social domains, the number of substantive factors that would have to be identified and measured is overwhelming; we hope instead to offer here a theory of the middle range by restricting our focus to work role adaptation. Finally, we concentrate on work behaviors that are not directly job performance, either quality or quantity. The satisfaction–performance relationship has been described as complex (Fischer, 1980). Weiss and Cropanzano (1996) noted that people experiencing negative affect are distracted from the task at hand. In our approach, people in the process of adapting to dissatisfying conditions may be distracted from performance, but whether that distraction would be detectable in the aggregate performance ratings commonly in use is doubtful at best, based on the voluminous data available. Interestingly, Cote (1999) recently published a study that suggests that *affect* predicted job performance better than job satisfaction, drawing on the distinction made by Write and Cropanzano (1997) between affect (emotional state) and satisfaction (evaluation of work environment). Because little other corroborating data exist to support the Cote (1999) findings, we leave it for now, although noting its theoretical interest. We believe that adaptation to dissatisfaction inherently involves a distraction from performing job duties, but we do not add performance explicitly in our model.

We expect that work events will serve as triggers for satisfaction evaluation and emotional reaction. In our view, dissatisfaction reflects an internal psychological state that is unpleasant, and therefore motivates employees to seek a means for reducing dissatisfaction. The search for an adaptive or coping response is one of two basic mechanisms driving a variety of behaviors at work, and it involves cognitive processing as an extension of evaluating job satisfaction, partially consistent with the perspective offered by Weiss and Cropanzano (1996). The other basic mechanism involves negative emotion, which is proposed to occur simultaneously with the realization of dissatisfaction. Events occur in work settings that trigger affective reactions (negative emotion) and evaluations (job dissatisfaction.) We expect that events may trigger emotion devoid of the rational process implied in job satisfaction evaluations sometimes for some people, and conversely some events may trigger satisfaction evaluations, with relatively less emotional content for other people and, at other times.[1] The results of each of these mechanisms (negative emotion, dissatisfaction) is hypothesized to lead to qualitatively different families of employee behavior (see Fig. 10.1).

Several behavioral families are hypothesized to result from either negative emotion or dissatisfaction. These behavior families are derived from the large body of theory and research described previously. Responding to Blau's (1998) critique, we propose additional behavioral categories beyond work and job withdrawal. Comparatively few such studies exist that

---

[1]Weiss and Cropanzano (1996) made a strong point of differentiating satisfaction from affect. We still hold the view that satisfaction, although a cognitive process, involves affect also.

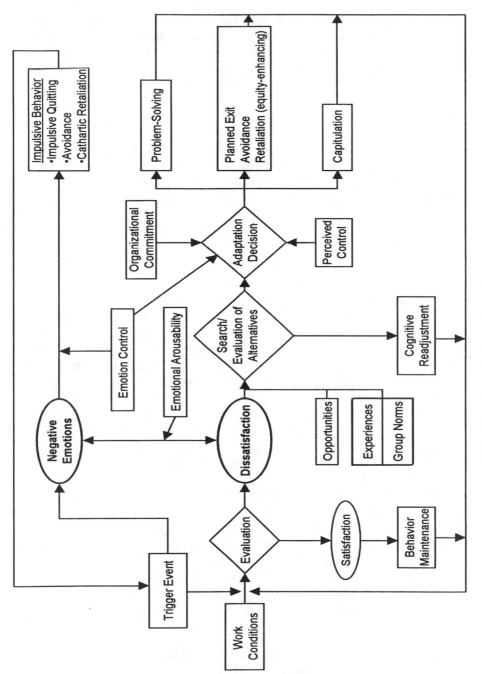

FIG. 10.1. A model of adaptive work behavior.

217

support more than two-factor behavioral families, yet we suggest more than two behavioral family categories, discounting the factor analytic results while drawing on the conceptual literature available as well as our own thinking and speculation. We propose four categories of adaptive behaviors that are driven by job dissatisfaction (*problem-solving, planned exit, planned avoidance*, and *equity-enhancing retaliation*). We also include *capitulation* as a fifth behavioral family response to job dissatisfaction, but as this is a "nonresponse" behavioral category, we believed it needed to be identified separately from the other four. In addition, we propose three categories of impulsive behaviors (*impulsive quitting, avoidance*, and *cathartic retaliation*), driven by the raw negative emotion of the moment. Each of these eight behavioral categories could encompass multiple, specific behavior indicators.

Adaptive Behaviors

We noted earlier that the two psychological events, raw negative emotion and job (dis)satisfaction, are the central motivational triggers to adaptive behaviors. A second basic premise of our model is that the organizing principal of a behavioral family stems from its effect on negative emotion and/or dissatisfaction. More specifically, behaviors are considered part of a family if there is a common effect that is perceived or anticipated in relation to negative emotion and/or job dissatisfaction. Some researchers clearly take the employer's perspective on the goodness or badness of a behavior. By contrast, the current model assumes the employee's perspective, as it is his or her adaptations that are of interest. That implies, of course, that conduct identified as "adaptive" by the employee may not be viewed that way by management in the organization.

Problem-solving responses represent constructive attempts to fix, reduce, or remove the source of dissatisfaction. These activities were called "attempts at change" in the original Rosse and Miller (1984) model, and are more commonly referred to as "voice" (Farrell, 1983; Withey & Cooper, 1989). Voice generally connotes an opportunity to be heard, which is certainly a part of what we term *problem solving*. However, there are other ways of reaching the goal of removing the source of dissatisfaction, so we have chosen problem solving as a more general description. It includes such behaviors as presenting problems to a manager, working with a supervisor or co-workers to change working conditions, making unilateral changes in how you do work (e.g., to make it less stressful or more rewarding), or joining a union to strengthen and amplify the message.

Planned exit corresponds to the category of *job withdrawal*, and includes decisions to quit, transfer, or retire in order to avoid the source of dissatisfaction. It is distinguished from impulsive quitting largely because exit is chosen explicitly as a means of adapting to the current, dissatisfying situation. By contrast, impulsive quitting involves no thought about what comes next.

Planned avoidance represents more short-term strategies for avoiding dissatisfaction, such as taking a day off, coming in late or leaving early, or avoiding meetings or duties while at work. It roughly corresponds to the *work withdrawal* category suggested by Hanisch and colleagues or to the *neglect* category proposed by Farrell (1983) and by Withey and Cooper (1989). Like *planned exit*, it is limited to behaviors that are chosen by the employee as a means of adapting rather than as impulsive behaviors.

Equity-enhancing retaliation broadens most conceptions of withdrawal/ adaptation by noting that violent or aggressive behavior can also represent a coping mechanism (Robinson, 1994). It includes aggressive behaviors that restore satisfaction by either increasing the employee's outcomes (e.g., stealing), reducing his or her inputs (e.g., sabotaging the production process), or reducing the outcomes of other employees (e.g., gossiping, backstabbing, or otherwise making life miserable for others). Again, a defining characteristic of these behaviors is that the employee can articulate the reason for the conduct.

Capitulation reflects the observation that some employees do not respond actively to dissatisfaction, at least in the short run. For example, consider an employee in a start-up company who learns through a news story that the CEO's compensation is 20 times greater than his own. Suddenly his previously acceptable salary looks meager, and the "family" culture of the company looks like a sham. Dissatisfied and feeling betrayed, he begins to look for a job at other dot.com companies. After some searching, he discovers that the salary gap he is experiencing is actually pretty typical and that his salary is more than competitive. As a result of readjusting his expectations, he has successfully adapted, even without making any behavioral changes. Another example of this category is actually closer to Hirschman's idea of *loyalty*, in that it involves waiting patiently for things to improve, such as when pay declines and work increases in response to a shift in demand for an employer's product or service. In most cases, however, this strategy is adaptive only in the short term (at best); unless the situation improves fairly quickly, the consequence for mental and physical health of "hanging in there" or, worse, giving up, can be quite negative (Rosse & Hulin, 1985).

Impulsive Behavior

One concern with our original model was that it requires a certain amount of rational evaluation on the part of employees, even while negative emotional states persist. That is, employees are presumed to engage in some sort of mental calculus that results in both an evaluation of whether they are satisfied and how they should respond if they are dissatisfied. It is also clear that some employees engage in behavior without much deliberation. We do not know the relative frequencies of either impulsive and deliberate responses. Is it reasonable to assume that most people engage in active dissatisfaction cognitive processing before engaging in the kinds of behavior we are discussing? It is quite possible that much behavior follows highly automated processing that may seem—even to the actor—to be spontaneous. Consider the employee who, once again, is insulted by his or her boss while making a presentation. Because that behavior has occurred before, and probably to other employees as well, she has already thought about her potential responses. Habit, based in part on prevailing norms and in part on prior active processing, predicts her immediate likely response, whether or not she is actively aware of her mental calculus at the moment of behavior.

But in some cases, impulsive behaviors clearly result. This includes the person who gets "fed-up" and just quits on the spur of the moment, with no thought (past or contemporaneous) about the consequences of the action or about alternative responses. Similar, less serious examples of what we previously described as *avoidance* would be the person who wakes up feeling tired, looks out the window to see that a cold rain is falling, and hits the "snooze" button on the alarm radio without ever asking himself how much work he needs to accomplish that day or how much sick leave he has remaining.

The third category of impulsive behavior, which we term *cathartic retaliation*, can be seen in the frustrated employee who verbally or physically assaults a fellow employee or supervisor just because it feels good at the moment.

As is evident in each of these examples, impulsive behavior is fundamentally different from the categories of *adaptive* behavior in two important ways. The first is that they are not driven by an attempt to improve the dissatisfying situation in a way most people would support. In fact, these kinds of impulsive behaviors can often be counterproductive. The second difference is that impulsive behavior is driven by an entirely different motivator than are the categories of adaptive behavior, a topic to which we now return.

Behavior Drivers

Following Weiss and Cropanzano's (1996) recommendations, our model includes two distinct psychological drivers of behavior: job (dis)satisfaction and workplace (negative) emotion. Although job satisfaction is seen as primary motivator of adaptive behaviors, workplace emotions are proposed to be the proximal cause of impulsive behaviors, as well as part of the job dissatisfaction process. In our original model, we did not know how to address how impulsive behavior might result in the face of dissatisfying conditions. In this version, we offer three speculative constructs to help understand if someone will act out impulsively or engage in a more deliberate process of evaluation. Specifically, we hypothesize that impulsive versus more thoughtful responses will hinge on the employee's *emotional arousability, emotion control,* and *emotional reserve.* We turn to discuss the evaluation process involving job satisfaction.We then discuss how emotional arousability, emotion control, and emotional reserve may serve to mediate if impulsive or deliberate behaviors result from dissatisfying conditions. We follow with a discussion of the direct connection betweeen affect and impulsive behavior.

Job Satisfaction

Most models of job satisfaction describe a process in which employees compare their perceptions of the work experience (both intrinsic and contextual factors) to their preferences (which are complexly determined by past experience, social comparisons, economic conditions, and other factors beyond the purview of the current chapter; Locke, 1976). The result of these comparisons is an evaluation of being either satisfied or dissatisfied; this evaluation is multidimensional, but with a strong underlying general or global factor (Smith, 1992).

Although job satisfaction is based on a summary evaluation of many stimuli, there is probably some sort of trigger event that stimulates the evaluation process. As long as situations are not changing, or changing only slowly, we do not routinely evaluate our satisfaction with a situation. It takes some particular trigger, event, or shock—such as learning that a co-worker is being paid more than you, being reassigned to a less challenging job, or even being asked to complete a job satisfaction survey—to activate a conscious reevaluation of the situation. Thus Fig. 10.1 shows a *trigger event* as moderating the linkage between work conditions (defined broadly) and the job satisfaction evaluation process.

A critical assumption in our model is that being dissatisfied has qualitatively different motivational and behavioral effects than being satisfied. Dissatisfaction is by definition unpleasant, and the fundamental motivational assumption underlying our adaptation model is that being dissatisfied creates a catalyst for action (Dawis, 1992). Satisfaction, by contrast, creates no motivation for behavior change; rather it encourages a continuation of the status quo.

Dissatisfaction plays a critical role in the adaptation process precisely because there is a pervasive tendency toward behavior maintenance rather than behavior change. Put simply, people are creatures of habit; all else being equal, behavior is likely to become routinized and persist with little conscious thought (Weiss & Ilgen, 1985). Indeed, both general motivational theories (Atkinson & Birch, 1978) and some theories of attendance (Fichman, 1974) suggested that the most interesting motivational question is the process by which behavior changes.

If employees evaluate their situation and conclude that they are dissatisfied, the next step is to review and evaluate different ways of responding. This is a complex process, and is influenced by a number of variables. One key variable is the employee's perception of external opportunities. A substantial literature shows that alternative job opportunities are a critical factor affecting turnover (Hulin, Roznowski, & Hachiya, 1985). We propose that alternatives play a similar role in affecting a wide range of adaptive behavior. For example, Withey and Cooper's test of the exit–voice–loyalty–neglect model is based on the assumption that the choice among these alternative strategies is based in large part on the perceived benefits and costs of each (Withey & Cooper, 1989). Costs, in turn, are strongly influenced by alternative job opportunities. For example, it is less risky to be absent, to goof off, or to complain if you believe there are plenty of other job opportunities should your employer choose to sanction your behavior.

Although perceived alternative opportunities have a general effect of increasing the range of adaptive options considered, two other factors have a more idiosyncratic effect. One is the individual's own past experiences, either directly experienced or vicariously appreciated from others. If workers learn that taking an occasional "mental health day" helps relieve stress, they will probably continue to consider this as an option in future stressful situations. Similarly, workers can learn from observing coworkers that one cure for boredom may be playing games on the job; this social learning can then influence their own adaptive behavior. Closely entwined in this process are the pressures of social norms. Behaviors that are accepted or even encouraged by group norms are more likely to be enacted than those that are counternormative (Johns & Nicholson, 1982).

One possible outcome of this evaluation of alternatives is *cognitive readjustment*. That is, one result of searching for and evaluating alternatives may be a conclusion that one's present situation is not as bad as initially thought. This adjustment to expectations then feeds back into the initial evaluation component of Fig. 10.1, and may lead to a state of relative job satisfaction (and thus behavior maintenance).

Alternatively, the search of alternatives may produce a set of behavioral options. In the next step in the proposed model, these strategies are evaluated and a response option is chosen. We propose that this decision step is affected by three key variables. The first of these is organizational commitment; feeling personally committed to the organization is hypothesized to increase the likelihood of problem-solving or capitulation responses, and decrease the likelihood of exit, avoidance, or retaliation. The second variable is perceived control; research suggests that employees who feel that they can have an impact on what happens in their firm are more likely to try to change dissatisfying conditions rather than withdraw or capitulate (Parker, 1993; Withey & Cooper, 1989).

The third category of variables hypothesized to affect the choice of adaptive strategy include *emotional arousability, emotional reserve,* and *emotion control.* Although these concepts appear in common use among clinical psychologists, we first came across the concepts of emotional control and regulation in research by Kanfer and associates on learning stages, and how psychological resource demands change as learners make transitions through each stage. A brief review of their work seems appropriate.

Learning theorists divide learning complex tasks (such as learning to run a business) into three phases. In first phase, called the *cognitive* phase, the learner begins to understand the basic task requirements and the rules for task engagement (Kanfer & Ackerman, 1996; Kanfer, Ackerman, & Heggestad, 1996). In this phase of learning, attentional resource demands are high (i.e., the learner must focus a great deal of attention on learning). Variations in cognitive abilities across learners relate substantially to performance scores. That is, students with high cognitive abilities learn faster, and so tend to perform better. In this phase, students tend to learn factual information and concepts relevant to the task (Ackerman, 1992; Anderson, 1987; Howell & Cooke, 1989).

The second phase, named the *associative* phase, involves strengthening associations developed in the first stage (Kanfer & Ackerman, 1996; Kanfer et al., 1996). In this learning phase, attentional demands decrease, whereas performance accuracy and speed increase. In this phase, facts and behaviors that go together are integrated into a routine (Ackerman, 1992; Anderson, 1987; Howell & Cooke, 1989).

In the *autonomous* third phase, there are minimal attention requirements as the task has become automatic for the learner (Kanfer & Ackerman, 1996; Kanfer et al., 1996). In this phase, performance is generally fast, accurate, and low-effort.

The challenge is to help move students through the three phases of learning. Strong emotional states, particularly negative states such as frustration or anger, interfere with learning. In contrast, mild positive feelings (e.g., how you might feel when receiving an e-mail from an old friend) favorably influence the manner in which information is organized, and improve the ability to integrate divergent information (Bretz & Thompsett, 1992). Kanfer and associates (1996) theorize that use of attentional resources to maintain positive emotions will be especially helpful in the first phase of learning, when high cognitive resource demands are present.

By contrast, learners face boredom as they approach the third, rather routine, phase of learning. Attentional resources that are directed toward motivational control techniques (such as self-set goals or competitions) will help keep focus on task during that phase. In summary, learners must direct attention to keep emotions in check early in learning, and motivational control late in the process to keep focused on task.

Kanfer and associates (1996) developed a simulation to teach air traffic controller skills, and trained novice controllers in a research program. The data from their studies showed, in part, that the correlation of a general cognitive ability measure with performance was strongest with first phase results and weakest with third phase results. This implies that differences in cognitive ability are more important early rather than late in learning. They also found an interaction involving general cognitive ability and the importance of emotional or motivational control. Specifically, lower cognitive ability learners were more likely to experience frustrations leading to negative emotions early in learning, when cognitive resource demands are high. Methods to encourage emotional control were more important for lower ability learners than their high-ability counterparts at this early phase in learning.

These research findings suggest that instructors could provide support for emotional control by bolstering learner efficacy expectations (Bandura, 1977). The self-efficacy expectations of learners can be enhanced by (a) persuasion, in which the instructor verbally assures the learners that they can be successful; (b) modeling, in which the learners are shown (live or on video tape) others, like themselves, who have been successful in previous training sessions; and (c) enactive mastery, in which the instructor takes steps to cause the learners to experience successes early in the training program (Gist & Mitchell, 1992; Gist, Schwoerer, & Rosen, 1989; Mathieu, Martineau, & Tannenbaum, 1993). Similarly, managers could support emotional control among workforce members using parallel techniques that are more appropriate to a workplace environment. We see value in applying these concepts to adaptation at work.

Emotional arousability we define as an individual difference variable with reference to affect intensity. Some people simply feel emotion very strongly, whereas others show almost blunted affective responses to rather sharp emotional cues and triggers. The more emotionally arousable the person, the more likely an impulsive act will follow, other things equal. We speculate that emotional arousability has a root in the neurobiology of our species, and is a relatively stable individual difference characteristic in the time periods covered in the model.

Emotion control is defined as a learned self-management skill. Someone who has considerable emotion control can feel very strongly internally, but show very little of that internal state, either verbally or nonverbally. A folk example would be someone who is especially adept at the card game, poker, where keeping the value of the card hand unknown to other players is a key skill to success. Someone strong in emotion control would be less likely to act impulsively, and more likely to deliberately evaluate the situation. *Emotional regulation* is another label for this same construct.

Emotional reserve is defined as the capacity to experience negative emotion-eliciting stimuli and still stay on task, undisrupted. It results from the interplay over time of emotion-triggering events, the person's emotional arousability, and the person's emotional control. Someone with a large emotional reserve can handle substantial, additional negative emotional and/or dissatisfying stimuli, and continue to stay on task. Someone who is low in emotional reserve cannot handle much more stimuli that trigger negative emotion and/or dissatisfaction and stay on task. One can imagine low emotional reserve people saying, "I can't take much more of this. . . ." When someone runs out of emotional reserve, then impulsive behaviors result. When emotional reserve remains, more deliberative processes should predominate.

Employees with greater emotional reserve can "tough out" situations that would create unbearable dissatisfaction for others, and are also likely to take a more stoic approach to how they adapt when they do feel dissatisfied. We speculate that, compared to those with low emotional reserve, those high in emotional reserve are more likely to wait for things to improve rather than taking matters into their own hands. Employees with better emotion control skills are also less likely to become dissatisfied, and to use problem-solving strategies when coping with dissatisfaction.

Turning to Fig. 10.1, we expect that emotional arousability will influence the intensity of emotional response to triggering events. In addition, we expect that emotion control will mediate if negative emotion causes impulsive conduct—the greater the emotional regulation, the more likely a deliberate evaluation becomes. Not shown visually in the figure is emotional reserve—when emotional arousal exceeds the person's emotion control, emotional reserve is exhausted and impulsive behavior occurs. However, that event can be depicted solely by emotional arousability and emotion control in the model.

WORKPLACE EMOTIONS

The second driver of behavior is negative emotional reaction, particularly in the form of anger. Weiss and Cropanzano (1996) suggest that emotional reactions occur in response to specific triggering events, such as being criticized publicly or finding out that a co-worker is being paid more than you. They suggest that these emotions lead to affect- (versus cognition-) driven behaviors. As shown in Fig. 10.1, these include such avoidance behaviors as being absent (or late, etc.) or impulsively quitting. In accordance with the frustration–aggression hypothesis (Berkowitz, 1989), this category also includes retaliatory behavior in which the "motive" is the emotional release provided by "blowing up," either at the source of the frustration or at a hapless bystander.

Unlike the case with job satisfaction, we presume that the relationship between strong negative emotions and impulsive behavior is relatively direct, and virtually simultaneous. Someone in this state is not a candidate for calm, rational discussion, as the raw negative emotion of the moment overwhelms any thoughtful process. As a result, the only moderator we propose is emotional reserve (the interaction of emotional arousability and emotion control skills.) Employees with greater emotional reserve have a larger capacity for negative affect, and are thus less likely to "go over the brink" and act impulsively. Here the factor is how much negative affect one can tolerate without responding. Emotion control skills pertain to how one copes with negative affect; employees with better-developed emotion control skills are less likely to respond impulsively to a given level of affect or frustration. Similarly, employees who are relatively unemotional are less likely to respond impulsively.

Other Model Characteristics, Issues, and Limitations

There are important characteristics and limitations in our model that should be noted. We use constructs that have been used in a variety of literatures by a variety of scholars. In a very real sense, our model can be seen as a special case of more general models of affect–behavior relations (Weiss & Cropanzano, 1996) and emotion and adaptation (Lazarus, 1991). Both of those sources are especially informative, and cover issues not addressed here. We simplify from those works to offer a model focused on workplace adaptive behavior. We offer speculation in the absence of strong or clear data, particularly concerning the role of emotional reserve. We have further work to do to embed our model in existing theory and data beyond what we have presented in this brief piece. We hope that the model will trigger other scholars to suggest improvements more consistent with extant theory and data.

Feedback Mechanisms

Because the underlying motivation for the adaptive behaviors proposed in the model is to cope with dissatisfaction, it is important to describe the consequences of behavior enactment. In general, enacting an adaptive behavior should decrease job dissatisfaction, but it is not expected that doing so will always have that effect. For example, an employee who is dissatisfied with pay may take a day off in order to reduce her contributions and thereby restore equity. However, if she or he is sanctioned for the absence, or finds an even bigger pile of work on the desk upon returning to work, the net effect on job satisfaction may be nil or even negative. For that reason, the feedback loop from adaptive behavior enactment leads to the evaluation and appraisal of work, where it combines with other factors to lead to a new cycle of evaluation, the result of which may or may not be increased satisfaction with work.

We also propose a feedback loop from impulsive behavior, although it is somewhat different from that for the adaptive behaviors. Since the driver of impulsive behaviors is negative emotion rather than job (dis)satisfaction, we do not assume that engaging in these behaviors will necessarily increase job satisfaction. Indeed, it is quite possible that some of these behaviors will produce consequences that will sharply reduce job satisfaction. Similarly, enactment of these behaviors may have different effects on negative emotions. Although absence, for example, has been described as a mechanism for "mood repair," aggressive behavior can also have a self-reinforcing effect in which negative emotions are perpetuated. (Although one category of impulsive behaviors is labeled *cathartic retaliation,* catharsis refers to the motivation for the behavior rather than its necessary consequence. Thus a person may lash out a co-worker because it "feels good" at the moment, yet later react to their own behavior with shame or even disgust.) Therefore, we propose a feedback loop in which enactment of impulsive behaviors serves as a trigger event that may affect subsequent emotions and that also prompts reevaluation of satisfaction with work.

Measurement Concerns

It is clear that measuring many of the constructs in our model will present substantial challenges. For example, emotional arousability makes a good deal of intuitive sense conceptually, but it is much less clear how we could reliably estimate this individual difference variable among employees. The same concern holds for emotion control, and several of the behavior categories as well. Operationalizing many parts of the model as presented would be difficult at best.

Modeling Stochastic Processes

It is important to emphasize that the model we are describing suggests a stochastic, rather than deterministic, relationship between behavior drivers and behaviors. That is, although we propose that a general lawful relationship exists between the two categories of behavior and their respective behavior drivers, these relationships are very much probabilistic in nature. This may be particularly evident in the case of negative emotions. We are all occasionally in a bad mood, but we do not necessarily act out our negative feelings. But if we are in a bad mood and yet another aversive event occurs, there may be an abrupt shift from inaction to impulsive—even violent—behavior. That is, there is likely to be a discontinuous relationship such that emotions produce serious behavioral reactions only after a threshold is reached. The point of this threshold in turn depends on the individual's emotional reserve and emotion control skills. A similar process may apply to the adaptive behaviors wherein a threshold of dissatisfaction may need to be broached before adaptive behavior is enacted. Or it may be that there are separate thresholds for different categories of behaviors, as is implied by a *progression of withdrawal* concept. If these processes are in fact stochastic, we should not expect linear relationships between either dissatisfaction or negative emotions and resulting behavior. One implication may be that cusp/catastrophe models are more appropriate to study these behavior processes than linear models.

Exogenous Factors

A final comment has to do with explanatory factors that are not included in the model. As we noted in the beginning of this chapter, our intent is not to explain or predict all examples of the behaviors that are described in Fig. 10.1. We agree with Blau (1998) and others that these behaviors are complexly determined, and that many instances of withdrawal in particular have minimal association with job satisfaction or negative affect. One important question is: What are the proportions of behaviors that can be explained by reactions to work? The answer would promote our theoretical understanding of how work factors affect behavior, and guide employers, who want to know where to focus when changing the workplace to reduce triggers for undesirable behaviors. We do think there are interesting ideas advanced by scholars in this general domain of research. Advances in theory, method, and data are still needed to sort out which among the ideas seem to map reality most closely. Although empirical results to date suggest that the proportions of behaviors influenced by work reactions are rather low, our hope is that a more complete representation of the multiple processes leading to these behaviors will ultimately substantially increase the proportion of explained variance, reflecting a model that captures enough of reality to be of interest to scholars and practitioners alike.

ACKNOWLEDGMENT

This manuscript is an expanded version of our presentation at the Illinois Conference of May 2000, held in honor of Dr. Charles L. Hulin. We are both grateful for all he has given to the profession and to us personally. Scholar, teacher, mentor, he continues to lead by example.

REFERENCES

Ackerman, P. L. (1992). Predicting individual differences in complex skill acquisition: Dynamics of ability determinants. *Journal of Applied Psychology, 77,* 598–614.

Anderson, J. R. (1987). Skill acquisition: Compilation of weak-method problem solutions. *Psychological Bulletin, 94,* 192–210.

Atkinson, J. W., & Birch, D. (1978). *Introduction to motivation.* New York: D. Van Nostrand.

Bandura, A. (1977). *Social learning theory.* Englewood Cliffs, NJ: Prentice-Hall.

Beehr, T. A., & Gupta, N. (1978). A note on the structure of employee withdrawal. *Organizational Behavior and Human Performance, 21,* 73–79.

Bennett, R., & Robinson, S. (2000). Development of a measure of workplace deviance. Journal *of Applied Psychology, 83,* 349–360.

Berkowitz, L. (1989). Frustration–aggression hypothesis: Examination and reformulation. *Psychological Bulletin, 106,* 59–73.

Blau, G. J. (1998). On the aggregation of individual withdrawal behaviors into larger multi-item constructs. *Journal of Organizational Behavior, 19,* 437–451.

Bretz, R., & Thompsett, R. (1992). Comparing traditional and integrative learning methods in organizational training programs. *Journal of Applied Psychology, 77,* 941–952.

Cote, S. (1999). Affect and performance in organizational settings. *Current Directions in Psychological Science, 8*(2), 65–68.

Dawis, R. V. (1992). Person–environment fit and job satisfaction. In C. J. Cranny, P. C. Smith, & F. F. Stone (Eds.), *Job satisfaction: How people feel about their jobs and how it affects their performance* (pp. 69–88). New York: Lexington Books.

Doob, L. W. (1947). The behavior of attitudes. *Psychological Bulletin, 84,* 888–918.

Farrell, D. (1983). Exit, voice, loyalty and neglect as responses to job dissatisfaction: A multidimensional scaling study. *Academy of Management Journal, 26,* 596–607.

Fichman, M. (1974). A theoretical approach to understanding employee absence. In P. Goodman & R. S. Atkins (Eds.), *Absenteeism: New approaches to understanding, measuring and managing employee absence.* San Francisco, CA: Jossey-Bass.

Fischer, C. (1980). On the dubious wisdom of expecting satisfaction to correlate with job performance. *Academy of Management Review, 5,* 607–612.

Fisher, C. D., & Locke, E. A. (1991). Job satisfaction and dissatisfaction: Enhancing the prediction of consequences. In P. C. Smith, C. J. Cranny, & E. F. Stone (Eds.), *Job satisfaction: Advances in theory and research.* New York: The Free Press.

Frayne, C., & Geringer, M. (2000) Self-management training for improving job performance: A field experiment involving salespeople. *Journal of Applied Psychology, 85,* 361–372.

Gist, M. E., & Mitchell, T. R. (1992). Self-efficacy: A theoretical analysis of its determinants and malleability. *Academy of Management Review, 17,* 183–211.

Gist, M. E., Schwoerer, C., & Rosen, B. (1989). Effects of alternative training methods on self-efficacy and performance in computer software training. *Journal of Applied Psychology,* 884–891.

Glomb, T. M. (1999, June). *Workplace aggression: Antecedents, behavioral components, and consequences.* Paper presented at the annual meeting of the American Psychological Society, Denver, CO.

Gupta, N., & Jenkins, D. (1982). Absenteeism and turnover: Is there a progression? *Journal of Management Studies, 1,* 539–559.

Hanisch, K., & Hulin, C. (1990). Job attitudes and organizational withdrawal: An examination of retirement and other voluntary withdrawal behaviors. *Journal of Vocational Behavior, 37,* 60–78.

Hanisch, K., & Hulin, C. (1991). General attitudes and organizational withdrawal: An evaluation of a causal model. *Journal of Vocational Behavior, 39,* 110–128.

Hanisch, K. A., Hulin, C. L., & Roznowski, M. (1998). The importance of individuals' repertoires of behaviors: The scientific appropriateness of studying multiple behaviors and general attitudes. *Journal of Organizational Behavior, 19*, 463–480.

Henne, D., & Locke, E. A. (1985). Job dissatisfaction: What are the consequences? *International Journal of Psychology, 20*, 221–240.

Herzberg, F., Mausner, B., Peterson, R., Capwell, D. (1957). *Job attitudes: Review of research and opinion*. Pittsburgh, PA: Psychological Services of Pittsburgh.

Hirschman, A. O. (1970). *Exit, voice, and loyalty: Responses to decline in firms, organizations and states*. Cambridge, MA: Harvard University Press.

Hollinger, R., & Clark, J. (1982). Employee deviance: A response to the perceived quality of the work experience. *Work and Occupations, 9*, 97–114.

Howell, W. C., & Cooke, N. J. (1989). Training the human information processor: A review of cognitive models. In I. L. Goldstein (Ed.), *Training and development in organizations* (pp. 121–182). San Francisco: Jossey-Bass.

Hulin, C. (1991). Adaptation, persistence, and commitment in organizations. In M. Dunnette & L. Hough (Eds.), *Handbook of industrial and organizational psychology* (Vol. 2, 2nd ed., pp. 445–506). Palo Alto, CA: Consulting Psychologists Press.

Hulin, C. L., Roznowski, M., & Hachiya, D. (1985). Alternative opportunities and withdrawal decisions: Empirical and theoretical discrepancies and an integration. *Psychological Bulletin, 97*, 233–250.

Johns, G., & Nicholson, N. (1982). The meanings of absence: New strategies for theory and research. *Research in Organizational Behavior, 4*.

Judge, T. A., & Hulin, C. L. (1991). Job satisfaction and subjective well-being as determinants of job adaptation. *Organizational Behavior and Human Decision Processes*.

Kanfer, R., & Ackerman, P. (1996). Self-regulatory skills perspective to reducing cognitive interference. In I. Sarason, G. Pierce, & B. Sarason (Eds.), *Cognitive interference: Theory, methods, and findings*. Mahwah, NJ: Lawrence Erlbaum Associates.

Kanfer, R., Ackerman, P., & Heggestad, E. (1996). Motivational skills and self-regulation for learning: A trait perspective. *Learning and Individual Differences, 8*, 185–209.

Lazarus, R. (1991) *Emotion and adaptation*. New York: Oxford University Press.

Locke, E. (1976). The nature and causes of job satisfaction. In M. Dunnette (Ed.), *Handbook of industrial/organizational psychology* (1st ed.). Chicago: Rand McNally.

Lyons, T. (1972) Turnover and absenteeism: A review of relationships and shared correlates. *Personnel Psychology, 25*, 271–281.

Mathieu, J. E., Martineau, J. W., & Tannenbaum, S. I. (1993). Individual and situational influences on the development of self-efficacy: Implications for training effectiveness. *Personnel Psychology, 46*, 127–147.

Miller, H. (1981). *Withdrawal behaviors among hospital employees*. Unpublished doctoral thesis, Department of Psychology, University of Illinois at Urbana-Champaign.

Mowday, R. T., Porter, L. W., & Steers, R. M. (1982). *Employee organizational linkages: The psychology of commitment, absenteeism, and turnover*. New York: Academic Press.

Necowitz, L. B., & Roznowski, M. (1991, April). *The relationship between negative affectivity, job satisfaction, and employee behaviors*. Paper presented at the Sixth Annual Conference of the Society for Industrial and Organizational Psychology, St. Louis, MO.

Organ, D. W., & Ryan, K. (1995). A meta-analytic review of attitudinal and dispositional predictors of organizational citizenship behavior. *Personnel Psychology, 48*, 775–802.

Parker, L. E. (1993). When to fix it and when to leave: Relationships among perceived control, self-efficacy, dissent and exit. *Journal of Applied Psychology, 74*, 949–959.

Pelled, L. H., & Xin, K. R. (1999). Down and out: An investigation of the relationship between mood and employee withdrawal behavior. *Journal of Management, 25*(6), 875–895.

Pulakos, E., Arad, S., Donovan, M., & Plamondon, K. (2000). Adaptability in the workplace: Development of a taxonomy of adaptive performance. *Journal of Applied Psychology, 85*, 612–624.

Robinson, S. L. (1994, August). *Explaining retreat, voice, silence and destruction: The impact of work context of employees' responses to dissatisfaction.* Paper presented at the annual meeting of the Academy of Management, Dallas, Texas.

Robinson, S. L., & Bennett, R. J. (1995). A typology of deviant workplace behaviors: A multidimensional scaling study. *Academy of Management Journal, 38*, 555–572.

Rosse, J. G. (1983). *Employee withdrawal and adaptation: An expanded framework.* Unpublished doctoral dissertation, University of Illinois, Urbana-Champaign.

Rosse, J. G. (1988). Relations among lateness, absence and turnover: Is there a progression of withdrawal? *Human Relations, 41*(7), 517–531.

Rosse, J. G. (1991). Understanding employee withdrawal from work. In J. Jones, B. Steffy, & D. Bray (Eds.), *Applying psychology in business: The handbook for managers and human resource professionals* (pp. 668–682). Lexington, MA: Lexington Books.

Rosse, J. G., & Hulin, C. L. (1985). Adaptation to work: An analysis of employee health, withdrawal and change. *Organizational Behavior and Human Decision Processes, 36*(4), 324–347.

Rosse, J. G., & Miller, H. (1984). Absence and other employee behaviors. In P. Goodman (Ed.), *Absenteeism: New approaches to understanding, measuring, and managing employee absence.* San Francisco, CA: Jossey-Bass.

Rosse, J. G., & Noel, T. (1996). Leaving the organization: Individual differences in employee withdrawal and adaptation. In K. R. Murphy (Ed.), *Individual differences and behavior in organizations* (pp. 451–504). San Francisco, CA: Jossey-Bass.

Roznowski, M., Rosse, J. G., & Miller, H. (1992, August). *The utility of broad-band measures of employee behavior: The case for employee adaptation and citizenship.* Paper presented at the annual meeting of the Academy of Management, Las Vegas, NV.

Rushton, J. P., Brainerd, C. J., & Pressley, M. (1983). Behavioral development and construct validity: The principle of aggregation. *Psychological Bulletin, 94*, 18–38.

Skarlicki, D. P., & Folger, R. (1997). Retaliation in the workplace: The roles of distributive, procedural, and interactional justice. *Journal of Applied Psychology, 82*(3), 434–443.

Smith, F. J. (1977). Work attitudes as predictors of specific day attendance. *Journal of Applied Psychology, 62*, 16–19.

Smith, P. C. (1992). In pursuit of happiness: Why study general job satisfaction? In C. J. Cranny, P. C. Smith, & E. F. Stone (Eds.), *Job satisfaction: How people feel about their jobs and how it affects their performance* (pp. 5–19). New York: Lexington Books.

Wanberg, C., & Kammeyer-Mueller, J. (2000). Predictors and outcomes of proactivity in the socialization process. *Journal of Applied Psychology, 85*, 373–385.

Weiss, H., & Cropanzano, R. (1996). Affective events theory: A theoretical discussion of the structure, causes, and consequences of affective experiences at work. *Research in Organizational Behavior, 18*, 1–74.

Weiss, H., & Ilgen, D. (1985). Routinized behavior in organizations. *Journal of Behavioral Economics, 14*, 57–67.

Weiss, H., Nicholas, J., & Daus, C. (1993). *Affective and cognitive influences on job satisfaction.* San Francisco, CA: Society of Industrial–Organizational Psychology.

Withey, M. J., & Cooper, W. H. (1989). Predicting exit, voice, loyalty, and neglect. *Administrative Science Quarterly, 34*, 521–539.

Write, T., & Cropanzano, R. (1997, August). *Well-being, satisfaction, and performance: Another look at the happy/productive worker thesis.* Paper presented at the annual meeting of the Academy of Management, Boston.

Modeling Organizational Behavior

Exploring Patterns of Aggressive Behaviors in Organizations: Assessing Model–Data Fit

Theresa M. Glomb
University of Minnesota

Andrew G. Miner
University of Illinois at Urbana-Champaign

Anger and its expression in aggressive behaviors are prevalent in organizations (Bureau of Labor Statistics, 1995; Northwestern National Life, 1993). Yet, we know little about the patterns of relationships among aggressive behaviors and how these behaviors unfold over time. Further, correlational and experimental methods, our standard research disciplines (Cronbach, 1957, 1975), are not particularly useful for investigating these issues. Although traditional methods have their own strengths, they all have the general disadvantage of being extremely limited in their ability to support the scope of causal models that are often desirable in social science (Seitz, Hulin, & Hanisch, 2000).

In this chapter, we use computational modeling to address questions about the patterns of relationships among aggressive behaviors and how these patterns unfold over time. We develop a conceptualization for the construct of aggressive behavior and use computational modeling to test four models of aggressive behavior against empirical data and against one another.

Computational modeling provides unique leverage to this investigation of aggressive behaviors because it may "simulate the outputs of complex, non-linear systems that, because of the interactions among components in the formal models, cannot be derived from, or attributed to, their specific components" (Seitz et al., 2000, p. 2). We treat aggressive behaviors as a complex, nonlinear system of interconnected attitudes and behaviors and use computational modeling to help us understand this system and its underlying processes.

Early research into aggression in the workplace was undermined by a focus on extreme, low base rate behaviors (e.g., homicide or physical assault; Folger & Baron, 1996). The approach taken in the current study is consistent with that taken by previous aggression researchers (Barling, 1996; Baron & Neuman, 1996; Folger & Baron, 1996; Neuman & Baron, 1998) that conceptualized a set of aggressive behaviors, rather than a focus on a single behavior. This approach has been used by Hulin and colleagues in studying withdrawal behavior. Computational modeling allows us to examine a broad array of behaviors and track their enactment over time, thereby avoiding the low base rate problem of studying extreme aggressive behaviors and permitting the study of patterns of relationships among aggressive behaviors.

Correlational and experimental methods fail to take into account dynamic feedback processes that are likely to operate over time among different behaviors (Hulin, 1991). Computational modeling can complement correlational and experimental designs by providing a means of testing propositions of dynamic models over time (Hanisch, Hulin, & Seitz, 1996). Instead of trying to control or ignore the complexity of human behavior, computational modeling embraces the dynamic, nonlinear, stochastic nature of behavior and models the implications of complex theories. When used in a way that complements data obtained from empirical studies, computational modeling can add to our understanding of behaviors captured as a cross-sectional snapshot in an organization. Computational modeling allows us to compare the output from multiple models with one another as well as with data obtained using other research designs (Munson & Hulin, 2000). In the current study of aggressive behavior, we examine the accordance of empirical data to data simulated under the theoretical assumptions of four models of aggressive behaviors using *WORKER* (Seitz, Hanisch, & Hulin, 1995), a computer program that simulates the functioning of individual behaviors within organizations over time. Comparisons of output from real organizations and WORKER modeled, virtual, organizations allow us to evaluate the usefulness of various dynamic models of aggressive behavior in an organizational setting.

We begin this chapter by reviewing prior research on aggression with the goal of translating current knowledge into models of aggressive behavior appropriate for use in computational modeling. We identify parallels between the functioning of aggressive behaviors and organizational withdrawal behaviors. We describe our approach to computational modeling of aggressive behaviors using WORKER. We also describe the cross-sectional data that we use both to generate the input for the models and to provide an empirical comparison for the data generated by WORKER.

CONCEPTUALIZING AGGRESSION

The Behavioral Construct of Aggression

Attention to violent behaviors in organizations has focused largely on extreme examples of aggressive behavior, particularly workplace homicide. Although the seriousness of workplace homicides and other extreme acts of aggression should not be dismissed, restricting our study to the most extreme forms of workplace aggression would not only create problems associated with low base rate phenomena (Hulin & Rousseau, 1980), but would also fail to represent adequately the construct space (Baron & Neuman, 1996; Greenberg & Barling, 1999).

Our conceptualization of aggression is similar to that of Neuman and Baron (1998), who define workplace aggression as "efforts by individuals to harm others with whom they work, or have worked, or the organizations in which they are presently, or were previously, employed" (p. 395) with the exception that we focus more on interpersonal forms of aggression rather than aggression directed at the organization (e.g., theft). The current study defines aggression as a behavioral construct (Baron & Neuman, 1996; Folger & Baron, 1996; Neuman & Baron, 1998) that includes a variety of harmful behaviors, such as yelling, swearing, talking behind someone's back, and physical assault. This behavioral construct approach enables the consideration of relations among a set of behaviors over time.

Theories of Aggression and Their Relations to Theories of Organizational Withdrawal Behaviors

Although WORKER was intended for use in modeling organizational withdrawal behaviors, we believe that the library of models simulated in WORKER are applicable to alternative organizational behaviors, including aggressive behaviors, for two reasons. One reason is the parallel in the conceptualization of the behavioral constructs of aggression and withdrawal and their placement in a broad attitude–behavior framework. The other reason is the generalizability of models explicating the underlying processes that link attitudes to behavior. The constructs of aggressive behaviors and organizational withdrawal behaviors have common characteristics: Both sets of behaviors should be conceptualized as broad behavioral constructs with dynamic interrelationships, and both are conceptualized as preceded by affective or attitudinal states.

Our approach to the behavioral construct of aggression is derivative of the work by Hulin and colleagues (Hanisch & Hulin, 1990, 1991; Hulin, 1991) in their program of research on organizational withdrawal. *Organi-*

zational withdrawal is defined as employees' attempts to remove themselves from their work tasks either permanently (e.g., turnover, retirement) or temporarily (e.g., absenteeism, tardiness). In Hulin and colleagues' research, they widen the lens to include a variety of behaviors that are representative of the broader behavioral construct of organizational withdrawal (e.g., wandering around looking busy, spending time on personal tasks), rather than focusing on low base rate, binary withdrawal behaviors such as turnover and absenteeism.

Our understanding of organizational withdrawal has benefited substantially from computational modeling (Hanisch et al., 1996; Munson & Hulin, 2000). We anticipate that computational modeling will also improve our understanding of workplace aggression by complementing traditional research methods that are inadequate to explore fully dynamic theories that involve complex, nonlinear interactions between aggressive behaviors and their antecedent conditions. We argue that the underlying process linking behaviors and their antecedent attitudes is similar for both aggressive and withdrawal behaviors. Both aggressive and withdrawal behaviors are preceded by some affective or attitudinal state. The presence of negative affectivity and the functionality of behavior in reducing the negative affectivity are key common elements in the process underlying aggression and organizational withdrawal.

Negative affectivity in the form of job dissatisfaction is an antecedent of organizational withdrawal behaviors, defined as attempts to remove oneself from the job situation (Hulin, 1991). Models of organizational withdrawal propose job satisfaction, or the affective response to one's job, as an antecedent of withdrawal, although the specific placement and operation of affect may be different in each model. These models presume that individuals seek to reduce the negative affect associated with their jobs by enacting withdrawal behaviors. Various alternative relationships between antecedent attitudes or affect and behavior are captured in the models of behavior simulated in WORKER. We hypothesize that aggressive behaviors also function to reduce negative affectivity and the underlying processes linking affect to behavior can be represented by the same models of behavior used to explain withdrawal behaviors.

In the past, aggression theorists have investigated the direct and indirect antecedents of aggressive behaviors in search of a general antecedent condition with explanatory power for aggressive situations (e.g., the frustration–aggression hypothesis; Dollard, Doob, Miller, Mowrer, & Sears, 1939; Miller, 1941). Recent conceptualizations, however, have focused on the role of negative affect rather than the source of the negative affect (e.g., frustration, injustice). A negative affective state is the mediating link between frustration and aggression in a recent revision of the frustration–aggression hypothesis offered by Berkowitz (1993). Berkowitz (1993) proposed "the negative affect is the fundamental spur to the aggressive in-clination" (p. 44) and "it is the degree of negative affect that matters, not whether [the frustration] is an insult or a thwarting" (p. 45). The emphasis in Berkowitz's reconceptualization is no longer on the specific antecedent frustration, but rather, on the negative affect that is created from the frus-trating condition. It is the negative affect that produces the instigation to aggress in this model. If the instigation to aggress results in an aggressive behavior, as opposed to an alternative response (Berkowitz, 1993), the ag-gression may result in a reduction of the negative affect experienced. Sev-eral other theories of aggressive behavior also postulate general mecha-nisms analogous to a reduction in negative affectivity associated with aggression enactment. Geen (1990) suggested that the reduction of nega-tive affect may be viewed as similar to the operation of catharsis. The insti-gation to aggress is reduced or eliminated following aggression, making subsequent aggression less likely. Bies, Tripp, and Kramer (1997) pro-posed a "thermodynamic" model of revenge in organizations. Their model postulates a process by which individuals "heat up" in reaction to a variety of perceived events and wrongdoings and then cool down through a variety of processes including venting, dissipating, and expressing their built-up emotional energy. The reduction of emotional energy through the expression of this energy is similar to the proposed process underlying the reduction of negative affectivity.

Our models of aggressive behavior assume this link between the reduc-tion of negative affectivity and aggressive behaviors. A common theme that runs throughout the models we now turn to is that behaviors are func-tional in reducing the underlying attitudinal or affective state that led to their enactment.

Models

We evaluate four models of aggressive behavior in organizations against the pattern of empirical data; the empirical data document the frequen-cies with which aggressive behaviors are enacted in a single time period in a real organization and the correlations or structure of these behaviors. These empirical data represent a correlational snapshot of the relations among aggressive behaviors of many separate individuals in an organiza-tion at one period of time. The computational models we are proposing allow us to produce simulated correlation matrices among aggressive be-haviors in a virtual organization resulting from the behaviors of many sim-ulated individuals behaving in accordance with the rules outlined by the four models. A major contribution of this study is that we compare the structures among aggressive behaviors estimated in two organizations, one real and one virtual. In the virtual organization, the rules by which behaviors affect each other and their antecedent attitudes are varied when testing the four different models. Our criterion for evaluation of these models is the degree of fit of the simulated correlation matrix among behaviors from many individuals acting according to the rules of the models to a parallel matrix from a real organization. There is no null hypothesis as such; rather, our method of asking which of four models seems to best fit our data is one of strong inference (Platt, 1964). The four models are independent forms of aggression, the spillover model of aggression, progression of aggression, and compensatory aggressive behaviors. Each model is described briefly. For further explanation of each model's functioning in terms of organizational withdrawal behaviors, see Hulin (1991).

The *independent forms model* is derived from a model originally proposed by March and Simon (1958) to explain the independence of absenteeism and quitting behaviors. It has been extended in WORKER to model each enactment of a behavior, in this case, enactment of each aggressive behavior, as essentially independent of the others. In this model, there are no direct linkages between the behaviors, with the exception that over time, behaviors will tend to be dampened by regression toward the mean level of behavior in the organization. This "self-organized criticality" removes the possibility that the level of enactment of any behavior can drift off to infinity. This model should produce structures reflecting independence of behaviors within any given time period, moderated only by the degree to which the antecedent attitudes are related to each other.

In proposing the *spillover model* Beehr and Gupta (1978) argued that behaviors should be positively intercorrelated—there should be a nucleus of behaviors that occur in concert. Thus, a frustrating work situation may generate several different aggressive behaviors at the same time. Relationships among these different aggressive behaviors can be expressed as conditional probabilities of one aggressive behavior occurring in a time period given that another aggressive behavior has occurred in that same time period. These spillover effects, from behaviors to other behaviors, occur independently of the indirect effects that enacted behaviors have on other behaviors through their effects on intervening attitudes and intentions (Hanisch et al., 1996). This model intuitively seems to make sense in terms of organizational aggression. The enactment of one behavior in an organization is unlikely to be an isolated event given the reciprocal nature of most aggression episodes. Rather, expressions of one form of aggressive behavior will spillover onto the enactment of other aggressive behaviors independent of the precipitating emotions or cognitions.

The *progression model* postulates that behaviors are enacted in an ordered sequence from least to most severe (Seitz et al., 2000). Each enacted behavior feeds back onto its antecedent attitude to the degree specified by the degree of belongingness of that behavior to the construct. Yelling vents anger or negative affect to the degree that it belongs to the construct of aggression; yelling should be less effective in reducing latent negative affect than should engaging in physical aggression, but more effective than talking behind the person's back. Over time, as behaviors become less functional in reducing the negative affect, extreme behaviors will be enacted more frequently compared to less extreme behaviors. For example, initially, physically aggressive behavior will be preceded by lower level behaviors such as yelling and enacting angry gestures, but over time, physical aggression will be more likely to be enacted because the individual will have progressed through the milder behaviors and found they have not reduced the negative affect. This model is similar to the "popcorn model" of aggression proposed by Folger and Baron (1996), in which emotional energy builds up over time until it explodes in some aggressive incident. If one extends this statement to include the enactment of lesser behaviors as negative affect inevitably builds up, then it may resemble the progression of aggression model.

The *compensatory behaviors model* postulates that any one of several behaviors may satisfy an attitudinal propensity (Seitz et al., 2000). This has implications for organizational interventions to partially block a specific behavior; because the behaviors function in a compensatory manner, blocking one will increase the likelihood that others will occur. Those behaviors that are sanctioned less may occur together. The behaviors that are heavily punished may produce weak relations with any other behavior because they will have low base rates. In the case of aggressive behavior, it is easy to see that some behaviors are much more severely punished than others (e.g., physical aggression is much easier to see and punish than is talking behind another person's back). Typically the passive and indirect cells of Buss's (1961) aggression framework may be enacted frequently under this model because other behaviors, although more direct and perhaps more functional, are heavily punished.

The complexity and dynamic nature of these models and difficulties inherent in studying the patterns of aggressive behaviors over time with traditional methods illustrates the benefits of computational modeling in the study of aggressive behaviors. This initial exploration into the nature of aggression using computational modeling attempts to examine the functioning of the models and the extent to which they can account for the pattern of behaviors observed in real organizations.

WORKER

The WORKER software we use to model aggressive behavior was developed originally to model organizational withdrawal behavior (Hanisch et al., 1996; Munson & Hulin, 2000). There is nothing inherent in the software, however that limits its application to withdrawal behavior. The software allows the modeling of complex systems of behavior, and the exploration of the emergent dynamic, nonlinear properties of models of those behaviors.

WORKER models organizational behavior mathematically using user-specified parameters such as the thresholds of behaviors, the degree to which any given behavior represents the underlying construct, the interrelatedness among behaviors, and the sanctions an organization imposes on each behavior. WORKER creates a sample of employees from user-specified age and tenure distributions of employees and simulates the attitudes and behaviors of each employee over a user-specified number of iterations (or time periods), in which employees may engage or not engage in any of a number of aggressive behaviors as a function of algorithms linking attitudes and behaviors stochastically. Enacting a given behavior has implications for that employee's level of negative affect. Exactly what those implications are depends on the model hypothesized to be operating. For example, in the compensatory model, behaviors are substitutable, so enacting any behavior causes the overall latent level of negative affect to be reduced and reduces the probability that other aggressive behaviors will be enacted in the current time period or iteration.

Any behavior can be seen as being caused by a number of events, resulting in seemingly random enactment of behavior. WORKER models this stochastic nature of behavior in two ways. The first way is by allowing the user to determine the degree to which the behaviors are intercorrelated by loading them differentially on a common vector. Behaviors that are weakly related appear to be acting in a random manner because they will be determined by many other factors besides the one that relates the behaviors to each other. The second is by including *1% rules* (Hanisch et al., 1996) that allow for unexpected behavior (i.e., behavior not explainable under the algorithms linking attitudes to behaviors) approximately 1% of the time. These properties allow the modeler to account for the fuzzy borders of the set of aggressive behaviors postulated by modern theories of aggression and to more realistically model the stochastic nature of real-world behavioral systems.

In order to use WORKER in the way that we are proposing, as a tool to assess the validity of models of behavior operating in a given organization, we need to specify a number of organizational and employee characteristics. For the behaviors in the model, we need to specify the structure among the behaviors, the threshold above which each behavior is likely to be enacted, the level of stochastic influence around that threshold, the organizational sanctions for engaging in a behavior, and the degree to which each behavior is a representative instance of, or belongs to, the construct of aggression. These parameters are necessary components to define each behavior as a member of the behavioral construct of aggressive behaviors. To create a more realistic modeling of our set of aggressive behaviors, we used empirically obtained thresholds and degrees of belongingness. The structure of the behaviors and the organizational sanctions were determined using empirical data collected for other purposes as logical proxies for this information. It is important to note that this primary set of inputs to the modeling software is obtained empirically and are not merely speculative.

METHOD

Participants

Pilot Sample. A total of 98 participants (50 women and 48 men) with a mean age of 18.5 years participated in a pilot study. The participants were undergraduates from a large, midwestern university who participated to fulfill an introductory psychology course requirement. The majority of the participants reported having had some exposure to the workplace in the form of part-time and full-time jobs, but little or no formal supervisory experience.

Sample 1. The first sample consisted of 115 employees (15 women and 100 men) from a large manufacturing corporation. Participants were selected to be approximately representative in terms of the gender and department and/or job category composition in the plant. The average tenure for employees from this company was 18 years, 3 months. Average age was 44.8 years. Management comprised 45% of the total sample.

Sample 2. The second sample consisted of 132 employees (69 women and 63 men) from a light manufacturing company. Attempts were made to select participants who had participated in a previous data collection to allow for cross-time comparisons. These cross-time comparisons were on variables not relevant to the current study. Additional participants were selected in proportions that were approximately representative of the plant in terms of job category and shift. The average tenure for employees was 4 years, 7 months. Average age was 36.2 years.

Sample 3. The third sample consisted of 93 employees (68 women and 25 men) from a large midwestern university who participated in a training session on violence in the workplace. Training participants received a questionnaire packet at the end of the training session and returned it via campus mail. The average tenure for employees from this organization was 10 years, 11 months. Average age was 44.7 years.

Questionnaire Administration Procedure

In all three samples and the pilot sample, participant groups were informed that they would be responding to a questionnaire designed to measure job attitudes, job experiences, personal characteristics, and questions related to interpersonal conflict, anger, and aggression. Following oral instructions given by the researcher and the signing of consent forms (Pilot Sample only), participants completed a questionnaire packet or completed it at another time (Sample 3). Sessions lasted approximately 15 to 30 minutes in the Pilot Sample and approximately 20 to 50 minutes in Samples 1 and 2.

Measures

A questionnaire was developed to assess the organizational and individual antecedents of the frequency with which people report experiencing aggression in organizations, the characteristics of angry encounters in the workplace, and the job, interpersonal, and personal outcomes of workplace aggression. For the pilot sample, additional measures were added in which participants were asked to indicate the extent to which they considered a list of 18 behaviors to be aggressive and the probability that someone who was angry would engage in these 18 behaviors on the job. The constructs relevant for this study are now described.

Frequency of the Expression of Aggressive Behaviors in Organizations.
The *Angry Experiences Scale (AES)* was constructed to assess the frequency with which respondents engage in and are the target of a variety of aggressive behaviors. Development of the scale relied primarily on two sources: structured individual interviews with 72 employees from three organizations concerning the antecedents, consequences, and characteristics of a workplace aggression incident, and the work of previous aggression researchers, particularly the work of Baron, Neuman, and colleagues (Baron & Neuman, 1996; Folger & Baron, 1996; Neuman & Baron, 1998). The Buss (1961) framework that classifies behavioral forms of aggression according to the dimensions of direct and indirect, active and passive, and verbal and physical aggression was also used to classify behaviors.

The AES has two separate 24-item scales; one in which respondents indicate whether they have engaged in the aggressive behavior described and the other in which respondents indicate whether they have been the target of the aggressive behavior described. The scale in which participants report the frequency with which they engaged in the aggressive behaviors is used in this study. Respondents were asked to indicate how frequently they had engaged in 24 behaviors using a 6-point scale ranging from *never* to *once a week or more*.

Degree of Aggressiveness. A scale was developed to assess the extent to which a behavior is considered aggressive. Respondents were asked whether 18 behaviors would be considered aggressive using a 7-point response scale ranging from *definitely not* to *absolutely yes*. The 18 behaviors in this scale are a subset of the 24 behaviors asked about in the AES. (These 18 behaviors were selected because they were used to collect data on specific aggressive encounters in another study.) These data give us an indication of the degree to which each behavior belongs to the fuzzy set of aggressive behaviors and are used to set the degree of aggressiveness parameters in the WORKER simulations. The 7-point response scale was rescaled to have a mean of .5 and a variance of .25, the appropriate range for WORKER input.

Behavioral Thresholds. To assess the likelihood that someone would engage in a given aggressive behavior when angered, respondents were asked to indicate how probable it was that someone who was angry would engage in a behavior on the job using a 5-point response scale ranging from *highly improbable* to *highly probable*. This scale asked about the same set of 18 behaviors in the aforementioned scale. These empirical data are used to set the thresholds in the WORKER simulations, the threshold above which an individual is increasingly likely to engage in a particular behavior. The 5-point response scale was also rescaled to have a mean of .5 and a variance of .25.

WORKER Simulation Procedure

Selection of Behaviors and Input Parameters. From the set of aggressive behaviors, six were selected for the WORKER simulations based on data from the Degree of Aggressiveness and Behavioral Threshold measures. Only six behaviors were used to enable clarity of exposition. Behaviors spanning the range of item mean values for the Degree of Aggressiveness and Behavioral Threshold were selected (i.e., behaviors with high, medium, and low degrees of aggressiveness and behavioral thresholds). Thus, behaviors varied in the degree to which they were considered aggressive and the likelihood that someone would engage in them if angry. Table 11.1 depicts the behaviors and the corresponding Thresholds and Degrees of Aggression.

Organizational sanctions can be set in WORKER to simulate the degree to which an organization discourages or encourages certain behaviors. Sanctions range from 0 to 1, with 1 representing a severe, negative sanc-

TABLE 11.1
WORKER Input Parameters for Thresholds, Degree
of Aggressiveness, Sanctions, and Loadings on the Common Vector

Behavior	Threshold[a]	Degree of Aggression[a]	Sanction[b]	Loadings on Common Vector
Making angry gestures (e.g., pound fists, roll eyes)	.3230	.4991	.65	.72
Insulting, criticizing another (including sarcasm)	.2992	.4351	.60	.71
Yelling or raising voice	.2915	.4768	.60	.71
Talking behind someone's back	.2846	.2794	.55	.61
Physically assaulting another	.5500[c]	.9106	.80	.42
Making threats	.5000[c]	.7493	.70	.70

Note. [a]Values derived from empirical data. [b]Sanction values can range from 0 to 1.0 and are scaled such that 1.0 = severe negative sanctions. [c]The original empirical values of .9764 and .7933 for physical assault and making threats respectively resulted in an abnormal functioning of the models. Thus, the values were reduced to their present values (.5500 and .5000) to allow for normal functioning.

tion. In these simulations, sanctions were set so that each behavior was either severely negatively sanctioned or moderately negatively sanctioned. The rank order of the sanctions was determined using data from a separate study in which the 24 behaviors of the AES were scaled in terms of severity (Glomb, 1998). Behaviors perceived as more severe were assigned greater organizational sanctions. As shown in Table 11.1, behaviors such as physical assault and making threats were severely sanctioned (.80 and .70), and others such as talking behind someone's back or yelling were moderately sanctioned (between .50 and .60).

The structure among behaviors can be represented by the loadings of selected behaviors on a common vector. In WORKER, one can set initial input parameters representing the loadings of each of the behaviors on a common vector. In this study, data from confirmatory factor analyses conducted on the behaviors in the AES scale were used to provide empirical basis for the loadings of the six aggressive behaviors. The loadings used in WORKER for the aggressive behaviors are presented in Table 11.1.

WORKER Simulations and Output. An organization with the input parameters described above and shown in Table 11.1 was created in WORKER and each of the four models was used to simulate aggressive behaviors over 40 iterations. Each iteration represents a behavior cycle or time period. We examined correlations among the behaviors at the midpoint (Iteration 20) and the final iteration (Iteration 40). These iterations were selected so as not to be too early for a system to stabilize while still allowing for some information about the unfolding of the system from the midpoint to the final iteration. Correlations among behaviors at Iterations 20 and 40 for each simulated model were compared to the empirical correlation matrices for Samples 1, 2, and 3, shown in Table 11.2, by calculating the root mean squared residual (RMSR).

The RMSR is a measure of the average of the residuals from the comparison of the empirical and simulated correlation matrices. However, caution must be taken in interpreting the RMSR values in this study for several reasons. First, these RMSR values should only be interpreted relative to one another rather than in comparison to an absolute value. The correlation matrices for the empirical and simulated data on which these calculations are based are subject to different sources of variance. Specifically, the empirical matrix contains variance from several sources: the true belongingness of behaviors to the latent construct of aggression, common variance across all measures due to rating/response set, and error variance. The WORKER simulated matrix will contain only the first of these, thus reducing the common variance among behaviors and attenuating the simulated correlations. Comparing these attenuated correlations from the simulated data to the empirical data serves to artificially inflate the RMSR values.

TABLE 11.2
Empirical Item Means, Standard Deviations, and Intercorrelations
Among Aggressive Behaviors for Samples 1, 2, and 3

| | Item | | Intercorrelations | | | | | |
Behavior	Mean	SD	1.	2.	3.	4.	5.	6.
1. Angry Gestures	1.89[a]	1.26	—	.18	.45	.13	.28	.27
	2.49	1.71		.53	.65	.47	.17	.44
	1.71	1.26		.26	.46	.38	—	.24
2. Insulting, criticizing	2.74	1.62		—	.30	.45	.12	.21
another	2.63	1.74			.46	.46	.12	.39
	2.57	1.47			.45	.54	—	.14
3. Yelling	2.43	1.33			—	.23	.32	.37
	2.75	1.88				.39	.10	.33
	1.83	1.22				.34	—	.13
4. Talking behind back	2.45	1.41				—	.18	.22
	2.21	1.60					.16	.39
	2.44	1.39					—	.06
5. Physical Assault	1.03	0.16					—	.55
	1.15	0.65						.59
	1.00	0.00						—
6. Making Threats	1.15	0.55						—
	1.32	0.87						
	1.03	0.23						

Note. [a]Means, standard deviations and intercorrelations for Samples 1, 2, and 3 are shown in the first, second, and third rows, respectively.

A second caution in interpreting the RMSR has to do with the assumption that the behavioral system has reached some point of equilibrium. Thus, the RMSR index, like other fit indices, is not appropriate for dynamic systems that may not be stable. Using the RMSR index for dynamic data would require that the underlying system has reached a point of stability, an assumption that may not be valid. However, there currently exist no measures for assessing the fit of dynamic systems, so the RMSR is used as a reasonable, albeit flawed, substitute.

A third caution in interpreting the RMSR is that it is concerned with distance, as opposed to rank. It may be that ranks are a more appropriate measure to use in these comparisons of simulated to empirical data. For all these reasons, caution should be used in interpreting results based on this imperfect index in the absence of a superior way to test the fit of dynamic data.

RESULTS

The parameters just described were input into WORKER and individual behaviors were simulated over time according to the rules of each model. The resulting correlation matrices among behaviors at the 20th and 40th iteration were compared to the empirical correlation matrices among behaviors from three organizations. To the extent that one model is a more accurate description of the dynamic processes occurring in the real organizations, the RMSR index of fit between modeled and real correlations will be lower than it is for other models. The RMSR values shown in Table 11.3 for all models and samples were between .10 and .38. Comparisons of the fit of the structure among behaviors between modeled and empirical data suggest that the structure of the data simulated by the independent forms model fits the structure of our empirical data best. RMSR values are lower than those of the other three models across samples and iterations. However, the limitations of the RMSR index as discussed limit us from drawing a definitive conclusion.

Examination of Table 11.3 also suggests that the degree to which the data produced by the simulated model is an appropriate representation of empirical data depends on the organization. The RMSR values for a particular model and iteration differ somewhat across the organizations. Differences in the degree to which the models fit the data for the three samples may suggest that the pattern of sanctions, thresholds, or degrees of belongingness and their operation in the simulations are more similar to those in operation in some organizations than in others. These differential fits across organizations demonstrate our inability to conclude that the independent forms model is superior to the others; alternative models

TABLE 11.3
Root Mean Square Residual Index of Fit Between
Empirical and Simulated Correlation Matrices

	20th Iteration			40th Iteration		
Model	Sample 1	Sample 2	Sample 3	Sample 1	Sample 2	Sample 3
Compensatory behaviors	.32	.26	.34	.37	.30	.38
Independent forms	.15	.19	.10	.18	.23	.14
Spillover forward	.21	.28	.16	.23	.30	.17
Progression	.25	.32	.21	.25	.32	.20

may have comparatively lower RMSR in other organizations. Nevertheless, the RMSR values suggest that the simulated correlation matrix produced by the independent forms model fits the empirical data best.

DISCUSSION

The current study explores the advantages of an alternative research method, computational modeling, and presents preliminary information about the appropriateness of models of aggression in organizations. Although results failed to generate overwhelming support for the superior fit of any one model, they do suggest that models may be differentially valid across organizations and also show the usefulness of computational modeling as a research tool to assess complex behavioral systems.

The lack of strong support for one model may be due to the problems encountered in comparing empirical data to simulated data. As noted, our empirical data is subject to sources of variance not present in the simulated data. These alternative sources of variance will be a limitation for any comparison of empirical data to simulated data that account solely for signal and not noise.

Further, alternative forms of empirical data may have more closely mirrored the behavioral processes and output simulated by WORKER. The optimal empirical data for comparison would assess individuals longitudinally and would enable us to compare the dynamic functioning of aggressive behaviors for individuals at various points in time. By comparing one iteration of the simulated model to the cross-sectional empirical data as we did in the current study, we are exploiting the features of WORKER that address the issue of time, yet we do not have the data to assess how our empirical organization changes over time. We are assuming that an iteration in WORKER is similar to the segment of time being tapped by the self-report AES scale. This limitation illustrates the necessity of considering and difficulty of accounting for organizational time in our research. That is, we do not know the speed at which these behavioral processes unfold. For example, the progression of aggression model states that individuals will progress through behaviors, but this model, as well as the others, provides little information about how quickly individuals will progress through behaviors. Using empirical data that more closely parallels the simulated output for comparison would provide superior information about the extent to which a given theoretical model is operating and answer important questions about how the processes operate over time.

One potential issue that arises on examination of the modeled output is the degree to which a system is stable, or at equilibrium. The similarity of the RMSR values between the 20th and 40th iterations for all models indicate that there is some fluctuation in the simulated correlations (because the real correlation matrix is constant), but that it is not large. In reality, we would expect the real correlation matrix to change over time if we had multiple measurements. However, if one makes the assumption, as we have, that the systems under investigation are relatively stable, then our approach of comparing modeled organizations with cross-sectional empirical data is reasonable.

The results of this study clearly demonstrate the importance of assessing behavioral constructs rather than single, low base rate behaviors, which are often the focus of research. The intercorrelations among behaviors in Sample 1, Sample 2, and Sample 3 suggest that aggressive behaviors are related in a consistent pattern (see Table 11.2). Research approaches that do not account for this interrelatedness and patterning among behaviors neglect the true nature of the underlying construct. Such approaches also fail to take advantage of the gains in reliability and validity offered by assessing multiple manifestations of a latent construct. As an illustration, imagine how different our interpretations and limited our information would be if we were to look solely at information on a single behavior, such as physical assault, rather than the correlations, patterns, and frequencies of multiple behaviors over time. This study illustrates the need for alternative research approaches that are capable of addressing questions about the structural and functional relations of complex behavioral constructs like aggression.

DIRECTIONS FOR FUTURE RESEARCH

Opportunities for future research are numerous. First, future simulations could expand the scope of the construct by including additional aggressive behaviors and their patterns of relationships over time. Second, additional data sets from different organizations could be used to determine the organizational boundary conditions on the operation of various models. Empirical data from different organizations regarding employees' perceptions of the organizational sanctions, behavioral thresholds, and degrees of belongingness could be used for input into WORKER to determine those boundary conditions. Differences in model fit across organizations found in the current study suggest that the input characteristics and their operation could be more similar to those in operation in some organizations than in others. If, as suggested by these results, different models operate differently in different organizations, interventions to reduce or redirect aggressive behaviors will need to be organization dependent. Third, WORKER's ability to create subpopulations, each having different input parameters can be used in future research to explore the effect of individual differences related to aggression (e.g., trait-anger, components of the Type A behavior pattern, negative affective disposition) on the enactment of behaviors over time.

CONCLUSION

Although this study may have raised more questions about the functioning of aggressive behaviors over time than it has answered, the methodology used to generate these questions, computational modeling, may be the only one capable of answering them. The issues raised in this study illustrate many of the complexities of human, organizational behavior in systems that are stochastic and dynamic—complexities that are not well addressed by traditional research methods. In conjunction with these traditional research methods, this innovative research tool is likely to prove invaluable for exploring the patterning of aggressive behaviors over time and investigating potential means of reducing organizational aggression.

REFERENCES

Barling, J. (1996) The prediction, experience, and consequences of workplace violence. In E. Q. Bulatao & G. R. VandenBos (Eds.), *Violence on the job: Identifying risks and developing solutions* (pp. 29–49). Washington, DC: American Psychological Association.

Baron, R. A., & Neuman, J. H. (1996). Workplace violence and workplace aggression: Evidence of their relative frequency and potential causes. *Aggressive Behavior, 22*, 161–173.

Beehr, T. A., Gupta, N. (1978). A note on the structure of employee withdrawal. *Organizational Behavior and Human Performance, 21*, 73–79.

Berkowitz, L. (1993). *Aggression: Its causes, consequences, and control*. Philadelphia, PA: Temple University Press.

Bies, R. J., Tripp, T. M., & Kramer, R. M. (1997). At the breaking point: Cognitive and social dynamics of revenge in organizations. In R. A. Giacalone & J. Greenberg (Eds.), *Antisocial behavior in organizations* (pp. 18–36). Thousand Oaks, CA: Sage.

Bureau of Labor Statistics, U.S. Department of Labor. (1995, August 3). News. *National census of fatal occupational injuries, 1994* [news release]. Washington, DC: Author.

Buss, A. H. (1961). *The psychology of aggression*. New York: Wiley.

Cronbach, L. J. (1957). The two disciplines of scientific psychology. *American Psychologist, 12*, 671–684.

Cronbach, L. J. (1975). Beyond the two disciplines of scientific psychology. *American Psychologist, 30*, 116–127.

Dollard, J., Doob, L. W., Miller, N. E., Mowrer, O. H., & Sears, R. R. (1939). *Frustration and aggression*. New Haven, CT: Yale University Press.

Folger, R., & Baron, R. A. (1996). Violence and hostility at work: A model of reactions to perceived injustice. In E. Q. Bulatao & G. R. VandenBos (Eds.), *Violence on the job: Identifying risks and developing solutions* (pp. 51–85). Washington, DC: American Psychological Association.

Geen, R. G. (1990). *Human aggression*. Pacific Grove, CA: Brooks/Cole.

Glomb, T. M. (1998). *Anger and aggression in organizations: Antecedents, behavioral components, and consequences*. Unpublished doctoral dissertation, University of Illinois at Urbana-Champaign.

Greenberg, L., & Barling, J. (1999). Predicting employee aggression against coworkers, subordinates and supervisors: The roles of person behaviors and perceived workplace factors. *Journal of Organizational Behavior, 20*, 897–913.

Hanisch, K. A., & Hulin, C. L. (1990). Job attitudes and organizational withdrawal: An examination of retirement and other voluntary withdrawal behaviors. *Journal of Vocational Behavior, 37*, 60–78.

Hanisch, K. A., & Hulin, C. L. (1991). General attitudes and organizational withdrawal: An evaluation of a causal model. *Journal of Vocational Behavior, 39*, 110–128.

Hanisch, K. A., Hulin, C. L., & Seitz, S. T. (1996). Mathematical/computational modeling of organizational withdrawal processes: Benefits, methods, and results. In G. R. Ferris, A. Nedd, J. B. Shaw, J. E. Beck, P. S. Kirkbride, & K. M. Rowland (Eds.), *Research in personnel and human resources management* (Vol. 14, pp. 91–142). Greenwich, CT: JAI Press.

Hulin, C. L. (1991). Adaptation, persistence, and commitment in organizations. In M. D. Dunnette (Ed.), *Handbook of industrial organizational psychology* (Vol. 2, 2nd ed., pp. 435–505). New York: Wiley.

Hulin, C. L., & Rousseau, D. M. (1980). Analyzing unfrequent events: Once you find them your troubles begin. *New Directions for Methodology of Social and Behavioral Science, 6*, 65–75.

March, J. G., & Simon, H. A. (1958). *Organizations*. New York: Wiley.

Miller, N. E. (1941). The frustration–aggression hypothesis. *Psychological Review, 48*, 337–342.

Munson, L. J., & Hulin, C. L. (2000). Applications of computational modeling to organizational behavior: Issues of model/data fit. In C. L. Hulin & D. R. Ilgen (Eds.), *Computational modeling of behavioral processes in organizations* (pp. 69–84). Washington, DC: American Psychological Association.

Neuman, J. H., & Baron, R. A. (1998). Workplace violence and workplace aggression: Evidence concerning specific forms, potential causes, and preferred targets. *Journal of Management, 24*, 391–419.

Northwestern National Life, Employee Benefits Division. (1993). *Fear and violence in the workplace: A survey documenting the experience of American workers*. Minneapolis, MN: Author.

Platt, J. R. (1964). Strong inference. *Science, 146*, 347–353.

Seitz, S. T., Hanisch, K. A., & Hulin, C. L. (1995). *WORKER: A computer program to simulate employee organizational withdrawal behaviors*. University of Illinois at Urbana-Champaign and Iowa State University.

Seitz, S. T., Hulin, C. L., & Hanisch, K. A. (2000). Simulating withdrawal behaviors in work organizations: An example of a virtual society. *Nonlinear Dynamics, Psychology, and Life Sciences, 4*, 33–65.

Chapter 12

Investigating Self-Presentation, Lies, and Bullshit: Understanding Faking and Its Effects on Selection Decisions Using Theory, Field Research, and Simulation

Robert A. Levin
Center for Human Function & Work, Boulder, Colorado

Michael J. Zickar
Bowling Green State University

This chapter presents the current state of our investigations into response distortion. *Response distortion*, or faking, occurs when people:

- Engage in presentation behavior, structuring or framing positively a presentation of truth
- Lie, presenting false information
- Use only expediency as the criterion for making representations, without regard for either truth or falsehood.

Response distortion is a fundamental phenomenon of human behavior. Response distortion has occurred since organisms began to transmit and receive information or signals from other organisms. It is inherent in the exchange of information itself and is enhanced whenever two parties have differential outcomes at stake. Faking in employment settings is not an isolated phenomenon but instead is consistent with how our world operates and with the central role that work plays in our world and in human lives. In our exploration of faking in personality testing in employment setting, our theoretical, empirical, and simulation results are all consistent with this broader context.

Our investigations of response distortion began when recommendations regarding faking were changing. For many years, the generally accepted view was that impression management would affect selection through effects on construct validity. Yet the more recent history of both research and wide practice led to an emerging consensus that faking would not affect personality testing. Researchers have argued that the validities of preemployment personality tests are unaffected by response distortion (e.g., Barrick & Mount, 1996; Hough, Eaton, Dunnette, Kamp, & McCloy, 1990). Adjustment of scores for faking was not recommended on the widely used Big Five personality instrument and selection measure, the NEO Personality Inventory, Revised (NEO–PI–R; Costa & McCrae, 1992). A large-scale study (Hough et al., 1990) and a meta-analysis (Ones, Viswesvaran, & Reiss, 1996) concluded that faking *can* occur but that faking and social desirability do not reduce the validity of selection decisions. The consensus seemed to be that faking on personality tests would not affect selection decisions.

These conclusions seemed counterintuitive to us. If respondents can fake (no one disputes that), and at least a small subsample of respondents do fake, concluding that "faking does not matter" seems misguided and potentially destructive. These conclusions and practices also seemed to be at odds with the perceptions of those involved most directly with using these tests. In our industrial work, employers express concerns that personality tests can be faked (see also Douglas, McDaniel & Snell, 1996) and individuals who take personality tests in these real-world employment settings report faking them (cf. Gilliland, 1995). Recommendations to not use faking scales (response distortion scales) also seemed to create a tautology for further research: Without administering faking scales, neither anomalous nor supporting data could be gathered in large-sample validation studies in realistic settings. Moreover, other researchers reported findings indicating that response distortion could impair the quality of hiring decisions by changing the rank ordering of applicants (Christiansen, Goffin, Johnston, & Rothstein, 1994; Rosse, Stecher, Miller, & Levin, 1998).

These differences pointed to two critical research needs. The first was to develop a more substantive conceptual foundation for faking strategies that might substantively affect employment selection decisions than is provided by the often vague and overlapping constructs of socially desirable responding and impression management (Leary & Kowalski, 1990). The second was to conduct empirical research, using both field research and simulation, with real applicants and real incumbents of real jobs for real companies using real tests to make real hiring decisions that had real financial consequences for the applicants hired and rejected, for the decision makers, and for the organization. Our concerns were confirmed by the results of large-scale meta-analytic studies, particularly Ones et al. (1996). The results of this study indicated that past research did not indicate that socially desirable responding affects validity correlations. In turn, this result pointed to a need for better conceptual and analytic models and a better understanding of the phenomena often lumped together as *socially desirable responding*. Consistent with the Ones et al. (1996) finding, we believe that such behaviors taken as a whole might not affect validity coefficients, but strategies embedded in these broader constructs might have particularly potent effects conveying substantial advantage to applicants who utilize them.

Our desire to develop a more focused conceptual and investigative approach was fueled by both methodological and substantive concerns with earlier studies. Our first concern lies with drawing broad inferences from meta-analyses of heterogeneous studies. The primary studies of Ones et al. (1996) used a wide range of constructs, all related to impression management and socially desirable responding. Moreover, they included studies conducted under simulated conditions, and widely ranging conditions. A meta-analysis of heterogeneous studies can be extremely useful to provide a starting point to investigate widely studied, vaguely defined constructs, but cannot logically provide an endpoint. The Ones et al. (1996) results admit of two possible conclusions, each logically inconsistent with its findings that validity coefficients were not affected overall by socially desirable responding. The first possible conclusion is that impression management and socially desirable responding do not distort selection decisions made based on preemployment personality tests. We believe that this conclusion is far too broad and cannot be logically inferred from the results, for doing so equates the lack of effect on correlation coefficients with no effects on selection decisions.

The second possible conclusion is that while impression management and socially desirable responding—as broad constructs—do not affect validity coefficients over the broad range of selection decisions, there are more specific and powerful effects on the validity of the decisions not apparent in a meta-analytic approach. These can come about in three ways: First, through specific strategies that substantively distort responses in ways that are particularly efficacious. Second, faking can work by creating effects that occur narrowly around the "critical points" of the distribution of an applicant pool involved in a selection decision. Third, faking can work by changing the validity of decisions without affecting the validity coefficient. The first two of these are the focus of our work here. The third concern, that validity coefficients are robust and insensitive to effects on relationships between tests and criteria themselves, is described in Zickar, Rosse, and Levin (1996) and Drasgow and Kang (1984).

From the field research, we knew that response distortion occurs and that it could affect rank ordering and applicant selection (Rosse, Stecher, Miller, & Levin, 1998). Now we wanted to know how. For that we turned first to developing a more focused theoretical understanding of the phenomenon of faking.

A CLASSIFICATION OF FAKING BEHAVIORS; TRUTH, FALSEHOOD, OR SOMETHING MORE?

There appear, initially, to be two broad classes of behaviors that form the basis for representations of truth and falsehood. The behaviors in the first class are primarily concerned with increasing the probability of selection by structuring the representation of truth, which we refer to as *presentation behaviors*. Of necessity, employers can only sample a small subset of an applicant's actual capabilities. Applicants who select a set of information that they deem will increase their likelihood of selection from entirely within their true set of capabilities engage in presentation behavior. As an example, a salesperson who has sold to a prestigious firm and an unknown firm might choose to focus on presenting information about selling to the prestigious firm.

The second class is characterized by increasing selection probability via the representation of falsehood, or *falsification behavior*. Much of the confusion over the nature of faking and much of the controversy over whether faking is benign or potent has come from considering faking only in dichotomous terms, that applicants might try to affect selection decisions either by selectively presenting information that is true (and possibly withholding relevant information also) or that is verifiably false (i.e., presenting false information).

The contemporary philosopher Harry Frankfurt (1986, 1988), however, moved beyond traditional neo-Platonist, two-class frameworks of *truth* and *falsehood* to create a third class of representation, one crucial to understanding faking and its effects. The neo-Platonists confounded the issue of truth and falsehood with issues of *intent*. Frankfurt formulated a third class of representation that is created without reference to truth or to falsehood but purely with regard to the expediency of the information at attaining the goal intended by the actor. By transcending truth and falsehood, this third class of information has potency beyond both truth and falsehood. Frankfurt's contribution to our theoretical model of faking is his identification of the efficacy of representations of information made without regard to truth or falsehood, instead made solely using expediency as the criterion for representations. This *expedient behavior* is a new third class of representation, especially efficacious for faking, for which Frankfurt's terminology is *bullshit*.

Expedient behavior, or bullshit, in a selection context, is characterized by increasing selection probability by the expedient behavior of creating and presenting a set of information that the actor believes will maximize the probability of selection, completely without regard to whether that information is true or false. We classify this behavior as *expedient* because truth and falsehood are no longer the basis for the presentation. The information presented is whatever is expedient at attaining the end, in this case of the offer of employment. The truth or falsehood of any statement are no longer evaluated by the presenter, only the expediency of the information. Thus, the actor constructs the representation that he or she believes will most increase the likelihood of selection. If truth or falsehood are evaluated by the actor, they are not evaluated for their own sake, but merely for whether they increase or impair the probability of the desired outcome.

This makes expedient behavior a particularly potent strategy for affecting selection decisions. Applicants who engage in expedient behavior will substantially increase their likelihood, in ways that affect rank ordering and the validity of selection decision, and can actually impair the validity of the selection system itself at its most critical point for selection decision. At the same time, these effects would not be apparent in more broad application of typical impression management scales, where they would be confounded with the other, more benign forms of faking.

Moreover, the efficacy of the expedient strategy is actually enhanced and made possible by a stable environment of honest responding (Johnstone & Grafen, 1993). Expedient presentation behavior will therefore be the most potent form of faking, one that is always present but never predominant, a pervasive form of faking that increases efficacy by increased selectivity by an employer and increased honesty in the overall applicant pool.

THE EFFICACY OF EXPEDIENT PRESENTATION

The efficacy of expedient presentation behavior, or bullshit, can best be differentiated by understanding the three other kinds of presentation behaviors in our framework that are also observed in job applicants, that are consistent with experimental results, and that do not influence selection decisions in the same way.

Background social presentation behaviors are those behaviors that an individual engages in as part of his or her regular conduct in a society that may have the effect of altering impressions, but are not performed with that intent in the selection setting. Wearing a suit to a job interview is a simple example of this behavior. Background social presentation might also be related to Paulhus's (1984) "self-deception" dimension on the Balanced Inventory of Desirable Responding, a type of responding that is often unconscious and possibly positively related to positive outcomes, such as mental health.

Situationally heightened self-presentation behavior, on the other hand, is behavior that is driven by the selection setting. The behavior is directed to maximizing the effective presentation of truthful information about one's qualifications in order to increase the probability of selection. We think of this behavior as "putting one's best foot forward," or presenting selectively the best information about one's actual qualifications in the best possible manner. Such behavior is similar to the behavior discussed in the sociologist Erving Goffman's (1959) seminal work on impression management. In Goffman's framework, people consciously select information to present to the "audience" (and hide other information) for the purposes of creating certain impressions.

Deceptive behavior (or lying), and expedient behavior (or bullshit), are as different from each other as they are from presentations of truth. Frankfurt (1988) differentiates between lying and bullshit by the scope and intent of the representation. In Frankfurt's scheme, a lie "is an act with a sharp focus" (p. 129). Lying "is designed to assert a particular falsehood at a specific point in a set or system of beliefs in order to avoid the consequences of having that point occupied by the truth" (p. 129). An example would be lying about a past criminal conviction.

Bullshit, on the other hand, is more sweeping in scope to Frankfurt (1988) and different in intent. With respect to scope, a person when bullshitting "does not limit himself to inserting a particular falsehood at a particular point . . . he is prepared to fake the context as well, so far as need requires" (p. 130). The faking of context contributes to bullshit's efficacy, and to the difficulty of detecting fakes that use bullshit. For in Frankfurt's words, "The essence of bullshit is not that it is *false*, but that it is *phony* (p. 128).

The *faking* that is characteristic of response distortion behavior—as in "faking good" on a personality measure—allows us to characterize this behavior as bullshit: expedient behavior performed with the intended outcome of creating a fake. Bullshit, in Frankfurt's (1988) words,

> differs from lies in its misrepresentational intent. The bullshitter may not deceive us, or even intend to do so, either about the facts or about what he takes the facts to be. What he does necessarily attempt to deceive us about is his enterprise. His . . . distinctive characteristic is that in a certain way he misrepresents what he is up to. (p. 130)

When one considers the nature of faking on preemployment personality testing, the characteristics of the behavior appear to be closer to bullshit than to lying: Faked information on a personality test is not identifiably false information, nor is it identifiably true. Faked personality information is itself a fake of a context for performance rather than of performance itself. And the applicant who fakes on a personality test deceives us about his or her enterprise: The applicant is not responding in order to provide either a true representation or a false representation of his or her personality. The applicant is responding in order to get a job.

Impact on Selection

How can each of the behaviors impact selection? The impact will be found in areas related to change in rank-ordering and job-relatedness of the behavior.

Background Social Presentation

In most cases, background social presentation will not affect rank ordering. Any reductions in rank-ordering effects are likely to be caused by lack of background social presentation, because most individual engage in it at significant levels.

Situationally Heightened Self-Presentation

If all candidates engage in situationally heightened self-presentation, changes in rank ordering may not occur. However, the findings of Rosse et al. (1998) would suggest that candidates may vary widely in such behavior. To reduce changes in rank ordering, practitioners need to be alert to the level of job-relatedness of heightened self-presentation. Kroger and Turnbull (1975) noted that people try to fit their actual qualifications to the stereotype of the desired job. Particularly, it will be important to avoid selecting against candidates lacking in heightened self-presentation, when this lack is not job-related.

Lying

Lying can produce change in rank-ordering by the omission or falsification of a piece of information. That omission or falsification can itself be verified as true or false by the target. Lying, when not detected, would generally result in a candidate being more likely to be selected for or more likely not to be selected against. Lying, when detected, is generally selected against.

The message about lying is: Verification of provided information is essential. Failure to verify will increase the probability of selecting individuals who, in fact, lack more qualifications or have more disqualifications relative to the applicant pool. Disqualification based on lying would rest on two criteria: Does the actual content of the truth change the individual's qualifications for the job? Does the act of lying change the individual's qualifications (including integrity) for the job?

Bullshit

Bullshit can affect selection in several ways. Bullshit at its essence in employee selection involves the creation or presentation of a phony or fake set of qualifications intended to maximize the fit between that set of qualifications and the described qualifications of the target. Heightened self-presentation, in contrast, seeks to maximize the fit between the actor's actual qualifications and these required by the target. In contrast to lying, which can be verified to be true or false, no single point in the set of qualifications created by the *skilled bullshit artist* (Frankfurt's (1988) term) will be able to be verified as false. The utility of the bullshit to affect selection may be *increased* if some points in the set of information can be verified as true.

Consequences of Bullshit for Selection. This aim of presenting a set of information that maximally matches the set of desired qualifications indicates why bullshit can have such significant consequences in selection. The skilled bullshit artist realizes his or her objective by achieving maximum fit between presented qualifications (independent of whether these are also actual qualifications) and the target's requirements, often appearing as a leading candidate in a pool. This could merely move an actor from a marginally lower position in a group of qualified applicants to a higher position. If the number of applicants selected is large with respect to the size of the pool of qualified applicants, and if the bullshitter's actual job qualifications are a reasonable approximation of those required, the subsequent effects on workforce performance could be small.

Under other conditions, though, the changes in rank ordering could be large and the performance consequences disastrous. Because with the bullshitter, in Frankfurt's words, "all bets are off" (1988, p. 131). The bullshitter's presented qualifications, after all, are intended solely to obtain an offer of employment. The actual match between the bullshitter's real qualifications and those required may be great, moderate or even nonexistent—and such differences are of no consequence to the bullshitter.

These consequences of faking will be greatest: First, when the change in rank-ordering changes the bullshitter from being ranked below a cut score to being ranked above the cut score. Second, when the applicant lacks, in fact, specific critical requirements for the job. Third, when the applicant, in fact, generally lacks the skills or experience required for the successful performance of the job, even though no single deficiency is task-critical. (Moreover, the percent of bullshitters in an applicant population would also affect the overall utility of the selection process.)

The consequences are best illustrated when the number of available positions is known to be small relative to the applicant pool, especially when that number is one. Under these conditions, the combination of the actor's expedient behavior and the target's decision-making behavior are particularly potent. When a single candidate is to be selected for a key position, particularly one high in power, prestige, or compensation, that position offers high relative rewards to a job seeker. The motivation and rewards for the applicant to increase the rank order of presented qualifications is high. There is no reward for increasing rank ordering incrementally, yet there is a substantial reward for increasing rank order in a quantum leap to the top of the pool. The relative utility of bullshitting over incremental response distortion strategies increases.

The possibility of selecting a fake is increased by the employer's decision-making requirements. Selecting a small number of candidates to fill positions from a larger applicant pool is a classic example of *satisficing* decision making (Simon, 1956). That is, decisions are made to obtain a satisfactory economic result in a simple, workable manner, rather than an absolutely optimal result.

In employee selection, the information used to assess the worth of a candidate's qualifications comes from the same source used to assess the certainty of those qualifications. The highest actual costs to organizations will be in instances of false positive selection of individuals whose performance is actually below the level required for the job, and even greater if work performance actually has a negative value, for example, though malfeasant or negligent behavior. Practitioners should be particularly alert to the possibility of bullshit when a candidate's qualifications are markedly superior to the rest of the pool and when a larger proportion of a candidate's qualifications cannot be verified or validated. Before any offer of employment is extended, the practitioner should ask this question about the candidate's qualifications: "What if this is all bullshit?"

MODELING FAKING ON PERSONALITY TESTS

With our problem now more focused by this theoretical model, we move to discussing our research that has investigated these concepts. Understanding faking is difficult when relying only on traditional data strategies. Field research provides us the opportunity to observe under real conditions, but for many phenomena, that observation remains indirect. Faking is such a phenomena, for to ultimately understand the nature of faking by field research alone, it would be necessary to identify a sample of applicants who would admit to faking. In lieu of this "ideal" sample, field research has provided a variety of indirect methods of studying faking. Our simulation approach is intended to move beyond inherent limitations of indirect observation by designating rather than identifying applicants as fakers and simulating what the effects on selection are of such designated fakers. The starting point for simulation research is the contributions provided by field research as well as the limitations of indirect observation. Modeling provides opportunities to explore phenomena that theory and field research cannot (Zickar, 2000). In turn, simulation in the absence of field data is apt to lose meaning even as it gains computational power (see Leontief, 1985).

Faking Scales

An indirect method for identifying fakers is to use scales that have been designed to identify people who are likely to be faking. The Minnesota Multiphasic Personality Test (MMPI) was one of the first personality instruments to include scales to identify dissemblers (Meehl & Hathaway, 1946). Since Meehl and Hathaway's work, there has been a proliferation of these scales. Other names for these faking scales are social desirability scales (Crowne & Marlowe, 1960), unlikely virtues (Hough, 1998), validity scales (R. Hogan & J. Hogan, 1992), and impression management (Paulhus, 1984). These scales do seem to have some validity, because samples that should have high amounts of faking (e.g., applicants or instructed fakers) tend to have higher means than samples that should have relatively low amounts of faking (e.g., job incumbents or instructed honest responders; Viswesvaran & Ones, 1999).

However, there are limitations to the faking scales approach. First, these indirect measures are fallible measures of faking, for the scales measure responses that correspond imperfectly with faked responses. Some honest individuals might receive high scores on these scales, and, improperly be classified as fakers (Zickar & Drasgow, 1996). Using these scales to identify fakers is problematic because there is always the possibility of labeling falsely an honest responder as a faker (i.e., a false alarm). The results of using these scales suggests that this false alarm rate is too high to warrant operational use (Zickar & Drasgow, 1996). Conversely, applicants' faking can be underreported if they fake in magnitudes that exceed the capacity of the impression management or response distortion scales, as has been observed under field conditions (Rosse et al., 1998).

A second limitation is that these scales can be faked but the faking may be undetected if sufficient instruction is given (Dwight & Alliger, 1997). For example, Kroger and Turnbull (1975) found that respondents were able to evade detection by the MMPI validity scales when portraying creative artists if they had job-related knowledge. Even earlier, Whyte (1957), in his essay, "How to Cheat on Personality Tests," advocated a similar strategy of consistently adopting a moderately well-adjusted (albeit odious) persona, neither virtuous nor vile, when answering personality test questions in an applicant setting. Such a persona would have few "unlikely virtues."

A final limitation is that there is a belief that some limited amount of socially desirable responding may be indicative of positive mental health and also may be correlated with performance in some occupations (see Block, 1965; Sweetland & Quay, 1953). Ones et al. (1996) concluded that social desirability scales did not correlate with important work-related criteria. There is, however, still some disagreement about this issue.

Clearly, given these limitations, it seems prudent not to assume that people who score high on faking scales are faking. A more prudent approach would be to collect ancillary evidence (whether of faking or of the quality of all information in an applicant's record) on applicants who score high on these scales.

Experimentally Induced Faking

Another method of studying faking is to instruct one sample to fake and another sample to respond honestly. This technique has been used extensively in conjunction with job incumbents (Young, White, & Oppler, 1991) and student samples (Schmit & Ryan, 1993). The problem with this type of research is that faking is dependent on the types of instruction given to respondents (see Zickar & Robie, 1999). The main problem, however, is that there is no guarantee that the magnitude and nature of faking would be the same across people who are instructed to fake as part of a study and those who are faking to obtain a scarce resource, a valued job (Kroger & Turnbull, 1975). It is possible that faking in a job context is tailored or targeted to perceived job characteristics, whereas faking in experiments might be more pervasive or as Kroger and Turnbull (1975) stated, utilize a more general "best self" technique (p. 48). Fakers in noncontextualized experiments might simply try to respond as if they were extremely sociable, intelligent, kind, and conscientious. Moreover, in many settings, responses may be affected by other needs to comply with the demands of the setting. Student settings may involve whatever behaviors that provide the simplest compliance required for course credit; in prisoner and military settings, there are substantive role conflicts between complying with experimental instructions to fake and complying with role-specific sanctions against faking. Therefore, the generalizability of instructed faking behavior may not generalize from the laboratory (usually the Introductory Psychology lecture hall) to the hiring hall.

Applicants Versus Incumbents

A third approach is to examine differences on faking scales and personality measures between samples of applicants and incumbents. Differences between the samples that occur are attributed to faking behavior in applicants. The advantage of this approach is that researchers examine behavior as it occurs naturally in the environment (i.e., applicant hiring) for which they wish to generalize. Moreover, to the extent that response distortion scales do measure faking, such comparisons test the prediction that response distortion is not different between applicants and incumbents.

Results of such studies (e.g., Rosse et al., 1998) do show that there are significant differences in response distortion scales scores between applicants and incumbents. Moreover, the Rosse et al. (1998) study showed that applicants scores differed from incumbents in ways that would be predicted by response distortion: applicants mean scores were more conscientious, extroverted, and emotionally stable than incumbents. The applicant versus incumbent approach, however, also presents several problems particularly amenable for addressing through simulation. Under many conditions, applicant and incumbent samples are not equivalent on other characteristics besides faking motivation and behavior. Applicant and incumbent comparisons have also shown differences in response distortion scores. These indicate the likelihood differences in faking behavior among applicants, as well as between applicants and incumbents. We explore models for such differences. But these also create a problem for comparative field studies. As Rosse et al. (1998) showed, there is large variability on faking scale indicators in applicant samples. This is consistent with the existence of different faking strategies, but it makes it difficult to relate a particular scale score to a particular level of faking. Some applicants might respond honestly because of moral standards or inability to fake. Other applicants might feel comfortable lying to obtain a valued job. Regardless, it is difficult to identify different types of faking present in applicant samples simply from scale scores.

A similar limitation is present in all data-based strategies of studying faking: It is difficult to identify fakers with certainty. It is important to the understanding of faking to differentiate fakers from honest respondents to understand their response processes. In lieu of being able to identify fakers in field studies, modeling faking allows us to designate respondents as fakers and to model the consequences on selection decisions of the behavior of these respondents.

The Value of Modeling

Modeling has been used extensively in fields like ecology where it is difficult to test the effects of certain variables. For example, modeling was used to determine the effects of building a dam on the preservation of an endangered species of a Texas snake (Quammen, 1996). In faking research, modeling can transcend limitations of empirical data techniques. Modeling allows researchers to precisely designate and control variables that are difficult to identify with empirical studies (e.g., faking behavior) and variables that are logistically impossible to manipulate (e.g., test validity or percentage of applicants who are faking). The modeler can designate or specify who is faking and define patterns of faking.

Our program of research has used computational modeling in addition to the empirical data methods previously mentioned to better understand the nature and consequences of faking. By studying the problem of faking from a variety of perspectives, we were able to counter these inherent limitations of each technique with the advantages of other methodologies. For example, the lack of external validity of the experimentally induced faking studies can be alleviated by testing the generalizability of those results to applicant versus incumbent studies. Modeling has been an extremely important aspect of this research program because it solves the inherent difficulty of not knowing who is faking under realistic conditions.

OUR COLLABORATIVE WORK
ON MODELING FAKING

Our collaboration was triggered by a symposium on faking at the 1995 annual meeting of the Society for Industrial–Organizational Psychology in which a discussant declared that research in the area of faking on personality tests leads to the conclusion that faking does not matter, and argued further that researchers who continued to pursue this topic were therefore wasting their creative energies. When Bob Levin and Joe Rosse talked with Chuck Hulin to get his reactions to the conclusion of this symposium, Chuck pointed out that Mike Zickar, then a graduate student at Illinois, was also interested in this problem. Challenged to provide data that would either substantiate or refute such a sweeping generalization, we designed a model that would allow us to examine whether faking had an effect on validity under what conditions.

Initial Modeling

Our initial model of faking used item response theory (IRT), which posits that responses to psychological items are a function of item properties (i.e., difficulty, discrimination, and guessing) as well as a respondent's latent or actual personality trait, commonly denoted *theta* (see Zickar, 1998, for an introduction to IRT). IRT is well-suited for conducting simulations because it is possible to derive specific models that can be used to predict how individuals with a specific level of a personality trait will respond to items with different features. For example, it is possible to use IRT models to predict that someone who is high in conscientiousness will have a 70%

chance to respond *Yes* to the item *Are you organized?* Conversely, someone who is low in conscientiousness might have only a 20% chance of affirming that item. An item response function (IRF) links an individual's standing on a personality trait with the probability of affirming that item. The shape of the IRF is determined by characteristics of the item (e.g., difficulty, discrimination). These IRT notions are crucial for most of the work that is reported in the following sections.

As a first step, we developed IRT-based models of items on the U.S. Army's Assessment of Background and Life Events (ABLE), a personality measure of traits hypothesized to be important for military success, based on a previous psychometric analysis of the ABLE (Zickar & Drasgow, 1996). Next, we hypothesized a model of respondent faking behavior: People who were faking responded to items as if their personality trait was augmented by a prespecified amount. This amount was varied to simulate differences in faking from slight exaggeration to what Levin (1995) called "bullshit" responding.

This model of faking was labeled the *theta-shift model*, based on the concept that fakers might respond by augmenting their latent trait, equivalent to shifting their theta value. A further assumption of this model is that items can be classified into two types—fake-prone and fake-proof items. As explained by Becker and Colquitt (1992), fake-prone items are ones that the content of the item is transparent, understood by respondents, and also difficult to verify. Although this is a simplifying assumption for the purpose of constructing the model, the assumption corresponds to research on item transparency. The theta-shift model assumes that people are more likely to respond with their true, stable theta on fake-proof items but that on fake-prone items they respond as if they had their theta incremented by a prespecified amount (i.e., the theta shift). A second assumption for the purpose of the model is that fakers will augment their scores in the proper direction, as also predicted by item transparency research. Of course, field research does indicate that a few applicants seem to fake in the wrong direction (Rosse et al., 1998), but for the purpose of the model, we are interested in understanding the effects on decisions of those who improve their probability of selection through faking. This theta-shift approach, therefore, guarantees that respondents who fake have an increased probability of choosing the correct answer.

In our simulations, we varied the faking magnitude (i.e., amount of theta shift) to simulate a range of faking, the validity coefficient (correlation between theta and a simulated criterion), and the percentage of respondents in a sample who were faking. This simulation was done using software custom-written in Turbo Pascal.

Our results suggest, first, that validity coefficients are relatively insensitive to even large amounts of faking, except when there is a relatively equal mixture of honest and faking responding (Zickar, Rosse, & Levin, 1996). Second, we demonstrated that people who were faking were likely to rise to the top of the rank-ordering of applicants. Therefore, top–down hiring using personality tests would result in an overselection of people who were misrepresenting themselves, yet would not change the validity coefficients. Previous research (Christiansen, Goffin, Johnston, & Rothstein, 1994) showed that rank-ordering of applicants had changed after partialing social desirability scores from content scales of the Sixteen Personality Factor (16PF) Questionnaire. Field research conducted simultaneously with our modeling research (Rosse et al., 1998), showed that cases high in response distortion rose to the top of the rank-ordering of applicants, and that respondents with high response distortion scores also had more desirable scores for personality traits (e.g., higher Conscientiousness). The additional contribution of our modeling research is to show that faking itself can and will produce these effects, and produce them in ways not detectable by correlation coefficients.

At the same time, a limitation of the modeling research was that the model of faking was too simple. Certainly, faking behavior is more complex than suggested by our model. Different respondents likely fake at vastly different magnitudes within the same sample. Respondents might also use different strategies to fake, instead of just different magnitudes. Another limitation is that items are not likely to be simply fake prone or fake proof, but the fakability of items is likely to range on some continuum. There may also be a relationship between the level of the latent trait and the magnitude of faking: Individuals who are high on a trait would not need to fake, or fake as much, which would result in a negative relationship between latent trait levels and magnitude of faking.

Any computational model of human behavior will be less complex than the behavioral system that is being modeled. The relevant question for modeling research relates not to the simplification itself but to the degree to which the specified model fits the existing data. Because of the inability to check the accuracy of some predictions, it is doubly important to verify as much of the model using data-analytic techniques based on the empirical data methods previously discussed. Simultaneously, it is important that we simulate the effects of a sufficiently wide range of parameter values to ensure that we include the true parameter value.

Differential Item Functioning Analysis of Faking

Toward these ends, two studies were conducted using differential item functioning (DIF) analysis. DIF analyses allow researchers to test whether items function similarly across distinct populations (see Raju, van der Linden, & Fleer, 1995). With DIF analyses, researchers can determine whether the difficulty and discrimination of items varies across populations. This can be important in determining the effects of faking on the functioning of items. In these two studies, we examined the effects of faking on how items functioned across two different respondent comparisons: experimentally induced fakers versus instructed-to-be-honest respondents (Zickar & Robie, 1999) and applicant respondents versus incumbent respondents (Robie, Zickar, & Schmit, 2001). These studies allowed us to answer several questions that would help us improve the fidelity of the Zickar et al. (1996) theta-shift model of faking, as well as answer several questions that have plagued faking research.

The first goal of this research was to determine plausible values for the magnitude of faking (i.e., the theta-shift). Previous meta-analytic research published after our initial modeling research provided "ballpark" estimates for the magnitude of faking. Viswesvaran and Ones (1999) found a mean effect size of .48 to .65 across Big Five constructs observed in studies of simulated faking. Within-subjects effect size were slightly higher, ranging from .47 to .93. These values, based on aggregations across a variety of studies and different personality instruments, provided a starting point for estimating the magnitude of faking. However, we expected that IRT-based estimates of effect sizes would be more precise: meta-analytic effect sizes are based on the mean difference of scale scores across conditions divided by the pooled standard deviation of the two groups' scale scores. With IRT-based estimates of latent personality traits, the separation of relevant variance from error variance is more accurate than traditional meta-analytic methods, which in turn provides more precise estimates of effect sizes.

In the Zickar and Robie (1999) comparison of instructed fakers versus instructed honest respondents, the magnitude of the effect size depended on the type of instructions given to the fakers. One faking condition, ad-lib faking, instructed respondents to fake without any explicit directions on how to fake. This condition had effect sizes that ranged from .63 to .82. In another condition in the same study, the coached faking sample presented sample items to the participants and instructed them on how to fake those items. This condition had mean effect sizes that were much higher than the meta-analytic effects and the ad-lib faking effect sizes. They ranged from .96 to 1.51. This second faking condition might represent an upper bound for faking magnitude. The difference between the effect sizes for ad-lib faking and coached faking also demonstrate the potential efficacy of skilled faking, and the potential devastating effects on selection decisions of treating all faking similarly, when effect sizes in fact vary greatly. This first study provides a perspective on what magnitudes of score increases are possible through faking. We also wanted to learn what magnitude of faking occurred in actual practice.

The analysis of applicants versus incumbents in the second study (Robie et al., 2001) provided an estimate of the magnitude of faking expected to occur in actual practice. The incumbents were managers for a large national service organization and the applicants were applying for these same managerial-level positions. Across a variety of scales, the effect sizes of the differences between the two samples ranged from .29 to 1.13 ($M =$ .68), values similar to the ad-lib faking samples and similar to the meta-analytic effect sizes of Viswesvaran and Ones (1999).

In both studies, we examined whether the IRT-based item response functions (IRFs) differed across the conditions. Based on the IRFs, it is possible to determine the discrimination and difficulty of each item and to examine whether there are differences across conditions. For example, it may be possible that faking makes items less discriminating and less difficult. If there are mean differences in scale scores across conditions, but no differences in IRFs, then the theta-shift model would be supported, that faking is simply a process of exaggerating existing traits in the desired direction, rather than engaging in a distinct process of creating faked responses, which in turn affects item parameters and may threaten the construct validity of the scale.

In the Zickar and Robie (1999) comparison of experimentally induced faking, there appeared to be some differences in IRFs across conditions, although these differences were not pervasive. Thirty-six percent of the items demonstrated differences across at least one faking condition. Many of these differences were due to faking respondents who were less likely to endorse the most negative option compared to honest respondents. In the Robie et al. (2001) comparison of applicants and incumbents, 38% of the items demonstrated differences across conditions. As with the previous study, we could not identify any item content or scale reasons for why some items produced differences and others did not.

These studies provided limited support to the theta-shift model and the concept that some faking is an exaggeration of the process that is used by honest respondents. It leaves open the possibility that faking involves a variety of behaviors, some consistent with the theta-shift model and some that involves a process of responding that is distinct from the process used when responding honestly. It would be fruitful to see future work directed at understanding better the mechanisms underlying faking.

Logistic Mixture Models Study of Faking

Both of these previously mentioned studies of differential item functioning make the assumption that all fakers use the same response process when faking personality items. Yet it is equally as plausible that applicants utilize a variety of faking strategies. The model outlined in Levin (1995) and in this chapter suggests that within any applicant sample, there should be a mixture of heterogeneous faking strategies. These strategies are posited to have different efficacies and different effects on validity.

A relatively new IRT technique called logistic mixture models (LMMs) allows us to determine whether there are heterogeneous samples within faking samples. These models combine latent class analysis with Rasch IRT modeling (Rost, 1997). Essentially, a computer program called Windows Mixture Rasch Analysis (WINMRA) seeks simultaneously to identify different samples within a sample and to estimate difficulty parameters for each item (von Davier & Rost, 1995). The computer also estimates the number of classes needed to represent the data. Based on this, it would be possible to identify different groups of individuals that respond to personality items in different ways. We suspected that different classes would be related to faking.

An LMM analysis was conducted on the two data sets previously mentioned (Robie et al., 2001; Zickar & Robie, 1999) to determine the number and nature of classes needed to represent different data sets. The analysis is ongoing (see Zickar, Gibby, & Robie, 2000) so the following results are preliminary. It appears that the honest and ad-lib fakers in the experimentally induced faking study can be represented by one class of respondents that share similar IRFs. The same model that fits ad-lib faking fits honest responding, which suggests that the process of responding is similar across the two groups of respondents.

In the coached faking samples, two classes are needed to represent the data. The first and most prevalent class describes a process that results in most respondents in the class choosing the most positive options. In this class, there also appears to be a previously unpredicted tendency for individuals who are extremely high in the personality trait to have a slightly higher probability of choosing the second most desirable option, rather than the most desirable option, compared to individuals who are estimated to be lower in the personality trait. This supports our earlier speculation that those who are already high in the personality trait might not exaggerate their responses.

The second class of individuals in the coached faking samples is similar to the classes of individuals found in the honest and ad-lib samples. The first class of individuals might be considered to be those who are engaging in what Levin (1995) called expediently heightened self-presentation, or bullshit, whereas the individuals in the second class of individuals could be considered to be in the simple exaggeration or situationally heightened self-presentation class. In the coached faking samples, the proportion of respondents engaged in bullshit responding appears to be about 50 to 60% depending on the scale being analyzed.

The LMM analysis (Zickar et al., 2000) of the applicant versus incumbent data identified two similar classes of individuals to the analysis of the first study—the expediently heightened presentation class and the honest or exaggerated class. In these data sets, however, both applicants and incumbents had a mixture of these two classes. In the incumbent samples, it appeared that about 65% of the samples were responding in the honest pattern, whereas 35% of the sample were in the expediently heightened presentation class. In the applicant samples, the percentages of class membership were reversed, with about 65% of the individuals falling in the expedient heightened presentation class, with the remainder in the honest and/or exaggerated class.

Conclusions of Modeling Studies

The results of all three modeling analyses of field and laboratory research (Robie et al., 2001; Zickar et al., 2000; Zickar & Robie, 1999) suggest that the theta-shift model used in the initial modeling research was too simple. Our further analyses suggest that there are two separate classes of respondents in both applicant and incumbent samples. This is consistent with our theoretical model. Future modeling research needs to include both classes of individuals.

NEW DIRECTIONS FOR FAKING RESEARCH

Studying faking through iterations of theory, investigation, and modeling allowed us to understand that faking constitutes an entire realm of behaviors, some perhaps benign, and others more negative. Our observations from field research and modeling suggest that expedient presentations, or bullshit, provide job applicants with a particularly powerful tool to increase their likelihood of selection. Our observations from field research and modeling are consistent with this prediction from our theory.

Faking exists in employment settings. Theory, observation, and modeling converge to tell us that faking by expedient representations can powerfully affect selection decisions. (We have investigated here the effects of candidates' representations on employer's decisions. Our findings suggest that employers' representations would likewise affect candidates' decisions by similar mechanisms.) As always with research, reaching one threshold of knowledge opens doors to new questions. One that particularly interests us is "How does faking work?"

We believe that faking is effective because in contexts where honesty is prevalent, increased selectivity increases vulnerability to faking. Indeed, we think that prevalence of honesty is necessary for the effectiveness of faking, enhances its power, and guarantees its continued existence. Much about faking, then, is inherent in the fundamental conditions of existence in our world, not just in our particular economic systems or selection practices. Put more strongly, the belief that faking does not exist in selection or is benign violates a fundamental precept for scientific work that there can be no "special laws," no part of the universe that operates in a way that contradicts what we know about the rest of the universe (without an explanation that is itself understandable in terms of what we know about the universe; after Brooks & Wiley, 1982).

Our further search to understand faking in employment selection as part of the broader existence of faking in our world has lead us toward these three areas of theory:

- Evolutionary game theory and faking and fitness in other organisms
- Information theory and signal-to-noise effects
- Social learning.

Evolutionary Game Theory

The selection "game" indicating the efficacy of "going big" under highly selective conditions is but one example of insights about faking that game theory can provide us. Even more intriguing are the insights of evolutionary game theory, which focus on identifying strategies that confer increased fitness on individuals and lead to the development of strategies that persist over time. Modeling studies of deception behaviors in animals yield conclusions strikingly similar to our own models (Johnstone, 1998; Johnstone & Grafen, 1993). As one example, similar to the differential efficacies of different amounts of faking at different selection ratios we discussed, cuckoo chicks exhibit differential volumes of crying, loud enough to enhance feeding from their host species' parents, crying louder than host brood chicks in all environments, but modulating crying volume to some constant volume above host chicks' crying volume (Johnstone, 1998).

One conclusion from combining our own research and evolutionary game theory models is that when "honest responding" is a stable strategy (Johnstone, 1998), then the presence of some amount of occasional deception, or faking, seems to follow as a consequence. If "dishonest responding" was pervasive in a hiring setting, for example, employers would not be able to rely on any information provided by applicants (e.g., about qualifications or availability for work) and hiring would not occur at all, leading to poorer outcomes for both applicants and employers. In turn, stability of honest responding provides the efficacy for the "occasional deception" that is analogous to the expedient bullshit strategy we observe in hiring. Increasing the prevalence of honesty increases the gains provided by faking. So long as honesty is stable, faking will exist and is inherent in a stable system of honest responding. Completely eliminating faking is impossible and there are substantial unintended consequences to efforts to reduce faking.

Information-to-Noise

Moreover, because neither *intent* to fake nor *knowledge* of true and false information can be postulated, for example, in newborn cuckoo chicks, we must look away from our traditional understanding of faking in the employment setting, to information theory, to better understand how faking might arise, and how it might be perpetuated. Resolving a signal effectively (e.g., to be able to receive it as a true signal or use it for a decision) works better when the signal is much stronger than noise and far more difficult when the strength of noise and signal are more equivalent in size. It then becomes difficult or impossible to differentiate the bits of information received that are signal (equivalent to actual latent traits, or theta) from those that are noise (or faked information).

Faking can arise from the very nature of signals themselves, and take advantage of inherent conditions robustly, in several ways. First, the presence of faked information can itself increase the noise in the environment. Second, a faker can take advantage of (or be more effective in) inherently noisy environments, such as selection decisions occurring with limited information, time, and validity. Finally, and most intriguingly, we postulate that a particularly potent faking mechanism is that faking may act to add faked information directly to a signal, so that it appears to the receiver as an increase in signal rather than as noise. This not only creates a stronger signal but also creates an environment in which the signal-to-noise ratio is distorted, which in turns leads the receiver or decision maker to have even more unwarranted confidence in the information provided in the faking-augmented signal.

Any signal is a probabilistic distribution of meanings. This feature of inanimate signals would have been inherent as signaling arose among organisms. Any given signal pattern thus admits of more than one meaning, which creates the conditions for faking to exist.

Social Learning

Human signaling today is probabilistic. We speculate that faking itself would have a significant enough adaptive impact to create adaptive value for signals with a narrower probability distribution and fewer potential meanings. Characteristic signaling, faking behaviors, and detection behaviors could arise spontaneously under these conditions in a wide range of settings. Some behaviors would naturally reoccur in many different settings without any need for transmission from setting to setting. Other more unusual or efficacious behaviors could be readily transmitted through the process of social learning. Laland and Reader (1999), for example, have found that schools of fish can be induced to stable patterns of suboptimal foraging behaviors of swimming to food and that these behaviors likely reduce visibility to predators, analogous to the stability of the suboptimal behavior of faking in an environment of stable honest responding. Once a suboptimal foraging pattern is introduced into a school of guppies, the pattern will propagate through the school and persist over time (Laland, 1996). Faking and detection behaviors can arise and persist similarly, even if the behaviors themselves appear to be initially rare or do not appear to be optimal across all conditions.

Response distortion and faking can be understood most usefully, then, when investigated as an integral part of human work and life. By working to understand faking and response distortion through theoretical development and empirical research, we come to a better understanding of faking itself, the impact of expedient representations, and the profound effects on selection decisions. We also come to understand better how faking appears help us to better understand the profound effects on work and life in general and on selection decisions. We can see how expedient representations can profoundly affect selection.

ACKNOWLEDGMENTS

We acknowledge Charles Hulin, Sherman Levin, R. C. Mercure, Jr., Chet Robie, and Joseph Rosse for their helpful contributions.

REFERENCES

Barrick, M. R., & Mount, M. K. (1996). Effects of impression management and self-deception on the predictive validity of personality constructs. *Journal of Applied Psychology, 81,* 261–272.

Becker, T. E., & Colquitt, A. L. (1992). Potential versus actual faking of a biodata form: An analysis along several dimensions of item type. *Personnel Psychology, 45,* 389–406.

Block, J. (1965). *The challenge of response sets.* New York: Appleton-Century Crofts.

Brooks, D., & Wiley, E. (1988). *Evolution as entropy: Toward a unified theory of biology* (2nd ed.). Chicago: University of Chicago Press.

Christiansen, N. D., Goffin, R. D., Johnston, N. G., & Rothstein, M. G. (1994). Correcting the 16PF for faking: Effects on criterion-related validity and individual hiring decisions. *Personnel Psychology, 47,* 847–860.

Costa, P., & McCrae, R. (1992). *Revised NEO Personality Inventory (CEO PI–R) professional manual.* Odessa, FL: Psychological Assessment Resources.

Crowne, D. P., & Marlowe, D. (1960). A new scale of social desirability independent of psychopathology. *Journal of Consulting Psychology, 24*, 349–354.

Deshon, R. P. (2000). Computational models of personality and faking. In D. Ilgen, & C. L. Hulin (Eds.), *Computational modeling of behavior in organizations* (pp. 109–113). Washington, DC: American Psychological Association.

Douglas, E. F., McDaniel, M. A., & Snell, A. F. (1996). The validity of non-cognitive measures decays when applicants fake. *Academy of Management 1996 Proceedings*, 127–131.

Drasgow, F., & Kang, T. (1984). Statistical power of differential validity and differential prediction analyses for detecting measurement nonequivalence. *Journal of Applied Psychology, 69*, 498–508.

Dwight, S. A., & Alliger, G. M. (1997, April). Using response latencies to identify overt integrity test dissimulation. In M. McDaniel (Chair), *Faking on non-cognitive measures: The extent, impact, and identification of assimilation*. Symposium conducted at the annual meeting of the Society for Industrial and Organizational Psychology, St. Louis, MO.

Frankfurt, H. G. (1986). On bullshit. *Raritan, 6*, 81–100.

Frankfurt, H. G. (1988). *The importance of what we care about: Philosophical essays*. New York: Cambridge University Press.

Gilliland, S. W. (1995). Fairness from the applicants' perspective: Reactions to employee selection procedures. *International Journal of Selection and Assessment, 3*, 11–19.

Goffman, E. (1959). *The presentation of self in everyday life*. New York: Anchor Doubleday.

Hogan, R., & Hogan, J. (1992). *Hogan personality inventory manual*. Tulsa, OK: Hogan Assessment Systems.

Hough, L. M. (1998). Effects of intentional distortion in personality measurement and evaluation of suggested palliatives. *Human Performance, 11*, 209–244.

Hough, L. M., Eaton, N. K., Dunnette, M. D., Kamp, J. D., & McCloy, R. A. (1990). Criterion-related validities of personality constructs and the effect of response distortion on those validities. *Journal of Applied Psychology Monographs, 75*, 581–595.

Johnstone, R. A. (1998). Game theory and communication. In L. A. Dugatkin & H. K. Reeve (Eds.), *Game theory and animal behavior* (pp. 94–117). New York: Oxford University Press.

Johnstone, R. A., & Grafen, A. (1993). Dishonesty and the handicap principle. *Animal Behaviour, 46*(4), 759–764.

Kroger, R. O., & Turnbull, W. (1975). Invalidity of validity scales: The case of the MMPI. *Journal of Consulting and Clinical Psychology, 43*, 48–55.

Laland, K. N. (1996). Is social learning always locally adaptive? *Animal Behaviour, 52*, 637–640.

Laland, K. N., & Reader, S. M. (1999). Foraging innovation in the guppy. *Animal Behaviour, 57*, 331–340.

Leary, M., & Kowalski, R. (1990). Impression management: A literature review and two-component model. *Psychological Bulletin, 103*, 34–47.

Leontief, W. (1985). Theoretical assumptions and nonobserved facts. In W. Leontief (Ed.), *Essays in economics: Theories, theorizing, facts, and policies* (pp. 272–282). New Brunswick, NJ: Transaction Books.

Levin, R. A. (1995, May). *Self-presentation, lies, and bullshit: The impact of impression management on employee selection*. Paper presented at the annual meeting of the Society for Industrial and Organizational Psychology, Orlando, FL.

Meehl, P. E., & Hathaway, S. R. (1946). The K factor as a suppressor variable in the Minnesota Multiphasic Personality Inventory. *Journal of Applied Psychology, 30*, 525–564.

Ones, D. S., Viswesvaran, C., & Reiss, A. D. (1996). Role of social desirability in personality testing for personnel selection: The red herring. *Journal of Applied Psychology, 81*, 660–679.

Paulhus, D. L. (1984). Two-component models of socially desirable responding. *Journal of Personality and Social Psychology, 46*, 598–609.

Quammen, D. (1996). *The song of the dodo: Island biogeography in an age of extinctions.* New York: Scribner.

Raju, N. S., van der Linden, W. J., & Fleer, P. F. (1995). IRT-based internal measures of differential functioning of items and tests. *Applied Psychological Measurement, 19,* 353–368.

Robie, C., Zickar, M. J., & Schmit, M. (2001). Measurement equivalence between applicant and incumbent groups: An IRT analysis of personality scales. *Human Performance, 14,* 187–207.

Rosse, J. G., Stecher, M. D., Miller, J. L., & Levin, R. A. (1998). The impact of response distortion on preemployment personality testing and hiring decisions. *Journal of Applied Psychology, 83,* 634–644.

Rost, J. (1997). Logistic mixture models. In W. J. van der Linden & R. K. Hambleton (Eds.), *Handbook of modern item response theory* (pp. 449–463). New York: Springer.

Schmit, M. J., & Ryan, A. M. (1993). The Big Five in personnel selection: Factor structure in applicant and nonapplicant populations. *Journal of Applied Psychology, 78,* 966–974.

Simon, H. (1956). Rational choice and the structure of the environment. *Psychological Review, 63,* 129–138.

Sweetland, A., & Quay, H. A. (1953). A note on the K scale of the MMPI. *Journal of Consulting Psychology, 17,* 314–316.

Viswesvaran, C., & Ones, D. S. (1999). Meta-analysis of fakability estimates: Implications for personality measurement. *Educational and Psychological Measurement, 59,* 197–210.

von Davier, M. V., & Rost, J. (1995). *WINMRA: Windows Mixed Rasch Model Analysis* [computer program]. Kiel, Netherlands: Institute for Science Education.

Young, M. C., White, L. A., & Oppler, S. H. (1991). *Coaching effects on the Assessment of Background and Life Experiences (ABLE).* Paper presented at the meeting of the Military Testing Association, San Antonio, TX.

Whyte, W. H., Jr. (1956). *The organization man.* New York: Doubleday.

Zickar, M. J. (1998). Modeling item-level data with item response theory. *Current Directions in Psychology, 7,* 104–109.

Zickar, M. J. (2000). Modeling faking on personality tests. In D. Ilgen & C. L. Hulin (Eds.), *Computational modeling of behavior in organizations* (pp. 95–108). Washington, DC: American Psychological Association.

Zickar, M. J., & Drasgow, F. (1996). Detecting faking on a personality instrument using appropriateness measurement. *Applied Psychological Measurement, 20,* 71–87.

Zickar, M. J., Gibby, R., & Robie, C. (2000). *Uncovering different faking styles in applicant, incumbent, and experimental data sets: An application of multi-group IRT analyses.* Manuscript in preparation.

Zickar, M. J., & Robie, C. (1999). Modeling faking at the item-level. *Journal of Applied Psychology, 84,* 551–563.

Zickar, M. J., Rosse, J., Levin, R. (1996, May). Modeling of faking in a selection context. In C. L. Hulin (Chair), *The third scientific discipline: Computational modeling in organizational research.* Symposium conducted at the annual meeting of the Society for Industrial and Organizational Psychology, San Diego, CA.

Chapter 13

Models of Organizational Withdrawal: Information and Complexity

Steven T. Seitz
Andrew G. Miner
University of Illinois at Urbana-Champaign

> *The best way to evaluate a new model is to ask: What can we learn and do with the model that we couldn't have learned or done before we had it.*
>
> —Charles Hulin

Theories of organizational behavior are often more complex than the data available to test them. Despite the limitation of data, at least five partially overlapping theories have been proposed to account for behavior in the domain of organizational withdrawal, or behaviors intended to remove one from one's work or work organization. Hulin's work in conceptualizing withdrawal behavior constructs and articulation of five alternative withdrawal models provides a context in which to study relations between information load and prediction using computational models. In this chapter, we demonstrate that these five models can be arrayed on a single dimension of *information load*. Using this dimension, we explain why the models make qualitatively different predictions about behaviors. We then show how predictions from high-information load theories are particularly sensitive to stochastic shocks, whereas the low-information models produce results that are largely impervious to such shocks.

The relation between information load and prediction highlights a crucial conundrum in the relation between theory and data. Theories that paint a faint landscape on the domain of inquiry produce a similar picture over smooth and rough terrain. That is, theories that make vague predictions, or are not high on the dimension of information load, tend to fit many different kinds of data. Theories that paint a vibrant landscape produce sharply different pictures for different terrain. In short, when the a priori probability of the prediction is low, meaning that the theory brings a lot of information to the domain of inquiry, the prediction may have several, substantially different, variants with slight changes in external factors. When the a priori probability of the prediction is high, meaning that the theory brings little information to the domain of inquiry, the prediction will be robust despite differences in external factors.

Suppose that I bring a motorcycle helmet and cheesecloth into the classroom and look for places that each might fit. The helmet is very structured and unforgiving; its fit is more or less restricted to a human head, and one not too large at that. The cheesecloth has less structure, and its flexibility allows it to be draped over desks, chairs, back packs, and so on, in addition to human heads. The a priori probability that the helmet will fit anything in the room is low; we know from experience that it is made for a human head and little else will do. The a priori probability that the cheesecloth will fit anything is high; we know from experience that this flimsy cloth will take the contour of virtually anything of greater structure than itself. A small helmet will not even fit a large head; here, a slight variance in external factors (size of the head) determines whether we can use the helmet at all, or even whether it provides minimum safety for heads smaller than the designated size range for that helmet. We have no such problems with the cheesecloth. It is robust despite differences in the objects over which it is draped. The helmet is like a theory with a lot of information; it has considerable a priori structure and the elements of the world to which it conforms are finite indeed. The cheesecloth is like a theory with little information; it has little a priori structure and it seems to cover a variety of objects with the same gauzy dexterity.

GENERAL FRAMEWORK—BEHAVIORAL CONSTRUCTS

Psychologists have known for years that there are myriad problems involved with the study of single behaviors. Single behaviors are badly distributed and are poor estimators of underlying constructs. Yet, until Hulin's articulation of a multiple behavior approach to the study of withdrawal behavior, organizational researchers systematically focused on single behaviors such as absenteeism or withdrawal. Hulin, in a chapter for the 1991 *Handbook of Industrial and Organizational Psychology*, used a medical analogy to make the case against using a single behavior to represent a construct. He pointed out that medical researchers interested in the construct of allergies would be misguided if they only studied watery eyes. Although watery eyes certainly indicate the presence of an allergic reaction, they are not present in every allergic reaction. Watery eyes can also be caused by other constructs, such as sadness, or a cold. Obviously it would be ridiculous to do whole studies of allergics where the only outcome under scrutiny was watery eyes. Following this same logic, it would be equally ridiculous to study turnover as an outcome in and of itself. Instead, Hulin and colleagues have emphasized the utility of studying families of behaviors related to psychologically and physically withdrawing from one's job or organization (Hanisch & Hulin, 1990, 1991; Hanisch, Hulin, & Roznowski, 1998; Roznowski & Hansich, 1990; Roznowski & Hulin, 1992).

MODELS OF ORGANIZATIONAL WITHDRAWAL

The use of the multiple behaviors to represent a single construct solves some research problems while generating others. One is the question of whether there is a pattern or order inherent in the behaviors' relation to the underlying construct. Specifically, although it is easy to know the variance that a set of behaviors have in common, this does not tell us in what order they are enacted, if there is any order at all. Hulin (1991) identified five different models of the patterning or ordering among withdrawal behaviors that have been proposed in the organizational behavior literature. Each model can be represented by a set of rules that govern the patterning of behaviors over time. For illustrative purposes, let us assume we have a behavioral family such that three behaviors, I, J, and K, are mutually exclusive and exhaustive of the repertoire of possible behaviors that can be enacted. Thus,

Repertoire   {I, J, K}

Using these three behaviors, we distinguish five models and operationalize them in propositional calculus.

Independent Forms

The *independent forms model* is derived from a model originally proposed by March and Simon (1958) to explain the independence of absenteeism and quitting behaviors. In this model, there are no direct linkages between the behaviors. Behaviors occur independently of one another and each behavior feeds back only upon itself. Stated in propositional form:

- If Behavior I was enacted in the previous time period, decrease the likelihood by 50% that Behavior I will happen.

- If Behavior J or K were enacted, do nothing.
- Choose the behavior with the highest likelihood of being enacted and enact it.
- Move on to the next time period.

Compensatory

The *compensatory behaviors model* postulates that any one of several behaviors may satisfy an attitudinal propensity (Hill & Trist, 1955). According to this model, an occurring behavior will decrease the likelihood of other behaviors occurring as well. Stated in propositional calculus:

- If Behavior I was enacted in the previous time period, decrease the likelihood that Behavior I will happen by 50%.
- If Behavior J or K were enacted, decrease the likelihood that Behavior I will happen by 33%.
- Choose the behavior with the highest likelihood of being enacted and enact it.
- Move on to the next time period.

Spillover

In proposing the *spillover model,* Beehr and Gupta (1978) argued that behaviors should be positively intercorrelated; there should be a nucleus of behaviors that occur in concert. Relationships among these different behaviors can be expressed as conditional probabilities of one behavior occurring in a time period given that another behavior has occurred. These spillover effects, from behaviors to other behaviors, occur independently of the indirect effects that enacted behaviors have on other behaviors through their effects on intervening attitudes and intentions (Hanisch, Hulin, & Seitz, 1996). Stated in propositional form:

- If Behavior I was enacted in the previous time period, decrease the likelihood that Behavior I will happen by 50%.
- If Behavior J or K were enacted, increase the likelihood that Behavior I will happen by 25%.
- Choose the behavior with the highest likelihood of being enacted and enact it.
- Move on to the next time period.

Alternate Forms

The *alternate forms model* suggests that behaviors are merely alternate forms of the underlying construct (Mobley, 1977; Rice & Trist, 1952; Rosse & Miller, 1984). It suggests that all behaviors are essentially substitutable for one another. For example, being late for work serves essentially the same function in terms of addressing the underlying causal construct as does being absent from work or taking a long lunch break. Stated in propositional form:

- Decrease the likelihood that any behavior will happen by 33%.
- Choose the behavior with the highest likelihood of being enacted and enact it.
- Move on to the next time period.

Progression

The *progression of withdrawal* model postulates that behaviors are enacted in an ordered sequence from *least* to *most severe* (Baruch, 1944; Melbin, 1961; Rosse, 1988). This model suggests not only that behaviors will be related to an underlying construct, but that they will be enacted in an ordered sequence. Behaviors that are least severe are enacted early in one's tenure, progressing through more extreme behaviors, until the decision to leave the organization is made. This model imposes the most structure on the behavioral construct because it explicitly specifies an order of behavioral enactment. Stated in propositional form:

- Order the behaviors from least extreme (Behavior I) to most extreme (Behavior K).
- If Behavior I was enacted in the previous time period, increase the likelihood that Behavior J will happen by 25%.
- If Behavior J was enacted, increase the likelihood that Behavior K will happen by 25%.
- Choose the behavior with the highest likelihood of being enacted and enact it.
- Move on to the next time period.

Information Load

The five models differ in the relations predicted among multiple behaviors. Independent forms is the baseline model. As just described, it assumes no relation among behaviors. Two other models (compensatory and spillover) assume generalized relations between any behavior that occurs and the remaining behaviors in the repertoire. The fourth model, alternate forms, is a special case of the compensatory model, where the degree of likelihood reduction is assumed equal for all behaviors in the repertoire. The fifth model, progression of withdrawal, assumes a specific ordered relation between behaviors.

To demonstrate, again let us assume that the behavioral repertoire consists of three behaviors I, J, and K:

Repertoire   {I, J, K}

Now suppose we restate the models in terms of conditional rates of change where rate of change is represented by δ:

Independent Forms	$\delta(i \mid j)$	$=$	$\delta(i \mid k)$	$=$	$\delta(i)$
Compensatory	$\delta(i \mid (j,k))$	$<$	$\delta(j,k)$		
Spillover	$\delta(i \mid (j,k))$	$>$	$\delta(j,k)$		
Alternate	$\delta(i \mid (j,k))$	$=$	$\delta(j \mid (i,k))$	$=$	$\delta(k \mid (i,j))$
Progression	$\delta(j \mid i)$	$>$	0		
	$\delta(k \mid j)$	$>$	0		
	$\delta(i \mid (j,k))$	$=$	0		
	$\delta(j \mid k)$	$=$	0		

The rate of change comparisons indicate that the progression of withdrawal model contains considerably more information than the other four models and it accordingly imposes a strong theoretical expectation on empirical data. The alternate forms model contains more information than either the spillover or compensatory models by virtue of its specification of equality of conditional rates of change. The alternate forms model is the equality condition of the compensatory model. If the researcher adjusts the compensation for other behaviors (J, K) to equal the feedback on Behavior I when i occurs, the compensatory model becomes the alternate forms model. The compensatory and spillover models contain less information than progression or alternate forms. The only logical difference between the spillover model and the compensatory model is that the feedback from I to (J, K) has the opposite sign. The independent forms model contains the least information of all, with no conditional constraints placed on behaviors.

Summary

Under positivist views of science-as-cumulation, the researcher needs to be little more than a passive gatherer of data. The data, in turn, supposedly reveal secrets through standard data analytic routines now widely available. The *postpositivist* view emphasizes the connection between theory and data, or rather, the intellectual iteration between conception and measurement. It is in this context that we view theories in an information-load framework, that is, how much does the conceptual framework say about existential referents, and conversely, how well do observations allow us to differentiate between and among competing theories. It is the marriage between theory and data, with an emphasis on realism that motivated the use of computational models to study organizational behavior. If lower information models, such as independent forms, were the way the world really works, it ironically would require less empirical data for confirmation than would the higher information models, such as the progression of withdrawal.

Our goal in this chapter is to make explicit the complexity inherent in our models of behavior and to suggest how information load at the conceptual level maps to complexity at the observational level. Seemingly different propositional calculi may produce similar simulation outputs. These similarities are due to the similar information load in the theories and force us to shift focus from different parameter values and even different local rules and focus instead on the degree to which the theory imposes structure or order on the empirical world. Those theories that say very little will produce outputs that look like other theories of similar low information load precisely because the signal to noise ratio is very low. Those theories with high information content will produce unique outputs because the signal-to-noise ratio is high. These same high information theories are more sensitive to seemingly small changes in the conditions under which the models operate or small changes in the input parameter values. It should be noted that the questions being explored here may not be accessible to traditional methods, and that selecting among competing models may require much study before we properly understand the conditions under which one or another model can be either validated or rejected. Essentially, our goal is to explain the differences in complexity produced by different models of organizational behavior and describe the implications of these differences.

METHOD

Five models of behavior were translated into mathematical statements about the relationship among three behaviors. These statements took the form of expected outcomes from the enactment of a behavior. Three behaviors, I, J, and K, were modeled over time to determine the patterning among behaviors inherent to the models. The behavioral repertoire was limited to three and every actor executed a behavior in each iteration for simplicity of presentation.

Our output for the first stage of analyses is the average likelihood of engaging in specific behaviors for people in the simulated population. The likelihood that a person would engage in a behavior was scaled 0 to 1 and constrained so that the total likelihood across all behaviors being modeled was equal to 1. Thus, when there are three behaviors being modeled, the average for all three is constrained to be .33. The initial likelihood for all three behaviors were determined by random draw from a uniform 0, 1 distribution, rescaled so that the sum of the likelihoods would equal 1.

This metric was tracked over 50 behavior cycles, where a behavior cycle represents one enactment of one behavior by everyone in the population. We averaged across 30 different runs of the model with different random initial values. This was done to ensure that the output does not represent nuances present in specific initial random values for likelihood.

Biased Replacement Manipulation

Organizational behavior is probabilistic, not deterministic. In order to determine the effects of stochastics on the models, we implemented a mechanism to introduce noise into the signal of the model. Adding this variable allowed us to test the effects of one source of error variance on the output of the models.

The variable we chose to manipulate was that of individuals in the modeled population exiting. These individuals are replaced with new individuals who have different likelihood of engaging in behaviors. This would be akin to individuals randomly leaving the organization and having their replacements drawn from a uniform labor pool. We implemented three levels of this variable: 25% of the population is replaced every round with individuals with likelihood of .33, 5% is replaced at .33, and 25% is replaced at a random value between 0 and 1. Levels of the replacement variable introduce randomness, or stochastics, into the models in that this variable interferes with the rather deterministic models.

WORKER Modeling

The initial simulations were implemented in spreadsheet format to provide simple and direct control over the algorithms. We now take advantage of the computational complexity available through WORKER, the software program designed by Seitz, Hanisch, and Hulin (1995) for computational modeling of withdrawal behaviors in organizations.

We created a simple organization of 100 individuals, ages 18 to 65, uniformly distributed. Five behaviors were included in the simulations: daydreaming, wandering around, tardiness, absenteeism, and turnover. For the progression model, these were ranked in severity from daydreaming to turnover. All five were equally loaded on a common underlying vector of worker withdrawal (.9). Finally, we did introduce an age bias into the simulation, so that age was positively associated with withdrawal (.9). This means that individuals were more likely to leave the organization as they got older. The simulations were run 30 times for each model and the aggregated results are used in the following analyses.

RESULTS

Initial Modeling

Exploratory runs using the five models outlined suggested that there were two types of models. The first type produced essentially the same patterning among behaviors regardless of the settings of the external biasing factors. This first type included the independent forms model, the compensatory forms model, and the spillover model. The second type of model responded to the introduction of bias by producing output that was qualitatively different than the model without bias. Both the alternate forms model and the progression of withdrawal model acted in this qualitatively different manner when bias was introduced. This qualitative difference in patterning of output is indicative of a nonlinearity. Specifically, there is something about the two models in the second category that causes random shocks to influence them much more strongly than similar shocks influence the three models in the first category. An examination of the information contained in each of the models provides insight into the reason why two models behaved differently when bias was introduced.

Figure 13.1 depicts the baseline output for the five models. The first page indicates the output from the independent forms model. The x-axis is time and the y is the average likelihood that a person in the population would engage in a behavior. Three lines plot the likelihood for each of the three behaviors in question. Inspection of this graph reveals that the model predicts cycling through all three behaviors, given that the behavior with the highest likelihood is always the one that is fired.

The next two pages in Fig. 13.1 also show this cycling through behaviors. These models, the compensatory and spillover models, produced output similar to the independent forms model. Recall that these two models, plus the independent forms, have less information than the alternate forms and progression of withdrawal models.

The last two pages of Fig. 13.1 contain output from these latter two models. The output from these two models is qualitatively different than the first

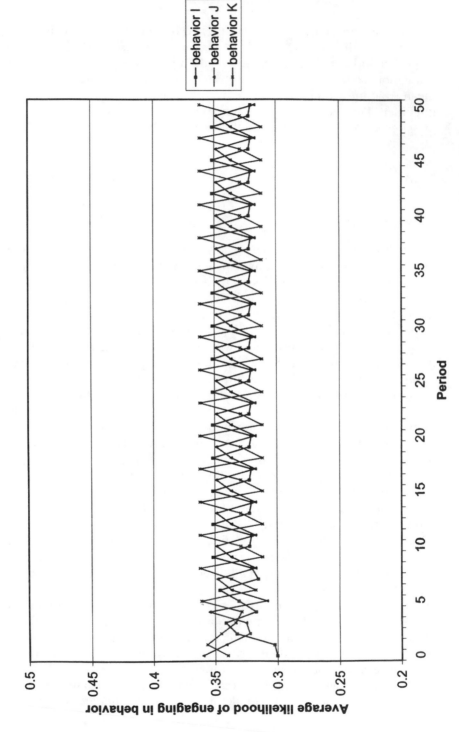

FIG. 13.1 (*this page and following*). Aggregated output for five models: Baseline settings.

Compensatory

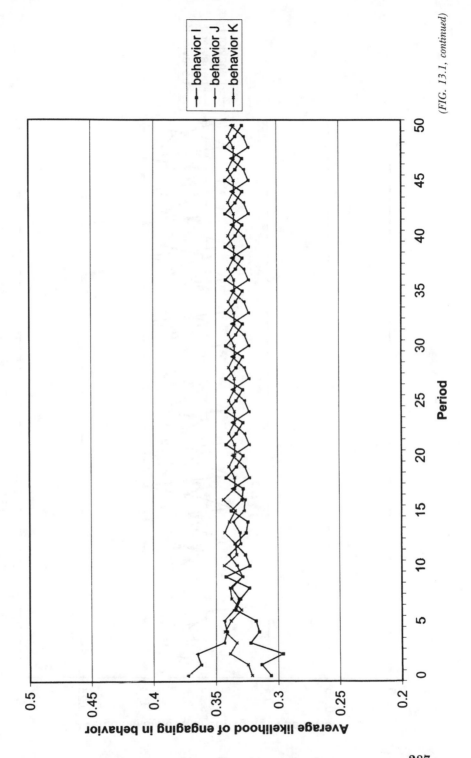

(FIG. 13.1, continued)

Spillover

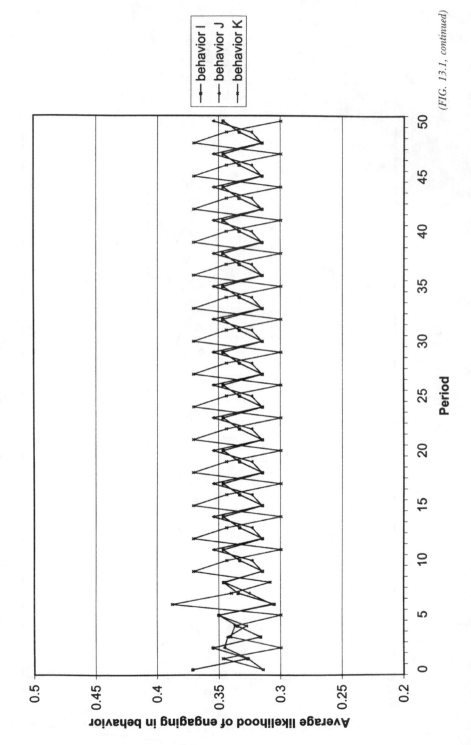

(FIG. 13.1, continued)

288

Alternate

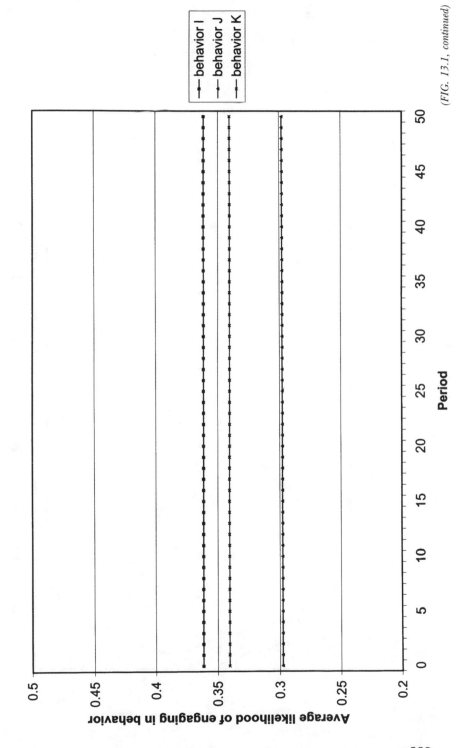

(FIG. 13.1, continued)

Progression

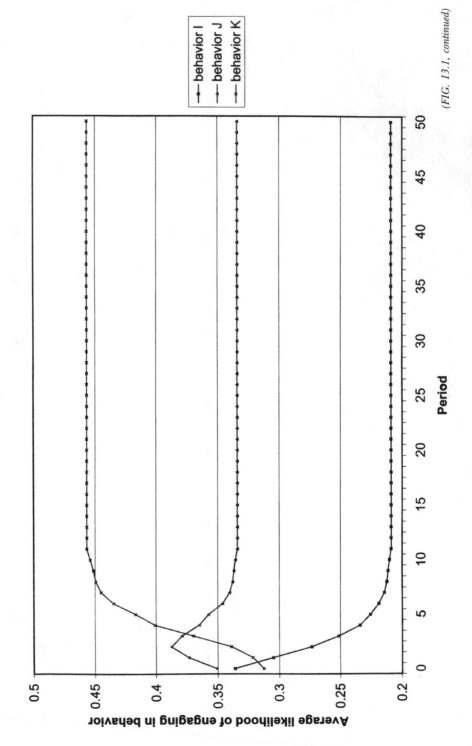

(FIG. 13.1, continued)

290

two. Rather than predicting cycling among behaviors, these models predict a relatively stable state. This state is reached immediately in the case of alternate forms, and after a short period in progression. Apparently, greater information is associated with prediction of stable patterns of output.

Figure 13.2 depicts the same five models, but under slightly different conditions. We have introduced a biasing condition to obscure the signal of the model. As just described, we reset the likelihood of engaging in behaviors under this condition to .33 for 25% of the cases. This condition is akin to removing a randomly selected 25% of the population under study in each round and replacing them with individuals from the uniform labor pool. Inspection of the pages of the graph illustrates that the general pattern of cycling of the first three models, independent forms, compensatory, and spillover, remained intact, albeit with lower amplitude. The last two models, shown in the last two pages of the figure, demonstrate qualitatively different patterns from those shown in the previous figure. The introduction of the biasing condition caused the two models with the highest information load to qualitatively change their behavior.

Figure 13.3 contains output from the same biasing condition, but instead of replacing 25% of the population every round, we only replaced 5%. The first three pages illustrate that the independent forms, compensatory, and spillover models all behaved roughly the same way, with amplitudes between the baselines and 25% conditions. The last two pages, alternate forms and progression, show a slower convergence on the .33 value than did the 25% condition.

Figure 13.4 is another variation on the biasing condition. This time, we replaced 25% of the population every round, but instead of replacing individuals with the original likelihood values (.33), we set the vector of behavioral likelihood to be sampled from a random series of numbers between 0 and 1. This would be akin to losing 25% of the organizational population and hiring individuals without a selection system from a variable labor pool. Inspection of Fig. 13.4 reveals that only one model appears to be exhibiting behavior qualitatively different from the other four. Although the signal of the alternate forms model appears to be washed out by this degree of extraneous variance, the signal of the progression model appears to manifest itself through the noise. The rank order of behaviors over most of the timeline is as expected under the verbal statement of the model, and is identical to that observed in the baseline condition.

Independent Forms

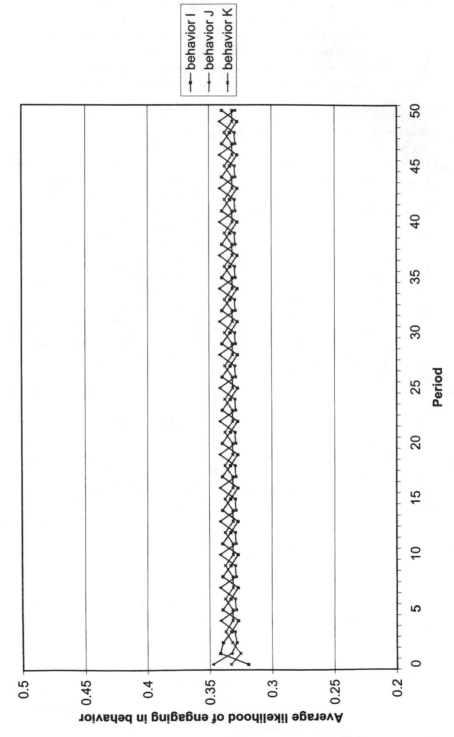

FIG. 13.2 (*this page and following*). Aggregated output for five models: 25% biased replacement.

Compensatory

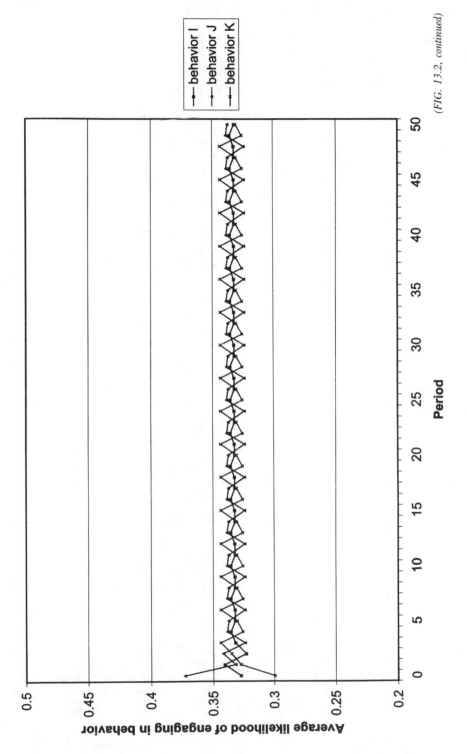

(FIG. 13.2, continued)

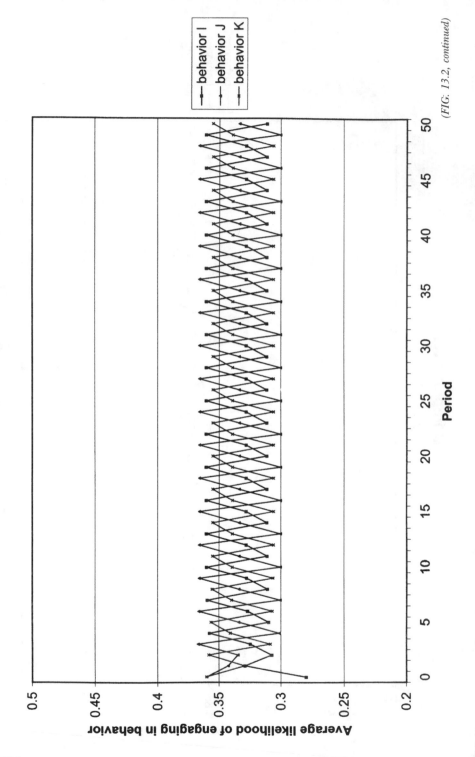

(FIG. 13.2, continued)

Alternate Forms

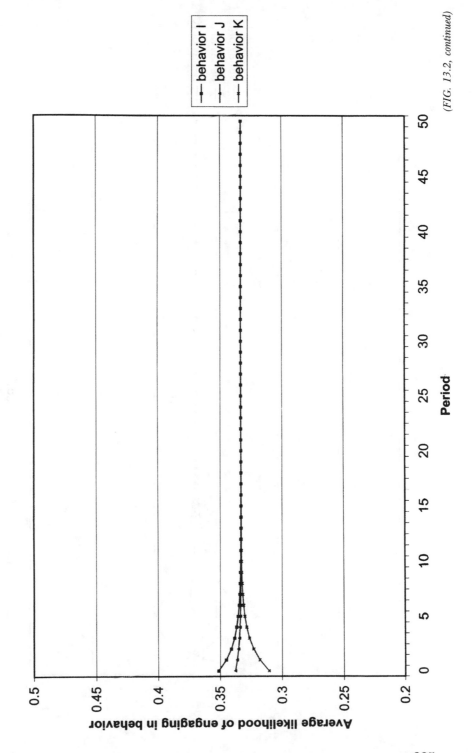

(FIG. 13.2, continued)

Progression

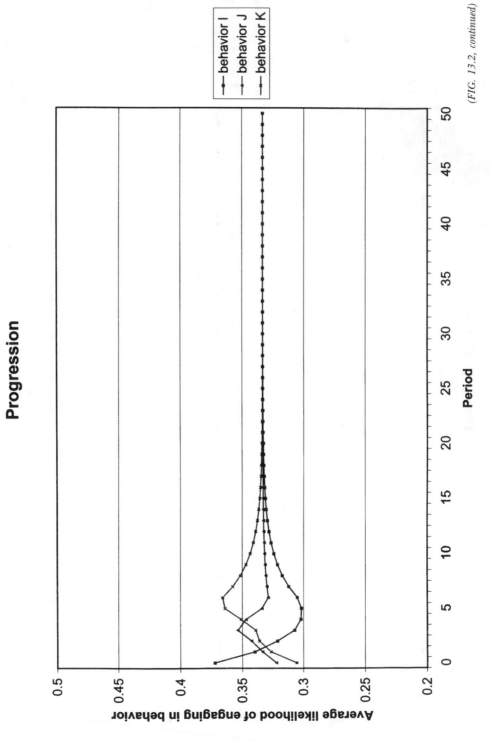

(FIG. 13.2, continued)

296

Independent Forms

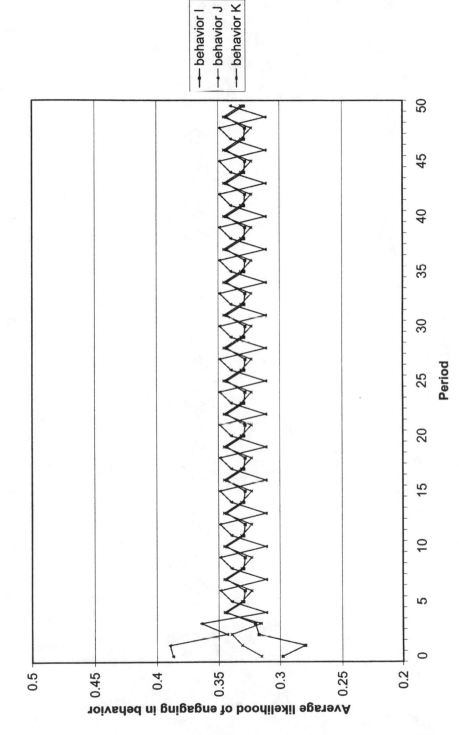

FIG. 13.3 *(this page and following)*. Aggregated output for five models: 5% biased replacement.

Compensatory

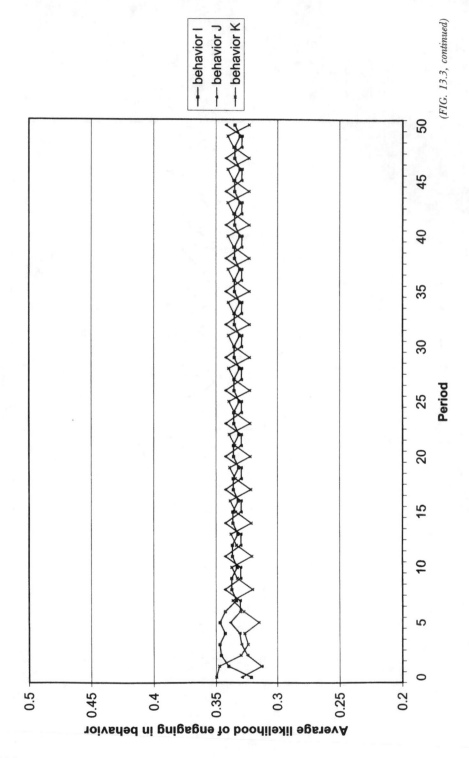

(FIG. 13.3, continued)

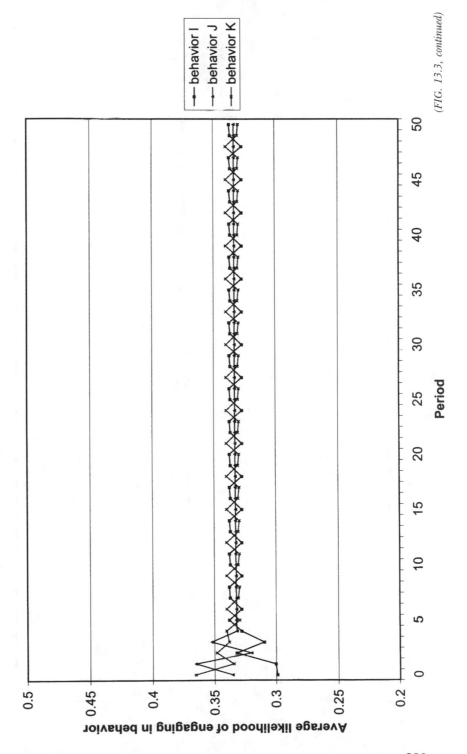

Spillover

(FIG. 13.3, continued)

Alternate Forms

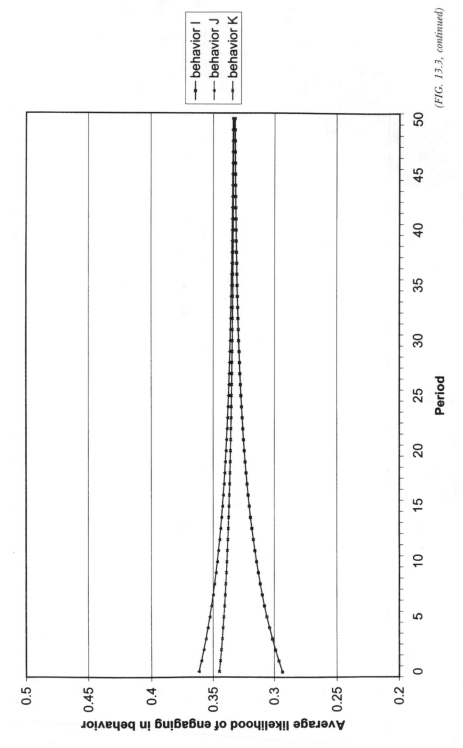

(FIG. 13.3, continued)

Progression

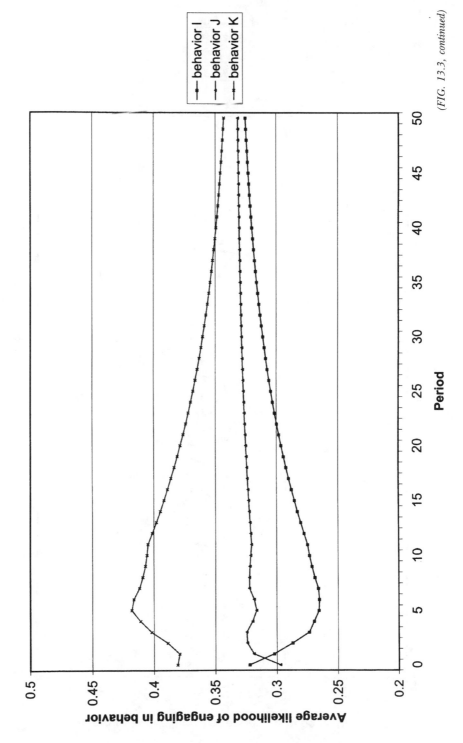

(FIG. 13.3, continued)

301

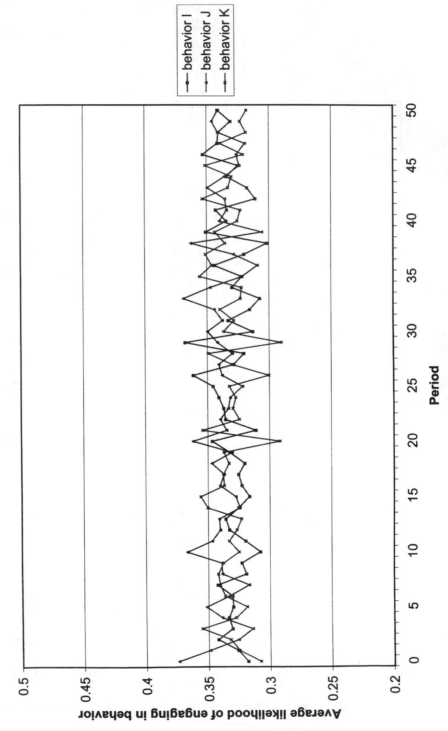

Independent

FIG. 13.4 (*this page and following*). Aggregated output for five models: 25% random replacement.

Compensatory

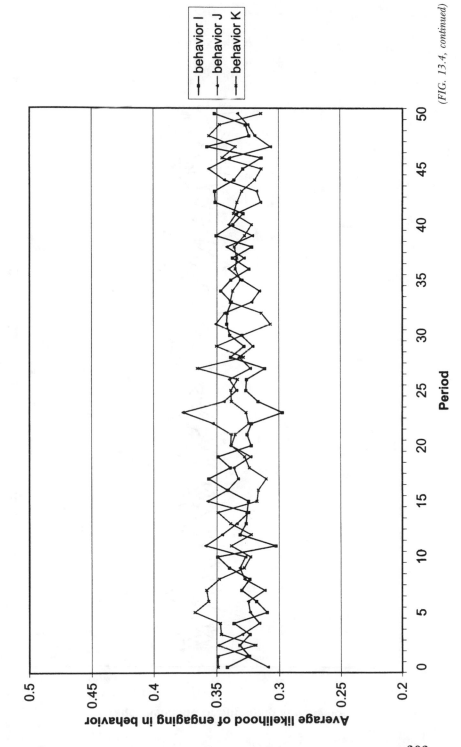

(FIG. 13.4, continued)

Spillover

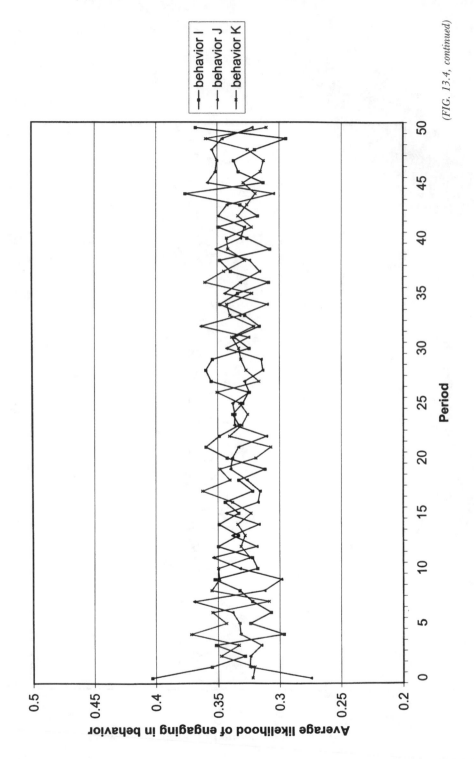

(*FIG. 13.4, continued*)

Alternate Forms

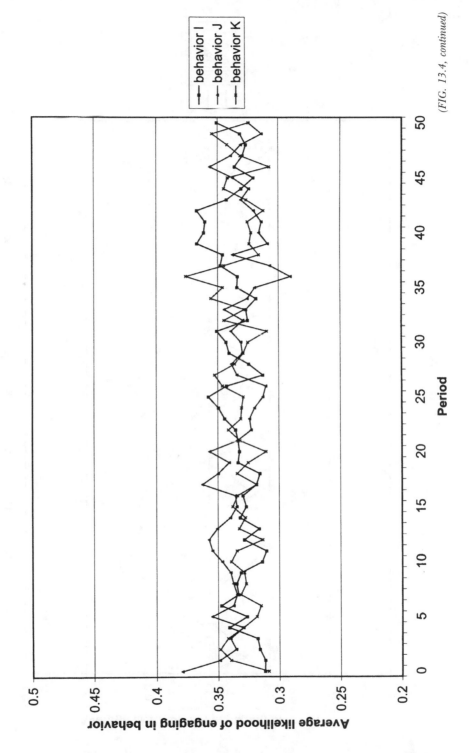

(FIG. 13.4, continued)

305

Progression

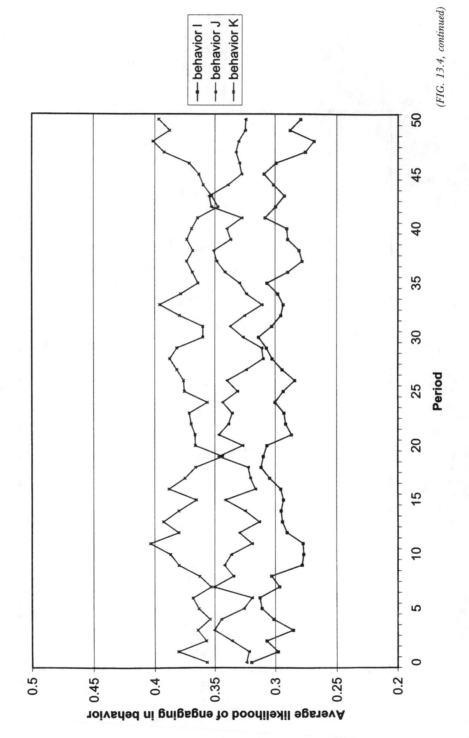

(FIG. 13.4, continued)

WORKER Modeling

WORKER replicates many of the results reported thus far, so we do not reproduce those here. We are interested in comparing the simulation results for the independent forms model, a low-information theory, and the progression of withdrawal model, a high-information theory in WORKER's more rigorous modeling environment.

Figure 13.5 compares two variants of the progression model with the independent forms model. These comparisons look only at workers 60 years of age and older. Recall that we introduced a correlation between age and withdrawal in the initial setup. One of the progression runs and one independent forms run uses a turnover counterfactual, namely, when the turnover behavior occurs, the individual is still not permitted to exit the organization. There is, therefore, no replacement. The second progression run (and a second independent forms run not shown in the graph) does permit exit upon turnover. The upper line in Fig. 13.5 depicts the progression run without exit, whereas the lower two lines represent the progression with exit and the independent forms without exit. (The independent forms with exit is similar to the independent forms without exit and has been dropped from the graph for clarity.) When the extreme behavior (turnover) results in the exit of an employee, the "censored trace" of turnover for the other employees looks remarkably like that generated by independent forms, with or without replacement. (Look at a similar impact of the replacement variable on the progression model depicted in Fig. 13.1 and Fig. 13.2.)

Figure 13.6 makes a similar comparison, except that we focus on workers under 25 years of age at the outset of the simulation. The structural patterns are similar to those reported in Fig. 13.5, with the progression without turnover replacement standing above the patterns with replacement for progression and with or without replacement for independent forms. The only difference is in the level at which the equilibration occurs for the progression model without exit upon turnover; it is higher for the older workers than for the younger workers.

Now let us combine these two factors: the relation of withdrawal to age and whether turnover results in exiting an organization. Figure 13.7 has two sets of bivariate panels. The top panel compares the overall behavior surface for the independent and progression models when turnover results in the exit of the disaffected workers and the entry of random replacements. The x-axis shows the age of the worker, the y-axis is time (30 cycles), and the z-axis is the proportion of workers exhibiting turnover for any time/age coordinate. The second panel makes a similar comparison but turnover does not result in exit or replacement.

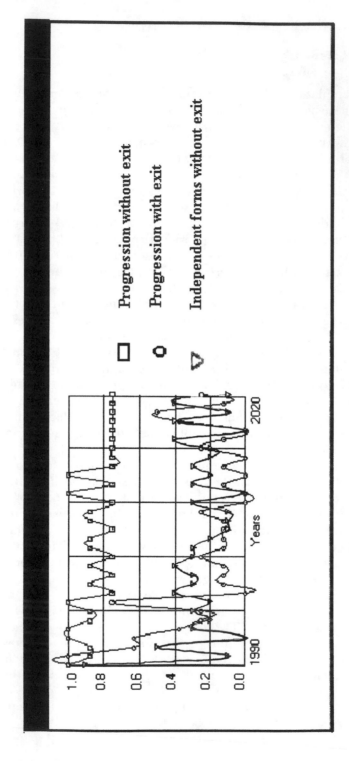

FIG. 13.5. Older worker turnover, with and without exit, for progression and independent forms.

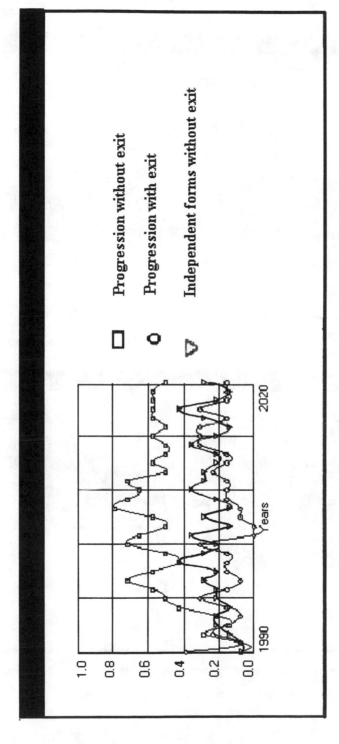

FIG. 13.6. Younger worker turnover, with and without exit, for progression and independent forms.

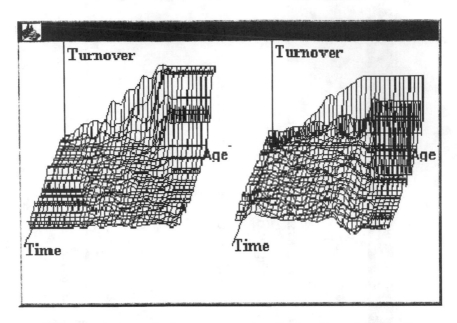

Turnover: Independent vs. progression (both with replacement).

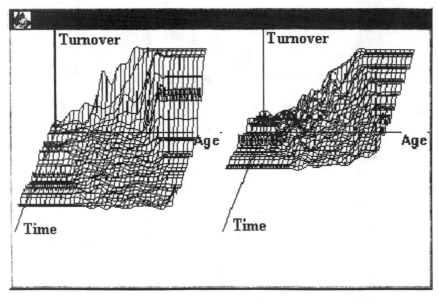

Turnover: Independent vs. progression (both without replacement).

FIG. 13.7. Bivariate turnover comparisons, independent forms and progression of withdrawal.

The finding that low-information theories are relatively unaffected by extraneous sources of variance is illustrated by noting the similarity of the response surfaces for the independent forms under either replacement condition. In both conditions, the pattern of the surface is remarkably similar. Note further that the diagonal river running through the bivariate surface represents a modestly rolling terrain painted by 30 aggregated runs of the original members of the simulation as it unfolds over the 30 cycles per run. The progression terrain is more rugged in both pictures, but it is especially steep and rugged when there is no replacement. Because this ruggedness characterizes a response surface, any modest change in either calendar time or age of the worker could result in sizable shifts in the behavior of workers vis-à-vis turnover.

There are real-world circumstances under which the particularly steep and rugged response surface for the progression model might become factual as opposed to counterfactual. This is precisely the impact of environmental changes, such as growing unemployment, where disaffected workers stay on despite their large withdrawal propensity. Similarly, carrot or stick policies that offer incentives or disincentives to slow turnover may similarly keep disaffected people in the organization. The result of having individuals with high likelihood of turnover without actual turnover is a large volatility of extreme withdrawal behaviors because the leveling influences of exiting and replacement have been muted.

To clarify, the high-information model, progression, suggests that a single extra factor (exit and replacement) has a large impact on the expected behavior of the population. This impact is nonlinear. Levels of this one variable cause changes in other variables (age) to result in large differences in the response surface.

This last statement, that the progression model may produce dissimilar results as a function of small changes in initial conditions or the operation of different stochastic factors from time to time, is very similar to the statements made by catastrophe theory. We conversely see far less evidence of such behavior in the independent forms model. The higher information load of the progression of withdrawal model may lead to predictions (response surfaces) that are considerably more nonlinear than those flowing from low-information theories such as independent forms. Similarly, these high-information theories produce response surfaces that are more sensitive to a wider range of external factors (e.g., aging, exit/replacement).

DISCUSSION

If simplicity were the sole guide to choosing among competing theories, then independent forms would be an attractive theory because it is so robust (or impervious to exogenous forces). The problem, of course, is that if the real world shows sensitivities between withdrawal and exogenous forces, then we need a theory that can rise to the challenge, even though the "world" it predicts is neither smooth nor simple. The choice among competing theories in the postpositivist era must look at the mileage we gain from high-information over low-information theories in prediction and explanation. For the ancient Egyptians, the weather looked remarkably similar from day to day, year to year. For the ancient Mesopotamians, there could be high variation in weather from day to day and season to season. Their respective religions modeled these differences, with gods of stasis and permanency in Egypt and gods of turmoil and fickleness in Mesopotamia.

The world of organizations is likely as heterogeneous as the life experiences of the ancients. For some organizations and for some purposes, the soft illumination cast by low-information models may be all that is needed for management and planning. For other organizations and other circumstances, such as rapid growth or downsizing, the floodlight cast by high-information models may be needed to guide managers and planners through the pitfalls of seemingly rapid change.

The key here is the coupling or uncoupling of seemingly exogenous processes with a set of withdrawal behaviors. The high-information models suggest coupling; the low-information models dismiss or ignore it. Whether coupling occurs is part of the empirical process. For example, do unemployment rates in a given employment sector affect withdrawal behaviors of individuals in organizations operating in the studied sectors? In casting dim or bright lights, these models tell us how to look—for what and why. In this respect, the theory and data are married.

Simulating the predictions of models over time is an important way to assess the information carried in the rules of the model. Models with more information will diverge from other models, and the null model, to make specific predictions about the data. Conversely, models with less information will produce output that is similar to output produced by other models with little information, and similar to the output of the null model. Researchers deriving theoretical statements using static data might misinterpret the output of one model, as the operation of another model, especially if the model carries little information and systems operating under its rules are impervious to external variables.

In summary, we believe that there is much to be gained from analysis of our models, apart from "real world" empirical data. This is especially true when it is difficult to gather the kind of data that would allow us to choose among different models. Our results demonstrate that some models of behavior carry more information than others. Systems operating according to the rules of high-information models behave in a nonlinear, and more complex, fashion in response to external variables. It is both useful and necessary to understand the theoretical implications of our models. One way to "discover what we can learn and do with a model that we couldn't have learned or done before we had it" is to generate output under different conditions. After doing so, we can both understand our models better as well as know where in the empirical world to search for validating evidence.

REFERENCES

Baruch, D. W. (1944). Why they terminate. *Journal of Consulting Psychology, 8,* 35–46.

Beehr, T. A., & Gupta, N. (1978). A note on the structure of employee withdrawal. *Organizatonal Behavior and Human Performance, 21,* 73–79.

Hanisch, K. A., & Hulin, C. L. (1990). Job attitudes and organizational withdrawal: An examination of retirement and other voluntary withdrawal behaviors. *Journal of Vocational Behavior, 37,* 60–78.

Hanisch, K. A., & Hulin, C. L. (1991). General attitudes and organizational withdrawal: An evaluation of a causal model. *Journal of Vocational Behavior, 39,* 110–128.

Hanisch, K. A., & Hulin, C. L. & Roznowski, M. (1998). The importance of individuals' repertoires of behaviors: The scientific appropriateness of studying multiple behaviors and general attitudes. *Journal of Organizational Behavior, 19,* 463–480.

Hanisch, K. A., Hulin, C. L., & Seitz, S. T. (1996). Mathematical/computational modeling of organizational withdrawal processes: Benefits, methods, and results. In G. R. Ferris, A. Nedd, J. B. Shaw, J. E. Beck, P. S. Kirkbride, & K. M. Rowland (Eds.), *Research in personnel and human resources management* (Vol. 14, pp. 91–142). Greenwich, CT: JAI Press.

Hill, J. M., & Trist, E. L. (1955). Changes in accidents and other absences with length of service: A further study of their incidence and relation to each other in an iron and steel works. *Human Relations, 8,* 121–152.

Hulin, C. L. (1991). Adaptation, persistence, and commitment in organizations. In M. D. Dunnette & L. M. Hough (Eds.), *Handbook of industrial organizational psychology* (Vol. 2, 2nd ed., pp. 435–505). New York: Wiley.

March, J. G., & Simon, H. A. (1958). *Organizations.* New York: Wiley.

Melbin, M. (1961). Organizational practice and individual behavior: Absenteeism among psychiatric aides. *American Sociological Review, 26,* 14–23.

Mobley, W. H. (1977). Intermediate linkages in the relationship between job satisfaction and employee turnover. *Journal of Applied Psychology, 62,* 237–240.

Rice, A. K., & Trist, E. L. (1952). Institutional and subinstitutional determinants of change in labor turnover. *Human Relations, 5,* 347–372.

Rosse, J. G. (1988). Relations among lateness, absence, and turnover: Is there a progression of withdrawal? *Human Relations, 41,* 517–531.

Rosse, J. G., & Miller, H. E. (1984). Relationship between absenteeism and other employee behaviors. In P. S. Goodman & R. S. Atkin (Eds.), *Absenteeism: New approaches to understanding, measuring, and managing employee absence* (pp. 194–228). San Francisco: Jossey-Bass.

Roznowski, M., & Hanisch, K. A. (1990). Building systematic heterogeneity into work attitudes and behavior measures. *Journal of Vocational Behavior, 36,* 361–375.

Roznowski, M., & Hulin, C. L. (1992). The scientific merit of valid measures of general constructs with specific reference to job satisfaction and job withdrawal. In P. C. Smith, C. J.

Cranny, & E. F. Stone (Eds.), *Job satisfaction: How people feel about their jobs and how it affects their performance*. New York: Lexington Books.

Seitz, S. T., Hanisch, K. A., & Hulin, C. L. (1995). *WORKER: A computer program to simulate employee organizational withdrawal behaviors*. University of Illinois at Urbana-Champaign and Iowa State University.

Seitz, S. T., Hulin, C. L., & Hanisch, K. A. (2000). Simulating withdrawal behaviors in work organizations: An example of a virtual society. *Nonlinear Dynamics, Psychology, and Life Sciences, 4,* 33–65.

Author Index

Subject Index

Note: An *f* or *t* immediately following a page number indicates a figure or table; an *n* immediately following a page number indicates a footnote on that page.